Early Texas Birth Records

1838-1878

Compiled By:

Alice Duggan Gracy
Jane Sumner
Emma Gene Seale Gentry

Southern Historical Press, Inc.
Greenville, South Carolina

This volume was reproduced from
A personal copy located in the
Publisher's private library

Please direct all correspondence and orders to:

www.southernhistoricalpress.com
or
SOUTHERN HISTORICAL PRESS, Inc.
PO BOX 1267
Greenville, SC   29601
southernhistoricalpress@gmail.com

Originally published: Easley, SC.   1978
Copyright 1978 by: Silas Emmett Lucas, Jr.
ISBN #0-89308-130-2
All rights Reserved.
Printed in the United States of America

It is a truism with genealogists that more often than not the choicest bits of information appear by chance, in the most unexpected of places, or come through the most unlikely channels.

What more unlikely channel could one imagine than the Texas Constitution of 1869?

The exceptional value to genealogists of one provision of that document and of a subsequent law putting it into effect were revealed only after Miss Jane Sumner, attorney, who, while working in the records of numerous counties, continued to notice an old, dark-brown, leatherbound book, marked on the outside, Record of Births, and on the inside, Van Beek, Barnard & Tinsley, Blank Book Makers, Saint Louis. No. 15123.

Inquiry into the beginning dates of county birth records consistently evoked the reply that birth records were not kept in Texas until 1903; hence the birth records begin in 1903.

How then does it happen that in many counties, which were organized by 1869 and even slightly later, there is this Record of Births, containing registrations made in the 1870's?

By the Reconstruction Acts of Congress in 1867, Texas and Louisiana were joined together to form one of the five Military Districts into which the South was divided following the Civil War.

One of these Acts directed that:

When the people in any one of the states shall have formed a constitution conforming with the Constitution of the United States and framed by a convention of delegates elected by the qualified voters according to the provisions of the Fourteenth Amendment, the state will be restored to representation in Congress.

Texans duly selected delegates to a constitutional convention, which assembled in Austin on June 1, 1868. The delegates quickly began discussing matters not related to their legal business; consumed the funds allotted for their work, before completing the new frame of government; adjourned; reconvened in December 1868; finally began concentrated work on the proposed Constitution a short ten days before the date for adjournment; and consequently adjourned sine die on February 8, 1869, still having failed to write in its entirety a new constitution.

Nevertheless, "its (the Convention's) work was gathered up under orders of the military officers, published as the Constitution of 1869, and accepted by the electorate" in a referendum held in July 1869.

Even though this Constitution of 1869 was not popular with those subject ot it. it contained one provision of great import to future genealogists, namely, Section 29 of Article XII, "General Provisions."

This article was framed by the standing committee on "General Provisions," composed of:

Chairman, Morgan C. Hamilton, Bastrop County.
        G. W. Whitmore, Smith County.
        James Winwright Flanagan, Rusk County.
        M. L. Sorrell, Limestone, Navarro, Hill counties.
        Wm. M. Varnell, DeWitt, Victoria, Jackson,
                Calhoun counties.

J. P. Newcomb, Bexar, Wilson, Kerr, Bandera,
Medina, Uvalde, Kinney, Maverick,
Edwards, Zavalla counties.
Robert K. Smith, Galveston, Harris counties.
W. J. Phillips, Wharton, Matagorda counties.
M. L. Armstrong, Lamar County.

Mr. Hamilton's report to the Convention contained the Committee's recommendation that:

Provision shall be made, under adequate penalties, for the complete registration of all births, deaths and marriages, in every organized county of this State.

Happily, the Convention later adopted this policy, and by a comfortable majority. The Thirteenth Legislature implemented this stipulation of the 1869 Constitution on May 3, 1873, by passing "An Act of Provide for the Registration of Births":

Section 1. Be it enacted by the Legislature of the State of Texas, That it shall hereafter be the duty of the Clerks of the District Courts of this State to make and keep in their offices a register of all persons born in their respective counties.

Section 2. Be it further enacted, That in order to enable the several clerks to perform the duty prescribed in the first section of this Act, it is hereby made the duty of the several County or Police Courts of this State to furnish the clerks with well bound books, with appropriate headings and properly ruled into columns. That said book shall be so ruled as to have one column for the name of the person to be registered; one column for the names of the father and mother; one column for date of births; one column for the color of the parents; and one column for the sex.

Section 3. Be it further enacted, That it shall be the duty of the father and mother to have the registry of all children born unto them, after the passage of this act, within six months after such birth; and any father or mother, guardian or person, having charge of such child, neglecting the performance of the duty prescribed in this Act, shall be fined in the sum of five dollars for every month said duty may be neglected.

Section 4. Be it further enacted, That the several clerks of this State shall keep a complete index of the persons so registered, and may demand and receive from the person having such registration done, the sum of ten (10) cents for each person so registered. Approved May 3, 1873.

The registration of births in Texas counties at this early period continued as directed until the Constitution of 1876 was adopted, in February of that year, after which the Fifteenth Legislature passed "An Act to Repeal 'An Act to provide for registration of Births.'" This statute of repeal was approved August 21, 1876, to take effect ninety days after adjournment.

Though most counties dutifully stopped recording at the appointed time, many continued to list births through the 1880s and 1890s.

For the compilers of this information, the questions were: how to make this invaluable information available to genealogists? And how to present this apparently little known bit of Texas history?

Initially, we made a survey of the counties in Texas. Of them 106 were organized too late to be affected by the 1873 bill.

Obviously then we had to visit personally each of the remaining 148 counties in search of the old book with its priceless records.

As of November 1968, the three of us have visited 73 counties (see map), of which 25 counties have the original book, or, as in a few instances, have transcribed these records verbatim into another volume, such as: "Road Minutes A," or "Marriage Record A."

But whenever and wherever found, they are unmistably the birth registrations ordered by the Constitution of 1869 and provided for by the Thirteenth Legislature, because of their form, which is always: child's name; parents' given names or initials and father's surname; date of birth; color; sex.

Since the registrars often did not make an entry under the column "Color," we have omitted it altogether. As a rule the mother's maiden name was not noted, the exception being in the German communities, where it was frequently included. The maiden names have been alphabetized along with the family surnames.

The birth records in this book cover the years 1873, 1874, 1875, with some few scattered through 1876, 1877 and 1878, but the bonus is that when registering a child born during one of these years, the parents often would list all of their previous children, so there are many quite early dates.

The records herein are from the following counties:

Austin	Colorado	Kendall
Bandera	Comal	Lavaca
Bastrop	Comanche	Lee
Bell	DeWitt	Medina
Bexar	Fayette	Menard
Brazos	Gillespie	Nacogdoches
Burnet	Grimes	San Saba
Caldwell	Hays	Travis
		Victoria

We wish to express to the County Clerks in these 73 counties visited our appreciation for their invaluable assistance. March, 1969

Two years later, many miles travelled, and the 75 remaining counties visited, we have completed Volume Two of Early Texas Birth Records, 1838-1878. This accomplishes our goal of visiting the 148 counties which were organized in time to have recorded births in the 1870s, and of getting this data into print.

The counties covered in this book are:

Anderson	Gregg	Nueces
Cameron	Jasper	Rusk
Cass	Kaufman	Somervell
Cherokee	Lamar	Upshur
Dallas	Marion	Washington*
Fannin	Navarro	Webb

*used by permission of the University of Texas Archives.

The birth records are closed in the following eight counties: Coleman, Harris, Houston, Jackson, McLennan, San Patricio, Tarrant, and Wilson. In these counties a specific name will be checked, but whether the old birth records exist, we could not learn.

In the predominantly Spanish communities we found, as in the German ones, that the county clerks frequently included the mother's maiden name in recording the birth of a child. These maiden names have been alphabetized along with the surnames.

We were disappointed that the Cooke County Clerk was unable to locate the "Baby Book," as he denotes the volume. While Starr County did not have the early birth records, we were interested to find that the originals of the first county records are across the Rio Grande at Camargo, Mexico, and that only copies exist in the Texas county.

H. Clyve Riddels, County Clerk of Navarro County, writes: "Most of the footprints man leaves on the sands of time wind up in the office of the County Clerk." Where the records are carefully preserved and in order, the county clerk is usually one who appreciates and interests himself in the history of his area and who realizes that the county records are the basic source for that history.

FIRE, WATER, TIME, NEGLECT, and MOVES of county records from one building to another, have taken a frightful toll of our county records. Of the 148 counties visited, only 43 had the records we sought--gone forever vital information on these early settlers.

Alice Duggan Gracy

Jane Sumner

Emma Gene Seale Gentry

November 1971

Volume I

COUNTY	PARENTS	CHILD	DATE
Bexar	AARON, Emma (See Samuel Moritz)		
Caldwell	ABBOTT, James G. & Mary C.	Zelma Price	20 Aug 1874
Grimes	ABERNATHY, G. H. & C. C.	Walter H.	21 Aug 1873
Comal	ABRAHAMS, Phil & Rachel	Joseph Emanuel	4 Apr 1878
Comanche	ABRAMS, W. H. & F. E.	Park Milton	4 Jun 1875
Bexar	ACKERMANN, Louisa (See F. W. Reinarz)		
Brazos	ACRES, Geo. & Anna (Glovin)	Nettie C.	7 Sep 1878
Nacogd.	ACREY, Abner & Harriet O.	Cora D.	15 Nov 1873
Nacogd.	ACREY, Silas & Eliza A.	James E.	11 Oct 1873
Bexar	ADAM, Anton & Mary Ann (Palm)	Margarette Marie	6 Oct 1867
		John Anton	2 Jan 1870
		Charles Joseph	15 Apr 1872
		A. C.	25 Dec 1874
Kendall	ADAM, Conrad & Adalbertha	Kathinka	7 Sep 1857
		Therese	20 Aug 1859
		Emilie	No date
		Julius	No date
		Bertha	No date
		Emma	No date
Bandera	ADAMIETZ, A. & F.	Ann	23 May 1873
	(1875 entry spelled ADAMITZ)	Adolph	17 Jun 1875
Bandera	ADAMIETZ, J. (?) & C.	Alexis	No date
Lavaca	ADAMS, Alfred & Easter	Jas. Dillard	10 Jun 1874
Burnet	ADAMS, H. C. & M. M.	Walter	10 Nov 1874
Lavaca	ADAMS, H. R. & Sarah	Samuel	26 Feb 1874
Comanche	ADAMS, J. Q. & Mary Ann	Maggie	17 Aug 1873
Burnet	ADAMS, Rich'd. & Sarah	Other Lee	5 Jun 1874
Kendall	ADLER, Friedrich & Juliana	Emma Pauline	14 Aug 1875
Comal	AHLEMEYER, Charlotte (See Wilhelm Boenig)		
Comal	AHRENS, Friedrich & Friederika		
		Auguste	24 Aug 1865
		Louise	10 Jan 1867
		Edward Friedrich	8 Apr 1869
Bell	AIKEN, J. H. & L. C. Elmer	Dameron or Dawson	13 Jun 1875
Bell	AIKEN, J. W. & A. E.	John Garrett	2 Jul 1874
Lavaca	AIRHEART, Jno. M. & N. E.	Jas C.	18 Jul 1874
DeWitt	AIRHEART, Wm. L. & Mary E.	Wm. Allen	8 Apr 1872
		Clarinda I.	8 Jan 1874
		Olive	3 Nov 1875
Bexar	AKIN, Margaret E. (See Stephen G. Burton)		
Hays	AKIN, P. C. & Eveline	Ida May	8 Nov 1874
Bastrop	ALANISI, Galvino & Antonia	Callistoro	14 Oct 1874
Kendall	ALBE, Jose & Rhody	Frank	14 Jan 1873
		Josephine	16 Jan 1875
Austin	ALBERT, Hy & Catharine	Pauline	16 May 1873
Gillespie	ALBERTHAL, John A. & Maria	Bertha	10 Dec 1873
Comanche	ALBIN, J. J. & Mary E.	Theodocia Ann	14 Jan 1875
Bexar	ALCOG, Paulina (See Adolph Scholz)		
Nacogd.	ALDERS, J. F. & Mary E.	Mary E.	4 Jun 1874
Comanche	ALDRIDGE, Jno. P. & A.M. Archibald Allen Anderson		
			19 Nov 1875
Victoria	ALEXANDER, Daniel & Adelein		
	(Silverstun)	Lewis	8 Jan 1873
Colorado	ALEXANDER, Edwin H. &		
	Emily C.	Edwin Franklin	27 Nov 1873
Fayette	ALEXANDER, F. F. & L. E.	William Calvin	23 Dec 1871
		Lucy Emma	30 Nov 1874
Bexar	ALEXANDER, George &	John Henry	13 Apr 1874
	Josephine		
Bastrop	ALEXANDER, Henry Harrison &		
	Harriet E. (Parkerson)	Abner	15 Oct 1873
Caldwell	ALEXANDER, J. L. & Mattie	Lousana	13 Dec 1874
Comanche	ALEXANDER, J. S. & A. J.	Mary Luella	27 Mar 1875
Bell	ALEXANDER, J. T. & J. A.	J. T.	4 Feb 1875
Burnet	ALEXANDER, Joseph & Margaret	Ellen	18 Aug 1873

1

COUNTY	PARENTS	CHILD	DATE
Caldwell	ALEXANDER, Joseph & Matilda	Henry	12 Sep 1874
Colorado	ALEXANDER, O. W. & N. L.	Lina Bell	30 Apr 1875
Bexas	ALEXANDER, Robert & Jennie		
	(Goodell)	Robert	9 Aug 1873
	(1875 Entry spelled Goodwell)	May	23 Feb 1875
Burnet	ALEXANDER, Robert G. &		
	Emily	Emily Pomelia	2 May 1874
Burnet	ALEXANDER, S. & A. C.	Della P.	8 Oct 1874
Burnet	ALEXANDER, Wm. & Jane	Annie	16 Sep 1873
Bastrop	ALFORD, Buck & Parthine	Wm.	16 Jul 1874
Lee	ALFORD, Samuel & Mary E.	Thomas Monroe	9 Jun 1874
Brazos	ALLDREDGE, J. J. & Cassa	Elisha B.	19 Sep 1873
Bexas	ALLEN, James P. &		
	Mary M. (Bailey)	Lewis	4 Feb 1877
Austin	ALLEN, John W. & Mary J.	William Arthur	9 Sep 1874
Burnet	ALLEN, W. S. & Martha J.	James H.	16 Apr 1875
Victoria	ALLEN, William &		
	Sarah Florence (Glass)	Florence Anna	16 Dec 1873
Burnet	ALLEN, William W. &		
	Sarah E.	Amos Elbert Robert	5 Sep 1874
Burnet	ALLSUP, D. E. &		
	Charlotte J.	Mary Orlena	19 Jan 1875
Bexar	ALTMANN, Josephine (See Diedrich Heye)		
Bexar	ALVARES, Francisco &		
	Felicita (Herrera)	Danujaria	10 Mar 1874
Fayette	ALWINE, J. D. C. (See Friderich W. Geo. Kuhls)		
Brazos	AMATO, Peter & P. O.	Frank	28 Jul 1875
Kendall	AMMAN, Albert & Emma	Albert	8 Sep 1875
Kendall	AMMAN, Carl & Catherine	Anna	18 Jan 1874
Fayette	AMSLER, Eliza (See Charles Welhausen)		
Austin	AMTHOR(?) K. F. L. (See Hartmann A.E. John)		
Lavaca	ANDERSON, A. B. & Mollie	Mary	19 Apr 1874
Bexar	ANDERSON, Aaron & Chaney		
	(Tobin)	Litton	13 Jun 1873
		Eugene	7 Mar 1875
Bandera	ANDERSON, Charles & S. A.	Charles	18 Sep 1875
Nacogd	ANDERSON, Irvin & Maria	Thomas H.	27 Nov 1873
Lavaca	ANDERSON, J. H. & M. J.	Bertha	31 Oct 1874
Fayette	ANDERSON, Miles & Rachel	Miles	22 Jan 1874
Bell	ANDERSON, R. D. & Callie	Rufus D.	2 Aug 1874
Bell	ANDERSON, V. H. & M. M.	V. H.	Aug 1874
Bandera	ANDEWALD, J. & A.	Mary	No date
Austin	ANDREAS, Fritz & Bertha	Emma	26 Oct 1873
		Fritz, Jr.	8 Feb 1875
Bandera	ANDRES, John L. & M. C.	David Ellsworth	8 May 1874
San Saba	ANDREWS, J. N. & J.	Etta	20 Dec 1874
Brazos	ANDREWS, Wm. & Priscilla	Phillip	1873
		Richard Phillips	26 May 1873
		Felix	10 Oct 1875
Travis	ARCHER, Osceola &		
	Minnie W.	Annie Elizabeth	13 Sep 1873
Comanche	ARGO, H. D. & S. J.	Mary Lizzie	10 Feb 1874
Gillespie	ARHELGER, William &		
	Catharine	Ida	26 May 1873
Gillespie	ARLT, August & Catharine	Anna Auguste	23 Sep 1873
Sah Saba	ARMINGTROUT, G. P. & Mary A.	Robert Owens	19 Apr 1875
Bell	ARMSTRONG, D. H. & J. F.	Claude	7 Feb 1875
Austin	ARMSTRONG, David & Clarissa	Charles	16 Oct 1873
Brazos	ARMSTRONG, Thomas & Sarah	Harry	1 Jun 1875
Bell	ARMSTRONG, W. M. & N. J.	Wm. Alex	13 Mar 1874
Austin	ARMSTRONG, W. T. & Margaret	A. E.	11 May 1858
		W. F.	15 Jan 1861
		Miller Francis	1 Jul 1863
		James Franklin	25 Feb 1868
		Maggie Lydia	10 Nov 1870
		Robert Lee	26 Jan 1874

COUNTY	PARENTS	CHILD	DATE
Burnet	ARNETT, A. M. & E. A.	John Alexander	16 Aug 1874
Burnet	ARNETT, D. N. & Ophelia	Ellenora Field	26 Dec 1873
Lavaca	ARNIM, Albert & Louisa	John Ernst	10 Sep 1873
		Lucy Fannie	20 Feb 1876
Comal	ARNOLD, Anna (See Rudolph Richter)		
Nacogd.	ARNOLD, Ode (See Peyton F. Edwards)		
Bexar	AROLD (ARNOLD?), Sarah Anna (See John Ochse)		
Bexar	ARTZO, ?? & ??	Lilly Cecilie	3 Sep 1873
Lee	ASSETIR, John & Mary	William Laspley	26 Dec 1874
Lee	ATCHISON, R. N. & M. E.	Edgar Hubbard	24 Feb 1876
Lee	ATCHISON, Robert N. &		
	Margaret E.	Addie Maud	2 Dec 1873
Burnet	ATER, A. M. & Francis E.	Hattie	6 Aug 1873
Bexar	ATKINSON, Ellen (See John Weik)		
Bexar	AUGUR, Jacob &		
	Katherine Jane (Dodge)	Carrie Heath	3 Jan 1875
Travis	AUSTIN, C. F. & Anna P.	Thos. F.	18 Dec 1873
		Mattie A.	3 Oct 1875
Bell	AUSTIN, F. K. & M.A.C.	Dora Eliza	28 Mar 1874
DeWitt	AUTERY, J. E. & Loucy	S. J.	May 1876
Lavaca	AUTRY, George W. & Mary A.	Walter Lay	30 May 1874
Bexar	BADDO, Benhardt & Rosalia		
	(Notre)	William	19 Apr 1874
Bexar	BADDO, Mary (See Peter Hehn)		
Austin	BADER, G. H. & Henriette	John Ernst Otto	24 Jan 1874
Victoria	BAECKER, Phillip &		
	Victoria (Wagner)	Joseph Adrian	8 Sep 1873
Comal	BAER, Helene (See Nicolaus Manger)		
Comal	BAETGE, Maria (See Christian Pantermuehl)		
Bexar	BAETZ, Emilie (See Henry Elmendorf)		
Bexar	BAETZ, Joseph & Margareta		
	(Schaeffer)	Max	27 May 1873
Victoria	BAGGETT, Annie F. (See William Shry)		
Bastrop	BAILEY, Burril & M. E.	Robt. H.	21 Jan 1874
Austin	BAILEY, Isaac & Sallie	Amanda	Sep 1874
Bexar	Bailey, Mary M. (See James P. Allen)		
Bell	BAIRD, B. H. & M. E.	Martha Washington	29 Jul 1874
Colorado	BAKER, B. M. & Jennie	Drew Cunningham	5 Feb 1875
Travis	BAKER, D. W. C. & Mary E.	Julia	6 Jun 1873
San Saba	BAKER, J. W. & Elizabeth	Ann Elizabeth	4 Apr 1875
Bell	BAKER, Jno. & E. J.	Martha Ellen	17 Aug 1875
Caldwell	BAKER, T. H. & Adelaide	Anne Adelaide	4 Jun 1874
Hays	BAKER, W. F. & Eugenia B.		
	(twins)	Berta & Bertha	11 Jul 1874
Bexar	BAKER, Wm. C. &		
	Adelade (Kleabe)	Pearl Adelade	11 Sep 1876
Lee	BAKER, Wm. M. & A. S.	Mills	13 Oct 1874
Bastrop	BAKER, Wm. R. & E. A.	Callie Pope	18 Jul 1873
Bexar	BALDUS, Theodore & Annie		
	(Byan)	Ethel Clara	16 Apr 1874
Bexar	BALDWIN, Winnifred (See Henry Semlinger)		
Austin	BALKE, Christian & Mary	Edward	20 Dec 1874
		Malena	18 Dec 1875
Bexar	BALL, Joseph & Sally (Keller)	Matilda	3 Feb 1875
Bexar	BALL, Peter & Louisa (Schorf)	Frank Joseph	21 Jun 1873
	(1874 Entry spelled Louise)	William	27 Jul 1874
Grimes	BALLARD, E. W. & E. J.	Sarah .L.	18 Mar 1875
Lavaca	BALLARD, James & Alice	Addison	11 Jul 1874
Bastrop	BALSER, Chas. & Mary	Bruno	5 May 1876
Fayette	BANKS, Ida Waldron (See Charles Ferdinand Fordtran)		
Comanche	BANNER, Wm. & Fannie	Stephen G.	27 Feb 1874
Colorado	BAPTISE, Louis & Laura	Louis	15 Oct 1873
Bexar	BARBECK, Herman & Pauline		
	(Biesenbach)	Pauline Christine	30 Mar 1876
		Bertha	23 Dec 1877
		Reimer	6 Sep 1879

3

COUNTY	PARENTS	CHILD	DATE
Hays	BARBEE, James G. & Sarah E.	Sallie Etta	No date
Hays	BARBEE, John J. & Cornelia M.	Sarah	7 Aug 1873
Hays	BARBER, Henry E. & Rachel T.	Henry E. Jr.	9 Jul 1874
Comanche	BARCROFT, J. D. & P. J.	Conrad Paschal	9 Aug 1873
		Martin Beron	11 Jan 1875
Bexar	BARDENWERPER, Carl Christian & Wilhelmina (Kummel)	Max Alex	16 Jan 1856
		Hedwig Anna	24 Sep 1864
Austin	BARING, Albert & Johanna	Albert E.	23 Jan 1874
Colorado	BARING, O. A. & Josephine	O. E.	16 Dec 1874
Bell	BARLEY, J. L. & S. A.	Myrta Alline	25 Dec 1874
Bexar	BARNHART, John J. L. & Ann (Nichols)	Byrum Nichols	6 Jul 1874
Victoria	BARNS, Thomas & Rosanna (Williams)	Levi	17 Oct 1873
Bexar	BARRERA, Juan E. & Julia C. (Cadena)	Agustin	28 Jan 1876
Caldwell	BARRINGTON, M. & L.	Ebner B.	11 Jul 1875
Lavaca	BARRON, J. B. & E. T.	Wm. H.	30 May 1874
Lavaca	BARRON, W. H. & Martha F.	Nancy J.	4 Feb 1874
Lavaca	BARRON, W. L. & E. V.	Sarah E.	1 Jan 1875
Comal	BARTELS, Marie (See Heinrich Hoeke)		
Travis	BARTHOLOMEW, E. C. & E. E.	Claude Morley	21 Jun 1873
Bexar	BARTOLOME, Manuel & Ygnacia (Rocaberte)	Maria Virginia	17 Oct 1874
		Jose	20 Jan 1878
Burnet	BARTON, James H. & Martha M.	John Franklin	7 Apr 1874
		Susan Angeline	9 Apr 1876
Burnet	BARTON, Robert T. & Mary Ellen	Lizzie Beatrice	21 Oct 1875
Bell	BARTON, S. L. & R. J.	Alvin	15 Jul 1875
Austin	BARZACK, Stevan & Louisa	Frederick William	18 Aug 1874
Comal	BASEL, William & Susanne (Brussler)	Betty	11 Feb 1855
		William	23 Apr 1857
		Julius	12 Feb 1859
Austin	BASLE, Ben & Sina	Reese	10 Aug 1874
Gillespie	BASSE, Oscar & Mathilde	Dorette Meta	1 Sep 1875
		Auguste Amanda	26 Mar 1874
Gillespie	BASSE, William & Louise	Auguste	30 Sep 1875
Burnet	BATEMAN, W. S. & Alice V.	Charles Halsey	19 Dec 1875
Hays	BATES, Perry & Sarah	Sinnett	19 Feb 1874
Bexar	BAUER, Pauline (See Edward Schmidt)		
Nacogd	BAUGH, M. V. & Nancy	Hollis R.	1 Apr 1876
Bastrop	BAUHOFF, F. & Annie	Edward	1 Sep 1873
Bexar	BAUMBERGER, Annie (See Joseph Treuer)		
Fayette	BAUR, A. & B.	Selma	5 Mar 1876
Nacogd.	BAXTER, Westley & Everline	John W.	20 Dec 1873
San Saba	BAYLIS, George & Mildred	Imogene	13 Jan 1875
Fayette	BAYLOR, G. W. & A. I.	Mary M.	29 Jun 1874
Bell	BEACH, J. F. & ?	Clara Emma	10 Mar 1874
Travis	BEALL, Duval & Jennie	Helen	21 Sep 1873
Lee	BEAMAN, J. W. & Mary W.	Beulah Canary	15 May 1875
Brazos	BEARD, J. T. & Elizabeth	Sidney T.	18 Mar 1874
Travis	BEAUMONT, G. N. & M. E.	Laura Catherine	15 Jan 1875
Comanche	BECK, Josiah & C. J.	Solomon	2 Jul 1874
Bexar	BECK, Lucian P. & Louise A.	Lucian P.	10 May 1871
		Hettie Maude	5 Sep 1873
Bexar	BECKER, Reinhold & Bertha (Gribbom)	Hedwig Amalie	21 Jun 1866
		Helena Wilhelmina	27 Apr 1868
		Max Fridolin	18 Aug 1869
		Hulda Emilie	17 Feb 1875
Bexar	BECKER, Theresa (See Charles Hitzfelder)		
Bandera	BEEKMAN, A. M. & Mary M.	Joseph Francis	18 Apr 1874
Colorado	BEEMAN, A. L. & A. E.	Annie Luter	30 Aug 1873

4

COUNTY	PARENTS	CHILD	DATE
Medina	BEETZ, Anton & Catharina	Rosaly	19 Apr 1875
Bexar	BEEZEIBOCH, Henrieta (See William Esser)		
Comal	BEHNSCH, Julius & Louisa (Gramm)	Adolph Gustav (Otto)	14 Feb 1875
Austin	BEHRNS, John & Emma	Henry	2 Jun 1874
Bexar	BEITEL, Elizabeth (See John Illg)		
Bexar	BELL, David & Eliza C.	Eliza C.	1 Sep 1872
		Emeline S.	7 Nov 1874
Hays	BELL, George & Martha L.	Olive E.	19 May 1873
Bell	BELL, J. K. & E. A.	James M.	19 Jul 1875
DeWitt	BELL, James & Mary	Carrie L.	31 Aug 1874
Austin	BELL, John P. & L. A.	Lucy	22 May 1874
Brazos	BELLINGTON, John W. & Julia A.	Clara Eliza	13 Dec 1874
Kendall	BELORA, Paul & Ernestine	Emilie	5 Sep 1873
Austin	BEMBRY, Ishmael & Emeline	John	3 Feb 1875
Victoria	BENHAM, Martha J. (See Gilbert Onderdonk)		
Comal	BENNER, Josephine (See Albert Dreiss)		
Bexar	BENNER, Susana (See Edward Anton Seffel)		
Comal	BENNER, Tony (See Edgar Ernst Schramm)		
Lavaca	BENNETT, J. W. & Fanny	Louisa	18 Aug 1875
Bexar	BENNETT, John W. & Sarah J.	Wm. Edward	11 Jul 1873
Lee	BENNETT, Robert B. & Rubelia	Pearl Virginia	27 Apr 1874
		Haywood	30 Dec 1875
Brazos	BENNEVILLE, M. J. & Z. C.	Blanche	26 Feb 1873
		Alice	26 Dec 1875
Comal	BENOIT, Joseph & Gertrude (Schlippes)	Heinrich	25 Dec 1874
Bexar	BEPPERT, Mary (See M. Zoller)		
Kendall	BERGMANN, Anton & Ernstine	Bertha	22 Nov 1868
		Joseph	8 Mar 1870
		Emma	5 Feb 1872
		Anna	1874
Kendall	BERGMAN, Christoph W. & Anna	Heinrich	11 Dec 1871
		Carl	23 Apr 1873
		Emma	2 Jul 1875
Bexar	BERNAL, Juan Pedro & Roberta (Reyes)	Tomasa	11 Apr 1874
Bexar	BERNARD, Louis & Sarah	Angel	29 Jul 1873
Austin	BERNER, Felix A. & Catharine	Maggie Eliza	10 Aug 1874
Comal	BERNHARD, Hieranimus & Adel (Reszcynski)	Thekla	2 Jul 1875
Comal	BERNHARDT, Lina (See John P. Lehde)		
Bexar	BERNHEIM, Louis & Sarah (Stron)	O. Angel	29 Jul 1873
Nacogd.	BERRYHILL, Thomas & Rutha J.	Christopher C.	14 Aug 1873
Lavaca	BESSANT, Benja. & Nancy	Christopher C.	18 Jul 1874
Bexar	BETZER, Raemond & Johanuetta (Sannees)	Willie Eliza	14 Jun 1875
Austin	BEYER, Leopold Max Ottomar & Mary	Justine Klara Ida	3 Dec 1875
Gillespie	BIBERSTEIN, H. R. & Lina	Herrman	4 Oct 1875
Bexar	BIESENBACK, Pauline (See Herman Barbeck)		
Bexar	BIGGAR, James Henry & Bridget J. (McDermott)	John	19 Aug 1877
		James Henry	12 Oct 1879
Bexar	BIHL, Charles A. & Eliza (Russi)	Chas. Alfred	26 Dec 1873
		Georg D.	8 Dec 1874

5

COUNTY	PARENTS	CHILD	DATE
Medina	BILHARTZ, Frank Haver &		
	Louisa Mary	Frank Haver	10 Sep 1874
	(1874 Entry spelled Mary Louisa)	Joseph	1 Apr 1876
Caldwell	BILLINGER, Edmund & Arminda	John Carnot	6 Jan 1875
Gillespie	BILLINGS, William Riley &		
	Ellen	Louisa Elisabeth	11 May 1873
		John	3 Apr 1875
Hays	BILLINGSLY, Canol & Eliza	Ora Ann	17 Dec 1874
Bastrop	BILLINGSLY, John H. & R. O.	Catherine	16 Aug 1873
		Cora	3 Sep 1874
Victoria	BILSTEIN, Anna (See Emeil Urban)		
Bexar	BIPPERT, Fred &		
	Bertha (Gueldner)	Fred'k. Albert	8 Jun 1874
	(1875 Entry Spelled Birda Gueldner)	Clara Sophia	29 Dec 1875
Medina	BIPPERT, John &		
	Catherine E.	Henry Jacob	30 Aug 1874
Gillespie	BIRCK, Peter & Lina	Emil	17 Nov 1874
Hays	BIRMINGHAM, E. L. & L. C.	Bessie S.	15 Sep 1874
Bexar	BIROZ, Marie (See George Mandry)		
DeWitt	BISCHOFF, Henry August &		
	Alma	Henrietta Alma	12 Jan 1876
Lavaca	BISHOP, B. F. & Emily	Ellen L.	4 Feb 1875
Lavaca	BISHOP, J. C. & ?	Lilley N.	22 Feb 1874
Fayette	BISHOP, John Rufus &		
	Maggie A. (Gillespie)	Willie Lee	20 Nov 1873
Lavaca	BISHOP, Lewis & Sarah J.	Jas. Ray	23 Mar 1874
Lavaca	BISHOP, R. & Martha	Chas. M.	11 Nov 1874
San Saba	BISHOP, S. G. & R. B.	Bessie Lee	11 Apr 1875
DeWitt	BISSETT, H. H. & Ann E. J.	Henry J.	7 Sep 1872
		George Wesley	31 Mar 1874
Lavaca	BISSETT, John H. & M. F.	John T.	5 Sep 1874
Bexar	BITTER, H. W. &		
	Francisca (Winckler)	Anna Ottilia	18 Dec 1873
Bexar	BITTERS, William H. &		
	Henrietta (Sorge)	Charlotte	23 Feb 1870
		Wm. Henry	28 Jul 1871
		Dan Charlie	25 Jul 1873
		Louise Elise	8 Jan 1876
Bell	BLACK, D. A. & Tenny (twins)	Alice & Ellen	12 Nov 1874
Burnet	BLACK, Wm. P. & Louisa	Permelia Ann	11 Sep 1874
Burnet	BLACKBURN, William A. &		
	Sarah A.	Robert Lee	12 Nov 1874
Nacogd.	BLACKWELL, Nathan & Mandy	Nathan	25 Dec 1873
Austin	BLAIR, Jacob & Wilhelmine	Benjamin Ferdinand	12 Feb 1876
Bell	BLAIR, W. B. & M. A.	Mallory	10 Dec 1873
	(1875 Entry spelled Wm.B. & M.A.)	George E.	7 Nov 1875)
Austin	BLAKE, S. Reese &		
	Julia Meshaw	Mary Louise	10 Feb 1875
Austin	BLAND, Thornton & Clarissa D.	Alice	7 Apr 1875
Cladwell	BLANKENSHIP, B. & Eurma	Frank H.	27 May 1875
Bexar	BLIND, Robert & Anna (Elsner)	Anna Catherine	9 Dec 1874
		Emile Ferdinand	28 Jul 1876
Bexar	BLOTZ, Frank & Agnes (Fink)	Frank Willie	3 Feb 1873
		Frank Louis	19 Jun 1874
Bexar	BLOTZ, Frank &		
	Catherine (Nagel)	Mary Caroline	13 Aug 1867
Hays	BLUM, C. Frederick &		
	Johanne H. C.	Egon	18 Oct 1874
Travis	BLUMENTRITT, Louis &		
	Caroline	Jane Caroline	9 Dec 1874
Bell	BOATRIGHT, E. & F. A.	John Wm.	16 May 1874
Lavaca	BOCK, Charles & Catherine	Anna	5 Jul 1873
Travis	BOCK, Edward & Julie	Mathilde	9 Dec 1870
		Edward	15 Dec 1872
		Theodore	17 Jul 1874
		Guido	12 Jul 1876
		Harry	15 Sep 1878

COUNTY	PARENTS	CHILD	DATE
Austin	BOEBEL, Gustav & Mary	Emma Charlotte	9 Apr 1874
Comal	BOECKMANN Von, Edgar &		
	Emma (Fuchs)	Edgar	2 Feb 1874
		Elise	12 Feb 1876
Medina	BOEHLE, Friedrich & Antje	Wilhelmina	1 Sep 1873
Austin	BOELSCHE, Friederich &		
	Caroline	Henry	14 Mar 1876
Comal	BOENIG, Whilhelm &		
	Charlotte (Ahlemeyer)	Louis	14 Apr 1875
Bexar	BOERNER, Johanna (See Joseph Heinen)		
Medina	BOHLEN, Ernst August & Folke	Frederick Herman	12 May 1873
Kendall	BOHNERT, Anton & Friedericka	Moritz	20 May 1869
		Antonia	24 Nov 1870
		Gottfried	18 Sep 1872
		Wilhelm	31 Aug 1874
Bexar	BOLDING, Annie B. (See W. A. Wallace)		
DeWitt	BOLDT, Lebrecht & C.	Robert	1 Mar 1874
DeWitt	BOLDT, Wm. & Mary	Matilda	18 Dec 1875
Nacogd.	BOLTON, Elijah & ?	Joseph M.	31 Dec 1874
San Saba	BOMAN, F. R. & M. V.	Cora Martha	6 Aug 1874
DeWitt	BOMBA, Joseph & Bellie	Ludwig	24 Aug 1873
Gillespie	BONN, Peter & Caroline	Richard	7 Mar 1875
Austin	BONNER, Dan & Mary	Mary J.	17 Oct 1874
Bexar	BONNET, Henry Daniel &		
	Josephine (Breitenstien)	Ida Caroline	2 Apr 1874
Bexar	BONNET, Wm. & Katie A.	Katie Ann	7 Nov 1873
Bexar	BOOKER, Ralph & Lucy	Della	3 Sep 1873
Burnet	BOOKER, Josiah & Nancy	Francis Rosa	12 Apr 1874
Grimes	BOOKMAN, F. D. & Lucy	Isiah	20 Aug 1873
Grimes	BOOKMAN, Green & Harriet L.	Lydia	2 Feb 1874
Grimes	BOOKMAN, W. C. & A. O.	Ida Lillian	28 Jan 1874
Bexar	BORCHERS, Henry &		
	Josephine (Stroyhmeyer)	Emma	3 Aug 1876
Lee	BORNEMAN, Henry & Wilhelmina	William Ernst	9 Feb 1874
		Chas. William	15 Apr 1875
		Marie Wilhelmina	
	(1875 - sic)	Amelia	8 Nov 1875
Bexar	BORTICK, M. Z. (See D. W. Heard)		
Comal	BOSE, Emil von &	Albert Heinrich	
	Caroline (Startz)	Julius	26 Dec 1878
Comal	BOSE, Heinrich Adolph von &		
	Marianne (Coers)	Theodor	24 Sep 1848
		Moritz	7 Oct 1853
		Emil	28 Feb 1857
		Clara	15 May 1859
		Robert	28 Feb 1861
Bexar	BOTHWELL, E. H. &		
	Isabilla D.	Isabella	21 Mar 1875
Burnet	BOULTINGHOUSE, Calvin &		
	Alice	Emily	20 Mar 1875
Bexar	BOWEN, Mary (See Dr. J. J. Gaenslen)		
Caldwell	BOWERS, Geo. T. & S. A.	Charles Lee	11 Nov 1873
Travis	BOWLES, J. S. & M. E.	Albert Sidney	5 Jan 1874
Bastrop	BOWLING, W. R. & Mary A.	Euli Jean	12 Feb 1874
Comanche	BOWMAN, John & Elizabeth	William Gainer(s)	23 Jul 1874
Bexar	BOYD, Haywood & Cora (Settles)	Lucy Ellen	5 Jun 1874
Nacogd.	BOYETT, Jefferson B. &		
	Mary Ann	Levi Allen	18 Sep 1873
Victoria	BRACKEN, Lizzie (See Henry Conrad Franz)		
Austin	BRADBURY, Thos. H. &		
	Margaret	Mary Alice	3 Sep 1873
Bexar	BRADER, Anna (See Friederick Emelienberg)		
DeWitt	BRADFORD, Jesse V. &		
	Eliza B.	Eliza Prudence	18 Oct 1874
Bexar	BRADFORD, M. H. &		
	Annie (Thompson)	George Anna	8 Apr 1875

COUNTY	PARENTS	CHILD	DATE
Hays	BRADFORD, Samuel & Popy (Merriwether)	Mattie E. B.	29 Mar 1874
Bexar	BRADLEY, Ada (See Jacob Waelder)		
Bastrop	BRADSHAW, W. H. & L. C. (twins)	Laura & Rosa	26 Feb 1874
Hays	BRADY, Amanda (See George McNeal)		
Bastrop	BRAHM, H. & Anna M.	Anna Catharina	3 Jun 1874
Bexar	BRAMIGH, Clara (See H. L. Degener)		
Hays	BRANDENBURGH, John H. & Lydia A.	Maud	12 Apr 1875
Bexar	BRANDIS, ?? & Dortheo (Brandis)	Dortheo (sic)	16 Jul 1874
Lavaca	BRANON, J. D. & J. A.	Katie C.	29 Dec 1873
Bexar	BRASFIELD, Soloman & Margaret (Hodges)	Lewis	6 Sep 1876
Travis	BRASS, G. M. & Amelia	G. M.	8 Sep 1874
Austin	BRAUN, August Ferdinand & Frederika Rebecca	Bertha Otilie Henriette Wilhelmine	5 Feb 1875
Kendall	BRAUN, Charles & Elizabeth	Carl Otto	16 Sep 1869
Comal	BRAUN, Emil & Caroline (Brumme)	Mathilde	16 Apr 1874
Hays	BRAUNHOLZ, John & Dorothea (Twins)	Volentine & Oscar	14 Mar 1874
	(Note: Line drawn through above entry)		
		Ernst & Otto	14 Mar 1874
San Saba	BRAZIL, Jesse & Eliz. J.	Finettie May	12 Dec 1874
Gillespie	BREHMER, Friedrich & Marie	Wilhelm	21 Mar 1875
Comal	BREHMER, Karl Friedrich Wilhelm & Emma (Hartung)	Louisa Alma	28 Sep 1875
		Agnes Emma	16 Apr 1878
Medina	BREITEN, J. N. & Ursula	August	16 Sep 1873
Bexar	BREITENSTIEN, Josephine (See Henry Daniel Bonnet)		
Bexar	BRENDEL, John & Dorothea	Emil	24 Oct 1851
		Hermann	6 Jan 1855
		William	29 Mar 1858
		Adam	18 Dec 1860
		Maria	23 Nov 1862
Bexar	BRENTONS, Louise (See Charles Harnisch)		
Bastrop	BRENZEL, Anton & Theresa	Anton	25 Oct 1874
Colorado	BRETSCHNIEDER, Egmont & Agnes	Clotilde	18 Dec 1873
Gillespie	BRETZMANN, Gustav & Sophie	Aurelie	21 Oct 1874
Austin	BREWER, B. D. & Susan E.	McLaran	23 Jan 1875
Bexar	BREWER, Mary (See Mathew Rossman)		
Austin	BREWER, Rufus H. & Isabella	Sarah Francis	12 Mar 1874
		(sic)William Augutus	16 Oct 1875
Bexar	BRIAM, Louis & Antonia (Lieck)	August	4 Aug 1858
		Carolina	17 Jul 1860
		Julia	26 Dec 1861
		Louis	17 Oct 1864
		Antonia	27 Jun 1869
		Hans	15 May 1871
Caldwell	BRIDGES, J. P. & L. F.	M. L.	3 Mar 1876
Bexar	BRIDON, Emma (See Henry McDowel)		
Nacogd.	BRIDWELL, William S. & Josephine A.	Thomas F.	3 Oct 1873
Grimes	BRIGANCE, A. F. & A. M.	Wm. Lewin	11 Jan 1875
Grimes	BRIGANCE, C. W. & Kate A.	May Willie Rhoennal	14 Feb 1875
Bexar	BRIGGS, I. Y. & Z. G.	Emma	27 Nov 1875
Bexar	BRIGGS, James Theodore & Zilla (Clark)	Mabel Etta	26 Apr 1874
Lavaca	BRINKLEY, J. W. & Mary A.	Leroy	29 Dec 1874
Victoria	BROCKER, Rosina (See August Scherer)		
Bell	BROADNAX, O. W. & C.	Wm.	8 Sep 1874
Brazos	BROGDON, Wm. Joseph & Laura (Cook)	Lucy Hix	11 Jun 1879

COUNTY	PARENTS	CHILD	DATE
Bell	BROOKMAN, W. L. & V. C.	Charlie	10 Sep 1872
Bell	BROOKMAN, W. &. & J.	Annie H.	21 Oct 1874
San Saba	BROOKRESON, Fed.(?) & Talitha	Tallitha Bell	28 Sep 1873
Hays	BROOKS, Francis A. & Rhoda	Francis M.	28 Jan 1874
		Roby. Westley	2 Jan 1876
Lee	BROOKS, R. W. & Amelia (sic)	Francis Asbory	15 Apr 1875
Bexar	BROTZE, Anna (See Julius Lieck)		
Hays	BROUN, Jesse & Sytha (John)	Robert	10 Jan 1875
Lee	BROWDER, Francis Marion & Cynthia Louvina	John Wilson	26 Apr 1874
Caldwell	BROWN, A. J. J. & Virginia	Wm. Aaron	10 Mar 1874
Travis	BROWN, Albert & Jennie Ann	Coke	30 Nov 1873
San Saba	BROWN, Asa R. & Mary S.	? (M)	12 Jun 1874
DeWitt	BROWN, Ben & Mary R.	Robt. Ben	28 Jan 1874
	(twins)	Ursula & Everett	7 May 1876
Bandera	BROWN, Caleb & Mary M.	Thomas Evans	11 Jul 1875
Hays	BROWN, E. S. & H. A.	Mary Hunt	24 Feb 1875
Nacogd.	BROWN, Ezekiel M. & Maria Josephine	Wm. Edgar	23 Feb 1868
		Robert Farmer	10 May 1870
		James Ezekiel	27 Jan 1872
		Dove Warner	18 Sep 1876
Bexar	Brown, Irene (See Joseph Volney Shiner)		
Kendall	BROWN, J. C. & Martha Jane	Diana Jane	1 Sep 1873
Fayette	BROWN, J. Calhoun & Olivia (Dancy)	Ella Deborah	20 Dec 1874
San Saba	BROWN, James F. & Alice	Guy McNeal	20 Jun 1874
San Saba	BROWN, Jasper W. & Clara	Bettie	13 Aug 1873
		Edna	12 Apr 1875
Hays	BROWN, John R. & Sarah Ellen	Edwin Green	4 Jan 1874
Bexar	BROWN, Kate (See James Clavin)		
Comanche	BROWN, M. B. & G. B.	Margaret Octavia	14 Sep 1874
Victoria	BROWN, Mary Louisa (See James Rives)		
Bexar	BROWN, Wm. & Mary	Henry	14 Mar 1875
Bexar	BRUCE, Gabriel C. & Mary	Leder Chrisiner	15 Feb 1875
Travis	BRUEGGERHOFF, William & Mary	Louis	18 Sep 1874
Comal	BRUMME, Caroline (See Emil Braun)		
Bastrop	BRUNDIDGE, B. A. & Lucy A.	Ada E.	24 Sep 1873
Comal	BRUSSLER, Susanne (See William Basel)		
Lee	BRYANT, B. B. & Isabella	Maggie Fleta	16 Feb 1873
Bexar	BRYANT, Neppa (See Wm. R. Carson)		
Bexar	BUCHANAN, George & Sarah (Morris)	Alick	2 Mar 1874
		George	1876
Lavaca	BUCHANAN, John & Lizzie	Eleanor	5 Feb 1874
		John Jr.	11 Oct 1875
Austin	BUCHMANN, John & Minna	Emiel	12 Mar 1875
Victoria	BUCHRIG, Wilhelmina (See Conrad Lackner)		
Bandera	BUCK, E. & Mary	Robert Edward	8 Mar 1874
Bexar	BUECHLER, P. A. H. & Anna (Mozygenda)	Elizabeth	25 Oct 1874
Travis	BUECHNER, Christ. & Mary	Herman Justus	8 Jun 1874
Austin	BUESCHER, Gottfried & Agnes	Hugo	5 Apr 1874
Bell	BUFORD, R. P. & Lucy	Grace Alice	15 Sep 1873
Victoria	BUKFIN, M. V. (See E. M. Philips)		
Brazos	BULLARD, Henry Mildred (See Frank George Hill)		
Burnet	BUMAM, Robert T. & Isabell	John H.	14 Sep 1873
Lee	BUNTING, James & Sarah E.	Williamson	6 Apr 1874
Hays	BUNTON, John & Julia (Scott)	John D.	18 Apr 1874
Bexar	BURELL, Theresa (See Eugene Dietrich)		
Bexar	BURG, Emma (See Adolph Weber)		
Nacogd.	BURK, B. T. & Sallie	Jane	4 Oct 1874
Nacogd	BURK, John T. & M. J.	Bettie English	11 Jan 1874
		James Washington	11 Jan 1874
Austin	BURKE, Louis & Sene	Ginnie	1874

COUNTY	PARENTS	CHILD	DATE
Lavaca	BURKETT, Nathan B. & Catherine	Ophelia Clementine	3 Jan 1874
Comal	BURKHARDT, Alvine (See Franz Wersterfer)		
Bexar	BURKHARDT, Fredk. & Amelia (Hoffman)	William	28 May 1874
Bell	BURKS, Silas & M. L.	Sarah July	3 Jul 1875
Hays	BURLESON, Ed & Emma	Mary K.	14 Dec 1873
Burnet	BURLESON, J. C. & M. J.	Sidney Estes	7 May 1874
Hays	BURLESON, Joe R. & E. E.	Joseph R. Jr.	16 Oct 1873
Hays	BURLESON, Maggie (See Jackson McMillan)		
Lee	BURNS, C. C. & Matilda	Walter A.	26 Apr 1874
Lee	BURNS, E. A. & M. J.	Mary C.	1875
Bell	BURNS, W. I. & E. A.	Mary E.	12 Oct 1875
Bexar	BURRIS, Marranda (Anthony Earhart)		
DeWitt	BURROW, August & Emilia	Emilie	25 Jan 1874
Nacogd.	BURROWS, E. M. & M. J.	R. D.	7 Jan 1874
Nacogd.	BURROWS, J. L. & Mary H.	Lilly	25 Mar 1876
Lavaca	BURT, W. D. & M. L.	R. O.	1 Jul 1873
Comanche	BURTON, J. B. & Marretu	Creed Holmes	15 Dec 1874
Bexar	BURTON, Stephen G. & Margaret E. (Akin)	Charles Woodson	22 May 1859
		Mary Evaline	2 Oct 1862
Comal	BUSCH, Emma (See Franz Heimer)		
Comal	BUSCH, Johann Christian & Anna (Knibbe)	Albert Heinrich Hermann	22 Jul 1874
Austin	BUSHWAL, Frank & Mattie C.	Lula Francis	1 Dec 1873
Comal	Buss, Carl & Ottilie (Lorenz)	Heinrich Ad.	23 Jun 1857
		Gustav	25 Dec 1858
		Dorothea	23 Dec 1860
		Maria	12 Jul 1864
Nacogd.	BUTLER, Samuel & Ashia M.	Samuel W.	9 Nov 1873
Grimes	BUTY, W. F. M. & S. E.	Herbert	27 Feb 1875
Bexar	BUTZ, Minna (See John Henry Schaefer)		
Bexar	BYAN, Annie (See Theodore Baldus)		
DeWitt	BYARS, J. M. & M. E.	Thomas Edgar	10 Aug 1873
Lavaca	BYARS, W. E. & Emily	Wm. L.	12 Nov 1873
	BYARS, W. H. & M. O.	John Bruce	7 Jun 1873
Lavaca	BYRN, R. & Mary	J. W.	6 Feb 1874
		Ada	12 Nov 1875
Bexar	BYRN, Virginia (See Robert C. Symington)		
Nacogd.	CADE, Thomas & Nancy	William H.	28 Sep 1874
Bexar	CADENA, Julia C. (See Juan E. Barrera)		
Fayette	CADWELL, J. A. & M. E.	Leticia Lucas	16 Jul 1873
Hays	CADY, J. C. & Cynthia	Marinda Alice	1876
Hays	CADY, J. D. & Winnie	Loren Erastus	6 Aug 1873
Victoria	CAIN, Bettie (See Louis C. Wheeler)		
Bastrop	CAIN, T. C. & M. E.	Annie Laurie	20 Dec 1875
Bastrop	CALDWELL, C. G. & M. R.	Jesse Oliver	4 May 1873
Bexar	CALDWELL, Geo W. & Lydia E. (Williams)	Arthur Brooks	8 Oct 1872
		Mary Roberta	23 Jul 1875
Bexar	CALDWELL, Mary (See John C. Crawford)		
Hays	CALDWELL, Robert M. & Mary E.	Georgie	26 Jun 1873
		Robert Milam Jr.	20 May 1875
Nacogd.	CALHOUN, B. A. & J. E.	E. V.	22 Apr 1875
DeWitt	CALHOUN, Jno. R. & Annie D.	Alvin	Jul 1873
		Chas. Reynolds	No date
DeWitt	CALHOUN, Saml. & Nancy E.	Lew Smith	11 Jan 1874
Bexar	CALLAGHAN, James & Mary (Grenet)	Marie E.	19 Sep 1873
Gillespie	CALLAN, Chris. C. & Sue, Jr. (sic)	Almon Orson	1 Jan 1875
Travis	CALLAWAY, C. M. & L. E.	Charles Kendall	11 Aug 1874
Grimes	CALLAWAY, J. M. & S. M.	Reba	29 Dec 1874

10

COUNTY	PARENTS	CHILD	DATE
Colorado	CALLER, J. H. & L. L.	James W.	21 Aug 1873
		Mary E.	16 Aug 1875
		(sic) Olivia A.	21 Jul 1872
Austin	CALLOWAY, George & Rosetta	Lee	2 Jul 1874
Kendall	CAMMACK, R. H. & Martha V.	Minnie Vilora	14 Jan 1873
		George A.	15 Jan 1875
Grimes	CAMP, M. M. & D. E.	William Burleson	3 Nov 1873
Nacogd.	CAMPBELL, Burl & Asilee	William H.	14 Oct 1873
Comanche	CAMPBELL, D. A. & C. N.	Elma Blanche	20 Sep 1875
Burnet	CAMPBELL, D. C. & Matilda	Mary Lee	12 Jul 1873
Caldwell	CAMPBELL, J. W. & E.	Carroll Elmer	12 Dec 1874
Austin	CAMPBELL, James & Sallie	Ira Lee	11 Oct 1874
Nacogd.	CAMPBELL, James L. & Ann J.	Zipora J.	25 Mar 1875
Bexar	CAMPBELL, Kate (See C. H. Merritt)		
Austin	CAMPBELL, Wm. T. & Sue	Eula	15 Aug 1873
Comanche	CANNACK, J. W. & N. J.	Wm. Lee	16 Feb 1875
Hays	CANNON, Chas. R. & Laura	Beulah Benton	Feb 1875
Bastrop	CANTWELL, James & Narcissi	Stepen (sic)	5 Jun 1874
Brazos	CAR, Henry & Sallie	Margurate	15 Jan 1862
Bastrop	CARDENES, Bartolo & Eugenia	Vanitta	7 Sep 1874
Bell	CAREY, E. W. & A. M.	Ada Viola May	2 Feb 1875
Medina	CARLE, Joseph & Catharine	John	24 Sep 1874
Lavaca	CARLILE, Jas. W. & Mary S.	Emma L.	14 Dec 1874
Hays	CARNAHAN, Wallace & Mary S.	Hart	30 Jan 1874
Comanche	CARNES, C. W. & Sallie	Edna Earle	20 Nov 1873
Comanche	CARNES, David & Caroline	Wade	26 Oct 1873
Nacogd.	CARNES, William F. & Louisa A.	Lourina (sic)	28 Jul 1874
Bexar	CAROTHERS, Sarah (See James S. Smith)		
Hays	CARPENTER, Cyrus M. & Charlotte A.	Mary Cornelius May	27 May 1875
Victoria	CARPENTER, Sallie F. (See Isaac P. Keibbe)		
Hays	CARPENTER, Shawnee & Susan A.	Shawnee Thomas	20 Feb 1874
Caldwell	CARPENTER, W. W. & M. J.	Luetta	5 Apr 1875
Colorado	CARRUTH, E. B. & Bettie	John Mc(sic)	29 May 1874
Bexar	CARRUTHERS, Andrew Ed & Frances (Ives)	Geo. Cupples	18 Dec 1875
		Andrew M.	8 Oct 1878
Austin	CARSEN, G. W. & Julia	Edward	19 Nov 1874
Victoria	CARSNER, Mary T. (See D. W. Kay)		
Lavaca	CARSON, J. W. & J. A.	John	16 Oct 1874
Hays	CARSON, James & Louisa	Francis	6 Feb 1874
Lee	CARSON, R. P. & E. June	Willie Hassel	3 Oct 1875
Bexar	CARSON, Rev. Wm. R. & Neppa (Bryant)	Nancy Caroline	30 Jan 1874
Kendall	CARSTANJEN, Rudolph & Ottilie	Ida	15 Nov 1871
		Rudolph	4 May 1876
Colorado	CARTER, C. R. & Jennie	Robert Ashley	6 Oct 1873
Austin	CARTER, Wilkins & Amanda	William	3 Dec 1874
Bell	CARTWRIGHT, J. T. & Maggie	Ida	14 Mar 1875
Nacogd.	CARTWRIGHT, L. M. & Mary F.	Jimmie E.	13 Jul 1873
Fayette	CARUTHERS, S. & A.	Stella	12 Dec 1873
Bandera	CARVER, Richard T. (? or G?) & M. M.	Joel	12 Dec 1874
Bandera	CASEY, S. C. & L. E.	Charlotte Eveline	9 Feb 1874
Nacogd.	CASPER, Joseph A. & Josephine	John Oswell	13 Aug 1873
		Wm. H.	9 May 1875
Burnet	CASS, Daniel E. & Louisa	Jessie Epps	12 Jan 1875
Baxar	CASTANOLA, Margaerite (See Charles Marucheau)		
Bexar	CASTELLAW, Helena (See Antonio P. Rivas)		
Bexar	CASTILLO, Manuel De Yturri & Helena (Garza)	Roberto de Yturri	9 Dec 1873
Nacogd.	CASTROW, Narcis & Mary	James T.	7 Jan 1872
		Neva Lenora	12 Jan 1875
		Eva Gabriella	9 Sep 1878

COUNTY	PARENTS	CHILD	DATE
Travis	CASWELL, Timothy & Julia	Minnie Amelia	11 Jul 1873
Burnet	CATE, James A. & Eliza J.	Mary Ellen	9 May 1875
Bell	CATER, J. & Nancy	Bab	19 Sep 1874
Burnet	CATES, R. H. & C. J.	Wooten Wesley	27 Jul 1874
Burnet	CATES, W. T. & Matilda A.	Esther Arnetta	6 Mar 1875
Bell	CAUTHON, J. B. & Sallie	Wm. Harvey	31 Dec 1874
Burnet	CAVIN, B. H. & Amanda M.	Rutha Ann	8 Sep 1873
		Minda Ellen	29 Dec 1875
San Saba	CAVNESS, D. P. & S. J.	Amanda Stella	8 Oct 1874
San Saba	DAVNESS, W. H. & Sarah	Henry Cliburn	20 Dec 1874
Hays	CEPHAS, Jos. & Isabella	Victoria Eva	6 Apr 1873
		Olive	16 Jan 1875
Bexar	CERNAL, (?) Rafugia (See Antonio Lopez)		
Burnet	CHAMBERLAIN, John T. &		
	Martha J.	James H.	9 Jan 1875
Bastrop	CHAMBLISS, L. L. & Mary J.	Louamna (sic)	29 Apr 1873
Lavaca	CHANDLER, O. & F. E.	Clara F.	1 Sep 1874
Nacogd.	CHANEY, P. G. & Sarah E.	Martha G.	20 Aug 1875
Hays	CHAPMAN, W. T. & M. A.	Willie	28 Feb 1874
Austin	CHAPPELL, Thomas & Adeline	Grant	13 Feb 1875
Bexar	CHAVES, Erasmo J. &		
	Antonia (Rodriquez)	Eloise F.	16 Jan 1874
Bexar	CHAVES, J. A. &		
	Gertrudes (Rivas)	Dora Yuana	1 Feb 1875
Bexar	CHAVEZ, Tomasa (See M. R. Garcia)		
Lavaca	CHENEY, A. P. & M. C.	Marion P.	18 Feb 1874
Lavaca	CHERRY, A. A. & S. F.	Minnie Earl	13 Sep 1873
Burnet	CHESSER, C. C. & Mandosha	Calvin Cornelius	8 Jun 1874
Brazos	CHESTERFIELD, Edward & Kate	Ella	6 Apr 1874
Bell	CHILDERS, D. Y. & M. A.	Andrew Young	30 Dec 1874
Lavaca	CHILDRES, W. G. & Ann	Henry T.	15 Jun 1874
Bexar	CHILDS, Mary (See Coteland Goodrich)		
Bexar	CHILTON, Emilie V. (See Willie H. Maverick)		
Victoria	CHIPLEY, Richard S. &		
	Mary (Skaggs)	Edmond Lee	22 Sep 1874
Bandera	CHIPMAN, David & Harriet	Thomas Henry	2 Aug 1875
Burnet	CHRISTIAN, John & Emma	Catherine	23 Jun 1874
Nacogd.	CHRISTOPHER, W. L. &		
	Martha Jane	Mary M.	31 Jul 1875
Nacogd.	CHRISTOPHER, William L. &		
	Rabecca	William L.	19 Nov 1875
Hays	CHUMNEY, W. C. & L. R.	James Edward	10 Mar 1874
Lavaca	CLARE, T. B. & Ann E.	J. B.	29 Mar 1876
Bandera	CLARK, A. & E. J.	Olive Rebecca	1 Mar 1874
Bell	CLARK, A. & S. A.	Lorada	30 Apr 1873
Bexar	CLARK, Francis (See Wm. Webb)		
Caldwell	CLARK, H. E. & S. E.	Hugh Caruthers	10 Jan 1875
Burnet	CLARK, J. R. & S. P.	Adelia Elizabeth	9 Feb 1874
Bandera	CLARK, P. C. & M. J.	Armentha Jane	20 Jan 1875
Lavaca	CLARK, S. A. & Susan	Marvin	3 Jul 1875
Bell	CLARK, S. J. & C. A.	James Walten	4 Mar 1874
Caldwell	CLARK, T. F. & E. J.	Della Elizabeth	2 Jan 1875
Lee	CLARK, Wm. R. & Sarah E.	Catherine	4 Feb 1874
		Mary A. O.	13 Mar 1875
Burnet	CLARK, William T. & Fannie	Adella	14 Nov 1874
		Edmund Carl	22 Mar 1876
Bexar	CLARK, Zilla (See James Theodore Briggs)		
Brazos	CLARKE, Frank & Paulene	Edith Morehouse	9 Nov 1874
		Josephine	30 Jan 1876
Bell	CLARY, A. H. & M. E.	Mary Viola	15 Jun 1873
Bell	CLARY, S. S. & Mary	Adah	No date
Bell	CLARY, W. S. & S.	Malony A.	14 Sep 1873
		Leona Jane	2 Mar 1875
DeWitt	CLASS, C. F. & Bertha	Emile Caroline	18 May 1873
Bexar	CLAVIN, James & Kate (Brown)	Geo. Innocent	7 Nov 1874

COUNTY	PARENTS	CHILD	DATE
Comal	CLEMENS, Whilhelm & Kathinka	Wilhelm Heinrich	20 Sep 1873
	(von Coll)	Walter	19 Oct 1874
Caldwell	CLIATT, Zach T. & Jennie M.	Lela Annie	10 Nov 1872
		Vela Taylor	30 Oct 1875
Bandera	CLICK, M. C. & N. J.	Ida	4 Oct 1874
Austin	CLIETT, Waller C. & Jodie	Anna Roberta	27 Aug 1874
Hays	CLOPTON, Anthony &		
	Margaret S.	Sarah E.	22 Sep 1873
Lavaca	CLOSE, E. S. & Sarah J.	Mary E.	9 Jun 1873
Lavaca	CLOSE, J. S. & Sarah V.(twins)	Thos. M. &	
		Lillen E.	4 Nov 1874
Lavaca	CLOSE, W. L. & R. E.	Sarah A. or E	12 Aug 1874
Austin	CLOUD, Green & Renza	Rosetta L.	15 Jan 1875
Bexar	COCHRAN, George B. &		
	Julia (Newton)	Thomas B.	8 Sep 1874
Austin	COCHRANE, Nehemiah & Florence	Carrie Emma	13 Feb 1874
		John Feilding	16 Feb 1876
Hays	COCREHAM, David E. &		
	Emma W.	Katie Celia	29 Apr 1874
Comal	COERS, Marianne (See Heinrich Adolph Bose)		
Lee	COFFMAN, W. H. & N. C.	Bill Jo	5 Feb 1875
Bexar	COHEN, Adolph M. & Theresa	Emanuel	15 Jan 1875
Comanche	COKER, J. W. & Laura	Robert Sanford	20 Jul 1875
Comanche	COKER, L. T. & Mary A.	Francis (sic)	
		Elmina	22 Sep 1874
		Joel Henry	19 Sep 1876
Comanche	COKER, P. L. & Fannie J.	David Thompson	31 Jan 1874
Comanche	COKER, R. C. & Mary U. (twins)	Emery Joseph &	
		Emily Josephine	24 Feb 1874
Grimes	COLDWELL, Orville B. & M.D.	Jane Rodney	26 Mar 1874
Kendall	COLE, Charles R. & Mary A.	Alfred J.	12 Aug 1874
Lavaca	COLEMAN, Chas. & Emely	Kate	31 Jul 1874
Austin	COLEMAN, George W. &		
	Georgeana	Levy Ann	5 Jul 1875
Lavaca	COLEMAN, T. B. & M. J.	Earnest H.	23 Jul 1874
Lavaca	COLEMAN, W. H. & C. R.	Hugh M.	16 Nov 1874
Victoria	COLLIER, Gilbert &		
	Caroline (Fryer)	Prescilla Jane	6 Aug 1873
Lee	COLLIER, J. W. & Lalitha	Ella Gertrude	9 May 1876
Colorado	COLLIER, Kit & Ann	Hattie	12 Jul 1875
Austin	COLLIER, Stephen & Hannah	William	17 Dec 1874
Caldwell	COLLINS, Clarence B. & Lou M.	Chester Tuttle	12 Dec 1874
Austin	COLLINS, Frank & Bettie	John Henry	1 Feb 1875
Lavaca	COLLINS, John A. & E. D.	John H.	22 Jan 1874
Bexar	COLLINS, Joseph &		
	Artie (Holladay)	James Foster	21 Dec 1868
		Robert Joel	30 Dec 1870
		Zelima	5 Dec 1872
		Custer Lee	28 Apr 1875
Austin	COLLINS, Kinchen & Mary	Linda Peach	12 May 1874
Nacogd.	COLLINS, Lee G. & E. M.	Lee G.	4 Jul 1873
Bexar	COLLMANN, Henry &		
	Josephine (Stanish)	Adolph	20 Jul 1873
Travis	COLVIN, G. & E. A.	Lillian	10 Aug 1874
Hays	COMBS, David S. &		
	Eleanora A.	Nora Burruss	6 Feb 1874
Hays	COMBS, James H. & Fannie A.	Robt. Lee	11 Aug 1873
Bell	CONDREY, L. T. (or S.) &		
	G. P.	Nancy M.	30 Oct 1873
Caldwell	CONNALLY, C. M. & Malissa	Dan Triplett	24 Jun 1874
Bexar	CONNELLEY, Bettie H. (See Richard H. Neal)		
Lavaca	CONNOWAY, W. A. & M.	Rosie Lee	4 Oct 1873
Bexar	CONRAD, Catharine (See Robert Meyer)		
Comal	CONRADS, Clemens &		
	Emma (Wallis)	Anna Catherina	
	August	Marie	28 Sep 1860

COUNTY	PARENTS	CHILD	DATE
Comal	CONRADS, Clemens & Emma Cont.	Thekla Clementine	2 May 1862
		Clementine Emma	
		Laura	28 Apr 1864
		Arthur Clemens	
		August	20 Feb 1866
		Nanni Mathilde	30 Jul 1869
		Clemens Johann	1 Dec 1877
		Waldemar Clemens	
		Joseph	1 Dec 1877
Comal	CONRING, Ernst & Elise (Muller)	Meta Clara	30 May 1874
Comal	CONRING, Georgine (See Christian Heinrich Holtz)		
Comal	CONRING, Marie Charlotte (See Hermann Emil Fischer)		
DeWitt	COOK, Caswell W. & Rebecca E.	King Thomas	23 Aug 1874
San Saba	COOK, G. B. & H. A.	Omega	31 Dec 1873
DeWitt	COOK, George S. & Martha A.	Charles Ervin	30 Nov 1874
Brazos	COOK, Laura (See Wm. Joseph Brogdon)		
San Saba	COOK, P. A. & Amy E.	Tully F.	21 Feb 1876
Austin	COOK, W. U. & M. E.	Zada Elizabeth	9 May 1874
Nacogd.	COON, Edwin F. & S. R.	John P.	24 Jun 1873
Bell	COOPER, F. P. & A. C.	Abbidena	4 Aug 1874
Comanche	COOPER, T. L. & H. E.	Nona Leoti (e)	10 Jan 1874
Bastrop	COPE, Jas. B. & Laura Lee	William Dade	7 Jul 1873
Bastrop	CORBELL, F. H. & M. E.	Sarah V.	9 Feb 1874
Bastrop	CORBELL, P. C. & E. C.	Mary S.	26 Mar 1874
Kendall	CORLEY, Frank & ??	Frank Hamer	16 Dec 1874
Comanche	COTTRELL, J. H. & Mary	Alice Lillian	23 Jan 1874
Bexar	COTULLA, Mary (See Christian M. Wolcken)		
Comanche	COUCH, W. H. & Jane	Susana	19 Sep 1873
Brazos	COULTER, Jno. W. & Nannie A. (Robinson)	Walter J.	16 Feb 1875
Nacogd.	COUNCIL, J. C. & M. M.	W. P.	8 May 1873
Lee	COWAN, D. B. & E. J.	R. Wood	Oct 1874
Bell	COWAN, R. J. & Melissa	Leona	16 Nov 1873
DeWitt	COX, H. H. & Caroline	Cora Rosali	16 Feb 1875
Travis	COX, J. F. & Nancy	Elizabeth Ellen	16 Dec 1871
		Willis Hampton	27 May 1874
Nacogd.	COX, Margaret A. H. (See James A. Day)		
Bexar	COX, Nannie (See J. T. Hunter)		
Bastrop	COX, W. H. & Nancy Ann	John Franklin	7 Oct 1873
Bell	COX, W. W. & S. A.	Hattie	12 Jun 1873
		Walter Clarence	30 Nov 1875
Bexar	COY, Andres & Anita	Alex	12 Sep 1876
Hays	COZBY, Isaac O. & Emily F.	Norman Berry	12 Nov 1873
		Amy Pearl	21 Jul 1876
Nacogd.	CRAIN, Giles B. & Sarah E.	Giles R.	16 Nov 1871
		Hulon Taylor	18 Aug 1874
		Richard Lycurgers	31 Dec 1875
		Wm. Oscar	19 Jan 1878
Nacogd.	CRAIN, John W. & Maneurah P.	William A.	3 Feb 1873
Brazos	CRAMER, Ceasor & Ellen	Ceasor	20 Apr 1874
Comanche	CRAMER, Josiah & Sarah E.	Jesse Selena	11 Sep 1874
Kendall	CRAVEY, Chas. H. & Mary	Alzoda	16 Nov 1874
Bell	CRAWFORD, E. S. (or G.) & M. J.	Robt. Hy Lee	20 Sep 1873
Colorado	CRAWFORD, George B. & Jennie O.	Jessie R.	23 Aug 1875
Bexar	CRAWFORD, John C. & Mary (Caldwell)	Annie Y.	23 Sep 1874
Bexar	CRAWFORD, John C. Jr. & Mary Ester (Miles)	Edward Miles	25 Nov 1875
		Mary Ann Miles	28 Sep 1876
Bell	CRAWFORD, M. A. & M. A.	Garie Lang	11 Jul 1874
Gillespie	CRENWELGE, Christian & Elizabeth	Henriette Louise	22 Apr 1875

14

COUNTY	PARENTS	CHILD	DATE
Gillespie	CRENWELGE, Friedrich & Johanne	Lydia	10 Nov 1874
Gillespie	CRENWELGE, Georg Wilhelm & Dorothea Sophie Christiane	Dorothea	6 Feb 1874
Gillespie	CRENWELGE, Peter & Eleonore	Otto Friedrich	12 Sep 1873
		Alfred Heinrich	15 Apr 1875
Gillespie	CRENWELGE, Philipp & Minna	Ludwig	5 May 1874
Kendall	CREWS, Thos. C. & Cora C.	Nancy Ann	22 Feb 1873
		Cassandra	31 Dec 1874
Comanche	CREWS, W. K. & E. P.	Laura Lettie	27 Feb 1874
Nacogd.	CRISP, Duncan C. & E. T.	Jessie	12 Sep 1875
DeWitt	CRISWELL, J. H. & M. J.	Thomas S.	27 Jul 1873
Bexar	CROKER, Annie (See Thos. A. Dwyer)		
Brazos	CROSS, N. J. & M. C.	Viola W.	6 Jan 1876
Nacogd.	CROUCH, William & S. E.	Walter S.	17 Apr 1874
Bexar	CROW, James & Harriet	Londres James	22 Apr 1875
Hays	CROWE, John F. & E. P.	John Finley	21 Mar 1874
Caldwell	CRUNK, R. J. & Florida	Ethel	13 Oct 1873
		W. R.	12 May 1875
Hays	CRUSE, J. S. & Mary K.	Indianola	23 Feb 1874
Hays	CUDE, John M. & Nancy N.	Thos. Nathaniel	20 Apr 1874
Bandera	CULLEN, T. J. & N. G.	Lucy	7 Jun 1874
Lavaca	CULPEPPER, J. L. & Margaret (Twins)	J. M. (M)	
		J. M. (F)	3 Jun 1873
Austin	CUMINGS, W. L. & Dicey A.	Anna Bell	21 Nov 1874
Burnet	CUMMINGS, C. C. & Mary	Wm. Rozelle	10 May 1874
Lavaca	CUMMINGS, D. M. & V. B.	Grant	29 Aug 1874
Comanche	CUNNINGHAM, R. F. & S. A.	Kinlock Falcones	23 Mar 1874
Bell	CURB, A. M. & F. J. (twins)	Anasew(?) Edwin & Martha Etta	5 Jul 1874
Brazos	CURD, B. M. & A.	Ellen M.	7 May 1875
Comanche	CURRY, J. S. & S. C.	John Virgil	29 Dec 1873
		Claude Rupert	26 Sep 1875
Brazos	CURTIS, J. S. & Fannie O.	Jimmie Y.	18 Nov 1875
Travis	CUSTARD, Wm. & Clara	Ellen	6 Oct 1873
Austin	DABNEY, C. I. & Bettie	Smith	30 Oct 1874
Austin	DABNEY, C. I. & M. A.	Ella May	15 Oct 1874
Austin	DABNEY, Edwin T. & Annie G.	Lucie A.	7 Nov 1874
Lavaca	DABNEY, Geo. R. & Louisa	Eugene	1 Jan 1874
Hays	DAILEY, Basil & Julia A.	Julia Antionette Mae	1 Nov 1874
Hays	DAILEY, David W. & Mary B.	Samuel George	20 Aug 1873
Hays	DAILEY, Thos. P. & Mary C.	John Pierce	2 Nov 1873
Lee	DALRYMPLE, William & Mrs.(sic)	Buel (Jesse)	28 Oct 1874
Caldwell	DANCHY, A. R. & G. S.	Mattie A.	28 Feb 1874
Fayette	DANCY, Olivia (See J. Calhoun Brown)		
Brazos	DANDRIDGE, Sam'l & Emily	Wm.	3 Dec 1875
Hays	DANFORT, A. O. & Hattie	Edna	27 Sep 1874
Hays	DANIEL, A. R. & M. J.	Benj. Franklin	2 Oct 1875
Brazos	DANIEL, Bailey & Maggie	Dusey	9 Jul 1873
Hays	DANIEL, J. B. & Susanah	Elijah Benjamin	12 Sep 1874
		Margaret S.	12 Dec 1875
Hays	DANIEL, James B. & Susan	Isaac Ross	29 Jun 1873
Lavaca	DANIEL, Joseph R. & M. R.	David C.	28 Nov 1874
Gillespie	DANNHEIM, William & Sophie	Theador Louis	30 May 1874
DeWitt	DARROS, Louis & ??	Anna	15 May 1874
Bexar	DASHIELL, Geo. R. & Kate (Ringgold)	Walter Richardson	11 Jul 1873
Caldwell	DAUGHERTY, H. M. & N. C.	Mattie Maud	23 Aug 1873
Comanche	DAVENPORT, C. W. & M. H.	Frances Eugenia	3 Mar 1874
		William Edward	28 May 1875
Brazos	DAVIS, ?? & Fanny	Joe	31 May 1875
Austin	DAVIS, Adam & Caroline (Sherrod)	Isam	Aug 1873
Brazos	DAVIS, C. T. & Laura A.	Geo. Thos.	7 Nov 1875
Hays	DAVIS, Chas. W. & Margery C.	Mary Ellender	20 Jun 1875

COUNTY	PARENTS	CHILD	DATE
DeWitt	DAVIS, Daniel & Amanda Caroline	Robert Winfield	24 Oct 1874
Burnet	DAVIS, David & Mary	Young	5 Mar 1875
Hays	DAVIS, Francis N. & Arlelia	Hubbard Edwin	13 Oct 1873
Brazos	DAVIS, Geo. W. & Corrie	Chas. A.	30 Jan 1874
Austin	DAVIS, Henry & Mary L.	William Henry Mathena	15 Sep 1874
Grimes	DAVIS, Henry & Nancy	Robert	28 Jan 1875
Austin	DAVIS, Hiram & Kate	Ellen Hannah	Mar 1875
Kendall	DAVIS, J. W. & Eliza	Martha Ann	No date
Hays	DAVIS, John E. & Emily C.	Francis Adelia	3 Oct 1874
		Robt. Pierce	5 Apr 1876
Hays	DAVIS, Jno. H. & Nancy C.	Reuben Marshall	30 Aug 1874
Kendall	DAVIS, John I. & Ann Keziah	Mildred Ellen	16 Jul 1874
Bastrop	DAVIS, M. V. & Sarah	Jonathan M.	29 Feb 1874
Burnet	DAVIS, Robt. W. & ?	John Calvin	27 May 1875
Hays	DAVIS, Thomas J. & Jane	H. N.	13 Feb 1875
Colorado	DAVISON, Wm. G. & Belle	Nannie A.	10 Jan 1873
Nacogd.	DAWSON, William & Tu(?)	Archey Bone	10 Aug 1873
Hays	DAY, C. Perry & Anna	Addison P.	26 Oct 1873
Nacogd.	DAY, Eli A. & Susan R. (sic)	Anloinette H.	4 Mar 1874
		Harriet May	6 May 1876
Nacogd.	DAY, Henry & Candis	Benjamin A.	14 Feb 1874
Nacogd.	DAY, James A. & Margaret A. H. (Cox)	Joseph R. T.	31 May 1873
		Marvin	1 Jan 1875
Kendall	DAY, Thos. F. & Ottilie	Josephine	5 Nov 1874
Bell	DEAN, T. W. & E. C.	C. P.	8 Mar 1874
Brazos	DEAN, W. H. & Alice	Willie	18 Jun 1872
		Rubie	18 Mar 1875
Bexar	DEATON, E. F. & Mary (Prescott)	Eva Fannie	22 Mar 1873
Bexar	DEATS, Geo. S. & Rebecca (Rice)	Joseph West	21 Mar 1874
Kendall	DEATS, Servis(?) M. & Mary I.	Joseph A.	16 Jul 1862
		Julius F.	1 May 1866
		Allethia E.	7 Nov 1867
		Paul S.	27 Dec 1869
		Joshua E.	28 Oct 1872
		Inez M.	9 May 1874
Lavaca	DEBORD, James & Martha	John F.	4 May 1875
Bexar	DE CORAY, Catherine (See David Defresne)		
Bexar	DEGEN, Charles & Elizabeth (Fink)	Alvina	11 Jan 1874
Bexar	DEGENER, Bertha (See Christoph Rhodius)		
Bexar	DEGENER, H. L. & Clara (Bramigh)	Else	21 Oct 1875
Bexar	DELGADO, Manuela (See Casimiro Guerra)		
Bell	DENNIS, J. C. & M. V.	Romeo Dilliard	18 Mar 1874
Nacogd.	DENT, Jesse & Mary	E. J.	20 Jun 1874
Bexar	DERR, Mina (See Louis Duerler)		
Austin	DERSCHKA, Joseph & Paulina	Gustav	15 Jan 1875
Burnet	DESPAIN, James R. & Mary J.	Jocephus	16 Aug 1874
		Doc.	23 May 1876
Austin	DEUTLER, Laurence & Annie	Annie	25 Dec 1874
Austin	DEUTLER, M. & Catharine	Fritz	12 Aug 1874
Lavaca	DEW, L. M. & E. M.	Mary E.	17 Jan 1874
Bandera	DHUGOS, C. & A.	Dominic	No date
Bandera	DIAL, Joseph & N. J.	Mary D.	21 Oct 1874
DeWitt	DIAL, Richard & Laura	Mary Eliza	16 Jul 1873
Bexar	DIAS, Martina (See Domingo Rodriguez)		
Caldwell	DICKERSON, F. L. & S. E.	Hugh	20 Jan 1875
Lee	DICKEY, Wiseman & Martha Jane	Wiley Guy	Jul 1874
Grimes	DICKSON, Dan & Madeline	Martha Caroline	22 May 1875
Grimes	DICKSON, Jr. J. L. & Clara	Beulah	24 Sep 1875

COUNTY	PARENTS	CHILD	DATE
Bexar	DIEFENBACH, Emilie (See Alexander Sartor, Jr.)		
Kendall	DIENGER, Carl & Dorothea	Emma	15 Oct 1857
		Joseph	17 Aug 1859
		Lina	20 Sep 1861
		Louise	9 Aug 1863
		Carl	25 Dec 1865
Fayette	DIESING, William & Sophie	Hermann	15 Nov 1873
Kendall	DIETERT, Henry & Amalie	Gnorst.(?) A.	28 Oct 1867
		Bertha	2 Dec 1869
		Amalie	23 Oct 1872
Kendall	DIETERT, Wilhelm & Rosa	Theordor	18 Feb 1861
		Emil	6 Dec 1862
		Ida	3 Jun 1864
		Edward	3 Jul 1866
		Ernst	5 Apr 1868
Bexar	DIETRICH, Eugene & (Burell) Theresa	Emily	22 Oct 1869
		Eugene J. B.	15 Nov 1872
		Edward L.	7 Aug 1874
Gillespie	DIETRICH, Maria	Peter	15 Dec 1874
Gillespie	DIETZ, John & Lisette	William	1 Jul 1873
Brazos	DILLARD, Ben & Lucy	Benjamin	23 Dec 1875
Caldwell	DILLARD, Wm. & Mary A.	Ann	23 Nov 1874
Bexar	DILLON, Arthur & Jane (Niel)	J. W. Henry	9 Mar 1874
Bexar	DILLON, Edward & Margarete (Fitzgerald	James Charles	21 May 1874
Comal	DINTLEMAN, Valentine & Cynthia (George)	Daniel Webster	18 Apr 1872
		Charles Monroe	13 May 1874
Bexar	DINZE, Elize (See C. F. Kroeger)		
Victoria	DITMAR, Ernestine W. F. (See Samuel Klein)		
Austin	DITTERT, August & Anna	Antoine	27 Apr 1874
Austin	DITTERT, Christian & Marie	Christian	28 Aug 1874
Colorado	DITTMAN, Charles & Anna	Henry Aug.	3 Sep 1873
Bexar	DITTMAR, Albrecht & Emmy (von Rehfines)	Lili	20 Jan 1875
Gillespie	DITTMAR, Martin & Elizabeth	Sophie	22 Oct 1874
Austin	DIXON, G. B. & Julia N.(?)	Sarah	10 Jul 1874
Hays	DIXON, Henry W. & Melissa S.	Edward Lee	16 Dec 1873
Hays	DIXON, Henry W. & Sarah M.	Helen	19 Apr 1875
Hays	DIXON, James A. & Harriett F. (twins)	Ada & Ida	22 Jun 1874
Hays	DIXON, Joshua T. & Mary L.	John T.	25 Nov 1873
Lee	DOAK, A. V. & Mattie	Vernon	21 Apr 1874
		Elizabeth	11 Jun 1876
Bexar	DOBBIN, John & Lavina (Wier)	??? (F)	26 Apr 1874
Lee	DODDS, Chas. A. & Mary Francis	Martha A.	15 Nov 1873
Bexar	DODGE, Katherine Jane (See Jacob Augur)		
Fayette	DODSON, Sam & Rosetta	Roselia R. B.	11 Mar 1876
Travis	DOHME, Ferdinand & Mary	Louis	17 Mar 1867
		Ferdinand	16 Nov 1868
		Emma	11 Nov 1873
Travis	DOHMEN, W. A. & Thecla M.	Franz Joseph	13 Feb 1874
Bexar	DOLAN, Mollie (See Adolph Ripstein)		
Bell	DOMDSON, W. T. & A.	Alice Rebecca	17 Jul 1874
Lavaca	DONELLY, John & Mary J.	H. H.	20 Nov 1873
Gillespie	DONHEIM, Wm. & Sophie	Adolph	19 Jan 1876
Bell	DONLEY, L. J. & Mary	Thomas P.	30 Sep 1875
Bell	DONLEY, T. B. & C. J.	Annette	27 Dec 1875
Bell	DONOVAN, J. T. & V. M.	Edward Spontz	22 Jul 1874
Comanche	DOOLEY, J. S. & M. J.	Margaret Ellen	23 Sep 1874

COUNTY	PARENTS	CHILD	DATE
Lavaca	DOOSE, Wm. & Anna	Christopher A.	4 Feb 1875
Comal	DOPPENSCHMIDT, Jacob &		
	Dorette (Kappmeier)	Anna	30 Sep 1871
		Wilhelmina	19 Apr 1873
		Wilhelm	10 Oct 1875
San Saba	DORAN, Wm. R. & Mary E.	Nancy Polina	12 Apr 1874
Burnet	DORBANDT, Christian & Ann	William Edward	5 Apr 1874
Austin	DORSETT, W. A. & Emma	Buela	11 Aug 1874
Grimes	DORSEY, E. W. & H.	Henry Lewis	21 Jan 1874
Lee	DOUGLASS, J. C. & Ophelia	Lucy	4 Oct 1873
Lee	DOUGLASS, T. S. & ?	Homer	29 Sep 1874
DeWitt	DOVE, Andrew & Dania	Harry Archibald	26 Jan 1874
Bexar	DOWNEY, Catharine (See W. H. H. Huston)		
Travis	DOWTY, Sam. J. & Helen V.	Samuel Seelye	27 Mar 1874
Brazos	DOZIER, T. J. & E. C.	Jas. L.	9 Jul 1875
Burnet	DRAK, J. W. & Texana	James Walter	21 Dec 1874
Bexar	DREISS, Adolph &		
	Elizabeth (Fritzez)	Albert	11 May 1874
Comal	DREISS, Albert &		
	Josephine (Benner)	James Edw.	16 Sep 1853
		Mathilde Amalie	5 Nov 1854
		Bertha Louise	8 Jan 1856
		Richard	26 Sep 1857
		Mathilde	9 Jan 1859
		Gustav	12 Nov 1861
		Eugen	31 Jan 1863
		Albert	30 Jun 1864
Bexar	DREISS, Edward &		
	Emmy (Mourean)	Theckla	21 Oct 1879
Bexar	DRESEL, Rudolph & Augusta		
	(Schleicher)	Gustav	8 Sep 1861
Gillespie	DRESSEL, Rudolph &		
	Bertha (Plage)	Emil	9 Jul 1858
Comal	DREYER, Dorothea (See Heinrich Steuer)		
Bexar	DRISH, Louisa (See Fred Whithoff)		
Hays	DRISKILL, William Z. &		
	Sarah E.	Samuel N.	10 Dec 1873
Nacogd.	DRIVER, Amos & Coke C.	Elijah	2 Sep 1873
Austin	DROS, F. & Rosalie Valeska	Rosalie	9 Jun 1875
Comanche	DRYER, Henry & Augusta	Doretha	9 Oct 1873
Lavaca	DRYSSE, Ernest & Mary	Lilly	2 Feb 1875
Lavaca	DUBOSE, J. B. & Elmira	Thos. Freddy	15 May 1875
Lavaca	DUBOSE, Wm. S. & N. C.	J. E.	1 Jan 1874
Lee	DUDLEY, Sam & Cinthia	John	Sep 1874
Bexar	DUERLER, G. A. &		
	Lena (Werner)	Alfred	21 Oct 1875
Bexar	BUERLER, Louis & Mina (Derr)	Edw'd. A.	30 Sep 1874
		Amelia	6 Mar 1876
Bexar	DUFF, Eleanor T. (See Michael Glynn Turquand)		
Bexar	DUFRESNE, David & Catharine Cora Maria Catharine Cora		
	(1874 Entry "Catherine DeCoray") Maria		5 Aug 1873
	(Twins) Emmanuel		22 Jul 1874
		Martin David	22 Jul 1874
Bexar	DUGAN, Wm. J. &		
	C. Gertrude (Gambia)	Bertha Louise	15 Oct 1874
Hays	DUGGAN, Alston & Eliza P.	Julia Claudia	6 Sep 1873
Bexar	DUKES, John R. & Mary C.	Susan C.	17 Mar 1876
Bexar	DULLNIG, A. &		
	Henrietta (Pohn)	Emma Amand Sophia	24 Sep 1875
Bexar	DULLNIG, Christn. &		
	Mary Bollwick (Schulz)	Thusnelela	10 Jul 1874
Bexar	DULLNIG, Jacob & Johanna	Henry	18 Aug 1874
Bexar	DULNIG, George &		
	Francis (Werner)	Carolina Amanda	11 May 1874
	(Twins)	Johane Sophie	11 May 1874
		Julia	12 Jan 1876

COUNTY	PARENTS	CHILD	DATE
San Saba	DUNCAN, R. J. & L. A.	Mary Caroline	26 Oct 1874
Bandera	DUNLAP, Robert & S. D.	Robert	5 Jun 1875
Comanche	DUNLAP, T. J. & B. E.	Martha Edna	1 Jan 1875
Brazos	DUNN, ?? & Sarah	Thos. W.	18 Oct 1874
Comanche	DUNN, M. & S. A.	Martha Caroline	24 Mar 1874
		Laura Ann	17 Jan 1875
Nacogd.	DUPREE, Nelson & Fanny	Allen Archer	16 Feb
Lavaca	DUPREE, Sam & Susan	Wm.	21 Dec 1873
Colorado	DURLAND, Lewis & Emma	Lewis	24 Mar 1874
Nacogd.	DURRETT, T. H. & Mary A. V.	Sarah L.	22 Sep 1873
Nacogd.	DURST, M. H. (See R. H. Irion)		
Bastrop	DUVE, J. J. & A. C.	Rosalie Lina	3 Jul 1871
		Carl Fredrich	27 Jan 1873
		Louisa Augusta	23 Feb 1875
Bexar	DWYER, Eliza (See James Jones)		
Bexar	DWYER, Jos. E. &		
	Annette (Magoffin)	Patrich Anthony	17 Dec 1874
Bexar	DWYER, Thos. A. &		
	Annie (Croker)	John Twohig	18 Oct 1873
Bexar	EARHART, Anthony &		
	Marranda (Burris)	Anthony Cosgrove	24 Jul 1872
		Susan Nora	21 Jun 1874
Bell	EASON, A. C. & Justin	Wilbourn	23 Mar 1875
Hays	EASTHAM, John H. & Eliza P. (Twins)	Albert L.	30 Jun 1875
		Alfred R.	30 Jun 1875
Caldwell	EASTWOOD, James & I. H.	Adelia D.	24 Feb 1875
Hays	EBERHARD, Edwin &		
	Anna Martha	Harry	20 Dec 1873
Bexar	EBERHARDT, Louis &		
	Josephine (Matton)	Richard Willie	3 Nov 1872
DeWitt	EBERHARDT, Thomas C. &		
	Frederika Eliza	Carolina Lenora	13 Jun 1875
Comanche	EBERHART, F. J. & N. A.	Lizie Bell	17 Jan 1875
Austin	EBERS, Herman & Emma	Alice Mary	11 Jan 1876
Austin	ECKELBERG, L. & Louise	Antine Renate	8 Oct 1873
		Ferdinando	28 Jun 1875
Gillespie	ECKERT, Ludwig & Lisette	Clara	3 Apr 1874
Gillespie	ECKERT, Rudolph & Louise	Rudolph Wilhelm	5 Nov 1873
		Amalia	15 Feb 1876
exar	ECKHARDT, Emily Victoria (See G. Schmeltzer)		
DeWitt	ECKHARDT, Robt. C. &		
	Caroline L.	Marcellus G.	14 Jun 1873
		Hedwig Eugenie	15 Jul 1875
DeWitt	ECKHARDT, Wm. L. & Mary	Auguste L.	10 Jun 1873
		Richard H.	30 May 1875
Bexar	EDENS, H. B. &		
	Eliza Ann (Helms)	Sarah Jane	9 Oct 1873
		Hugh G.	9 Dec 1874
Bexar	EDENS, N. A. &		
	Mary F. (Grigsby)	William Grigsby	24 Feb 187_
Bexar	EDINS, Margaret E. (See Wm. W. Sproul)		
Nacogd.	EDWARDS, Peyton F. &		
	Ode (Arnold)	Clara Sarah	3 Sep 1873
Austin	EDWARDS, Pink & Amelia	Nona	8 Feb 1875
Grimes	EDWARDS, Thomas & Rose	Amanda Alice	5 Oct 1874
Hays	EDWARDS, Thomas R. & Annie E.	Anna May	17 Jan 1874
		Roscoe	25 Jan 1876
Grimes	EDWARDS, W. O. & G. E.	J. W. P.	21 Aug 1873
Burnet	EFFINGAR, Mike & S. J.	Maggie H.	1 Sep 1874
DeWitt	EGG, Isaac & Hellen	Alfred	28 Aug 1875
Bexar	EICKE, Juliana (See Frederick Willgehausen)		
Austin	EIDMAN, F. G. & Martha E.	Frederick Gustav	1 Oct 1874
Austin	EIDMAN, Seamen O. & Virginia	Cattie May	28 Jun 1874
Bexar	EISERLOH, Peter &		
	Margareta (Kraus)	Maria	21 Aug 1872
		Margareta G.	20 Jul 1874

COUNTY	PARENTS	CHILD	DATE
Medina	EIT, Theodor & Louisa	George D.	8 Sep 1873
		Mary	8 Dec 1875
Bell	ELAM, W. N. & A. C.	W. Nile	18 Sep 1875
Comal	ELBEL, Gottlieb &		
	Auguste (Seekatz)	Alma	23 Nov 1874
DeWitt	ELDER, M. M. & L. M.	James Mathews	10 Oct 1873
DeWitt	ELDER, Phillip T. & Sarah S.	Thomas B.	12 Jun 1874
Burnet	ELDRIDGE, Dan & Julia A.	Henry E.	13 Feb 1874
		Clement Ambrose	6 Aug 1875
Bell	ELKINS, H. D. & M. J.	Nancy	1 Jan 1874
		Franklin	30 Apr 1875
Gillespie	ELLEBRACHT, William & Maria	Maria Henriette	9 Jul 1873
Brazos	ELLINGTON, D. C. & Polly	D. C.	6 Feb 1876
Bell	ELLIOTT, A. & M. (N) J.	Lockey	15 Mar 1875
Bell	ELLIOTT, R. T. & E. F.	Harry Miller	25 Jul 1873
Austin	ELLIOTT, William & Adeline	Rebecca	10 Dec 1874
San Saba	ELLIS, Henry W. & M. A.	Amelia	30 Aug 1874
Bell	ELLIS, W. G. & C. J.	John W.	27 Jul 1875
Caldwell	ELLISON, A. A. & L. C.	Augustus Lou Ella	3 Oct 1874
Caldwell	ELLISON, Jacob L. & M. A.	George Gordon	1 Nov 1874
Hays	ELLISON, Thos. H. & Sarah B.	Hue Branch	19 May 1874
Bexar	ELMENDORF, Emil &		
	Emilie (Heitiz)	Charles	6 Oct 1873
		Gustav E.	3 Sep 1875
Bexar	ELMENDORF, Henry &		
	Emilie (Baetz)	Helen A. M.	8 Oct 1874
Bell	ELMORE, M. & L. T.	Claudy E.	14 Jul 1873
		Mathias	6 Sep 1875
Austin	ELOLF, August & Matilda	Charles	17 Oct 1873
Bexar	ELSNER, Anna (See Robert Blind)		
Bexar	EMANUEL, S. E. & Mary Fannie	Fannie Louisa	1 Nov 1873
Bell	EMBREE, J. W. & T.	Gillian	7 Nov 1874
Bexar	EMELIENBERG, Friederick &		
	Anna (Brader)	Cacilia	28 Jul 1872
		Kurt	25 Nov 1874
Austin	ENGELKING, Fritz &		
	Anna F. (Trenckmann)	Clara Helene	4 Oct 1873
Bexar	ENGLEHART, Teodore &		
	Elisa (Ludwig)	Ida	21 Aug 1873
		Willie	6 Nov 1874
Austin	ENGLISH, Hiram B. & Annie E.	Mary Bell	15 Jul 1874
Nacogd.	ENNIS, J. M. & A. L.	Euallia	4 Nov 1874
Travis	ENOCHS, J. A. &		
	Eliza Harriet	Eliza Harriet	19 Aug 1873
Austin	ERMLER, Henry & Bettie	Anna	26 Oct 1874
Comal	ERNST, Heinrich &		
	Johanna (Kohlenberg)	Heinrich Wilhelm	27 Feb 1873
		Martha Johanna	19 Apr 1875
Bastrop	ERWIN, J. P. & L.	Wm. Walter	28 Feb 1874
Bastrop	ERWIN, Lucurgus & Mary V.	Julia R.	3 Sep 1874
Bastrop	ERWIN, W. N. & M. H.	Jonathan M.	19 Feb 1874
Fayette	ESCHENBURG, Charles & Anna	Agnes	12 Nov 1868
		Robert Lee	3 Feb 1870
		Mary	12 Jul 1872
		Charles	3 Nov 1873
		Gustav A.	27 Feb 1875
Bexar	ESSER, William &		
	Henrieta (Beezeiboch)	??? (M)	29 Oct 1874
San Saba	ESTEP, J. N. & Louisa	J. N., Jr.	21 Oct 1875
San Saba	ESTEP, S. & Jane	Amanda Lee	21 May 1874
Austin	ETLINGER, Peter & Elise	Margaret	10 Feb 1874
Medina	ETTER, Jacob & Catharine	John Albert	16 Nov 1874
Lavaca	EVANS, A. T. & Mary J.	Dora Ann	16 Jan 1874
		Oscar Lee	29 Nov 1875
Travis	EVANS, Clark O. & Martha M.	Joseph W.	20 Aug 1874
Bell	EVANS, J. N. & L. M.	Mary Belle	15 Aug 1873

COUNTY	PARENTS	CHILD	DATE
Bexar	EVANS, Sally (See Henry Weir)		
Comal	EVERETT, M. & Mary P.	William Elbert	26 Aug 1874
Hays	EVERITT, Thomas J. &		
	Sarah E.	Eloise	4 Jan 1874
Gillespie	EVERS, Henry & Johanna	Otto	26 Aug 1874
Lavaca	EVINS, A. W. & E.	James W.	9 Apr 1874
Hays	EZELL, Green B. & Eliza C.	Ledford & Wilford	31 Jul 1873
Austin	FABIAN, Robert & Sarah	Surmantha Calonia	12 Aug 1874
Bastrop	FALCONI, Josef & Artemisa	Maria	8 Aug 1874
Austin	FALK, Gustav & Elizaberto	Herman	27 Sep 1873
Nacogd.	FALL, J. C. & Larra E.	Willie B.	28 May 1871
		Susan R.	11 Nov 1874
Colorado	FALWELL, John & Charlotte	Alma S.	13 Oct 1873
Lee	FARISS, W. H. & Amelia S.	Oscar Peery	1 Sep 1874
Bell	FARLEY, E. & L. J.	James Adkisson	24 Jan 1875
Burnet	FARQUHAR, A. N. & C. C.	James Anderson	8 Mar 1875
Burnet	FARQUHAR, D. J. & M. N.	Effa J.	22 Oct 1874
Burnet	FARQUHAR, F. M. & Samira	Thomas Marion	6 Nov 1874
Travis	FARR, Thomas Jefferson &		
	Sarah Ann	Thomas Jefferson	3 Mar 1874
Lavaca	FARRER, H. H. & Sarah I.	Stephen S.	18 Jan 1874
Bell	FARRER, J. & M. E.	Wm. Washington	27 Oct 1873
Lavaca	FARRINGTON, A. G. & Amanda	Robt.	5 Jan 1874
Lavaca	FARRINGTON, John W. & A.	Willia Addie	27 Feb 1875
Medina	FASELER, Gerd H. & Christine	George	27 Apr 1874
Comal	FAUST, Joseph &		
	Ida (Forcke)	Walter	26 Jul 1878
Grimes	FAW, Lemuel & Hannah	Margery Anna	27 Jan 1875
Bell	FAY, E. W. & Emma C.	Catharine L.	No date
Victoria	FAY, John & Sophia (Sitterle)	William	3 Dec 1873
San Saba	FEAZLE, Ashley & Mary Delila	Alice Keziah	20 Nov 1874
DeWitt	FECHNER, Edward & Herrmina	Robert	24 Jul 1873
Bell	FEDDEMAN, J. A. & M. A.	Joseph M.	16 Feb 1875
Austin	FEDFORD, Aaron & Louisa	James Patrick	14 Jul 1873
		Prince	6 Jul 1875
Austin	FEDFORD, Brister & Alabama	Allie Lee Thomas	4 Sep 1875
Bexar	FEIDERMANN, Josephine (See Joseph Fischer)		
Bexar	FELDTMANN, Eliza (See Wm. Small)		
Kendall	FELLBAUM, Gottlob &		
	Elisabeth	Carl	30 May 1866
		Wilhelm	26 Sep 1872
		Elise	13 Jun 1874
Gillespie	FELLER, Charles & Magdalena	Emil	4 Jan 1876
Gillespie	FELLER, Chas. & Maria M.	Alize	12 Mar 1874
Austin	FELLER, Gottlieb & Agnes	Maria	5 Oct 1873
Bastron	FELLOWS, W. G. & Mary	John	25 Jun 1875
Comal	FELTNER, August &		
	Wendeline (Ridel)	Carl Gottfried August	30 Apr 1874
		Anna Auguste Wendeline	2 Nov 1870
Nacogd.	FENLEY, W. H. & M. J.	William C.	26 Sep 1873
Victoria	FENNER, F. A. & Mssie?		
	(Sturgess)	Mildred Blanche	23 Mar 1875
DeWitt	FERBER, John & Lone ?	Minnie M.	17 Feb 1873
Burnet	FERGISON, Balous E. &		
	Mary L.	James E.	27 Oct 1873
Brazos	FERGUSON, B. G. & Mattie G.	Mary Francis	11 Nov 1874
Bell	FERGUSON, J. E. & F. P.	Alx McGowen	7 Jul 1874
Bell	FERGUSON, J. G. & Charity	Wm. A. Udley	8 Apr 1874
Brazos	FERGUSON, John & Josephine	Ellen	11 Oct 1873
		Walter L.	29 Dec 1874
Lavaca	FERNAN, Christian & E.	F. P.	29 Jun 1873
Lavaca	FERNAN, H. C. & E.	Emelia	14 Sep 1875
Bexar	FEST, M. (See S. Kunkie)		
Austin	FICK, John & Henriette	William	28 Apr 1874
Burnet	FIELD, M. A. & M. C.	Sam	22 Jul 1874
Burnet	FIELDER, J. W. & S. A.	Laura Alice	18 Nov 1874

COUNTY	PARENTS	CHILD	DATE
Travis	FIELDS, J. D. & Mary F.	Eleanor Hibernia	3 Sep 1873
Austin	FIFE, J. H. & Mary E.	Oliver	25 Jan 1875
Bexar	FILE, Emily (See Charles August Fischer)		
Bastrop	FINCH, J. J. & Martha Texas	Allan Travis	1873
Grimes	FINCH, John B. & Mary E.	Mary W. T. (?)	21 Nov 1875
Austin	FIND, Daniel & Wilhelmina	Daniel	12 Aug 1873
Bexar	FINK, Agnes (See Frank Blotz)		
Bexar	FINK, Elizabeth (See Charles Degen)		
Lavaca	FINK, Isaac & Anna	Minnie	4 Jan 1876
Bexar	FINK, Kate (See C. L. Wurzbach)		
Kendall	FISCHER, Andreas & Wilhelmine	Wilhelm	6 Dec 1874
Bexar	FISCHER, Charles August & Emily (File)	Mary Augusta	30 Aug 1875
Bexar	FISCHER, Dorotea (See Charles Ochse)		
Kendall	FISCHER, Friedrich & Jenny	Bertha	9 Feb 1875
		Ehrich August	25 Jan 1877
		Othman Ewald	19 Jul 1879
Comal	FISCHER, Hermann Emil & Marie Charlotte (Conring)	Alexander Hermann	24 Sep 1866
		Carl Moritz	29 Nov 1867
		Hilmar Ferdinand	18 Apr 1871
		Hermine Emilie	11 Jun 1874
		Emil	23 Jul 1876
Gillespie	FISCHER, Herrmann & Elizabeth	Daniel	9 Jul 1874
Comal	FISCHER, Johann Heinrich & Auguste (Koch)	Ferdinand	23 May 1873
		Ida	13 Oct 1875
Bexar	FISCHER, Joseph & Josephine (Feidermann)	Maria Rosa	6 Jun 1876
Austin	FISHER, A. P. & Ada B.	Ada Beula (sic)	13 Mar 1875
		(sic) Edna Fredonia	28 Feb 1875
Burnet	FISHER, Alexander & Sarah J.	Franklin	7 Aug 1875
Austin	FISHER, James M. & Mary Ann	Ada Lockett	12 May 1875
Bexar	FISHER, Jennie (See Wallace Mitchell)		
Hays	FISHER, O. A. & Mary S.	William Harper	12 Apr 1875
Lee	FISHER, Sophronia (See Henry Hosea)		
Hays	FISHER, Sterling & Martha J.	Hancock A.	12 Feb 1874
		Lula Daisey	23 Jul 1876
Colorado	FITZGERALD, Alexander & Flora A.	Ernest	14 Dec 1874
Bexar	FITZGERALD, Margarete (See Edward Dillon)		
Lee	FITZBERALD, R. E. & M. A.	H. H.	2 Jan 1874
Lee	FITCH, Collins & Martha C.	William Azel	9 Apr 1875
Caldwell	FLEMING, ?? & ??	Samuel Lee	28 Dec 1875
Bastrop	FLETCHER, J. A. & C. A. C.	Chas. F.	23 Jun 1874
Fayette	FLEWELLEN, W. T. & Mary E.	Lucy	1 May 1876
Brazos	FLIPPEN, Wm. H. & Simie	Edgar	7 Mar 1876
Comal	FLOEGE, Hermine (See A. L. Kepler)		
Bexar	FLORES, Marcos E. & Josefa (Rivas)	Marcos	20 Mar 1874
Caldwell	FLORIDA, J. R. & Mary B.	Benjamin J.	24 Nov 1873
Caldwell	FLOWERS, H. M. & Elizabeth	Martin	6 Oct 1874
Austin	FORESTER, August & Susanna D.	John	4 Jan 1875
Comal	FOERSTER, Bertha (See Heinrich E. Jentsch)		
Comal	FOERSTER, F. W. & Bacha (Schneider)	Emil	30 Jul 1873
	(Friedrich Wilhelm)	Anna	27 Apr 1875
Comal	FOERSTER, Louise (See Lebrecht Weidner)		
Medina	FOLK, Friedrich & Auguste	Laura Johanna Rosina	10 May 1874
		Louisa Elisab. C.	15 Sep 1876
Lavaca	FOLK, Joseph & Mary	Louis	5 Apr 1874
Burnet	FOMBY, Wiley & Mary	Wiley	14 Jul 1874
Comal	FORCKE, Ida (See Joseph Faust)		

COUNTY	PARENTS	CHILD	DATE
Hays	FORD, George & Eliza.	Almo	13 Mar 1874
Grimes	FORD, John & Roxacy Ann	Margaret	9 Jul 1875
Lavaca	FORD, Presley & Mildred	Adella	23 Dec 1873
Travis	FORD, S. W. & Nannie	Lizzie	6 Nov 1873
		Tennie	17 Sep 1875
Brazos	FORD, Spencer & Mary	May Kate	3 Mar 1876
Fayette	FORDTRAN, Charles Ferdinand &		
	Ida Waldron (Banks)	Lilla	23 Oct 1874
		Nellie	20 Dec 1875
Fayette	FORDTRAN, E. H. & A. L.	?? (M)	17 Sep 1875
Comanche	FOREHAND, G. W. & L.	George Washington	19 May 1875
Travis	FOREHAND, William & Alice	John	16 Jul 1873
Grimes	FORSGARD, J. W. & (S. or L.)	J. (S. or L.) F.	26 Aug 1873
Bastrop	FORT, H. H. & S. A.	Wm. C.	9 Apr 1875
Austin	FORT, T. C. & Ellen J.	Sarah Ann	30 Jul 1874
Caldwell	FORTUNE, R. W. & Frances E.	John	10 Oct 1874
Lavaca	FOSTER, A. G. & Emiline	Thos. P.	6 Jun 1873
Travis	FOSTER, Edlie P. &		
	Mary Francis	James B.	13 Nov 1873
Brazos	FOSTER, M. B. & Aletha	Thos. C.	18 Jul 1875
Lavaca	FOSTER, T. B. & Mary B.	Alberta	15 Feb 1874
Burnet	FOWLER, H. C. & R. T.	Laura Lee	20 Jul 1874
Travis	FOWLER, W. S. & Mattie G.	Rupert	23 Jul 1873
Lee	FOWLER, Wiley & Susan	Abram W.	18 May 1874
Bexar	FRANK, A. B. &		
	Sarah (Lindheim)	Carrie	26 Nov 1873
		Nettie	1 Oct 1875
DeWitt	FRANKE, Aurelius & Mina	Nathalia	28 Sep 1873
DeWitt	FRANKE, Emil & Henrietta	Otto	6 Mar 1872
		Hellena	28 May 1873
Burnet	FRANKLIN, John W. & Mary E.	Lucien B.	25 Jan 1875
Bell	FRANKLIN, R. & F. E.	John M.	28 Apr 1874
Burnet	FRANKLIN, Wm. & Mary	Sadie E.	14 Jul 1873
Victoria	FRANZ, Henry Conrad &		
	Lizzie (Bracken)	Henry Gotlieb	20 Nov 1874
Caldwell	FREASIER, Ben E. & O. E.	Lola Maud	15 Sep 1874
Kendall	FREEMAN, A. S. & Margaret E.	Hermann	26 May 1874
Caldwell	FREEMAN, B. H. & Matilda	Sarah K.	17 Jun 1875
Hays	FREEMAN, James & Amanda M.	James Earl	14 Apr 1874
DeWitt	FREHNER, Jacob & Caroline	Anna Caroline L.	15 Mar 1874
Austin	FREITAG, Albert & Augusta	Phillip	21 Aug 1875
Caldwell	FRENCH, S. L. &		
	Minerva Hazel F.	James Leslie	3 Jan 1875
Fayette	FRENZEL, Charl. F. &		
	Wilhelmine	Anvin Otto	24 Aug 1873
Bandera	FRICK, C. H. & Mary	Henry William Adolph	11 Jan 1876
Bexar	FRIEDLANDER, Rosa (See Sala Sulnon)		
Hays	FRIEDSAM, Herman & Elizabeth	Alba	1 May 1873
		Andras San	4 Mar 1874
Colorado	FRIEMANN, Adolph &		
	Pauline (neé Lisiecka)	Rosalie	7 Oct 1878
Gillespie	FRIESS, Adam & Magdalena	Fried.	15 Jun 1874
Bell	FRINK, J. O. & F. A.	Wm. Oscar	14 Dec 1873
Comanche	FRITTS, C. S. & S.	Sewillow May	25 Dec 1873
Comanche	FRITTS, W. H. C. & M. L.	Dona Cathrine	8 Sep 1875
Bexar	FRITZE, William &		
	Anna (Gembler)	Ida	2 Nov 1872
		Andreas	22 Jun 1874
		Louis	9 Mar 1876
Bexar	FRITZEZ, Elizabeth (See Adolph Dreiss)		
Kendall	FROEBEL, H. G. & Therese	Agnes	4 Apr 1855
		Rudolph	22 Jun 1857
		Hilmar G.	27 Jul 1860
Bexar	FROMME, Charles &		
	Laura (Longwell)	Frank	3 Dec 1875
		Augusta Alvina	6 Apr 1877

COUNTY	PARENTS	CHILD	DATE
DeWitt	FROMME, Rudolph & E.	E.	15 Mar 1875
Fayette	FROSCH, Henry & Wilhelmine	Laura	9 Jun 1874
Bexar	FROST, Sallie (See Sam Maverick)		
Lee	FRY, Jos. H. & Mary M.	Jessie	12 Jan 1874
Hays	FRY, William B. & Georgia A.	Robert Earle	19 May 1874
Victoria	FRYER, Caroline (See Gilbert Collier)		
Comal	FUCHS, Emma (See Edgar Von Boeckmann)		
Victoria	FUHRMAN, Catharina (See Michael Weber)		
Brazos	FULKUSON, Isaac & M. L.	Sam'l Vance	17 Apr 1874
Nacogd.	FULLER, B. F. & Josephine	Franklin O.	2 Nov 1873
Lavaca	FULLER, Cade & Sarah	Mittie	18 Apr 1874
Lavaca	FULLER, Calvin & Sarah	Maggie	21 Dec 1873
Nacogd.	FULLER, D. F. & Josephine	Milford	15 May 1875
Nacogd.	FULLER, Henry C. & Francis	Minna Octavia	30 Dec 1873
Bell	FULLER, J. F. & E. J.	J. F., Jr.	2 Jun 1873
Nacogd.	FULLER, William H. & Nancy	Ollie	9 Feb 1874
Hays	FURR, C. & Beneta	Andrew James	29 Jan 1874
DeWitt	GAEBLER, Charles & Bertha	Caroline	Mar 1875
Bexar	GAENSLEN, Dr. J. J. & Mary (Bowen)	George Ralph	25 Mar 1875
Bell	GAGE, J. C. & Ophelia	Lillia	14 Sep 1873
Fayette	GAGE, Marion & ??	Mary Jeanett	Oct 1874
Comanche	GAISEN, J. M. & Drucilla	Clarence Elmo	14 Jul 1874
Travis	GALAWAY, Hosea & Sarah Adeline	Sarah Adeline	17 Aug 1873
Caldwell	GALBREATH, ?? & ??	Wm.	27 Jan 1875
Caldwell	GALBREATH, P. B. & J. M.	Geo. F.	27 Jan 1875
Caldwell	GALLAGHER, J. F. & H.	Annie H.	19 Jun 1874
Bell	GALLAT. ?? & A. G.	Minnie	27 May 1874
Bell	GALLAT, H. & A. J.	Henry	13 Jan 1875
DeWitt	GALLE, Charels (sic) & Louise	Sophia	16 Jul 1875
Bexar	GAMBIA, C. Gertrude (See Wm. J. Dugan)		
Bastrop	GAMBLE, Geo. & Maria E.	Maria G.	15 Nov 1873
Gillespie	GAMMENTHALER, G. & Helene	Elisabeth	8 Apr 1874
Bell	GANGERO, ?? & ??	Beltona	20 Mar 1876
Bexar	GARCIA, M. R. & Thomasa (Chavez)	Alejandro	6 Jun 1875
Caldwell	GARCIA, Rosalio & Nancy	Samuel	10 Nov 1874
Hays	GAREY, James H. & Mary F.	Mary Elizabeth	14 Sep 1874
Lavaca	GARNER, A. J. & Mary E.	Mary E.	10 May 1874
Bexar	GARRERA, Joaquin & Joseta (MacLenies)	Joaquin	22 Mar 1874
DeWitt	GARRETT, William M. & Margarett A.	James Terry Patterson Smith	21 Jan 1874
Bell	GARRISON, J. T. & S. M.	Maud Alice	12 Oct 1874
Victoria	GARRISON, Ottile (See L. F. Mack)		
Bexar	GARZA, Helena (See Manuel de Yturri Castillo)		
Kendall	GASS, Jacob & Louise	Ida	10 Jan 1875
Kendall	GATES, Aug. Valentine & M.A.	Eugene Valentine	29 Oct 1859
		Cathrina Isabella	26 Feb 1862
		John Alb. S.	16 Mar 1866
		Minnie L. G.	3 Oct 1867
		Chas. Harnoch	25 Jul 1869
		M. Maggie	13 Sep 1871
		Eudora Jane	7 Apr 1874
		Mary Lee	29 Aug 1876
Kendall	GATES, Sam'l B. & Mathilda	Wm. Valentine	6 Oct 1874
San Saba	GAUNY, J. N. & Sarah E.	Ada Ward	15 Oct 1873
		J. N., Jr.	20 Nov 1875
DeWitt	GEHRING, Angus C. H. & Lina	Chas. A. H.	24 Dec 1874
Bastrop	GEIS, Chr. (sic) & Barbara	Maria Bartha	30 Sep 1874
Gillespie	GELLERMANN, Ferdinand & Charlotte	August Wilhelm	15 Sep 1873
Bexar	GEMBLER, Anna (See William Fritze)		

COUNTY	PARENTS	CHILD	DATE
Bexar	GEMBLER, Cathrene (See Edmond Lieck)		
Bexar	GEMBLER, Mary (See William Piper)		
Comal	GEORGE, Cynthia (See Valentine Dintleman)		
Comal	GEORGE, Enoch Ben &		
	Caroline (Sattler)	Wilhelmine	Dec 1873
Comal	GERLICH, Gustav &		
	Sophie (Holdermann)	Alma	19 Oct 1873
Bexar	GERLOFF, Andres &		
	Catharine (Hoffmann)	?? (M)	21 Jul 1874
Bandera	GERSDORF, Charles & Frances	J. B.	No date
		Frances	3 Apr 1876
Colorado	GERSTENBERGER, Eduard & Ema	Hugo Ed.	18 Feb 1876
Comal	GEUE, Wilhelm &		
	Emilie (Staats)	Emma	9 Jun 1873
Hays	GIBSON, B. M. & Martha	Elfie	4 Jan 1874
Bell	GIBSON, Jno. A. & Mary D.	Margaret Agnes	8 Mar 1875
Bandera	GIBSON, W. E. & S. J.	Aznion(?)	17 Feb 1874
Bexar	GIBSON, W. R. &		
	Frances L. (Thrall)	Bessie	10 Sep 1872
		Mable R.	14 Oct 1873
		Ellen T.	3 Dec 1874
Comal	GIESECKE, Adolph &		
	Emilie (Groos)	Marie Ernestine	13 Jun 1874
Burnet	GIESECKE, Albert & Ottilie	Richard August	5 Dec 1874
Comal	GIESECKE, Julius &		
	Whilhelmine (Groos)	Wilhelm Emil	30 Jun 1874
Hays	GIESEN, William & Louisa	Clara	30 Apr 1873
		William	30 Jun 1875
Austin	GILBERT, Herman & Caroline	Sophia Anna	8 Dec 1872
		Melissa Bertha	2 May 1875
Burnet	GILDART, Thos. & Mozelle	Carleton M.	11 Aug 1873
Hays	GILES, George & Matilda F.	George Andrew	10 Mar 1874
Kendall	GILES, John I. & Doretta	Leelan	3 Oct 1872
		Frederic	17 Jul 1873
		Betty	22 Jan 1875
Fayette	GILLESPIE, Maggie A. or E.	(See John Rufus Bishop)	
DeWitt	GILLETT, J. F. & M. E.	Staten Hudson	14 Jan 1875
Hays	GILLETT, John S. &		
	Frances C. Kerr	Carrie Ethel	12 Dec 1875
Burnet	GILLIS, R. C. & M. E.	Christiana	18 Aug 1873
		Carrie	30 Jun 1875
Kendall	GILLMORE, James & Lucy Ann	James Albert	20 Feb 1875
Lavaca	GILMER, A. M. & Susan	Airs.	7 Jul 1873
Hays	GILMORE, E. A. & Aquilla	Wm. Bennett	6 Dec 1873
Lee	GILMORE, J. S. & M. A.	Dora Alice	2 Oct 1873
DeWitt	GIPS, Frantz & Anna	Frantz Otto	19 Dec 1875
Burnet	GIPSON, James C. & E. C.	John H.	18 May 1874
Bexar	GLAESER, John E. & Friedrica	Amelia	11 Jun 1867
		Julius Herman	5 Jan 1871
		Arma Matilda	13 Feb 1873
		Emma	22 Apr 1875
Bexar	GLASER, Augusta P. (See S. W. Morris)		
Bexar	GLASER, Harmon &		
	Augusta (Komoruff)	Molly L.	9 Mar 1873
Victoria	GLASS, Sarah Florence (See William Allen)		
Bastrop	GLASS, W. S. & Jane	Frank M.	3 May 1873
Comal	GLENEWINKEL, Carl &		
	Marie (Heinemeier)	Wilhelm	22 Sep 1873
Austin	GLENN, Wm. B. & Lisette	Walter William	14 Dec 1875
Austin	GLENN, William I. & Mary E.	Robert Pilley	14 Nov 1874
Lavaca	GLOUSE, F. & Eliza	Freda	29 Sep 1874
Bastrop	GLOVER, Chas. H. & M.	Henry E.	25 Jul 1873
Hays	GLOVER, Eli & Rachael	Ruben Belvin	15 Aug 1874
Colorado	GLOVER, Will & Martha	Jennie	16 May 1875
Brazos	GLOVIN, Anna (See Geo. Acres)		

COUNTY	PARENTS	CHILD	DATE
Comal	GOBEL, Ferdinand & Wilhelmine (Roege)	Hermann Heinrich	27 Nov 1873
Travis	GODBEY, William & Margaret	James Willis	28 Dec 1873
Gillespie	GOEHMANN, August & Catharine	Otto	21 Oct 1874
		Sophie	19 Jun 1876
DeWitt	GOEHRING, August & Adeline	Ferdinand	16 Sep 1876
DeWitt	GOEHRING, Fred & Charlotta	Mary H.	17 May 1876
Bastrop	GOERTZ, John & Antonette	Phil.	12 Aug 1874
DeWitt	GOHLKE, F. Rudolph & Auguste	Anna	5 Nov 1874
DeWitt	GOHLKE, William & Louise D.	Maria A. L.	28 Dec 1873
DeWitt	GOHMERT, F. B. & Catherin	Hedwig	2 Sep 1874
DeWitt	GOHMERT, R. B.(?) & M. D.	Emilie T.	5 May 1873
	(1875 Entry spelled Robert P. & Mary		
		Johanna Virginia	Sep 1875
DeWitt	GOHMERT, R. W. & Justine	Mary C. E.	22 Aug 1873
	(1875 Entry spelled GOHMERT, Rud. W.)		
		Ida Justine	2 Dec 1875
DeWitt	GOHMERT, Wilhelm & Sophia	Friedrich Wilhem (sic) Gustav	26 Aug 1874
DeWitt	GOHRING, F. A. & C.	Adolph A.	28 Oct 1873
DeWitt	GOHRING, William & Alvona	Henry Willie	17 Jul 1874
Austin	GOINS, A. M. & Martha E.	Margaret Elizabeth	29 Oct 1875
Gillespie	GOLD, Jacob & Elisabeth	Clara	12 Apr 1874
Gillespie	GOLD, Jacob & Johanne	August	28 May 1874
Gillespie	GOLD, Peter Jr. & Auguste	Clara	30 Aug 1873
		Friedrich	28 Sep 1875
Gillespie	GOLD, Peter & Henriette	Emil	27 Jul 1875
Gillespie	GOLD, Wilhelm & Caroline	Franz	19 Sep 1875
Bexar	GOLDFRANK, M. & Bertha (Pfieffer)	Gertrude	6 Aug 1875
Colorado	GOLDSCHMIDT, Robert & Mary	John	18 Dec 1873
Lee	GOLDSTEIN, H. & Bertha	Max	25 Apr 1874
Victoria	GOLLA, Julia (See John Sherer)		
DeWitt	GOLLE, Wm. & T.	Terresa Wilhelmine	19 Feb 1874
Bexar	GOLOFF, Eleanor (See Emile Labroche)		
Kendall	GOMBERT, Hermann & Threse	Anna	21 Dec 1872
Bell	GOODE, J. A. & E. E.	Reuben John	6 Oct 1873
Austin	GOODE, John W. & Callie	Fay	9 Jan 1875
Bexar	GOODELL, Jennie (See Robert Alexander)		
Grimes	GOODMAN, B. & Ernestine	Theresa	26 Oct 1873
		?? (M)	26 Oct 1873
Bastrop	GOODMAN, J. H. & M. M.	Lula A.	29 Sep 1874
Bexar	GOODRICH, Coteland & Mary (Childs)	Joseph H.	1 Mar 1875
Brazos	GOODSON, J. M. & M. R.	T. E.	12 Dec 1874
Victoria	GOODWIN, Marion G. (See A. B. Peticolas)		
Grimes	GOREE, J. & Fannie W.	Longston J.	9 Dec 1873
Comanche	GOSSETT, L. J. & Harriet M.	Martha Emily	19 Jan 1874
Burnet	GOTCHER, T. J. & Fannie A.	Robert E. L.	3 Dec 1874
Victoria	GOUGLER, Betty (See Henry Kuykendall)		
Bexar	GOULON, Anna (See Aransas Prescott)		
Kendall	GOURLEY, T. M. & S. A.	Wm. Newton	22 Nov 1871
		Thos. M.	4 Oct 1874
Kendall	GOURLEY, W. P. & Elizab. E.	John Patton	17 Jan 1870
		Thos. Jeff.	18 Jun 1872
		Wm. Losien	2 Dec 1874
Austin	GRAF, Hermann & Rosa	Katie	17 Oct 1874
Medina	GRAFF, Carl & Justine	Caroline	21 Dec 1875
Austin	GRAFF, Wm. Franke & Caroline	Mary	11 Dec 1874
DeWitt	GRAHAM, W. H. & M. L.	Mary Agnes	24 Nov 1875
Comal	GRAMM, Louisa (See Julius Behnsch)		
Lavaca	GRANBERRY, W. L. & Mary	Amos F.	15 Dec 1874
Colorado	GRANGER, James & Lucy	Dick	28 Dec 1874
Bastrop	GRASS, Thomas Y. & E. A.	Thomas Y.	14 Jul 1873

COUNTY	PARENTS	CHILD	DATE
Kendall	GRASSO, Fritz & Sidonie	Adolph	16 Sep 1876
		Alwine	3 May 1878
		Else	6 Nov 1879
Bell	GRATEHOUSE, A. D. & M. A.	Stellar	13 Jun 1874
Victoria	GRAVES, W. P. & Louisa	Julia	20 Oct 1874
Comanche	GRAVIS, P. W. & Mary	James Stephen	8 Feb 1875
Comal	GRAVIS, Susan Elizabeth (See George H. Pfeuffer)		
Comanche	GRAY, Crocket & Caroline	Wm.	15 Mar 1874
Bell	GRAY, J. C. & R. C.	I. P.	26 May 1874
Bell	GRAY, J. D. & M. W.	Hiram Damon	6 Sep 1873
Brazos	GRAY, T. & Julia	Selana	1 Sep 1874
Hays	GREEN, B. F. & Kate	Wm. Robt.	6 Aug 1873
Hays	GREEN, Ed. J. L. & Eliza J.	Edwin	5 Apr 1875
Burnet	GREEN, G. E. & M. R.	Ula Zoe	29 Mar 1875
Lavaca	GREEN, G. W. & Francis Udora	Mary K.	1 Mar 1873
Fayette	GREEN, Harris F. & Mary M.	Jesse T.	12 Oct 1874
Hays	GREEN, J. H. & Martha A.	Frances Lucinda	18 Nov 1874
DeWitt	GREEN, L. B. & S. A.	Jos. J. (? or G?)	28 Apr 1875
DeWitt	GREEN, N. E. & S. O.	M. V. C.	20 Apr 1874
		N. H.	21 Dec 1875
Colorado	GREEN, Rowan & Leonora Dixie	Rowene Erie	5 Feb 1874
		Moirtle Elizabeth	No date
Comanche	GREENE, J. W. & Dora	Lucy	25 Jan 1875
DeWitt	GREENE, N. E. & ??	?? (M)	19 Dec 1875
Bastrop	GREEN, R. A. & S. A.	Minnie K.	24 Mar 1874
Austin	GREEN, Solomon & Lucy	Henrietta	4 Jul 1874
Bell	GREEN, W. P. & Emily F.	Eula	9 Jul 1873
		James Claude	14 Jul 1874
Bexar	GREENE, Simon P. & Margaret J.	William H.	2 Jun 1873
	(1875 Entry spelled GREEN)	Thomas Francis	13 Nov 1875
Grimes	GREENWOOD, F. B. & Annie Q.	Willie Wood	22 Aug 1874
Caldwell	GREGG, David & Josephine	Annie Davis	15 Oct 1875
Travis	GREGG, Richard & Mary	Ethel	19 Jun 1874
DeWitt	GREGORCZKY, John & Albina	Ludwig	16 Aug 1873
Lavaca	GREGORY, A. D. & Martha	Sam	20 Jun 1873
Bexar	GRENET, Mary (See James Callaghan)		
Bell	GRESHAM, J. N. & M. F.	Robert Oate	23 Aug 1873
Bexar	GRIBBOM, Bertha (See Reinhold Becker)		
Bell	GRIFFIN, D. C. & Nancy	Moses	26 Jun 1874
Lavaca	GRIFFIN, J. W. & Mary D.	L. B.	16 Jan 1874
Nacogd.	GRIFFIN, Robert C. & Elzir(i)a	Benjamin P.	27 Sep 1873
		J. C.	9 Jun 1875
Lavaca	GRIFFITH, L. M. & Ann E.	Kate	20 Jan 1874
Bexar	GRIGSBY, Mary F. (See N. A. Edens)		
Bastrop	GRIMES, A. W. & Lottie A.	Elizabeth	29 Jan 1875
		Wm. B.	19 May 1876
Bell	GRIMES, J. J. & Lucy J.	Alice Edney	4 Nov 1874
Nacogd.	GRIMES, John M. & P.	John M.	20 Nov 1874
Bell	GRIMES, L. P. & S. H.	Robert L.	4 Dec 1874
Nacogd.	GRIMES, Monroe & Sarah	Adolphus Y.	7 Sep 1873
DeWitt	GRIMES, S. F. & Cora L.	Ann Mary	18 Sep 18
		Sterling F.	8 Jan 1874
Lavaca	GRISSOM, J. J. & Rosealee	Polly C.	2 Jan 1874
Austin	GRISWOULD, Wm. M. & Elizabeth	John Oliver	3 May 1874
Comanche	GRNIER, Samuel & Lydia J.	Mary Belah	25 Jan 1874
Gillespie	GROBE, Ernst & Rosalia	Alwine	22 Oct 1875
Gillespie	GROBE, Fritz & Mathilda	Christine	24 Jul 1873
	(1874 Entry : Friedrich GROBE)	Heinrich	1 Oct 1874
Gillespie	GROBE, William & Clara	Emilie	3 Jul 1875
Kendall	GROENKE, Helene (See Gottfried Knoepfli)		
Bexar	GROOS, Charles & Hulda (Moureaa)	W. T. Elise	11 Mar 1871

COUNTY	PARENTS	CHILD	DATE
Bexar	GROOS, Charles -- Cont.	Helene	26 Oct 1872
		Emilie W.	20 May 1874
Comal	GROOS, Emilie (See Adolph Giesecke)		
Bexar	GROOS, Frederick &		
	Anna (Siemering)	Clara	23 Nov 1875
Bexar	GROOS, Gustav &		
	Anna (Willrich)	Elize Fredricke	27 Oct 1866
		Arna Franciska	29 Apr 1869
		Otto	14 Mar 1873
		Wilhilmine	30 Jul 1875
		Gustav	2 Feb 1879
Comal	GROOS, Gustav F. &		
	Medwig (GROOS)	Gustav Whilhelm	8 Jun 1876
Comal	GROOS, Hedwig (See Gustav F. Groos)		
Bexar	GROOS, Louisa (See John E. Schertz)		
Comal	GROOS, Wilhelmine (See Julius Giesecke)		
Kendall	GROSSMANN, Heinrich & ??	August	31 Jan 1858
		Carl Joseph	21 May 1860
		Phil. Hermann	20 Jan 1864
		Maria Theresia	23 Apr 1870
DeWitt	GROSZE, Charles & Henrietta	Emma	3 Mar 1874
Bexar	GROTE, Henry &		
	Mathilda (Stubing)	Ferdinand	19 Dec 1869
		Gustav	14 Apr 1873
		Carls	10 Feb 1875
		Pauline	5 Jan 1877
		Alvina	18 Jun 1871
Bexar	GROTHAUS, Emile (See Dr. Theo Hertzberg)		
Bexar	GROTHAUS, F. C. &		
	Lina (Schorre)	Emilie Charlotte	23 Aug 1874
Comal	GRUENE, Johanna (See Johann Sippel)		
Travis	GRUMBLES, John D. & Liza J.	Stephen Pomeroy	8 Oct 1873
Comal	GRUPE, Friederike (See Friedrich Schulze)		
Bexar	GUELDNER, Bertha (See Fred Bippert)		
Bexar	GUERRA, Casimiro &		
	Manuela (Delgado)	Antonio	16 Mar 1874
Travis	GUEST, Alexander H. &		
	Catherina	Emma Landor	20 Apr 1875
Victoria	GUGERHEIM, Rose (See Simon Levy)		
Hays	GULLETT, John T. & Ximera M.	Harriett R.	24 Mar 1873
Bexar	GUTIERRES, Augustin &		
	Virginia	Isabelle Virginia	19 Sep 1873
Victoria	GWINN, Wm. W. &		
	Mary E. (Newcomb)	William Elmer	28 Dec 1874
Bexar	HAAG, Christina (See Albert Lips)		
Kendall	HAAG, Friedrich & Charlotte	Heinrich Louis	22 Mar 1870
		Friedrich Otto	30 Sep 1871
		William Adolph	7 Jul 1873
Austin	HAAK, August & Emilie	August Henry	2 Nov 1874
Comal	HAAS, Wilhelm &		
	Emma Theresa (Mögelin)	Hellga Mathilda	20 Feb 1863
		Julius Franz	29 Apr 1864
		Louis Albert	8 Apr 1866
		Alvine Emma	
		Friederike	4 Sep 1868
		Oscar Wilhelm	8 Feb 1874
Medina	HAASS, Phillipp (sic) &		
	Hildegard	Sibila Hildegard	17 Dec 1871
		Emilia	21 Mar 1873
		Fritz Adolf	23 Sep 1874
		Marie Lidia	15 Mar 1876
Medina	HAASS, Valentine & Aalke(?)	George Louis	30 Mar 1874
Comal	HABERMANN, Ulricke (See Ferdinand Julius Heilig)		
Bexar	HADER, Dan &		
	Amanda Marie (Wisoff)	John Louis	30 Oct 1872
		Charles Emiel	16 Jan 1875

COUNTY	PARENTS	CHILD	DATE
Caldwell	HADNETT, J. M. & Delilah F.	?? (F)	21 Jul 1874
Bexar	HAENEL, Julius &		
	Emilie (Hartwig)	Emma	4 Sep 1857
Austin	HAGEMANN, W. A. & Marie	Johann Ernst Otto	23 Sep 1873
Gillespie	HAGEN, Louis v.d. & Clara	Otto	4 Jun 1874
Burnet	HAHN, A. C. & Mary J.	Anson Brady Jones	8 Oct 1874
Burnet	HAHN, C. H. & Mary C.	Thomas Cristof.	23 Dec 1874
Bexar	HAHN, F. & Cathrine (Venger)	Gustav Wm.	15 Jan 1874
Colorado	HAHN, Peter & Catharine	Henry Peter	15 Mar 1874
		Hattie Elizabeth	24 Apr 1875
Gillespie	HAHN, Peter & Lina	Emilie	9 Feb 1876
Fayette	HAIDUSEK, A. & A.	Jerome Ladislav	30 Aug 1875
Bexar	HAINEL, Anne (See Adolph Hensinger)		
Bell	HAIR, D. F. & I. S.	Helen Rebecca	2 Jun 1875
Lavaca	HAIRGROVE, Mark & F. E.	A. J.	21 Nov 1874
Caldwell	HALE, A. L. & H. F.	Anna Maude	31 Oct 1874
Burnet	HALE, C. & Mary E.	Miny	2 Apr 1874
Nacogd.	HALE, Henry C. & Mattie P.	Mary E.	7 Nov 1874
Lavaca	HALE, J. W. & Mary E.	Laura A.	4 Sep 1874
Bell	HALES, R. N. & M. J.	Martha Ann	8 Jun 1874
Bexar	HALFF, Mayer &		
	Rachael (Hart)	Henrietta	25 Sep 1867
		Alexander	5 Feb 1868
		H. Henry	17 Aug 1874
Bexar	HALFF, Salomon & Fannie (Leir)	Henry Leir	16 Nov 1873
		Minnie	12 Sep 1875
Victoria	HALFIN, Blonndi (See Charles A. Wertheimer)		
Victoria	HALFIN, Sol & Haidee (Stapp)	?? (M)	9 Oct 1875
Burnet	HALL, A. C. & Amanda	Wesley Levi	25 Feb 1874
Nacogd.	HALL, B. M. & R. P.	Ellis Houston	19 Dec 1873
Victoria	HALL, Charles A. &		
	Susan (Norris)	Nettie Ann	10 Jul 1873
		Charles Edward	2 Sep 1874
Caldwell	HALL, D. W. & A. C.	Jesse Maud	14 Oct 1875
Caldwell	HALL, E. W. & M. A.	F. O.	1 Dec 1874
Burnet	HALL, Henry W. &		
	Margaret J.	Sarah Agnes	6 May 1874
Austin	HALL, John H. & Sarah	P. H.	23 Jul 1876
Nacogd.	HALL, S. H. & Sallie	M.	25 Sep 1873
Burnet	HALL, T. P. & Zilphe	Wm. Alexander	15 Dec 1873
Victoria	HALSEL, Martha M. (See Joseph M. Van Norman)		
Nacogd.	HALTOM, James H. & M. L. A.	Mary L.	12 Nov 1873
Bell	HAMILTON, M. & ??	John William	17 Nov 1875
Travis	HAMMETT, Mary Susan (See Thomas Kirkpatrick)		
Comal	HAMPE, Friedrich &		
	Jacobine (Wolfshohl)	Albert	5 Jul 1874
Lavaca	HAMPIL, C. W. & Louisa	Julius W.	24 Aug 1875
Travis	HAMPTON, William & Sarah Ann	William Columbus	22 May 1873
Nacogd.	HAMRICK, T. W. & N. J.	Effa	18 Feb 1873
		Daniel E.	28 Nov 1875
Bell	HANCOCK, W. P. & A. E.	Chas. Thos.	16 Oct 1873
		Mary Helen	16 Aug 1875
Comanche	HANDLEY, John J. & Rhoda	Luretta	1 Mar 1874
Bastrop	HANDLIN, Margaret (See Jas. Robert Haynes)		
San Saba	HANDSHEY, W. O. & Sarah	Katie Vance	21 Dec 1874
Brazos	HANEMAN, Albert & Sarah E.	Sallie	20 Oct 1873
Travis	HANNA, R. H. & E. J.	John Austin	25 Dec 1880
Lavaca	HANNA, Wm. & Mary E.	John H.	3 Sep 1873
Bastrop	HANNAY, G. F. & Mollie E.	Robina Anna	12 Feb 1879
Bexar	HANNICH, Anton & Sophie	Katie	29 Jul 1874
Victoria	HANNIG, Julius & Emma (Krosh)	Maria Olga	25 Jun 1873
Fayette	HANS, D. & C.	Maxmilian	28 May 1875
Medina	HANS, Justin & Barbara	Mary Elisa	6 Nov 1875
Comal	HANSMANN, Christian &		
	Friederike (Timmermann)	Conrad August	2 Feb 1875
Lavaca	HANSON, C. H. & E. W.	Charles W.	16 Sep 1873

29

COUNTY	PARENTS	CHILD	DATE
Burnet	HANSON, John G. & Ida F.F.	Lorena Sophia S.	15 Jul 1874
Gillespie	HANSON, John G. & Ida	Mary Helen	15 Sep 1875
Grimes	HARBUCK, Wm. H. & Mary F.	Lula	1 Dec 1874
Nacogd.	HARDEMAN, Bunch & Fanny A.	Condy B.	20 Jun 1873
Hays	HARDIN, Benjamin C. &		
	Claracy J.	Claracy	23 Jan 1874
		Wm. Green	17 Feb 1876
Bexar	HARDING, Jane (See William Wallace)		
Bandera	HARDUK, C. & A.	M. C.	28 Oct 1874
Brazos	HARDY, Hammett & Molissa	Wm. Hammett	5 May 1876
Bexar	HARDY, Lucinda J. (See Wyatt Johnson)		
Bastrop	HARGROVE, J. F. & Anna	Mattie Bell	22 Aug 1878
Fayette	HARIGEL, H. & I.	Alfred August	15 Jun 1875
Austin	HARIGEL, Wm. & Bertha	Wilhelm Emil Lee	4 Jul 1875
Bexar	HARLOS, Catherine (See George Rittimann)		
Comal	HARLOS, Sophie (See Heinrich Neuse)		
Burnet	HARLOW, Elisha & E. J.	James Samuel	29 May 1875
Lavaca	HARMES, Frank & B.	J. Frank	27 Oct 1873
		Peter B.	15 Jun 1875
Lavaca	HARMES, Henry & ??	A. Christina	17 Sep 1873
Lavaca	HARMES, John & Elizabeth	Mary M.	18 Mar 1874
		Leo	18 Feb 1876
Austin	HARMS, John Frederick &	Auguste Dorothea	
	Johanne Margaret	Johanna	15 Aug 1873
		Johanna Marie	
		Margarethe	5 Oct 1875
Lavaca	HARMISS, Casper & Mary	Josephine	28 Dec 1875
Lavaca	HARMISS, Henry & Christina	Julius	15 Apr 1875
Hays	HARMON, James T. & Martha	Tibitha Cassandray	24 Sep 1874
Hays	HARMON, John S. & Sarah J.	Laura Tabitha	1 Feb 1875
Brazos	HARMAN, W. H. & Sarah E.	Willie Florence	16 Dec 1876
Burnet	HARNESS, Abel & Sarah E.	John Willis Blakey	12 Jan 1875
Bexar	HARNISCH, Charles &		
	Louise (Brentons)	Josephine Charlotte	18 Aug 1876
Hays	HARPER, William H. &		
	Jane L.	Rebecca M.	25 Sep 1873
Nacogd.	HARRALL, Dossett & Pink	Maria L.	21 Nov 1874
Lee	HARRELL, E. C. & Pauline G.	Maud O.	26 Mar 1874
San Saba	HARRELL, J. W. & P. L.	Virginia A.	27 Oct 1874
Brazos	HARRELL, W. A. & M. R.	??	24 Nov 1875
		Katie May	2 Jan 1876
Bell	HARRELL, W. H. & L. A.	Martha Ella	16 Dec 1873
Burnet	HARRINGTON, B. L. & Rocky	Andrew J.	5 Mar 1874
Burnet	HARRINGTON, R. & Percilla	Walter Wright	10 Nov 1874
Bell	HARRIS, A. J. & O. P.	Olivia F.	2 May 1874
Brazos	HARRIS, Alberta (See Tony Wilson)		
Lee	HARRIS, C. C. & S. A. S.	Charlie David	27 Sep 1875
Hays	HARRIS, Charles P. & Ellen A.	William Augustus	8 Jul 1875
Austin	HARRIS, Christopher & Annie	Mary Jane	
		Elizabeth	30 Jun 1875
Travis	HARRIS, Fleming & Rachel	Walter Elmer	5 Jun 1875
Lee	HARRIS, Lewis & Johanna	Moses	3 Apr 1876
Lavaca	HARRIS, W. J. & M. C.	Ruth A.	26 Jul 1874
San Saba	HARRIS, W. J. & S. J.	E. J.	17 Nov 1875
Lee	HARRISON, Benjamin & Amanda	Henry	13 Mar 1874
Victoria	HARRIS, William &		
	Jenette (Ragland)	Elisha	5 Oct 1873
Caldwell	Harrison, P. L. & M.	Elizabeth E.	27 Dec 1874
Lee	HARRISON, Thomas J. & Sarah	Jefferson	30 May 1874
Grimes	HART, H. C. & Sallie	John Bennett	15 Oct 1873
Bexar	HART, Rachael (See Mayer Halff)		
DeWitt	HARTMANN, A. C. & Josephine	Otto F.	24 Apr 1876
Bell	HARTRICK, W. T. J. & F. C.	Wm. Henry	4 Mar 1874
Comal	HARTUNG, Emma (See Karl Friedrich Wilhelm Brehmer)		
Bexar	HARTWIG, Emilie (See Julius Haenel)		
Bell	HARTWIG, L. & C.	Joab Robt. Pleasant	20 Jul 1874

COUNTY	PARENTS	CHILD	DATE
Burnet	HARWELL, J. S. & Mary L.	Almon Dean	20 Jun 1875
Burnet	HARWELL, J.S.H. & Francis R.	William Penn	24 Nov 1874
Bexar	HASDOFF, Eliso (See Chas. H. Hugo)		
DeWitt	HASDORFF, William & Mary	Josephine	23 Jul 1874
Gillespie	HASEL, J. P. & Christiana	Auguste Alsvine Sophie	14 Aug 1874
Bexar	HASENBERG, Fred & Emma (Nette)	Fred E. Adolph	22 Oct 1872
Fayette	HAST, C. F. & ??	Johannes	2 Mar 1875
Bell	HASTY, A. P. & S. C.	Louvina E.	16 Sep 1873
Fayette	HATCHETT, J. M. & Sarah	Jesse	27 Dec 1874
Caldwell	HATCHETT, Joseph & Mary E.	Wallace P.	27 Dec 1875
Nacogd.	HATHCOAT, Wm. B. & P. E.	E.	3 Nov 1873
Bexar	HAUCK, Joseph & Elizabeth (Maixnar)	Catharina	11 Mar 1874
Bexar	HAUEISEN, Friederick C. & Maria C. (Wrede)	Alfred Leopold	8 Dec 1861
		Ida Carolina	13 Oct 1864
		Hulda Emilie	18 May 1867
		Freiderick Louis	28 Sep 1869
		Maria Laura	8 Nov 1870
		Otto Fried.	23 Jan 1873
		Emil W. F.	21 Apr 1875
Bandera	HAUGHT, William A. & Sarah L.	Ida Leona	10 Mar 1875
Victoria	HAUSCHILD, Geo. Herman & Adele (Luder)	Otto Herman	14 Mar 1875
Bandera	HAY, George & Virginia	F. W.	9 Feb 1874
Bell	HAYDON, J. S. & T. A.	Lena	14 Feb 1875
Lavaca	HAYNES, Geo. L. & Nancy Jane	Nancy Ida	15 Sep 1873
Lavaca	HAYNES, J. H. & A. T.	Ada	4 Jan 1875
Lavaca	HAYNES, J. H. & M. A.	Amos	14 Dec 1874
Caldwell	HAYNES, Jas. E. & M. E.	Alice Luretta	11 Feb 1874
Bastrop	HAYNES, Jas. Robert & Margaret (Handlin)	Fannie Adelia	7 Jun 1861
Burnet	HAYNIE, Wm. & S. B.	Elizabeth	11 Mar 1875
Burnet	HAYS, Thos. M. & Mary A.	William M.	19 Oct 1874
Austin	HAYS, W. H. & M. C.	Mary Francis	25 Aug 1873
Austin	HAYWOOD, Henry & Ellen	Caladonia	20 Jul 1874
Bexar	HEARD, D. W. & M.Z. (Bortick)	John B.	3 Jan 1872
DeWitt	HEARD, Joel B. & L. A.	Willie Conizene	27 Apr 1875
Victoria	HEARD, Olie (See John S. Munn)		
Grimes	HEARNE, W. F. & Kate	Willie	23 Jan 1874
		Maurie	31 Mar 1875
Bandera	HEATH, Joseph & Mary	Elby Jane	4 Nov 1873
Victoria	HECK, Christian & Rosine (Rieg)	Charles William	2 Jun 1873
Lee	HECK, R. D. & Martha A.	Mittie	12 Jan 1874
Bexar	HECK, Rosa (See Chas. Kunzmann)		
Lee	HECK, W. F. & Melissa W.	Mary L.	12 Aug 1873
Lee	HECK, Wm. T.(?) (or F?) & Malissa E. (Moore)	Randall Davis	Jan 1875
		Randle Davis	15 Feb 1875
Comal	HEFFTER, F. Hermann & Molly Catharina (Spiess)	Lucy Charlotte	27 Jan 1861
	(1865 Entry Friedrich is spelled out)	Hermine Elise	15 May 1865
Travis	HEFFTER, H. O. & Mary Louisa	Mathilde Charlotta Attilie	27 May 1873
		Willy Hugo Frederick	2 Nov 1868
		Elizabeth Rosalie Mathilde	5 Mar 1870
Nacogd.	HEFLIN, S. R. & Sarah S. (? or L.)	Mary A.	15 Sep 1873
Bexar	HEHN, Peter & Mary (Baddo)	William	4 Nov 1874

COUNTY	PARENTS	CHILD	DATE
Bexar	HEIDELBERG, Lena (See Henry Kuhlman)		
Comal	HEIDEMEYER, Auguste (See Alex Hofmann)		
Bexar	HEILAMANN, Bertha (See A. Hornung)		
Comal	HEILIG, Ferdinand Julius &		
	Ulricke (Habermann)	Wanda Marie	28 Aug 1875
Comal	HEILIG, Otto &		
	Margaretta (Reszczynski)	Alexandra	8 Feb 1875
Bastrop	HEILIGBRODT, Ludolph & Julie	Clara	2 Feb 1875
		Julie	13 Sep 1876
Kendall	HEILIGMANN, Heinrich &		
	Johanne	Henry Fasben	20 Feb 1862
		Augustine	23 Sep 1865
		Emma	23 Jul 1867
		Anna	2 Jul 1870
		Louise	2 Dec 1871
		Mina	3 Apr 1872
		August	20 Dec 1873
		Ida	28 May 1875
Gillespie	HEIMANN, Aug. & Helene	Auguste	7 Jul 1873
	(1875 Entry Spelled Helena)	Henry	31 May 1875
Comal	HEIMER, Franz &		
	Emma (Busch)	Adele	19 Nov 1873
		Albert	22 Jun 1875
		Otto	4 Jun 1877
		Hermann	10 Jun 1879
Medina	HEIN, Hei & Catharine	William	4 Mar 1874
Bexar	HEINAN, Louise (See Joseph Lamm)		
Comal	HEINEMEIER, Marie (See Carl Glenewinkel)		
Bexar	HEINEN, Joseph &		
	Johanna (Boerner)	Emil	17 Nov 1874
Gillespie	HEINMANN, William & Maria	Maria	10 May 1875
Bexar	HEITIZ, Emilie (See Emil Elmendorf)		
Austin	HEITMANN, Christian D. &		
	Mary	Fritz Johan	20 Oct 1874
Bexar	HELMS, Eliza Ann (See H. B. Edens)		
Fayette	HELLMUTH, H. & L. F.	Rosa Mary	12 Feb 1859
		Clara Hermine	14 Mar 1866
		Hermann Gustav	12 Oct 1868
		Ella Laura	30 Mar 1874
Bastrop	HEMPHILL, G. & A. E.	Ann E.	10 Jan 1875
Bastrop	HEMPHILL, Jacob & E. V.	J. E.	30 Sep 1873
Bastrop	HEMPHILL, W. L. & Sarah Jane	Ardella	3 Jan 1874
Travis	HENDERSON, McD. & Elvira L.	James Thomas	19 Dec 1873
Bell	HENDRICK, C. L. & L. M.	Rosa L.	5 Mar 1873
		Charles A.	25 Sep 1875
Bell	HENDRICK, J. M. & M. A.	James Valpo	28 Nov 1875
Comal	HENNE, Louis August &		
	Emilie (von Stein)	Henriette Charlotte	23 Feb 1871
		Emmy Auguste	11 Sep 1873
		Louis August	14 Sep 1875
Lavaca	HENNESSEY, W. H. & Mary	Mary	28 Jul 1873
Lavaca	HENNESSY, T. H. & Sarah J.	Thos. J.	4 Apr 1874
Austin	HENNINGS, George & Clothilde	Julie	2 Jan 1875
Bexar	HENSINGER, Adolph &		
	Anne (Hainel)	Emma	31 Dec 1857
		Ottilie	25 Jun 1861
		Anna	21 Apr 1865
		Julia	15 Sep 1868
		Adolph	20 May 1871
		Edward	9 Jun 1874
		Matilde	22 Jan 1877
Victoria	HENSOLDT, Helena (See E. Melchior)		
Hays	HENSON, William & Jane	Martha J.	11 Sep 1873
Gillespie	HERBORT, Conrad & Dorothea	Adolph	27 Jan 1874
Kendall	HERBST, Carl Heinrich &		
	Sophie Dorothea	Emma	9 Nov 1858

COUNTY	PARENTS	CHILD	DATE
Kendall	HERBST, Carl Heinrich-Cont.	Albert	11 Oct 1860
		Rudolph	21 May 1864
		Robert	11 Aug 1866
		Theodore	21 May 1868
		Lillie	9 Mar 1870
		Ernst	8 Jun 1872
		Ida	6 Feb 1876
Bexar	HERFF, John A. &		
	Ida (Kampmann)	Herman Ferd.	24 May 1876
Medina	HERFURTH, John & Anna Barbara	Anna Maria	26 Oct 1875
Comal	HERING, Johann &		
	Caroline (Lorentz)	Richard	23 Nov 1873
Comal	HERING, Johann &		
	Paulina (Lorentz)	Anna	1 Nov 1875
Bexar	HERNANDEZ, Polonio &		
	Blasa (Martinez)	Estanislado	28 Sep 1873
Colorado	HERNDON, L. D. & ??	Eugene	13 Nov 1873
Colorado	HERNDON, Wm. & Mary V.	Boswell	4 Apr 1875
Austin	HERNER, Marcus & Emilie	William	2 Jul 1874
Lavaca	HERON, T. L. & E. E.	Adelia A.	12 Aug 1875
Bexar	HERRERA, Felicita (See Francisco Alvares)		
Kendall	HERRIN, I. (or) J. F. &		
	Elizabeth	Mary Ellen	19 Nov 1856
		Nancy Mathilda	15 Oct 1860
		Martha Francis	14 Aug 1864
		James Wesley	30 Sep 1868
Lavaca	HERRON, M. D. & M.	Alabama	4 Oct 1873
Bexar	HERTZBERG, Carl Frank &		
	Anna (Osing)	Carolina M.	16 Jul 1874
Bexar	HERTZBERG, Dr. Theo &		
	Emilie (Grothaus)	Edward Fried.	14 Jan 1860
		Emmy Charlotte	8 Apr 1863
		Hans Rudolph	1 Jul 1871
Lee	HESTER, Nicolas & ??	Bismark	17 Jan 1874
Bexar	HESTER, Viney H. (See Elijah B. Smith)		
Kendall	HEUERMANN, Wm. & Caroline	Wm.	8 Feb 1858
		George	26 Jan 1859
		Lina	19 Jul 1860
		Carl	2 Nov 1861
		Dorothea	2 Feb 1863
		Minna	20 Jan 1865
		Emma	No date
		Louis	23 Oct 1869
		Hermann	16 Oct 1871
		Emilie	15 May 1872
Colorado	HEYDRON, Christian & Louise	John H. F. W.	10 Jun 1873
	(1875 Entry spelled Heydorn)	W.	22 Jul 1875
Bexar	HEYE, Diedrich &		
	Josephina (Altmann)	Gerhard Anton	29 May 1874
Austin	HEYNE, Richard & Auguste	Robert	10 Nov 1873
Bell	HIATT, M. F. & H. C.	B. Bismark	3 Sep 1874
Bastrop	HICKSON, B. F. & Mary	Martha Jane	15 May 1874
Brazos	HIGGS, S. H. & B.	Emma Jane	23 Dec 1874
Bastrop	HIGHSMITH, W. A. & L. A.	Katie Lee	17 Feb 1874
Lee	HILDEBRAND, W. B. & Elsie	David Leon	16 Dec 1873
Austin	HILDEBRANDT, Edward &		
	Mary (Twins)	Louis & Laura	18 Sep 1875
Hays	HILL, C. & Aney D.	Oler(?)(orSler?)	19 Dec 1873
Bastrop	HILL, D. O. & Nannie	Thomas O.	28 Feb 1875
Caldwell	HILL, E. P. & M. A.	Wm. C.	31 Apr 1875
Brazos	HILL, Frank George &		
	Henry Mildred (Bullard)	May M.	25 Dec 1874
Austin	HILL, Louis & Melissa	Douglass	9 Jun 1875
Bastrop	HILL, R. T. & Lucinda P.	Anna (?) Lou	14 Nov 1873
Bastrop	HILL, Rebecca (See Michael Wolf)		
San Saba	HILLIARD, Wm. & Amand C.	Thos. Alex.	12 Feb 1874

33

Austin	HILLYARD, Martin & Scilla	Ira	4 Jun 1874
Austin	HIMLY, Charles & Lena	Helene	8 May 1877
Lee	HINES, R. B. & Sueritia H.	Marion Luther	1874
Fayette	HILDEBRAND, W. J. & N.	Walter J.	6 Jun 1873
Fayette	HILL, J. W. & Grace	Nina	19 Apr 1874
Lee	HILLIARD, A. A. & ??	Martha A.	14 Sep 1874
Bell	HINSHAW, J. & Rosa	Wm. Henry	7 Apr 1875
Bastrop	HINTON, J. R. & T. A.	Joseph Henry	27 Dec 1874
Comal	HINTZ, Wilhelmine (See Fried. B. Hoffmann)		
Austin	HINZE, Frank & Wilhelmine	Lydia	25 Jun 1873
Fayette	HINZE, Frederick & Louisa	Friederika M.	2 Oct 1874
Gillespie	HIRSCH, Jacob & Maria	Louis	23 Nov 1873
Bexar	HITZFELDER, Charles & Theresa (Becker)	Matthias Edward	29 Mar 1876
Comal	HITZFELDER, Maria (See Albert Kopplin)		
Lee	HOBBS, W. R. & E. J.	America	5 Dec 1874
Bandera	HODGES, F. M. & N. A.	Nancy Anne	29 May 1875
Bexar	HODGES, Margaret (See Soloman Brasfield)		
Caldwell	HODNETT, J. A. & Melissa A.	Johanna	14 Jul 1875
Comal	HOEKE, Heinrich & Marie (Bartels)	Emma Christine	9 Oct 1873
Gillespie	HOELZER, Joseph & Christine	Adolph	10 Feb 1876
Comal	HOERHOLD, Louise (See Moritz Suche)		
Bexar	HOERNER, Minna (See F. A. Piper)		
Bexar	HOFFMAN, Amelia (See Fredk. Burkhardt)		
Comal	HOFFMANN, Antonie (See Ferdinand Nehls)		
Gillespie	HOFFMANN, August & Sabine	Louis	25 Nov 1873
Bexar	HOFFMANN, Catharine (See Andres Gerloff)		
Comal	HOFFMANN, Fried. B. & Wilhelmine (Hintz)	Antonie Wilhelmine	31 Mar 1848
		Gustav August	19 Jul 1850
		Friedrich Edward	2 Dec 1851
		Heinrich Scipio	15 Jun 1853
		Elizabeth Theresa	25 Nov 1854
		Emma	28 Dec 1856
		Alwine	28 Mar 1860
		Agnes	5 Dec 1865
		Thekla	25 Mar 1868
		Franz Carl	31 Jul 1870
Bexar	HOFHEINZ, Daniel & Augusta (Voges)	Mathilda Olga	18 Dec 1875
Kendall	HOFHEINZ, Friedrich & Emilie	Emma	12 Sep 1874
		F. F. Adolph	4 Mar 1866
		S. Eduard	20 Feb 1868
		R. G. Hugo	12 Jul 1870
		C. E. Adele	22 Nov 1872
Comal	HOFMANN, Alex & Auguste (Heidemeyer)	Alfred Adolph	19 Sep 1874
Gillespie	HOHENBERGER, Robert & Clara (Twins)	Auguste & Anna	28 Feb 1875
Bell	HOLCOMB, F. N. & L. F.	Robert Newton	7 Jun 1874
Gillespie	HOLDEN, Caleb Baines & Margaret (Hunter)	Mortimer Thaddeus	14 Aug 1873
Gillespie	HOLDENHAUER, Aug & Johanne	Anna	17 Oct 1875
Comal	HOLDERMANN, Sophie (See Gustav Gerlich) (Holtermann)		
Bell	HOLECOMB, T. W. & Jane	Wilburn C.	31 Jul 1873
Bastrop	HOLEMAN, Joshua & Carolin	Perry Holdman?	1 Nov 1873
Bexar	HOLLADY, Artie (See Joseph Collins)		
DeWitt	HOLLAN, H. H. & Jane	Sam. Tilden	Jul 1876
DeWitt	HOLLAN, N. B. & Josephine	Fannie	Aug 1876
Comanche	HOLLAND, R. & Susan E.	Mary	7 Aug 1873
Brazos	HOLLAND, Wm. & Martha C.	Ida M.	19 Apr 1875
Hays	HOLLANDER, William & Martha A.	Mary Belle	12 Jan 1874

COUNTY	PARENTS	CHILD	DATE
Colorado	HOLLINGSWORTH, R. B. & J. A.	Phebe	1 Mar 1874
Bastron	HOLLOWAY, J. L. & R. E.	Winnie L.	17 Jan 1874
Bell	HOLMAN, W. S. & H. E.	Lewis W.	3 Aug 1874
Caldwell	HOLMES, E. W. & B. Z.	W. H.	25 Aug 1873
		Cornelia	15 Nov 1873
Bell	HOLMES, P. E. & Martha E.	Robt. Brelan	18 May 1873
Comanche	HOLMSLEY, F. M. & L. A.	James Europe	12 May 1874
Comanche	HOLMSLEY, J. M. & Aramintie	James Sutton	2 Oct 1873
Lavaca	HOLSTER, Felix & Teresa	Geo. E.	12 Jun 1873
Lavaca	HOLSTER, Leander & Serene	Mary Lilly	4 Sep 1873
Comal	HOLTZ, Christian Heinrich & Georgine (Conring)	Harry	24 Oct 1873
Gillespie	HOLYBERGER, Albert & Henriette	Carl Albert Friedrich	19 May 1873
Colorado	HOLZGRAFF, Charles & Lizzie	Mattie F.	6 Jun 1874
Comal	HOMBACH, Magdalena (See Heinrich Wilhelm Schorn)		
Austin	HOOD, C. W. & Missouri	Wallace A.	17 Jun 1875
Brazos	HOOD, W. S. & M. J.	Russell	23 Jan 1874
Burnet	HOOVER, Isaac L. & Mary R.	Henry Edward	18 Mar 1875
Bell	HOOVER, T. B. & A. S.	A. J.	10 Jul 1873
Bexar	HOPKINS, Bell (See George Williams)		
Hays	HOPKINS, Desmond P. & Mary L. C.	Clinton L.	29 May 1874
Bastrop	HORD, A. W. & Laura	Ziddie	14 Sep 1875
Caldwell	HORNER, J. M. & Mary A.	John A.	13 Jul 1874
Bexar	HORNER, Louisa (See George Jagge)		
Bexar	HORNUNG, A. & Bertha (Heilamann)	Bertha Teresa	2 Dec 1875
		August Louis	6 Mar 1878
Medina	HORNUNG, August & Catharine	Augusta	29 Nov 1872
		Regina	25 Feb 1875
Hays	HORTON, Thos. J. & Maggie M.	Herff McCarty	15 Nov 1874
Lee	HOSEA, Henry & Sophronia (Fisher)	George Washington	27 Jul 1875
Comal	HOSSE (See McCullogh, D. A.)		
Travis	HOTCHKISS, Martha Elizabeth (See Aaron Hill Whitten)		
DeWitt	HOUSE, Fred & Sarah	John R.	2 Oct 1855
		H. Jane A.	15 Feb 1858
		Annie C.	6 Oct 1859
		Laura F.	13 Oct 1861
		Martha E.	21 Aug 1865
		Christopher H.	10 Oct 1867
		Mary A.	27 Sep 1870
		Sarah E.	22 Aug 1872
		Henry S.	21 Nov 1874
San Saba	HOUSTON, John T. & Sarah E.	Thomas Archibald	27 Apr 1874
Burnet	HOWARD, J. B. & Martha M.	Martha Jane	12 Dec 1873
		Cora	4 Nov 1875
Burnet	HOWARD, J. G. W. & Martha	Mary	10 Aug 1874
San Saba	HOWARD, W. H. & Mary	Walter D.	28 Feb 1874
Grimes	HOWELL, Smith Judson & Mary Sue	Maud Gravis	31 Oct 1873
Lavaca	HOWERTON, D. B. & Ann	Daisy	5 Nov 1874
Lavaca	HOWLAND, E. P. & E. O.	Willie C.	21 Nov 1874
Bexar	HOYER, Lina (See Fridolin Wild)		
Austin	HUBNER, Hermann & Julie	Julie	22 Jan 1874
Lavaca	HUDDLESTON, P. W. & M. F.	Gabie	10 Aug 1873
		James B.	20 Jul 1875
Lavaca	HUDGEONS, Thos. & M. A.	Thos. M.	30 Jan 1874
Lavaca	HUDGEONS, W. R. & Avan	Arthur	15 May 1875
Brazos	HUDSON, Anson & Leandor	Albert	21 Jul 1873
		Edna	15 Apr 1875
		Felix Grundy	20 Mar 1876
Burnet	HUDSON, J. R. & J. C.	Julia	12 Nov 1874
Caldwell	HUDSON, M. M. & Lucy	Sarah Ann	29 Nov 1873

COUNTY	PARENTS	CHILD	DATE
Bandera	HUDSPETH, J. A. & A. E.	M. L.	8 Jul 1874
Bandera	HUDSPETH, J. B. & Letitia	Thomas F.	26 Jun 1875
Bexar	HUEBNER, Matilda (See Geo Schroeder)		
Bexar	HUEFFNEYER, Louise (See Herman Schleuning)		
Bexar	HUERTA, Rosa (See Santiago Vidal)		
Lavaca	HUGHES, David & F.	Martha	25 Dec 1874
Bexar	HUGO, Chas. H. &		
	Eliso (Hasdoff)	Lilly Eliso	27 Sep 1872
		Viola Frida	25 Nov 1874
Lavaca	HULL, Jacob & Ruth Jane	Jane Gabrila	13 Sep 1873
	(1875 Entry R. J.)	A. J.	26 Feb 1875
Gillespie	HULLER, Gustav & Anna	Henry Frederick	
		Gustav	23 Nov 1874
Nacogd.	HUMBER, John P. & Jane	Willis E.	8 Oct 1872
Bexar	HUMMER, Sarah Francis (See V. C. Ostrom)		
Lavaca	HUMPHREYS, Geo. P. & Mary A.	Wm. E. J.	30 Sep 1873
DeWitt	HUNT, F. P. & H. J.	Catherine D.	31 Aug 1873
Bexar	HUNTER, J. T. & Nannie (Cox)	Daisy	8 Oct 1873
		Horace L.	14 Jul 1875
Gillespie	HUNTER, Margaret (See Caleb Baines Holden)		
Bell	HUNTER, S. L. & P. A.	Charles Erwin	22 Jan 1875
Brazos	HUNTER, S. M. & C. L.	Sallie	19 Oct 1873
		Sam	9 May 1875
Bexar	HUNTRESS, Frank C. &		
	Francisca (Montes)	Thos. Richard	3 Apr 1874
		Anna Maria	15 Nov 1875
Bexar	HUPPERTZ, H. J. &		
	Mary F. (Parschal)	Ernestine L. G.	19 Feb 1874
Bell	HURST, J. M. & M. A.	Mary Charlotte	7 Apr 1874
		J. M.	22 Jan 1876
Bexar	HUSTON, W. H. H. &		
	Catharine (Downey)	Wm. Henry Harrison	21 Oct 1873
Travis	HUTCHINS, A. H. & Kathleen	Rufus Jones	14 Aug 1874
Colorado	HUTCHINS, Cornelius & Jane	Merrett	14 Mar 1873
Caldwell	HUTCHISON, A. J. & George	A. R.	1 Apr 1874
Bexar	HUTH, Louis Jr. & Lina	Emil Albert	19 Jul 1873
		Emma Amalia	5 Jan 1875
Comanche	HUTSON, J. M. & C. C.	Fannie	27 Sep 1873
		William F.	2 Jan 1876
Medina	HUTZLER, Nicolaus &		
	Marianna	Elizabeth	9 Aug 1874
Comal	IKELS, Meta (See Christian Meyer)		
Fayette	ILEY, V. H. & E. A.	Ruben	6 Jul 1874
Bexar	ILIG, John &		
	Elizabeth (Beitel)	Betta	2 Aug 1874
Brazos	ILLO, John & Mary A.	Amelia	6 Sep 1873
		Peter	22 Sep 1875
Kendall	INGENHUTT, Peter J. & Marie	Hubert	28 Aug 1863
		Paul	12 Apr 1868
		Hermann	16 Feb 1870
		Ernst	16 Jan 1872
Nacogd.	INGRAHAM, George F. &		
	Martha T.	Elsee R. (sic)	3 Dec 1874
Bastrop	INGRAM, R. & M. F. (Twins)	Milton	20 Oct 1873
		Marion	19 Oct 1873
Nacogd.	IRION, R. H. & M. H. (Durst)	R. D.	22 Jul 1875
Nacogd.	IRVIN, Harrite D. (See L. S. Taylor)		
Bexar	IVES, Frances (See Andrew Ed Carruthers)		
Burnet	IVEY (IVY), J. S. & S. E.	Carrie May	28 Mar 1874
Lavaca	JACKS, D. R. & A. M.	Chas. B.	15 May 1874
Burnet	JACKSON, A. M. & V. J.	Ira Francis	30 Nov 1874
Austin	JACKSON, Calvin & Temese	Betsey Ann	24 Jul 1875
San Saba	JACKSON, D. & E.	J. E.	30 May 1874
Burnet	JACKSON, Elias & ??	James Monroe	27 May 1875
Burnet	JACKSON, J. M. & S. E.	Phoeba Tennessee	15 Sep 1874

COUNTY	PARENTS	CHILD	DATE
Bastrop	JACKSON, Louis & Matilda	Amos	1 Sep 1875
Austin	JACKSON, Miles & Becky	William	15 May 1875
Brazos	JACKSON, Niel & Mag.	Carrie	1 May 1875
Bell	JACKSON, Thomas & Lucy	Rufus E.	20 Nov 1873
Lavaca	JACKSON, Thos. F. & Jennie	Lela Octavia	5 Sep 1873
Burnet	JACKSON, Z. R. & Sarah E.	Hetty Ann	31 Oct 1875
Gillespie	JACOBI, Peter & Catharine	Hillmar Otto	31 Jul 1873
Bexar	JACOBS, Caroline (See Samuel Mayer)		
Lavaca	JACOBS, John & Nancy J.	Thomas Lee	31 Aug 1875
Lavaca	JACOBS, John & Sarah	Donna	13 Feb 1875
Lavaca	JACOBS, John & U. J.	Edward	15 Jul 1873
Bexar	JAGGE, George &		
	Louisa (Horner)	George	17 Apr 1874
		Louisa	18 Feb 1876
Bexar	JAGGE, Lena (See Robert Storbeck)		
Bexar	JAGGY, Julia (See E. L. Richey)		
Bexar	JAMES, Henry &		
	Mille (Sappington)	Benjamin S.	16 Aug 1874
		Clara	1 Aug 1876
Bexar	JAMES, John & Annie (Milby)	John Herndon	13 Oct 1852
	(This concludes second listing below)		
		Thomas Milby	21 Oct 1854
		Vinton Lee	3 Jul 1858
		Annie Laura	26 Jan 1860
		Sidney Stirling	12 Jun 1862
		Mary Emma	18 Jul 1864
		Hugh Scott	13 Oct 1866
		Fannie Ellen	19 Aug 1871
		Flora Diana	29 Oct 1874
Burnet	JAMES, J. H. & Mary J.	Christian A.	20 Jun 1875
DeWitt	JAMISON, R. B. & M. J.	John H.	14 Jul 1873
Lavaca	JANCHER, John & Mary	Frankisca	1 Jan 1874
Comanche	JANES, A. J. F. & A. A.	Amanda Elizabeth	21 Mar 1874
Austin	JANSSEN, John & Eliza H.	Marie Catharine	17 Dec 1873
Lavaca	JAVIS, W. J. & Francis Ann	Geo. Emmit	15 Nov 1874
Bandera	JEFFERS, M. V. & Elizabeth	Thomas W.	14 Jan 1873
		Ophelia Denie	26 Jan 1875
Nacogd.	JEFFERSON, Isaac & Jane	John William	16 Nov 1873
		Josephine	Apr 1876
Austin	JEFFERSON, Thomas & Caroline	Hillyard	14 Jul 1874
DeWitt	JENDRZYI, Thom & Francis	Emanuel	26 Mar 1875
Hays	JENNINGS, A. J. & Mary E.	James Thomas	18 Jan 1874
		Byrd Owen	7 Dec 1875
Hays	JENNINGS, Jas. M. & Sarah	Robt. Lester	13 Sep 1875
Hays	JENNINGS, W. S. & Matilda E.	May L.	3 Aug 1873
	(1875 Entry spelled Jennings, William S.)		
		Lester S.	3 May 1875
Comal	JENTSCH, Heinrich E. &		
	Bertha (Foerster)	Albert Aug.	16 Jun 1874
		Hermann Edward	30 Sep 1872
Colorado	JERRELLS, A. H. & A. V.	Zula M.	23 Oct 1874
Bexar	JESSE, Maximillian T. &	Maxamillian	
	Aminda (Liebe)	Eugene	12 Sep 1875
Travis	JESSEN, Adelbert C. &		
	Ottilie W. A.	Elfriede Ottilie	8 Sep 1873
Travis	JESTER, Mary Catherine (See Newton Cain Moore)		
Austin	JOHN, Hartmann A. E. &		
	K. F. L. (Amthor?)	Ida Mary	30 Mar 1875
	(Twins)	Emelie Bertha	30 Mar 1875
Hays	JOHN, Sytha (See Jesse Broun)		
Bell	JOHNS, F. W. & P. A.	James Alva	15 Apr 1874
		George D. Elmer	20 Apr 1876
Burnet	JOHNSON, A. R. & Josie E.	Fannie	25 Nov 1874
Caldwell	JOHNSON, Albert C. &		
	Sallie A.	Mary Emma	5 Mar 1874
Bexar	JOHNSON, George &		
	Maria (Johnson)	Mary Luella	17 Jul 1875

COUNTY	PARENTS	CHILD	DATE
Colorado	JOHNSON, H. M. & Hattie B.	Mittie Sue	2 May 1874
Austin	JOHNSON, Henry & Auguste	Pauline	7 Sep 1873
Brazos	JOHNSON, Henry & Lucy	Andrew	17 Sep 1873
Bandera	JOHNSON, Harry & M. E.	Mary Alma	11 Aug 1874
Comanche	JOHNSON, J. W. & Susan E.	Missouri	3 Jul 1874
Caldwell	JOHNSON, James L. & A. E.	Susan Pearl	6 Jun 1874
Colorado	JOHNSON, Jessie H. & Laura G.	Emieola	9 Oct 1874
Bexar	JOHNSON, Maria (See George Johnson)		
Bexar	JOHNSON, Mary (See J. B. Sweeney)		
Travis	JOHNSON, Sam H. & Desdemona	Samuel William	18 Jan 1874
		Guy Augustine	11 Nov 1874
Travis	JOHNSON, Sam M. & Helen	Edith	10 Sep 1873
Bexar	JOHNSON, Susie G. (See Green Moorezel)		
Brazos	JOHNSON, Thedore B. & M. J.	Joseph E.	20 Oct 1873
Caldwell	JOHNSON, Thos. G. & Laura L.	Albert Casson or Carson	30 Jan 1875
Bell	JOHNSON, W. A. & M.	Joseph Sydney	8 Jul 1874
Lee	JOHNSON, W. L. & Mary A.	Nettie	25 Sep 1874
Bexar	JOHNSON, Wyatt & Lucinda J. (Hardy)	Agnes	14 Apr 1874
		Wyatt	16 Jan 1876
Travis	JOLLY, Cornelius & Bethnia	Abner Elijah	??
Caldwell	JOLLY, J. M. & D. A.	Ida May	15 Nov 1874
Brazos	JOLLY, Robt. E. & Elizabeth	Daniel Davis	21 Feb 1875
Bandera	JONES, A. G. & G.	Chloe	20 Nov 1874
Lavaca	JONES, C. W. & Hortense B. (Twins)	Sallie & Eugene	11 Mar 1874
Lavaca	JONES, D. C. & Amanda	Emma May	14 Feb 1875
Hays	JONES, David K. & Eliza A.	Robert Edna	9 May 1874
Hays	JONES, E. F. &.S. J.	Charley Robt. Lee	12 Jul 1874
Lavaca	JONES, Ed. W. & Hortense	Arthur Henry	4 Oct 1875
Austin	JONES, Frank & Catherine	Franklin	2 Jun 1873
Fayette	JONES, George W. & Francis (sic) E.	Henry Madden	26 May 1874
Fayette	JONES, J. C. & J. E.	Chas. Yancy	9 Jul 1873
		Mary L.	5 Apr 1875
Bell	JONES, J. C. & S. F.	Charles Barton	26 Jan 1875
Lee	JONES, J. N. & M. E.	Emma Hattie	3 Dec 1874
Bexar	JONES, James & Eliza (Dwyer)	James Henry	21 Aug 1874
Kendall	JONES, Jas. R. & Mollie E.	Laura Ann	23 May 1873
Brazos	JONES, John H. & N. E.	Horace Otto	17 Nov 1874
San Saba	JONES, John L. & Martha R.	Sarah Elizabeth	30 Dec 1873
		Katy	24 Mar 1875
Bastrop	JONES, John P. & Talitha Jane (Reding)	Margaret Belle	29 Jan 1874
		Tignal	3 Dec 1875
Lavaca	JONES, M. M. & Martha	Joel A.	28 Mar 1874
Nacogd.	JONES, Mack & Rachael	Oscar	1 Nov 1874
Lee	JONES, Nancy (See Peter R. Purcell)		
Bastrop	JONES, R. P. & M. L.	Newell Lee	8 Feb 1877
Bastrop	JONES, Robt. P. & M. E.	Henry C.	29 May 1875
Lavaca	JONES, Rufus & Bell	Leon Burt	15 Feb 1875
Bandera	JONES, Sam H. & M. J.	John A., Jr.	29 Dec 1872
San Saba	JONES, Samuel W. & Melissa	Hattie Belle	16 Jan 1874
		Amory Starr	29 Oct 1875
Fayette	JONES, W. B. & Mary	Guy Fountane	1 Apr 1874
Bell	JONES, W. S. & I. J.	Mary Alma	16 May 1874
Bastrop	JONES, Wm. & Annie E.	John Wm.	20 Jan 1874
Gillespie	JORDON, William & Lina	Edward Wm.	17 Sep 1873
Bexar	JOSEPH, Thomas & Emma (Standon)	Tommy	1 Jul 1874
Victoria	JOSHUA, Wm. & Jane	Abner	6 Dec 1875
Fayette	JOST, Louis & Pauline	Carl Wilhelm Ludwig	23 Apr 1873
Bastrop	JOURNAGAN, J. E. & M. E.	M. E.	1 Aug 1874

COUNTY	PARENTS	CHILD	DATE
Bandera	JUNTZKO (?) L. & H.	Anna	24 May 1873
Bandera	JURECZKI, Leonard & Rosilla	John	17 Dec 1874
Gillespie	KALLENBERG, William & Emma	Carl	2 Dec 1873
Gillespie	KALLENBERG, Wm. & Anna Cath.	Wilhelm Ernst	16 Sep 1875
Bexar	KALTEYER, Geo. H. &		
	Jane (Gloetzel)	Minnie	18 Feb 1874
		Fredrick	20 Jul 1875
		Stella	14 Oct 1878
Bexar	KAMPMANN, Ida (See John A. Herff)		
Fayette	KANIOKOVSKY, J. B. & M.	Julius Ottakar	9 Jan 1874
Comal	KAPP, Julie (See Rudolph Wipprecht)		
Comal	KAPPMEIER, Dorette (See Jacob Doppenschmidt)		
Comal	KAPPMEYER, Mathilde (See Wilhelm Karbach)		
Comal	KARBACH, Wilhelm &		
	Mathilde (Kappmeyer)	Auguste	22 Nov 1874
Bell	KARNES, W. K. & S. E.	Minnie Jane	6 Jan 1874
Lavaca	KARNICK, John & Tkler	Francisco	25 Feb 1875
Lee	KASPER, John & Hannah	Johanna Paulina	26 Dec 1873
DeWitt	KAUFFMANN, Emil & Amelie	Amelie C.	17 Oct 1873
	(1875 Entry Spelled Amilia)	Jane	9 May 1875
Bexar	KAUFMAN, Leonora (See Robert Matzdorf)		
Victoria	KAY, D. W. &		
	Mary T. (Carsner)	Wiley Christopher	26 Jun 1874
Victoria	KAY, Mary L. (See V. J. Rose)		
Travis	KEANESTER, Wm. V. & Mary H.	William Hill	17 Mar 1874
Bandera	KEESE, Thomas H. & A. T.	William R.	5 Sep 1873
		Warren Lockhart	13 Jan 1875
Bell	KEGLEY, Sem & S. A.	Jonar Florence	16 Mar 1874
Bexar	KEHN, Margareta (See Laurence Reymann)		
Victoria	KEIBBE, Isaac P. &		
	Sallie F. (Carpenter)	Irwin	25 Oct 1873
Brazos	KEITH, (?) Clara Elizabeth (See John Henry Wheeler)		
Hays	KELLAM, John P. & Sinia B.	Bascum H.	12 Jan 1874
	(1876 Entry reads (Kellam, Jno. P. & S. B.)		
		Nettie M.	23 Jan 1876
Medina	KELLER, Heinrich & Manja	Franz Martin	27 Dec 1875
Travis	KELLER, J. George & Ida	J. G. William	18 Nov 1873
Bexar	KELLER, Sally (See Joseph Ball)		
Austin	KELLNER, August & Ottilie	Alma	11 Dec 1874
Austin	KELLNER, Gottfried & Amalie	Gustav Max	25 Jan 1874
Bexar	KELLNER, Ida (See Wm. O. Kellner)		
Bexar	KELLNER, Wm. O. &		
	Ida (Kellner)	Alma	30 Sep 1873
Caldwell	KELLY, R. R. & Texana	Lybert Ann Eliza	3 Dec 1873
	(1875 Entry reads R. P.)	Wm. J.	18 Apr 1875
Caldwell	KELLY, T. E. & L. A.	Robert LaFayette	6 Nov 1874
Bell	KEMP, Z. & L. A.	Simeon R.	29 Mar 1874
Bexar	KEMPER, Fanny K. (See Wm. H. Young)		
Lee	KENNERLY, Joshua Harper &		
	Hannah	Thomas M.	24 Jan 1874
Caldwell	KENNEY, James & M. A.	Cora Bell	??
Bexar	KEOLVASSA, Josephine (See Wenzel Seffel)		
Comal	KEPLER, A. L. &		
	Hermine (Floege)	Alexander Louis	26 Mar 1867
Fayette	KERR, A. B. & Elizabeth	Mary Elizabeth	4 Oct 1874
Fayette	KERR, A. B. F. & Susan	Albert B. F.	22 Dec 1875
Travis	KESSEE, William & Jennie	Willie	13 Apr 1873
Gillespie	KESSLER, Carl & Emilie	Wilhelm	6 Feb 1874
DeWitt	KEY, G. W. & M. A.	A. E.	7 Aug 1873
Fayette	KEYLICH, F. & Anna	Augusta Cecelia	17 Aug 1873
Brazos	KIDD, Geo. & Kate B.	Mary Canan	5 Feb 1876
Medina	KIEFFER, Blaise & Louise	Felix	12 Feb 1874
Bastrop	KILLOUGH, E. T. & Elizabeth	Claudius Clay	15 Aug 1873
Nacogd.	KIMBROUGH, F. G. & M. E.	Ada M.	24 Feb 1875
Nacogd.	KMIBROUGH, J. B. & C.	J. D.	16 Jun 1873
Brazos	KINCANNON, W. C. & Eugenia	Susan E.	2 Dec 1874

COUNTY	PARENTS	CHILD	DATE
Burnet	KINCHELO, Louis C. &		
	M. Ruth	Eva Percilla	??
		Evaline	22 Dec 1874
Bexar	KINEHAN, John &		
	Annie (Maxfelt)	Emily	6 Oct 1873
Colorado	KING, Claiborne & Jane	Mollie Austell	5 Mar 1875
Victoria	KING, F. B. & L. E.	Ray	2 Nov 1874
Medina	KING, Isaac & Nellie	Emma	29 Dec 1873
		Lora M.	14 Dec 1875
Bell	KING, J. R. & Sarah	Mary E.	8 Sep 1873
Nacogd.	KING, R. P. & Amanda J.	W. D. H.	10 Aug 1875
Lee	KING, William & Amanda	Charly	14 Feb 1874
Nacogd.	KING, William A. & Mary Jane	Lara Francis	5 Jan 1874
		William A.	8 Jan 1876
Travis	KIRKPATRICK, Thomas &		
	Mary Susan (Hammett)	Arthur Benton	6 Apr 1877
		Edward Oliver	18 Oct 1879
Comal	KIRMSE, Hermann &		
	Sophie (Harloz)	Robert Wilhelm	22 Mar 1875
Bell	KISER, J. A. & N. J.	Ethelinda	17 Aug 1873
Bell	KISER, J. H. & M. E.	James Andrew	15 Oct 1874
Comanche	KITTLE, J. F. & M. J.	Benjamin Parrsons	6 Nov 1874
Gillespie	KLARNER, C. Philipp &		
	Caroline	Lina	3 Nov 1873
Austin	KLATT, Adolf & Christine	Robert	30 Jun 1874
Bexar	KLEABE, Adelade (See Wm. C. Baker)		
DeWitt	KLEBERG, Rand & M.	Caeser	20 Sep 1873
DeWitt	KLEBERG, Otto & Mary O.	Rud. Ferd.	22 Feb 1874
Bexar	KLEID, Peter &		
	Augusta (Neuman)	Eda	11 Mar 1873
		Annie	16 Aug 1874
Victoria	KLEIN, Samuel &		
	Ernestine W. F. (Ditmar)	Max George	2 May 1873
Bexar	KLEINE, Mary (See George Witte)		
Bexar	KLENNER, Clara (See Henry F. D. Wedemeyer)		
Fayette	KLOESEL, Franz & ??	Adolph	23 May 1873
Austin	KLOSS, Robert August &		
	Johanna	Ernst	8 Jun 1873
		Sophia	21 Nov 1874
Austin	KLUMP, August & Anna	Anna Henriette	24 Aug 1874
Austin	KNAFF, Charles & Helen	Charles	14 Oct 1874
Fayette	KNEIP, Ferdinand C. &		
	Emilie Sophia	Wilhelm Adolph	2 Mar 1874
Comal	KNIBBE, Anna (See Johann Christian Busch)		
Kendall	KNIBBLE, August &		
	Mary Elizabeth	Fridonia	23 May 1871
		Mary Elizabeth	11 Feb 1873
		Emma Jane	18 Mar 1875
Kendall	KNOEPFLI, Gottfried &		
	Helene (Groenke)	Gottfried	27 Jul 1876
		Hugo	4 Jan 1878
Austin	KNOLLE, Louis & Caroline	D. M. Helda	7 Dec 1873
Austin	KNOLLE, W. & Dora	Eda Wilhelmine	5 Jul 1875
Gillespie	KNOPP, 2nd. Jon. Jus &		
	Anna Margarethe	Louise Margarethe	4 Feb 1874
Lavaca	KNOX, J. W. & Martha A.	Mary Ann	12 Jun 1873
Lee	KNOX, W. A. & S. E.	Louis	24 Dec 1874
Caldwell	KOANSON, Joseph & A. E.	Fred R. William	17 Oct 1875
Comal	KOCH, Auguste (See Johann Heinrich Fischer)		
Bexar	KOCH, Friedrich &		
	Mena (Voges)	Emma	28 Aug 1874
	(1876 Entry reads W. C. Mina (Voges)		
		Bertha	3 Nov 1876
Comal	KOCH, Sophie (See Friedrich Voges)		
Austin	KOCH, Wilhelm & Mita	Anna Marie	27 Oct 1875
Lavaca	KOEHLER, Joseph & Mina	Mary	10 Jun 1875

COUNTY	PARENTS	CHILD	DATE
Gillespie	KOENIG, August & Sophie	Ludwig Adolph	21 Jun 1873
		Emil Carl	27 Mar 1875
DeWitt	KOENIG, Ed. & Agatha	Albert	Nov 1873
		Emma	17 Mar 1875
Bexar	KOENIGHEIM, M. & Elise	Abram	1876
Comal	KOHLENBERG, Johanna (See Heinrich Ernst)		
Lavaca	KOHLER, Fritz & Mary	Joseph F.	11 Sep 1875
Gillespie	KOHLMEYER, William & Susana	Anna	3 May 1874
		Wilhelm	22 Aug 1875
Colorado	KOHLOEFFEL, A. F. & Helena	Theodor	16 Jan 1874
		Friederich H. C.	9 Aug 1875
Colorado	KOHLLOFFEL, Wm. & Bertha	Adolph	9 Apr 1876
Bexar	KOMORUFF, Augusta (See Harmon Glaser)		
Lavaca	KOPECKGL, M. & Susan	Josephine	20 Jan 1875
Austin	KOPISCH, Arthur & Emilie	Auguste	20 Mar 1873
		Clara	19 Jan 1875
Comal	KOPPLIN, Alberta &		
	Maria (Hitzfelder)	Emma	13 Jan 1874
Gillespie	KORDZIK, Henry & Auguste	C. Otto	14 Dec 1874
Gillespie	KORKZIK, Julius & Hedwig	Ottilie Danielle	1 Mar 1875
Austin	KORFF, Charles & Helene	Agnes Amelia	25 Jul 1875
DeWitt	KORTH, Harman & Louisa	Robert	7 Oct 1874
DeWitt	KORTH, Julius & Bertha	Linna	8 Apr 1874
Gillespie	KOTT, Julius & Hedwig	Emilie	21 Feb 1874
Bexar	KOTULA, Ed & Mina (Sang)	Emila	26 Apr 1874
Bexar	KOTULA, F. C. & Francis (Pyka)	Frank Edwd.	4 Dec 1874
Austin	KOZIAN, Joseph & Mary	Antonie	1 1875
Bexar	KOZUB, Juliana (See Joseph A. Ripka)		
Bexar	KRAKAUER, Adolph & Ada (Zork)	Max	15 Aug 1874
Bexar	KRAKAUER, Max & Minna	Albert	16 Sep 1868
		Bertha	21 Jan 1871
		Matilde	14 Jan 1873
		Adolph	20 Jun 1875
		Julius	20 Sep 1878
Bexar	KRAMER, Amelia (See Fred Mesch)		
Austin	KRANCHER, J. H. & Johanne F.	Louise	24 Apr 1874
Bexar	KRAUS, Margareta (See Peter Eiserloh)		
Bexar	KRAUSE, A. T. & J. (Presler)	Anna Louise	1 Feb 1874
Austin	KRAUTER, John G. & Ottilie W.	Bertha Mary Susan	19 Aug 1875
Bexar	KRAWIETZ, August &		
	Caroline (St. Martin)	Clara Caroline	7 Jun 1873
		Mary Caroline	5 Nov 1874
		August Benhard	28 Jul 1876
Gillespie	KREPPEN, Ferdinand & Anna	Hugo	25 Sep 1874
Colorado	KRIECH, R. & Minna	Mary E. M.	15 Nov 1874
Nacogd.	KRINPER, John S. & E. H.	Thomas J.	26 Aug 1873
Bexar	KROEGER, C. F. & Elize (Dinze)	W. C.	25 May 1874
Victoria	KROSH, Emma (See Julius Hannig)		
Austin	KRUEGER, Henry & Henrietta	Paul	14 Jul 1874
Gillespie	KRUEGER, Louis & Johanne	Otto	22 Sep 1874
Gillespie	KRUEGER, Max & Emilie	Willie	2 May 1874
Austin	KRUEGER, William & Elise	Sophie	29 Apr 1873
		William Frederick	
		Karl	5 Jun 1875
Comal	KUBEL, Friedrich &		
	Rosa (Schneidner)	Anna	12 Jun 1876
Comal	KUEHN, Franziska (See Dr. William Remer)		
Bexar	KUEHNE, August &		
	Mary (Niggle)	Max Adolph	12 Aug 1874
Gillespie	KUEHNE, Chas. & Henriette	Heda	30 Sep 1874
Gillespie	KUENEMANN, Heinrich F. &		
	Doth. Elisa.	John Henry	3 Nov 1873
Kendall	KUHFUSS, William & Therese	Ottilie	15 Nov 1862
		Lina	27 Oct 1866
		Eduard	3 Jan 1870
		Emma	19 Apr 1874

41

COUNTY	PARENTS	CHILD	DATE
Bexar	KUHLMANN, Henry &		
	Lina (Heidelberg)	Ernst	4 Oct 1873
		Rudolph	5 Dec 1875
		Adolph	15 Jan 1878
Fayette	KUHLS, Friederich W. Geo. &	Edmund Fritz D.	17 Oct 1874
	J. C. D. Alwine	Augusta Alvenia P	21 Oct 1875
Comal	KUHN, Bernhard &		
	Sophie (Spangenberg)	Bernhard	14 Oct 1873
Victoria	KUHNE, Henry &		
	Eugenia (Willemien)	Leonora Minnie	4 Feb 1874
Bexar	KUMMEL, Wilhelmina (See Carl Christian Bardenwerper)		
Bexar	KUNKLE, S. & M. (Fest)	Louise	19 Aug 1873
Austin	KUNZA, Robert & Matilda	Franklin Julius	21 Apr 1874
Bexar	KUNZMANN, Chas. & Rosa (Heck)	Charles	16 Jun 1873
		Teressa	4 Sep 1874
Bexar	KURKA, Ed. & Maria (Wrobel)	Augusta	23 Jul 1868
		Charles	7 Feb 1870
		Ed.	2 Jan 1872
		Anton	9 Dec 1873
		Julie	26 Feb 1875
		Bertha	17 Apr 1877
		Maria	9 Jan 1879
Kendall	KUTZER, Reinhold & Pauline	Ida	28 Nov 1864
		Emma	5 Mar 1866
		Anna	15 Mar 1868
		Clara	31 May 1870
		Albert	7 Oct 1871
		Otto	20 Jan 1874
Lee	KUYKENDAL, I. H. & Kate	Felix R.	6 Mar 1874
Lee	KUYKENDAL, Joseph A. &		
	Sallie A.	W. H.	6 Jun 1860
		Iva I.	21 Apr 1873
Victoria	KUYKENDALL, Henry &		
	Betty (Gougler)	Hermena	3 Jul 1874
Bell	KUYDENDALL, M. J. & Mary L.	Wm. O. (?)	5 Sep 1873
Hays	KUYKENDALL, Wm. M. & Jennie	Minnie D.	10 Aug. 1873
Austin	KVETON, Mathias & Angelina	Winney	14 Jul 1874
Hays	KYLE, Felix & Martha	Martha	7 Oct 1873
Hays	KYLE, Robt. & Anna	_aute Turner	25 Aug 1873
Hays	KYLE, Samuel & Vina	Samuel Jr.	20 Jul 1874
Hays	KYLE, Thomas & Lou	Rose	28 Nov 1874
Comal	KYPFER, J. Albert &		
	Mina (Puls)	Ida	Aug 1872
		Hermann Albert	8 Feb 1875
Lavaca	LAAS, C. & Emma	Emma	6 Feb 1874
Austin	LAAS, Charles & Christiene	Meta	15 Mar 1874
Travis	LABENSKE, Daniel W. &		
	Mary Ann	Robert Lee	25 Feb 1875
Hays	LABENSKI, Chas. C. &		
	Fannie J.	Charles Milton Lee	21Apr 1876
Bexar	LABROCHE, Emile &		
	Eleanor (Goloff)	Mary	14 Aug 1876
Colorado	LACKEY, George &		
	Manerva Jane	Lillie Gray	5 1873
Victoria	LACKNER, Conrad &		
	Wilhelmina (Buchrigo)	Paul	17 May 1871
		Fritz	8 Jul 1873
		Sophie	2 Feb 1875
Medina	LACY, Earl & Jenny M.	Sue Jenny	21 Feb 1875
Burnet	LACY, G. W. & A. J.	Francis Hickman	27 Jul 1874
Burnet	LACY, M. H. & Martha	Susan Virginia	22 Jul 1874
Burnet	LACY, Mathew P. & Celest W.	John Edwards	14 Jul 1875
Bell	LAGRONE, G. W. & A. L.	George Allen	27 Dec 1874
Austin	LAHMANN, Ferdinand & Sophie	Emma	3 Nov 1874
Bexar	LAMM, Joseph &		
	Louise (Heinan)	Henry Joseph	16 Jan 1870

COUNTY	PARENTS	CHILD	DATE
Bexar	LAMM, Joseph--Cont.	Mary Fraker	22 Oct 1874
		Alfred Charles	14 Mar 1879
Lavaca	LAMOTHE, F. & S. J.	Sarah	24 Jan 1874
Bexar	LANDMAN, Jacob &		
	Carie (Wildenstein)	Alphas	12 Jun 1875
San Saba	LANDRUM, R. A. & E. D.	Loula May	6 Sep 1874
Gillespie	LANDRUM, Larkin & Mary Jane	Georgeann	27 Feb 1875
Burnet	LANDRUM, R. W. & Nola	Lula Elizabeth	1 Feb 1875
Caldwell	LANE, Bayless & P. C.	Samuel H.	8 Jul 1874
Caldwell	LANE, C. M. & Ann	Edward M.	16 Sep 1874
Caldwell	LANE, J. L. & M. A.	Annie Laurie	1 Sep 1874
Bastrop	LANE, N. N. & Caroline E.	Mary Elizabeth	8 Sep 1874
Caldwell	LANEY, J. W. & R. L.	Clarence Elgin	28 Sep 1875
Gillespie	LANG, August & Helene	Alexander Edmund	5 Jan 1875
DeWitt	LANG, Chas. & Alwine	Otto Ludwig	30 Sep 1875
		Richard Gustav	3 Feb 1878
Gillespie	LANGE, August & Magdalena	Certronio Adelheide	19 Sep 1873
Bexar	LANGE, Fredrich Wilhelm &		
	Maria Elizabeth	Wilhelm August	
		Ernst	13 Feb 1863
		Henriette W.E.	
		Hedwig	23 Jan 1865
		Daniel Fredrick	
		August	18 Jul 1870
		Herman Wilhelm	25 Aug 1873
		Louise Auguste	
		Maria	6 Feb 1876
Gillespie	LANGE, Helmuth & Mary	Louisa Johanne	30 Dec 1874
Gillespie	LANGE, Henry & Elisabeth	Frida	19 Jan 1874
Gillespie	LANGERHAUS, Heinrich &		
	Charlotte	Christine	5 Oct 1875
Bandera	LANGFORD, B. F. & A. J.	Ella	2 Jul 1873
		Nora Lee	31 Jul 1875
Bandera	LANGFORD, J. B. & E. J.	William Lee	No date
Bexar	LANGWELL, Arthur &		
	Mary Langwell	Edmund	12 May 1872
		Gustav	1 Feb 1875
Bexar	LANGWELL, Augusta (See F. Nagle)		
Bexar	LANGWELL, Leopold &		
	Mary (Stromeyer)	Henry August	30 Sep 1875
Lee	LANMAN, W. P. & Callie	Charles Marion	6 Oct 1874
Caldwell	LARO, A. & S. A.	Abram H.	8 Feb 1875
Gillespie	LARSON, James & Susanna	Emma Elisa	28 Oct 1874
Bexar	LASSNER, Edward &		
	Adolphine Lassner	August	29 Aug 1872
		Clothilde	22 Oct 1873
Austin	LAUGHAMMER, Charles &		
	Mathilda	Clara	17 May 1868
		Ellen	28 Oct 1874
Austin	LAUGHAMMER, Henry & Minna	Ulrich	10 Jun 1873
		Minna	10 Oct 1874
Lavaca	LAUGHTER, J. S. & Elizabeth	Milby Hunt	19 Apr 1874
Lavaca	LAUGHTER, T. L. & C. E. D.	M. Lee	11 Feb 1875
Colorado	LAUTERBACH, Richard &		
	Louise	Friedrich	11 Aug 1874
Bexar	LAVAL, Etienne & Josephine	Louise Antoinette	5 Mar 1873
Lee	LAW, H. D. & Harriet S.	Senorameiss	16 Jan 1874
Bastrop	LAWHON, D. B. & Lucy H.	Lucy A.	24 Sep 1873
Bastrop	LAWHON, J. C. & J. E.	John Irvin	9 Sep 1873
Bastrop	LAWHON, W. C. & Jane	A. J.	12 Jun 1874
Lee	LAWRENCE, Charles & Virginia	Charles Henry	2 Aug 1874
Lee	LAWRENCE, L. E. &		
	Leeanna P.	Henry Alexander	5 Apr 1875
Lee	LAWRENCE, Richard T. &		
	Mary Jane	James A.	Mar 1874
Lavaca	LAWRENCE, W. A. & Sarah E.	Delbert C.	5 Mar 1875

43

COUNTY	PARENTS	CHILD	DATE
Lee	LAWRENCE, W. R. & M. E.	Ada Francis	18 Aug 1875
Hays	LAWRENCE, Wash. & H.A.E.	George W.	25 Oct 1873
Hays	LAWSON, J. R. & Sue M.	Ina S.	2 Nov 1873
		Leslie Joe	9 Feb 1876
Bexar	LAYER, Constantin & Magdalena	Charles	25 Aug 1873
Nacogd.	LAYTON, G. B. & Nancy A.	Mary E.	24 Nov 1873
Nacogd.	LAYTON, H. A. & Elizabeth	Ann E.	7 Aug 1874
Lavaca	LAYTON, J. M. & Mollie	Bernard	26 May 1874
Hays	LEACH, T. V. & Georgia Ann	Mary Ann	15 Jun 1875
Hays	LEATH, Wm. A. & Margaret E.	May Upha	11 May 1873
		Ed Jenkins	24 Nov 1874
Bell	LEATHERMAN, J. G. & Annette	Mary Ann	10 Jul 1874
Bastrop	LEATHERWOOD, P. A. & ??	?? (M)	23 Aug 1873
Burnet	LECLARE, Paul & Malisa E.	Louis Alexander	6 Apr 1875
Lavaca	LEDBETTER, A. A. & J. G.	F. W.	29 Oct 1873
Fayette	LEDBETTER, James P. & E. Ladbetter (sic)	John Dancy	23 Dec 1873
Fayette	LEDBETTER, W. H. & T. Ledbetter	Gilbert Flournoy	22 Jun 1875
Comanche	LEE, D. N. & Mattie M.	Sula Senora	10 Jun 1874
Nacogd.	LEE, David & Cora E.	John	3 Jan 1876
Hays	LEE, David & Catherine G.	Almus Ruperty	23 May 1873
Travis	LEE, George W. & Sarah	Malcom	7 Jun 1874
Austin	LEE, James K. & Susan C.	Mary Emma	28 Oct 1873
Hays	LEE, Jerry W. & Mary A.	Wm. Fletcher	13 Jul 1873
Austin	LEE, Sterling & Charlotte	Lucy	10 Mar 1875
Comanche	LEE, W. T. & V. O.	Frank Zeuxis	2 Dec 1875
Colorado	LEESEMANN, C. J. G. & Elizabeth J.	Elizabeth Annie	16 Sep 1875
Nacogd.	LEGG, S. J. A. (See N. L. Raney)		
Lavaca	LEGGETT, J. W. & Josephine T.	Fanette Gabrila	20 Jan 1875
Lavaca	LEGGETT, T. J. & Margt	Charles	22 Dec 1874
Comal	LEHDE, John P. & Lina (Bernhardt)	Sphigenia Elmyra	10 Jan 1869
		Jule Philip	6 Aug 1871
		Hedwig Natalia	16 Nov 1873
Bastrop	LEHMAN, John T. & M. A.	Joseph	16 Mar 1874
Austin	LEHMANN, Ferdinand & ??	William	25 Sep 1876
Gillespie	LEHNE, Christian & Sophie	Anna	23 Jul 1874
Bastrop	LENTZ, H. C. & Nancy	Sarah Elizabeth	13 Jun 1874
Victoria	LEVY, Simon & Rose (Gugerheim)	Julius	1 Dec 1870
		Moses	31 Mar 1872
		Bella	5 Mar 1874
Bexar	LIEBE, Aminda (See Maximilian T. Jesse)		
Bexar	LIECK, Antonia (See Louis Briam)		
Bexar	LIECK, Edmond & Cathrena (Gembler)	Edward Fritz	11 Feb 1875
		Rudolph Adolph	11 Aug 1877
		Anna Sophia	15 Sep 1879
DeWitt	LEICK, Frederick E. & Clementine	Otto Henry	19 Apr 1875
Bexar	LIECK, Gertrude (See Christian Schaezler)		
Bexar	LIECK, Julius & Anna (Brotze)	Gustave	8 Jun 1873
		Robert	2 Jan 1875
Bexar	LEIGHTON, Charlotte Baxtor (See Alexander Sartor, Jr.)		
Bexar	LEIGHTON, Thomas B. & Francisca E. (Schmitt)	Thomas George	7 Nov 1873
		Edward A.	1 Feb 1875
Bexar	LEIR, Fannie (See Salomon Halff)		
Comal	LEITSCH, Auguste (See Paul Schmidt)		
San Saba	LEONARD, Levi & Lorena J.	Martha Canvada	8 Aug 1874
Caldwell	LEROY, W. H. & N. J.	John Albert	29 Sep 1873
		?? (M)	24 Dec 1875
Austin	LESCHPER, Adolph & Marie	Christopher	21 May 1874

COUNTY	PARENTS	CHILD	DATE
San Saba	LESSING, W. H. & ??	Mary E. T.	27 Jan 1875
Burnet	LESTER, William & Sarah Ann	William Walter	28 Sep 1875
DeWitt	LETTERMAN, H. A. & ??	Margareъta	
		Katharina Emma	27 Jul 1874
		August Engelhardt	" " "
Caldwell	LEVYSON, H. & J.	Alice	Feb 1874
Caldwell	LEVYSON, Siegfried & Flora	Abraham	31 May 1873
Burnet	LEWIS, Alexander & Mary Jane	James M.	12 Oct 1873
Burnet	LEWIS, Henry & Thankful H.	Samuel Virgil	9 Dec 1873
Burnet	LEWIS, J. M. & M. E.	Jacob Aaron	27 Jan 1875
Austin	LEWIS, James & Mahala	John	1 Jul 1873
Burnet	LEWIS, Robert & Josephine	Rodney T.	26 Feb 1874
		Edmund R.	10 Sep 1875
Lavaca	LEWIS, W. & Mat	R. H.	25 Dec 1873
Gillespie	LEYENDECKER, Johann & Bertha	Johann Carl	26 Apr 1874
Gillespie	LEYENDECKER, Joseph & Maria	William	4 May 1875
Kendall	LIGHT, John & Caroline	Jeeroders	26 Nov 1873
Kendall	LIGHT, Rubins & Mary	George	10 Dec 1873
DeWitt	LILLIE, W. H. & Ellen	Blanche	31 Oct 1873
Nacogd.	LILLY, John J. & Paulina	Alice Nueces	18 Jun 1874
		Lucinda Henrietta	24 Nov 1875
Bastrop	LINAM, John B. & Sarah E.	Martha E.	1 Feb 1874
Caldwell	LINCH, Lewis & E. A.	Wm. L.	12 Jan 1878
Kendall	LINDEMANN, Gustav & Auguste	Louise Minna	11 Apr 1874
		Anna Elisabeth	27 Oct 1875
Lavaca	LINDENBURG, F. & Augusta M.	Anna	14 Apr 1874
Bexar	LINDHEIM, Sarah (See A. B. Frank)		
Austin	LINGNAN, Frederick & Caroline	Herman	10 Nov 1874
Bexar	LIPS, Albert & Christina (Haag)	Emma Amelia	1 Sep 1875
Colorado	LISIECKA, Pauline (See Adolph Friemann)		
Travis	LITTLE, James M. & Catherine	Henry Ettie	14 Jul 1874
Nacogd	LITTLE, John M. & Sophia	Malphimea	17 Mar 1875
Nacogd.	LITTLE, Joseph W. & Mary J.	Henry Curl	15 Feb 1875
Brazos	LITTLEPAGE, S. C. & J. D.	Ben	16 Jul 1874
Travis	LITTMAN, Leopold & Hattie	Belle	15 Feb 1876
Nacogd.	LITTON, John & Elizabeth	John H.	10 Oct 1873
Lavaca	Livergood, J. H. & S. E.	No. Lee	7 Jun 1874
Fayette	LOCKMANN, J. B. & A. Lockmann	E. J. H.	2 Oct 1874
Gillespie	LOCHTE, Fritz & Charlotte	Otto	4 Jan 1876
Hays	LOCK, Wm. W. & Lavenia A.	John H.	21 Jun 1873
Burnet	LOCKETT, M. B. & Annie	Minnie Kate	23 Feb 1874
Austin	LOCKETT, Wesley & Mahala	Lucius	4 Sep 1874
Bexar	LOCKWOOD, A. J. & Mary (Stevens)	Albert Stevens	7 Aug 1871
		John Arthur	5 Jul 1873
Burnet	LOCKWOOD, Thomas & Martha A.	Frank Leslie	12 Aug 1873
Caldwell	LOE, J. T. W. & Nellie	Lola	8 Feb 1875
Austin	LOEWENSTEIN, B. & Caroline	Robert	12 Feb 1874
San Saba	LOFTIN, Gus W. & Ella	Stephen Walter	11 Nov 1873
		Lena V.	6 Aug 1875
Bexar	LOGWOOD, William & Lucy	Lucy	10 May 1874
		Wm. H.	27 Oct 1876
Gillespie	LONDON, Fr. & Julie	Ottoman	12 Jul 1875
		Nelly Lina Julie	12 Jan 1879
Lavaca	LONG, E. A. & Emma	E. P.	17 Oct 1874
Comanche	LONG, E. T. & S. E.	W. P.	25 Jul 1874
San Saba	LONG, F. H. & Mary J.	Nathaniel	6 Aug 1874
Lavaca	LONG, Geo. & Celia	Eugene T.	20 Jul 1874
Comanche	LONG, H. M. & Lydia	Horrie Madison	5 Feb 1875
Lavaca	LONG, Henry T. & Mary J.	Sarah E.	18 Feb 1875
Lavaca	LONG, M. A. & Elizabeth	Martha Jane	Feb 1875
Caldwell	LONG, T. H. & L. E.	Henry Abner	29 Nov 1874

COUNTY	PARENTS	CHILD	DATE
Bexar	LONGWELL, Laura (See Charles Fromme)		
Bexar	LOPEZ, Antonio & Rafugia		
	(Cernal)	Louis	17 Sep 1874
DeWitt	LORD, Geo. & Katharine	Pomona Bell	14 Sep 1875
Comal	LORENTZ, Caroline (See Johann Hering)		
Comal	LORENTZ, Paulina (See Johann Hering)		
Comal	LORENTZ, Ottilie (See Carl Buss)		
Hays	LOTT, Dardas & Charity	Joseph	27 Nov 1873
Austin	LOTT, Jacob & Eda	Mattie	25 Mar 1875
Grimes	LOUD, Samuel & Marza	Benjamin	23 May 1873
	(Twins)	James & John	23 Mar 1874
Comanche	LOUDERMILK, R. C. & Julia A.	James Bonnen	24 Jan 1874
Austin	LOUWINE, Gustav & Mary	Frederica	28 Jan 1875
		Gustav	6 Jun 1876
Brazos	LOVE, J. T. & G. C.	M. L. W.	1 Feb 1875
Bell	LOVE, J. W. & S. B.	Charles	28 Oct 1873
Nacogd.	LOVE, R. D. & Martha M.	John E.	13 Dec 1873
Lee	LOVE, W. E. & Huldah	Lena Shepard	22 Nov 1874
Burnet	LOW, J. B. & Eliza A.	Samuel E.	9 Apr 1875
Grimes	LOW, Luke & Julia	Samuel	20 Mar 1874
San Saba	LOWE, J. M. & J. L.	James Walter	17 Aug 1874
Bexar	LOWORKA, Amelia (See John Sowa)		
Colorado	LOWRY, J. C. & Ellen Virginia	William Andrew	5 May 1874
		Walter Bennett	12 Apr 1876
Gillespie	LUCKENBACH, Wm. & Anna Cath.	Anna Elise Betty	8 Aug 1874
Bastrop	LUCKET, H. P. & F. T.	Worth Moore	12 Jan 1874
Austin	LUCKO, Andrew & Rosalie	William	31 Dec 1874
Victoria	LUDER, Adele (See Geo. Herman Hauschild)		
Victoria	LUDER, Baldy & Mary		
	(Sifferman)	Laura	10 Jul 1874
Bexar	LUDWIG, Elisa (See Teodore Englehart)		
Bexar	LUDWIG, Franz Joseph &		
	Wilhelma Sophia (Sielher)	Franz Joseph	18 Dec 1857
		Wilhelma Josephina	16 Feb 1859
		Maria Johanna	13 Oct 1860
		Emma Cathna.	
		Christa.	15 Jul 1862
		Louis Albert	6 Jun 1864
		Catharina Christa.	9 Feb 1867
		Ida	1 Jan 1869
		Aminda Sophia	28 Dec 1870
		Karl	18 May 1872
		Felix Joseph	21 Nov 1873
Austin	LUEDEKE, Johan & Gertrude	Peter Emil	10 Nov 1873
		Catharine	28 Jan 1875
Austin	LUHN, Charles O. & Elise	Elise Minna	12 Oct 1874
		Beta Emilie	18 Sep 1875
Austin	LUHN, G. A. & Fredonia	F. W. Reinhardt	16 Sep 1874
Austin	LUHN, G. A. & Friedrike	Gustav Bernhard	3 Jun 1876
Austin	LUHN, Wm. E. & Emilie L. T.	Olga	17 Sep 1873
Bexar	LUTZ, Ventelin &		
	Minna (Ventland)	Maria	No date
Bell	LYELL, J. A. J. & M. S.	Mary	6 Oct 1873
		Wm.	8 May 1875
Hays	LYELL, William H. & Mary C.	Willie Corinne	2 Sep 1875
Nacogd.	LYNTACUM, Carter & Elvira	President	1 Dec 1873
Bexar	LYONS, Wm. & Anne (Quigley)	Ellen	6 Nov 1874
Medina	LYTLE, Samuel & M. Lucy	Margareth Lucy	21 Jun 1874
Grimes	McAFEE, M. D. & Hattie	John Perry	12 Jun 1875
Grimes	MCALPINE, Dr. J. A. & W. C.	Alexander D.	3 Feb 1875
Grimes	MCALPINE, Jr. W. K. & S. A.	James Franklin	2 Nov 1874
Gillespie	MCARTY, Adam & Margareth	Wilson	14 Dec 1873
Hays	MCBRIDE, S. B. & M. Belle	Amos Bender	1 Sep 1875
Colorado	MCBROOM, S. C. & M. E.	Alma Hester	8 Feb 1874
		Bettie	28 Jun 1875
Bell	MCBURNETT, Wm. & M. C.	Reuben Goode	11 Dec 1873
		Milford	4 Sep 1875

COUNTY	PARENTS	CHILD	DATE
Bexar	MCCALL, Tomas P. & Josephine (St. Martin)	Mattie Lee	22 Jun 1874
Brazos	MCCANN, J. F. & A.	Jimmy	20 Nov 1875
Hays	MCCARTY, Thomas J. & Mary E.	William Cyrus	20 Jun 1874
Bell	MCCASKILL, Albert & Annie B.	Mary Etta	22 Dec 1873
Bell	MCCASLAND, J. L. & M. F.	Samuel Benjamin	16 Mar 1874
Bell	MCCASLAND, J. P. & Annie	Samuel Coontz	2 Dec 1873
Bell	MCCAULEY, C. B. & L. E.	Cellena	29 Dec 1873
Caldwell	MCCAUSLAND, W. D. & S. E.	Nannie Harris	6 Jul 1875
Bexar	MCCLELLAN, Joe, Sr. & Bessie G.	Joe, Jr.	11 Mar 1877
Lee	MCCLELLAN, W. J. & Mary A.	Lucy	1 Jun 1874
Fayette	MCCOLLUM, A. D. & S. M.	Wilson A.	1 Dec 1873
Fayette	MCCOLLUM, John L. & Mary A.	John A.	31 Jan 1874
Brazos	MCCOMNICO(?), A. D. & L. M.	Frank W.	11 May 1873
Hays	MCCORD, James E. & Elizabeth	Su Clement	16 Jan 1869
		Mary Virginia	25 Feb 1871
		Thos. Morney	5 Jul 1872
		Julia Thompson	4 Sep 1874
Colorado	MCCORMICK, George & Myrah	George	15 Jul 1872
		Etta	6 Jan 1874
Burnet	MCCOY, A. L. & E. J.	Lilly Annie	11 Jul 1876
Comanche	MCCRARY, J. M. & B. E. S.	Mattie Sophronia	25 Dec 1873
Lee	MCCRIGHT, Marion & Sarah Ann	George Washington	10 Mar 1874
Nacogd.	MCCUISTIAN, Ben & Sally	Nancy	7 Mar 1874
		Henry	3 Apr 1876
Comal	MCCULLOUGH, D. A. & Sarah (Hosse)	Walter Sidney	12 May 1875
DeWitt	MCCULLOUGH, John & Dora	Wm. H.	31 Aug 1874
DeWitt	MCCULLOUGH, William & A. E.	Virginia	19 Nov 1873
		Dora	7 Jan 1876
Comanche	MCCURDY, C. C. & Mary L.	Nancy Jane	9 Apr 1873
		Cornelia	6 Oct 1874
Lee	MCDANIEL, R. T. & Martha	Thomas Jefferson	31 May 1875
Bastrop	MCDAVID, W. P. & M. E.	Florence	28 Apr 1874
Bexar	MCDERMOTT, Bridget J. (See James Henry Biggar)		
Brazos	MCDONALD, Chas. & Phillis	Lula	18 Oct 1875
Comanche	MCDONALD, J. A. & Mary A.	Sarah Ann	13 Apr 1873
Brazos	MCDONALD, John & Mollie	Daisie	27 Aug 1873
Caldwell	MCDONALD, Patrick J. & Sarah A.	Henry	26 Oct 1875
Comanche	MCDONALD, W. J. & J. P.(Twins)	Villula Leona	26 Oct 1874
		Almus Leo	27 Oct 1874
Bexar	MCDOWEL, Henry & Emma (Bridon)	Eleanora	28 Jun 1875
Bell	MCDOWELL, John & Caroline	Lula	20 Jan 1874
Caldwell	MCDOWELL, L. J. P. & K. L.	Horace Martin	11 Aug 1873
	(Twins)	Clarence J. P.	7 Feb 1876
		Kate L.	7 Feb 1876
Burnet	MCFARLAND, John T. & Martha	Minnie Florence	4 May 1875
Burnet	MCFARLAND, M. L. & S. K.	Wm. Alexander	28 Sep 1873
Hays	MCGEHEE, Charles S. & Sarah J.	Miles Humphries	17 Jan 1873
Hays	MCGEHEE, Chas. W. & Bettie	Jessie R.	9 Oct 1875
Hays	MCGEHEE, Wm. A. & Julia (Vernetta)	Anna Laura	9 Jul 1875
Bell	MCGINNIS, A. D. & N. A.	Vic. Bradford	28 Dec 1875
Caldwell	McGinnis, J. S. & M. A.	E. E.	7 Jan 1875
Caldwell	McGINNIS, W. & S. E.	Ella Nora	1 Jun 1873
Bell	MCGLOTHLIN, J. J. & M. C.	Robt. A. S.	7 Jan 1874
Victoria	MCGREW, Margaret A. (See C. L. Thurmond)		
Comanche	MCGUIN, J. M. & Margaret J.	Mary Elizabeth	12 Oct 1874
Bell	MCGUIRE, Robt. & Hanna A.	Louvie	15 Aug 1873
Bell	MCKAY, B. S. & D.	Sudie Roxana	12 Jun 1874
Bell	MCKAY, J. P. & J. C.	Katie Jane	28 Oct 1874
Caldwell	MCKEAN, W. A. & Ann E.	David Shilo(?)	
		Stranton	20 Sep 1874

47

COUNTY	PARENTS	CHILD	DATE
Comanche	MCKENZIE, J. E. & Nancy E.	Ellen	8 May 1875
Lee	MCKEOWN, Wiseman & Elizabeth	Cora Lawson	10 Jan 1874
Bexar	MCKIE, Robt. McPherson &		
	Katie (vanPelt)	Robt. vanPelt	1 Jul 1874
Austin	MCKINNEY, A. & Susan C.	Sarah Margaret	14 Nov 1873
		John Gardner	4 Sep 1875
Fayette	MCKINNEY, J. L. & B. M.	Richard L.	17 Nov 1873
Travis	MCKINNEY, Jas. P., Jr. &		
	Clara	Elizabeth Anna	27 Jul 1874
		Elvira Mary	18 Dec 1875
Bexar	MCKINNEY, Sarah J. (See John W. Bennett)		
Caldwell	MCKINNEY, W. N. & Mary E.	Clarence H.	8 Oct 1874
DeWitt	MCKINNEY, William J. &		
	Elizabeth A.	Mary Etta	14 Jun 1875
Fayette	MCKINNON, A. L. & Lucinda	Alice	15 Jun 1874
Caldwell	MCKINZIE, T. N. & Mary J.	Alice O.	30 Jun 1875
Nacogd.	MCKNIGHT, D. M. & O. C.	Alexander Hern	24 Oct 1874
DeWitt	MCLAIN, F. A. & S. A.	J. C.	4 Nov 1876
Travis	MCLAUGHLIN, C. E. & R. A.	Guy	11 Mar 1873
		Maud	8 Jan 1875
Bexar	MCLEARY, James &		
	Emily (Mitchell)	Mary L.	15 Dec 1870
		Emily Enid	10 Feb 1873
Austin	MCLEOD, Roderick & Christine	Birdy Alice	26 Sep 1874
Bell	MCMAHAN, J. D. & Sarah	John	8 Oct 1874
Bastrop	MCMAHAN, James & Charlotte	Ben	29 Jun 1875
Travis	MCMAHAN, Mary Elizabeth (See John Hughston Phillips)		
DeWitt	MCMANUS, W. J. & H. E.	Josephine C.	30 Jun 1873
Hays	MCMEANS, H. A. & Dora A.	Florence Ivey	27 Feb 1875
Brazos	MCMICHAEL, W. H. & Nora	Lucy Bell	13 Apr 1876
Hays	MCMILLAN, Jackson &		
	Maggie (Burleson)	Jane P.	15 Mar 1874
Bell	MCMILLAN, Robt. & S. J.	Mary Magdalane	15 Jul 1875
Brazos	MCMORDIA, A. & A. W.	Annett K.	19 Jul 1874
		Blackburn K.	19 Jul 1874
Hays	MCNEAL, George &		
	Amanda (Brady)	George Henry	2 Nov 1873
Burnet	MCNETT, A. J. & Sarah C.	Eliza Thomas	25 Sep 1875
Bastrop	MCPHERSON, O. G. & S. P.	Jane R.	23 Jan 1874
Travis	MCVEIGH, James D. &		
	Mary Francis	James Martin	23 Jul 1874
Hays	MCWILLIAMS, Albert & H.	Margetta	27 Nov 1874
Hays	MCWILLIAMS, James & March (Twins)	Margaretta	27 Nov 1874
		Albert H.	27 Nov 1874
Nacogd.	MCWRIGHT, Peter & Surena	Mariah	10 May 1874
Bandera	MAASS, William & Charlotte	Helena	11 Jul 1875
Burnet	MABRY, J. J. & Fannie B.	Ernest Demahler	27 Feb 1874
DeWitt	MACHAST, Henry & Augusta	Minna	7 Oct 1873
Lee	MACHIN, E. L. & N. A.	Sarah Adelaide	2 Jul 1875
Victoria	MACK, L. F. &		
	Ottile (Gareison)	Otto Frederick	2 Dec 1868
		Ottile Olga	15 Dec 1872
		Alma	15 Apr 1875
Bexar	MACLENIES, Joseta (See Joaquin Garrera)		
Lee	MADISON, J. S. & Rebecca	Addie Alabama	6 Feb 1875
		Hettie Texana	6 Feb 1875
Bell	MAEDGEN, G. A. & E.	James Isaiah	4 Jul 1874
Bell	MAEDGEN, M. & E.M.P..	Paul S.	25 Feb 1874
Grimes	MAGEE, Jr., F. W. & A. E.	Mary A.	24 Dec 1873
Lavaca	MAGEE, H. J. & Maggie	J. H.	17 Nov 1873
Kendall	MAGERS, Heinrich & Louise	Anna	27 Mar 1870
		Heinrich	4 Jan 1872
		Emma	9 May 1874
Burnet	MAGILL, Wm. H. V. &		
	Elizabeth A.	Robt. Franklin	8 Dec 1874
Bexar	MAGOFFIN, Annette (See Jos. E. Dwyer)		

COUNTY	PARENTS	CHILD	DATE
Austin	MAGRUDER, F. B. & Mollie	Henry Arthur	16 Feb 1875
Austin	MAHNKE, John F. & Ann	John Morris	16 Mar 1874
		Emma	15 Oct 1875
Bexar	MAIXNAR, Elizabeth (See Joseph Hauck)		
Bexar	MAIXNER, Margarette (See Thomas Marricom)		
Fayette	MAKER, Fritz & Marie	Marie	30 Jun 1874
Austin	MALESCHECK, A. & Josephine	Charles	26 Dec 1875
Lavaca	MALLICK, Ab & Kate	Stella	12 Apr 1874
Lavaca	MALLICK, Paul & Leo	Wm. Arthur	24 Aug 1873
Burnet	MALOY, Edwin J. & Francis	Netty Francis	24 Aug 1875
Bexar	MANDRY, George &		
	Marie (Biroz or Binz)	Marie Elizabeth	19 Jul 1875
		George Heribert	16 Aug 1877
Comal	MANGER, Nicolaus & Helene (Baer)	Elise	6 Jan 1874
Burnet	MANN, E. A. & C. J.	Martha Elizabeth	31 Jul 1874
Lavaca	MANNING, W. H. & Francis	David J.	12 Dec 1875
Austin	MANNING, William L. & Mary F.	Morris Edmund	13 Nov 1875
Travis	MANOR, Jo. J. & J. A.	Fannie	4 Aug 1873
Bexar	MARAWITZ, Jos. & Susan Oczko	John	20 Oct 1876
Bell	MARIOTT, J. W. & S. J.	James Wm.	8 Oct 1874
Travis	MARKLEY, Thomas J. & S. J.	Olga Josephine	29 Oct 1875
San Saba	MARLEY, S. H. & Ella	Cortenus Aldebron	13 Nov 1875
Lee	MARQUIS, R. T. & Martha S.	Thomas Jackson	30 Dec 1875
Bexar	MARRICOM, Thomas &		
	Margarette (Maixner)	George	13 Jul 1873
Kendall	MARSHALL, Anderson &		
	Prudy Ann	Luria Ann	14 Oct 1874
Bell	MARSHALL, R. P. & I. A.	Martha A.	29 Dec 1873
Bell	MARSHALL, Wm. B. & Martha Jane	James Williams	20 Sep 1873
Bexar	MARTIN, George M. &		
	Martha Julia (Merrick)	John Sims	15 Jul 1854
		Geo. Merrick	8 Sep 1855
		Julia Isabella	22 Nov 1856
		Mattie Martina	29 Jul 1859
		Stonewall Jackson	17 Sep 186
Caldwell	MARTIN, H. & Spencer J.	Maggie L.	26 Dec 1874
Comanche	MARTIN, H. R. & Martha J.	Martha J.	14 Jan 1874
Nacogd.	MARTIN, James A. & Susan E.	James F.	12 Sep 1873
Caldwell	MARTIN, M. A. & R.	Miles Burges	13 Nov 1874
Lee	MARTIN, M. C. & Mary E.	Emergy Seth	25 Jan 1874
Bexar	MARTIN, Martha (See Victor Rompel)		
Brazos	MARTIN, Patrick & ??	Patrick J.	23 Aug 1875
Grimes	MARTIN, Robert J. & Clarcinda	Ivar Guyton	26 Dec 1874
Bexar	MARTINEZ, Blasa (See Polonio Hernandez)		
Bexar	MARUCHEAU, Charles &		
	Margaerite (Castanola)	Felicite M.	5 Sep 1874
Lee	MASON, William &		
	Nancy Malinda	Lina E.	29 Jan 1874
Hays	MASSEY, A. J. & Martha A.	Louisa	24 Aug 1873
Hays	MASSEY, F. M. & Elizabeth	Margaret	28 Dec 1873
		Waul Lee	28 May 1875
Nacogd.	MAST, D. C. & Mary L.	Mattie S.	29 Jan 1874
Nacogd.	MAST, Milton & Nancy A.	Oscar F.	8 Jun 1874
Nacogd.	MATHEWS, E. N. & E.	Laura B.	3 Mar 1874
Lee	MATHIS, A. S. & Mary R.	Lydia M.	8 Oct 1873
		Lillie	28 Feb 1876
San Saba	MATSLER, J. T. & Mary Ann	Martha Elizabeth	11 Nov 1874
Hays	MATT, West & Jenny (Nance)	Charles	Mar 1875
Lavaca	MATTHEWS, E. F. & Mary B.T.	Jerome	27 May 1873
		John L.	14 Mar 1875
Caldwell	MATTHEWS, John & Janie	Lillian D.	22 Apr 1874
Austin	MATTHEWS, Mary (See Wm. L. Springfield)		
Bexar	MATTON, Josephine (See Louis Eberhardt)		
Lavaca	MATUSHAK, John & V.	Adolph	1 Jan 1874
Bexar	MATZDORF, Robert &		
	Leonora (Kaufman)	Carl	11 Apr 1875

COUNTY	PARENTS	CHILD	DATE
Lavaca	MAULDIN, Jno. W. & F. Josephine	Lawrine H.	27 Oct 1873
Bexar	MAURER, Joseph & Augusta (Zinck)	Albert	25 Dec 1865
		Joseph	26 Aug 1867
		William	20 Sep 1871
		Emeal	19 Jun 1874
Bexar	MAVERICK, Sam & Sallie (Frost	Samuel Augustus	3 Sep 1872
		John Frost	23 Mar 1874
Bexar	MAVERICK, Willie H. & Wmilie V. (Chilton)	Wm. Chilton	19 Feb 1875
DeWitt	MAXEY, David & Ann E.	Rice	1 Mar 1872
		Cora	24 Jun 1873
Bexar	MAXFELD, Sophia (See Otto Solms)		
Bexar	MAXFELT, Annie (See John Kinehan)		
Bell	MAXWELL, H. H. & Adelaide	Florence A.	29 Jun 1873
Lavaca	MAY, A. & Ella	Robt. E.	13 Nov 1873
Austin	MAY, Charles & Ottilie	Lena	15 Oct 1874
Bell	MAY, J. D. & Leoana	Robt. Lee	21 Apr 1874
Lavaca	MAY, Pat. & Mary A.	Sarah C.	1 Apr 1874
Comanche	MAYBARY, Wm. & Eliza	Henry Virgil	3 Dec 1873
Bexar	MAYER, F. & Jette (Steiner)	Max	3 Aug 1867
		Solomon	18 Jan 1869
		Fanny	2 Nov 1870
		Josephina	2 Sep 1872
		Therese	12 Nov 1874
Austin	MAYER, John & Catharine	Catharine	20 Jan 1874
Bexar	MAYER, Samuel & Caroline (Jacobs)	Max	2 Jan 1860
		Fanny	27 Aug 1865
		Freddy	4 Feb 1867
		Lily	5 Jul 1868
Bastrop	MAYNARD, C. B. & K. S.	Carrie Bell	Dec 1873
Hays	MAYS, John, Jr. & Parolee	Larkin B.	27 Jan 1874
DeWitt	MEADOWS, John H. & Elvira	George W.	27 Jan 1874
San Saba	MEANS, J. W. & M. E.	Mary Isabell	23 May 1873
Bexar	MEANS, Junius & Mary A. (Smylie)	Mary Eliza	7 Oct 1875
Bell	MEARS, Henry & Caroline	Nancy Elizabeth	21 Oct 1873
Fayette	MEBUS, R. & L.	Otto	29 Mar 1874
Gillespie	MECKEL, Bernhard & Sophie	Maria	22 Apr 1874
Kendall	MECKEL, Carl & Caroline	Emma	23 Feb 1873
Kendall	MECKEL, Daniel & Friederike	Hugo	1 Sep 1874
Kendall	MECKEL, Friedrich & Ernstine	Pauline	24 Aug 1855
		Cathrine	26 Dec 1858
		Louise	6 Sep 1861
		Carl	30 Jan 1864
		Friederike	25 Jun 1867
		August	6 Aug 1870
		Anna	27 Nov 1872
Nacogd.	MEDEAR, W. A. & Harriet	Mary Jane	14 Aug 1874
Bastrop	MEEK, J. M. & Elizabeth	James Westley	26 Jan 1874
Fayette	MEERSCHEIDT, Arthur & Lina	Otto	Dec 1873
Austin	MEINECKE, August & Henrietta	Berta Martha	25 Jun 1873
Hays	MEINERS, H.O.E. & Eugenie	Else Henriette Sophie	29 Nov 1874
		Eugene Herman George	1 Nov 1876
Victoria	MEISS, Elisabeth (See Joseph Sherrer)		
Victoria	MELCHIOR, E. & Helena (Hensoldt)	Ida Johanne	5 Sep 1873
		Rudolph Armien	18 Sep 1871
San Saba	MELTON, W. T. & M. F.	Willie Augusta	27 Apr 1874

COUNTY	PARENTS	CHILD	DATE
Fayette	MENEFEE, T. S. & Mary E.	Susan Ella	16 May 1874
Bexar	MENGER, Erich &		
	Mary E. (Phillippe)	Emilie	22 Mar 1874
		Rudolph August	15 Nov 1875
		Erich	6 Oct 1877
Nacogd.	MENIFEE, Walton & Mary	Arlie	30 Aug 1873
DeWitt	MENN, Fred & Johanna	Louise	18 Dec 1874
DeWitt	MENN, Henry & Emlia	Ida C.	11 Jul 1874
Caldwell	MERCER, Alex & M.A.M.	Ida C.	24 Oct 1875
Bexar	MERRICK, Martha Julia (See George M. Martin)		
Bexar	MERRITT, C. H. & Kate		
	(Campbell)	Clare Irene	29 Sep 1873
Comanche	MERRITT, D. G. & A. V.	Elisha	30 Mar 1874
Hays	MERRIWETHER (See Bradford, Samuel & Popy)		
Lavaca	MERTZ, D. & Anna	Edward W.	17 Apr 1874
Gillespie	MERZ, John & Gottliebe	Clara	4 Jan 1874
Bexar	MESCH, Fred &		
	Amelia (Kramer)	Theodore	6 Dec 1874
Comal	MEUSEBACH, John D. & Agnes	Max Reed	2 Mar 1857
Bexar	MEYER, Bertha (See Theo. Schleuning)		
Comal	MEYER, Christian &		
	Meta (Ikels)	Willie	23 Jul 1871
		Amanda	4 Oct 1873
Bexar	MEYER, F. Ignace &		
	M. Anna (Strandt)	Heribert	8 Mar 1861
		Charles Louis	21 Sep 1862
		Eliza Teresa	5 Mar 1864
		Marie	31 Mar 1866
		Edward	25 May 1868
		Perpetua	1 Sep 1869
		Catharine	14 Mar 1871
		Joseph	30 Dec 1872
		Anna	2 Jun 1874
		Emilie	8 Jan 1876
		Carolina	6 Feb 1878
		Cecilia	3 Dec 1879
Gillespie	MEYER, Friedrich & Anna	Emma	8 Nov 1873
Kendall	MEYER, Friedrich & Ernstine	Agnes	6 Aug 1861
		Anna	14 Nov 1869
		Carl	6 Apr 1873
		Walter	6 Sep 1874
Austin	MEYER, Henry & Adele	Emilia	28 Oct 1873
		Ernst	25 Dec 1874
Travis	MEYER, Phillipe Louis &		
	Louisa	Frieda Emilie	29 Sep 1874
Bexar	MEYER, Robert &		
	Catharine (Conrad)	Louis	24 Jan 1874
		Joseph	2 Jan 1876
Austin	MEYER, Theodore & Ida	Ernstine	28 Apr 1876
Lavaca	MEYER, Wm. & Freiderika	Charles	4 Jun 1874
Austin	MICHAELIS, William & Minna	Charles Ludwich	
		Herman	23 Oct 1874
Austin	MICHALLIS, Louis &		
	Wilhelmine	Emma	27 Jan 1875
Bexar	MICHEL, Alexander &		
	Helen (Oppenheimer)	Max O.	21 Jun 1865
		O. Bertha	20 Aug 1867
		O. Barney	24 Oct 1872
		O. Henry	13 Oct 1873
Bell	MIDDLETON, A. F. & S. J.	John R.	22 Jun 1874
Austin	MIDDLETON, Edward & Cynthia	Eliza	19 Jan 1875
Brazos	MIKE, D. & Mary	Lovie	23 Dec 1872
		Arthur Lee	1 Apr 1875
Bexar	MILBY, Annie (See John James)		
Bexar	MILES, ?? & Lina	Mary	14 Sep 1874
Bell	MILES, Chas. & L. J.	Sarah C.	15 Aug 1874

COUNTY	PARENTS	CHILD	DATE
Bexar	MILES, Mary Ester (See John C. Crawford, Jr.)		
San Saba	MILICAN, W. W. & M. F.	Moses Eugenia	20 Jan 1875
Austin	MILLARD, T.W.J. & Martha A.	Martha Ellen	26 Oct 1874
Grimes	MILLER, Charles & ??	Rudolph	17 Apr 1873
		Emma	7 Mar 1875
Travis	MILLER, Charles & Louisa	Pina(?) Evangeline	28 Aug 1875
Victoria	MILLER, Frederick & Aurelia (Zahn)	Martha	6 Dec 1873
Bexar	MILLER, George & Lucy (Smallwood)	Ellen	10 Nov 1874
		Ellen (again)	1 May 1877
Bell	MILLER, Geo. J. & Mary L.	Geo. E. B.	5 Oct 1873
Lavaca	MILLER, Henry & Augusta	Henry	14 Dec 1874
San Saba	MILLER, Hugh & Sarah A.	Elijah Hollen	18 Sep 1874
Colorado	MILLER, Hugo & Emma	Albert	31 Oct 1874
Caldwell	MILLER, I. J. & M. J.	Arthur	5 Jun 1875
Bell	MILLER, J. H. & Lou N.	Horace J.	22 Oct 1874
Lavaca	MILLER, James & Virginia	Addy Zue	30 Sep 1875
Bell	MILLER, Joe & Helena	Patrick Henry	22 May 1874
Bell	MILLER, John & M. B.	James Alex	1 Dec 1873
Bell	MILLER, Joseph L. & Margaret M.	Mary Susan	4 Sep 1874
Travis	MILLER, M. K. & Lucretia	Forest	2 Apr 1874
Bell	MILLER, R. C. & S. E.	James Eddie	29 Oct 1874
Travis	MILLER, W. A. H. & Kate	Mattie Bell	8 Oct 1874
Austin	MILLER, W. T. & Mary	James Henry	4 Aug 1874
Bastrop	MILLER, Wooas S. & Margarett	Cornelia E.	16 Apr 1874
Comanche	MILLICAN, P. D. & Sarah	Kieffer L.	14 Sep 1873
Comanche	MILLIGAN, J. W. & M. J.	Cloda Larnen	6 Jan 1874
Comanche	MILNER, J. & S. C.	Sally Rochester	17 Apr 1875
Travis	MILUM, Joseph & Mary Jane	Francis Elizabeth	18 Oct 1873
Comanche	MIMMS, J. A. & M. J.	Augusta	21 Jul 1874
Brazos	MIMS, Alfred & Caroline	Harry Lucius	13 Aug 1874
Fayette	MINDEN, Ditrich & Louisa von Minden	Henry	24 Oct 1874
Kendall	MINNICH, Ignaz & Barbara	Gustav	23 Apr 1853
		Anna	4 Sep 1855
		Pauline	2 Jun 1857
		August	29 Oct 1859
		Robert	6 Mar 1864
		Johanne	1 Oct 1866
Medina	MINNIMK, Friede & Antke	Christina	12 Jun 1875
Lee	MINSHAW, R. L. & Victoria	C. A.	27 Oct 1873
Travis	MINTER, J. C. & Evaline A.	Maud C.	16 Jan 1874
Austin	MINTON, Samuel A. & Martha A.	John Isaac	23 Mar 1875
Austin	MISSOURICA, John & Martha	John	Dec 1874
Hays	MITCHELL, Columbus C. & Julia	Nellie	7 Aug 1874
Bexar	MITCHELL, Emily (See James McLeary)		
Bell	MITCHELL, J. E. & S. A.	(Twins) Lou & Dru	7 Nov 1874
Burnet	MITCHELL, J. W. & M. A.	Lou Anna	6 May 1874
Brazos	MITCHELL, L. E. & A. D.	Edward Lewis	23 Sep 1874
		Wm. Travers	16 Jul 1876
Bexar	MITCHELL, Wallace & Jennie (Fisher)	Lenora Fisher	5 Nov 1874
Grimes	MIZE, D. M. & M. C.	J. V.	22 Jun 1873
Lavaca	MIZE, Wm. & Jane A.	Lewis	30 Oct 1875
Gillespie	MOEHLE, Heinrich & Marie	Alfred	16 Jun 1874
Gillespie	MOELLRING, William & Louise	William	31 Aug 1875
Lavaca	MOFFITT, T. H. & Amanda	Alice	1 Nov 1873
Comal	MOGELIN, Emma Theresa (See Wilhelm Haas)		
Bexar	MOKE, Leon & Isabelle (Souza)	Hortense	2 Oct 1874
Gillespie	MOLDENHAUER, August & Johanne	Susana Wilhelmine	23 Oct 1873

COUNTY	PARENTS	CHILD	DATE
Bastrop	MOLTON, D. M. & Lucinda	Aaula	1 Jul 1875
Bastrop	MONCURE, J. J. & A. J.	John Decherd	27 Aug 1873
Lee	MONROE, Sanders & Sarah Ann	B. F.	17 Apr 1874
Bandera	MONTAGUE, C. & L.	Rosa	12 Jun 1873
Bexar	MONTES, Francisca (See Frank G. Huntress)		
Nacogd.	MONTES, Pantalleon & Valentina	Larrance	5 Sep 1873
		Thomas	3 May 1875
Caldwell	MONTGOMERY, J. W. & Dora	Nora	16 Jul 1874
Colorado	MONTGOMERY, John J. & Fannie A.	Fannie Joe	12 Aug 1875
Comanche	MONTGOMERY, W. H. & J. S.	Geo. Belldo(ee) Dennis	4 Mar 1875
Bell	MOON, W. S. & M. E.	Wm.	5 May 1874
DeWitt	MOONEY, John & Maggie	Thomas M.	1876
Travis	MOORE, A. E. & S. S.	Mary Alice	26 Jul 1873
Bell	MOORE, C. R. & T. J.	Lillian Estella	9 Jul 1874
Lee	MOORE, Chesley & Josephine	Abbennier	1 Jul 1873
Bell	MOORE, D. P. & M. M.	Ann Moshell	21 Jan 1875
Bastrop	MOORE, Dyer & M. D.	Elwood	13 Aug 1875
Bastrop	MOORE, E. C. & L. A.	Dallas	27 Feb 1874
Travis	MOORE, E. T. & Maggie R.	Victor Cloud	4 Feb 1874
Brazos	MOORE, H. A. & Eliza	Daisy Rosaline	1 Nov 1876
Brazos	MOORE, H. M. & O. M.	Maud	29 Jan 1874
		Helen Earl	25 Aug 1876
Fayette	MOORE, Haywood & Mary	Cintha Naomi	1 Oct 1873
Bastrop	MOORE, J. W. & Mary	Walter L.	24 Feb 1874
Bastrop	MOORE, James & Sigur B.	R. W.	2 Oct 1873
Lee	MOORE, James M. & Matilda	Asa Thomas Jacob	19 Aug 1873
		Jessie David Ross	19 Aug 1873
Lee	MOORE, M. T. & Nellie	Albert O.	Nov 1875
Travis	MOORE, Newton Cain & Mary Catherine (Jester)	Atha May	6 May 1879
San Saba	MOORE, S. M. & E.	Mary E.	1 Feb 1871
		Amanda Jane	1 Feb 1873
Bell	MOORE, T. & Jane	Robert Edgar	9 Jun 1874
Kendall	MOORE, W. R. & Louisiana	Emma Alice	7 Feb 1872
		Haddie	15 Apr 1874
Bexar	MOOREZEL, Green & Susie G. (Johnson)	Mattie Green	31 Sep 1872
		Sarah Green	25 Oct 1874
Bexar	MORALES, Ignacio & Louisa (Schreiner)	Freddy	11 Sep 1874
Bandera	MORAVIETZ, Thomas & Frances	Sophie	7 May 1874
Bexar	MORAWIETZ, Jos. & Susan (Oczko)	Jadwiga	16 Oct 1874
Lavaca	MORELAND, W. H. & R. L.	M. F.	6 Aug 1874
Grimes	MORGAN, J. & M. A.	Sallie Eliza	2 Oct 1873
Lavaca	MORGAN, W. H. & Mary A.	Mary A.	31 May 1873
Bexar	MORITZ, Samuel & Emma (Aaron)	Clara	1 Feb 1874
		Solomon	6 Dec 1875
	(Twins)	Bertha & Esther	31 Jan 1877
Bastrop	MORRIS, A. A. & A. J.	Margaret C.	22 Sep 1875
Comanche	MORRIS, G. W. & N. P.	Ceclia May	6 Dec 1873
Caldwell	MORRIS, Geo. W. & Margaret	Joseph W.	15 Nov 1875
Austin	MORRIS, James & Louisa	John Henry	6 Sep 1874
Bell	MORRIS, John F. & Lizzie J.	Vernie R.	11 Jul 1873
Bastrop	MORRIS, N. A. & A. E. (Twins)	Jas. W. & Alma A.	20 Jun 1873
Bexar	MORRIS, S. W. & Augusta P. (Glaser)	Menie E.	2 Oct 1869
Bexar	MORRIS, Sarah (See George Buchanan)		
Lavaca	MORROW, J. F. & Louisa	J. F. Harry	4 Jun 1874
Nacogd.	MORTON, John B. & Amelia	V. D.	3 Oct 1873
Bell	MORTON, Jos. D. & Rachel	Wm. Russell	17 Mar 1874
Nacogd.	MORTON, Thomas & D.	Sallie	25 Sep 1873

COUNTY	PARENTS	CHILD	DATE
Medina	MOSBY, W. R. & Ann Jane	John C. Sullivan	13 Dec 1875
Lee	MOSER, Dan P. & M. G.	Thomas Percy	30 Nov 1874
Burnet	MOSES, Norton & Lucy A.	Andy	6 Jun 1874
Hays	MOSHER, Albert C. & Jane S.	Arabella J.	14 Nov 1873
Bell	MOSS, D. G. & Sophia	Annie Bell	14 Oct 1873
Bastrop	MOTON, David & Lucinda	Elizabeth	4 Oct 1873
DeWitt	MOTTING, H. & Augusta	Karl	29 Jan 1874
Bell	MOUNGER, ?? & ??	Ida Estelle	5 Jan 1875
Bexar	MOUREAA, Hulda (See Charles Groos)		
Bexar	MOUREAN, Emmy (See Edward Dreiss)		
Bexar	MOYE, Emilie (See Julius Piper)		
Bexar	MOZYGENDA, Anna (See P.A.H. Buechler)		
Nacogd.	MUCKLEROY, Anthony & Mary E.	Bertie	30 Sep 1873
		David W.	5 May 1875
Nacogd.	MUCKLEROY, J. H. & Mary E.	Margaret Roena	30 Sep 1874
Bexar	MUELLER, Carl Hubert & Emilia	Emilia	2 Dec 1871
		Elise	14 Aug 1874
		Fredrich Albert	15 Dec 1875
		Paul Joseph	24 Mar 1878
		Henriette	19 Sep 1879
		Chas. J.	5 Mar 1870
Austin	MUERE, Jacob & Henriette	Henriette	10 Mar 1874
Hays	MULKEY, Monroe & Lucy (Nance)	Columbus	12 Jun 1874
Bexar	MULLER, Agath (See Stephen Sherrer)		
Comal	MULLER, Elise (See Ernst Conring)		
Burnet	MULLINS, William & Eliza	William	8 Oct 1873
Austin	MUNGER, David R. & Lou M.	Eugene D.	19 May 1875
Victoria	MUNN, John S. & Olie (Heard)	Lora Dream	11 Oct 1874
Fayette	MUNN, Neil & Sarah V.	William Roy	23 Feb 1874
Burnet	MURCHISON, D. A. & Anetta	Sarah Ann	26 Jan 1874
Nacogd.	MURPH, T. J. & Olivia M.	Margaret Catherine	1 Aug 1873
Austin	MURPHY, Chas. & Ellen	Mary Ann	12 Nov 1874
Burnet	MURPHY, H. A. & Olivia	William M.	27 Mar 1875
Burnet	MURPHY, James G. & Nancy E.	John Glass	14 Feb 1874
	(Twins)	Edward Joel	
		Daniel Henry	6 Apr 1875
Victoria	MURPHY, M. & Julia (Teal)	Rosanna	23 Oct 1873
Bell	MURPHY, W. G. & M. A.	Edna Pearl	21 Jan 1874
Bexar	MURRAY, A. I. & Ellen (Revere)	Ida Louisa	27 Nov 1874
Austin	MURRAY, Caesar & Harriet	John	9 Feb 1875
DeWitt	MURRAY, David L. & N.A.E.M.	Nettie Ann	3 Apr 1868
		Mary Catherine	23 Mar 1870
		Peggy June	29 Oct 1871
		David Hugh Bunn?	7 Sep 1873
Austin	MURRAY, J. H. & Mary Lou	Nathan W.	11 Jan 1875
Austin	MURY, Jacob & Anna	Sophia	1 Jun 1873
		Sam	28 Jul 1875
Brazos	MUSE, H. E. & Fannie G.	Alice Erma	4 Apr 1876
Austin	MUSLOW, William & Christine	Herman	1 Sep 1874
Bell	MYER, C. F. & N. E.	E. W.	9 Sep 1875
Comanche	NABERS, W. J. & Actreamen(?)	Thomas Jefferson	15 Jul 1874
Comal	NAEGELIN, Eduard & Franzisca (Seekatz)	Franklin	13 Sep 1873
Bexar	NAGEL, Catherine (See Frank Blotz)		
Bexar	NAGEL, Frank Peter & Charlotte	Mary Matilda	11 Nov 1875
		Richard	27 Jun 1868
Bexar	NAGLE, F. & Augusta (Langwell)	William	27 Jun 1874
Hays	NANCE, Jenny (See West Matt)		
Hays	NANCE, Lucy (See Montoe Mulkey)		
Hays	NANCE, Thomas N. & Ola	Ezekiel T.	23 Sep 1873

COUNTY	PARENTS	CHILD	DATE
DeWitt	NAU, C. W. & Caroline	Johannes	24 Jun 1873
Bexar	NEAL, Richard H. &		
	Bettie H. (Connelley)	Claudius Reed	8 Mar 1875
Hays	NEAL, Stephen J. & Martha A.	Howard	31 Mar 1875
Lee	NEAL, William S. &		
	Martha A.	Frances E.	22 Mar 1874
		James M.	22 Mar 1874
Austin	NECKER, Charles & Ernstine	Bertha	11 Dec 1875
Comanche	NEELEY, F. H. & Sarah E.	Octavia	10 Sep 1873
Victoria	NEELY, Wm. J. &		
	Louisa F. (Roberts)	Alma Augusta	4 Apr 1873
Comal	NEHLS, Ferdinand &		
	Antonie (Hoffmann)	Selma Antonie	17 Oct 1867
		Friedrich Wilhelm	7 Dec 1869
		Ferdinand Gustav	2 Oct 1871
Caldwell	NEILL, Geo. F. & M. E.	George Ewell	30 May 1875
Austin	NELIUS, Charles &		
	Josephine	William	22 Nov 1874
Kendall	NELSON, F. H. & Annie	Francis John	3 Dec 1873
		James Frederic	20 Nov 1874
Nacogd.	NELSON, F. M. & Callie	Alice M.	10 Jun 1873
Nacogd.	NELSON, John B. & Sarah	Mary C.	17 Sep 1873
Bexar	NESTOR, Mary (See Emil Zinsmeir)		
Hays	NETHERLAND, Jo H. &		
	Margaret	Jane	24 Jan 1873
		Benjamin	22 Dec 1874
Bexar	NETTE, Emma (See Fred Hasenberg)		
Bexar	NEUMAN, Augusta (See Peter Kleid)		
Austin	NEUMANN, Hermann & Ida	Fred Wilhelm	22 Sep 1873
		Anton Robert	24 Dec 1875
Medina	NEUMANN, John & Josephine	Bernhart	5 Jan 1874
Medina	NEUMANN, Thomas & Julia	August Ed	21 Sep 1873
Victoria	NEUMEYER, Herman A. &		
	Mary Louisa (Sitterle)	William Adolph	16 Aug 1871
		Louisa Rose	20 May 1873
	(Twins)	Sophie Anna	20 May 1873
		Charles Theodore	29 Aug 1875
Comal	NEUSE, Heinrich &		
	Sophie (Harlos)	Wilhelm George	20 Dec 1873
Caldwell	NEW, J. B. & T. T.	Joseph E.	17 Feb 1874
Caldwell	NEW, W. H. & Mary	Mae Delenia	14 Jul 1874
Victoria	NEWCOMB, Mary E. (See Wm. W. Gwinn)		
Bandera	NEWCOMER, F. G. & H. N.	James Jackson	30 Mar 1875
Bell	NEWMAN, H. E. & O.	Margaret May	13 Aug 1874
Travis	NEWMAN, R. J. & M. C.	Malinda Catherine	22 Mar 1874
Lee	NEWSOM, Braxton & Ann	Mary Ella	8 Jan 1874
Bexar	NEWTON, F. McC. &		
	C. M. (Sibert)	Charles	2 Oct 1874
		Frank R.	4 Jan 1871
		Joseph Samuel	28 Jan 1873
Bexar	NEWTON, H. M. &		
	Lucinda E. (Smith)	S. H.	25 Oct 1870
Bastrop	NEWTON, J. D. & Mary A	Margaret L.	19 May 1874
Bexar	NEWTON, Julia (See George Cochran)		
Burnet	NEWTON, R. J. & Mary Ann	Sarah Elizabeth	10 Nov 1874
Bexar	NEWTON, S. G. & M. E. (Tompkins)	Jones T.	26 Oct 1874
Burnet	NEWTON, W. M. & M. C.	Viola	8 Apr 1874
Bell	NIBLING, F. & A. A.	Geo. Wm.	26 Nov 1874
Bexar	NICHOLS, Ann (See John J. L. Barnhart)		
Austin	NICHOLS, James W. &		
	Henriette	Albert Perry	14 Jul 1873
Kendall	NICKEL, Wilhelm & Marie	Heinrich	28 Jan 1873
		Marie	1 May 1875
Bexar	NIEL, Jane (See Arthur Dillon)		
Fayette	NIEMANN, Chas. & Ernestine	Albert L.	16 Feb 1874
Fayette	NIEMANN, Fritz & Louise	Emil	12 Nov 1873

55

COUNTY	PARENTS	CHILD	DATE
Fayette	NIEMANN, Fritz & Louise	Emil	12 Nov 1873
Bexar	NIGGLE, Mary (See August Kuehne)		
Medina	NIGGLI, Ferdinand &		
	Josephine	William	5 Dec 1873
		Adele	27 Dec 1874
Gillespie	NIMITZ, Ernest & Theresia	Louis Otto	21 May 1875
DeWitt	NITSCHE, Hermann & Anna	Adolph Louis	
		Hermann	13 Feb 1874
Bastrop	NIXON, W. J. & P. A.	Caroline	20 Nov 1874
Burnet	NOBLE, J. P. & Amanda	Delia Jane	1 Sep 1874
Grimes	NOBLES, J.P. & J.S.	Swannah	17 Oct 1873
Grimes	NOBLES, J. S. & Catherine	James Thomas	22 Oct 1873
DeWitt	NOELKE, Ferdinand & Alice P.	Montgomery	15 Jan 1873
		William Theodore	13 May 1874
Lavaca	NOLEN, J. W. & Fanny	Nanny	15 May 1874
Medina	NOONAN, William & Abby	Mary Rowina	30 Mar 1874
		Clara Elizabeth	25 Jan 1876
Burnet	NORRIS, C. J. & Sarah A.	Ida Dell	19 Jun 1874
Burnet	NORRIS, G. W. & Sarah E.	Lucy Jane	6 Jul 1874
Burnet	NORRIS, Solamon & Nancy	Benjamin A.	4 Nov 1874
Victoria	NORRIS, Susan (See Charles A. Hall)		
Burnet	NORRIS, Thos. M. &		
	Elizabeth	Luther Oscar	30 Jun 1873
		Martha Kansas	7 Feb 1876
		John	27 Nov 1874
Bexar	NORTON, R. C. &		
	Ellen H. (Whiteley)	Kirkwood W.	30 May 1874
Hays	NORWOOD, Cornelius & Mary	Lucy	15 Jun 1875
Bastrop	NORWOOD, W. J. & M. E.	Laura A.	30 May 1874
Travis	NOTEN, Thomas & Marian	Thomas	7 Dec 1873
Bexar	NOTRE, Roaslia (See Benhardt Baddo)		
Kendall	NOWLIN, James B. & Mary T.	Bobbie	20 May 1870
		William Albert	29 Feb 1872
		Frank	9 Aug 1873
Kendall	NOWLIN, R. W. & A. E.	Susan	5 Aug 1874
Bexar	NUCKOLLS, T. A. (See J. C. Stanfield)		
Burnet	NULL, A. C. & Mary	Oscar Lafayette	13 Oct 1873
Gillespie	NUNEZ, J. W. & Anna Maria	Dulce	25 May 1875
Lee	NUNN, William R. & Sarah J.	Joel Thomas	26 Aug 1874
Lee	NUNNS, Aaron & Betsy	Nancy	27 Jun 1875
Burnet	OATMAN, M. C. & S. C.	Harvey Cromwell	
		Hiram	21 Jun 1874
Lavaca	OBELGONER, H. & Mary A.	Sophia	5 Jul 1873
		Christine	6 May 1875
Comanche	OBRYANT, Dennis & Jane E.	Henry Harvey	11 Mar 1874
Bexar	OCHSE, Charles &		
	Dorotea (Fischer)	Lucy	10 May 1874
		William	25 Jan 1876
Bexar	OCHSE, John &		
	Sarah Anna (Arold)	Lillian Stella	4 Mar 1874
San Saba	O'CONNELL, Thos. N. & Kate	Maggie Neill	25 Nov 1875
Victoria	O'CONNOR, Dennis & Virginia	Josephine	13 Jun 1873
Bexar	OCZKO, Susan (See Jos. Morawietz)		
Comanche	ODELL, J. E. & E. J.	Lottie Clementine	14 Mar 1875
Burnet	ODEN, P. E. & Louisa	Albert & Miranda	15 Apr 1874
Hays	ODOM, Hugh S. & Manerva J.	Robert Britton	28 Feb 1874
Comal	OELKERS, Marie (See Ferdinand Simon)		
Austin	OHLENDORF, Charles & Minna	Lena	18 Dec 1875
Comal	OHLRICH, Carl &		
	Louise (Pantermuehl)	Carl	11 Oct 1874
Nacogd.	OLIVER, Sant & Amy	Ruth	15 Dec 1873
Fayette	OLLE, Chas. & T.	Otto	28 Feb 1873
Bexar	OLLIVARRI, Placido &		
	Micaela (Ximenes)	Solema	1874
Brazos	OLVERSON, Nelson & Minerva	Sam Lee	6 May 1875

56

COUNTY	PARENTS	CHILD	DATE
Victoria	ONDERDONK, Gilbert &		
	Martha J. (Benham)	Gilbert	5 Sep 1873
		Lillian	5 Sep 1873
Bexar	OPERT, Mary (See Aug. Santleben)		
Bexar	OPPENHEIMER, Anton &		
	Adelaide (Pheiffer)	Lilly	27 Jan 1874
Bexar	OPPENHEIMER, Helen (See Alexander Michel)		
Bexar	OPPERMANN, F. &		
	Mary (Ratzel)	Otto	15 May 1874
		William W.	23 Aug 1876
Bastrop	ORGAIN, B. & Dru F.	Kate D.	3 Apr 1874
Nacogd.	ORTON, John G. & Madora	Mattie L.	24 Sep 1874
Bastrop	OSBORNE, C. & A.	Demis	4 May 1873
Grimes	OSBORNE, W. F. & Alice E.	Ira (or Iva) McQueen	
	(Twins)	Alice Granger	10 Jun 1876
Lavaca	OSBOURN, M. S. & M. C.	Wm. Edward	27 Sep 1874
Bexar	OSING, Anna (See Carl Frank Hertzberg)		
Bell	OSTERHOUT, J. P. & J.	Junia Roberts	9 Apr 1874
Bexar	OSTROM, V. C. &		
	Sarah Francis (Hummer)	Edward	31 Oct 1873
Lee	OSTROWSKI, A. & L.	Mendel	16 Feb 1876
Fayette	OTKEN, F. C. & Hellener	Henry	5 May 1874
Fayette	OTKEN, George & C. C.	Louis F.	20 Jan 1874
Gillespie	OTTE, Friedrich & Dina	Ida	2 Sep 1873
Austin	OTTO, William & Mina	Mary	2 Feb 1874
Grimes	OWEN, Davis & Catherine	John H.	20 Oct 1874
Burnet	OWEN, E. A. & E. Jane	Lizie Rosalia	28 Feb 1874
Medina	OWEN, J. C. & Margaret E.	Joseph Columbus	Nov 1874
Hays	OWEN, Wm. H. & Elizabeth	Perdy Mathews	2 Aug 1874
Hays	OWENS, Jas. & Anges	Melvina Humphries	24 Mar 1876
Hays	OWENS, Oscar O. & Mahulda	Mary Ellen	15 Mar 1876
Bell	PACE, W. J. & Olive L.	Robert E. Lee	28 Jun 1873
Lavaca	PAGE, W. W. & Leoina	Charles T.	12 Sep 1874
Lee	PAIR, Drury T. & Eliza J.	Bettie Sarah	8 Feb 1874
		John Thomas	May 1875
Austin	PALM, A. & Sophie	Joseph	5 Feb 1872
		Hulda	30 Aug 1874
Bexar	PALM, Mary Ann (See Anton Adam)		
Bexar	PANCOAST, J. E. & Sarah E.	George J.	17 Aug 1873
Bexar	PANCOST, Aaron & Mary (Test)	Joseph Carrol	11 Apr 1874
Comal	PANTERMUEHL, Christian &		
	Maria (Baetge)	Ottilie	25 Apr 1872
		Paul	22 Sep 1873
		Olga	14 Feb 1875
Comal	PANTERMUEHL, Louise (See Carl Ohlrich)		
Bexar	PAPE, Augusta (See Gerard Storms)		
Comanche	PARKER, A. G. & Mary S.	Fanny Texanna	28 Oct 1873
Lee	PARKER, J. W. & Bettie	Norma	17 Feb 1874
Burnet	PARKER, L. J. & Tila M.	Eugene C.	17 Dec 1874
Burnet	PARKER, Riley V. & Mary E.	Oscar Erastus	15 Dec 1875
Bastrop	PARKERSON, Harriet E. (See Henry Harrison Alexander)		
Lavaca	PARR, G. S. & M. C.	Thebe	20 Feb 1875
Lavaca	PARR, J. M. & J. A.	Lillian R.	26 Mar 1875
Caldwell	PARR, James Z. & M. C.	William Gibson	2 Jul 1875
Lavaca	PARR, R. H. & Liddy J.	E.M.A.	24 Sep 1875
Nacogd.	PARRISH, David & L. C.	Ella May	1 May 1875
Nacogd.	PARRISH, William & Nancy A.	Richard J.	2 Sep 1875
Nacogd.	PARROTT, F. M. & J. E.	W. R.	9 Jun 1874
Nacogd.	PARROTT, H. H. & Sarah	Andrew W.	18 Mar 1874
Bexar	PARSCHAL, Mary F. (See H. J. Huppertz)		
Bell	PASS, W. J. & M.	Lillie O.	27 Jun 1873
		Minnie	3 Oct 1875
Lavaca	PATE, Andrew & Sarah	Mary Jane	9 Sep 1874
Nacogd.	PATE, C. T. & Elizabeth P.	M. E.	7 Aug 1873
		Emley E.	30 Nov 1874
		Wm. Riley	13 Jul 1876

| --- | --- | --- | --- |
Brazos	PATE, W. T. & Mary A.	Cora Lula	15 Aug 1875
Caldwell	PATTERSON, B. D. & Mary	Lula Duff	18 Mar 1875
Austin	PATTISON, Wm. R. & Fannie	Wm. R.	25 Sep 1873
Lavaca	PATTON, C. B. & Kate A.	Mary Dibrell	10 Nov 1874
Caldwell	PATTON, J. C. & A. J.	Andrew	Sep 1874
Gillespie	PAULUS, August & Roxie	Louisa	17 Aug 1874
Hays	PAYNE, D. T. & Mary Jane	John Lewis	4 Apr 1876
Bell	PEACOCK, S. & M. E.	Lela Emma	15 Feb 1875
Bell	PEARCE, W. Y & M. A.	John	6 Nov 1873
Travis	PEARSON, E. & Ann	Nancy Elizabeth	27 Jan 1874
Brazos	PEARSON, E. C. & Zelphia	Lovely	9 Feb 1874
		Homer	1 Oct 1875
Burnet	PEARSON, W. H. & A. A.	Willie May	8 Jun 1873
Travis	PEARSON, W. S. & S. E.	Allebie	15 May 1873
DeWitt	PEASE, S. K. & Susan (Twins)	Eddie & John	30 Mar 1875
DeWitt	PEAVY, D. B. & Margarett	Charles Druery	7 Aug 1876
Gillespie	PEHL, Peter & Mariana	Helena	22 Dec 1873
Comal	PELTZER, Anna (See Julius Tips)		
Colorado	PENDICK, R. P. & K. L.	Sophia	8 Aug 1874
Comal	PENSHORN, Bertha (See Hugo Bruno Wetzel)		
Comal	PENSHORN, Sophie (See Wilhelm Ullrich)		
Lee	PERKINS, A. G. G. & Jennet P.	Oscar Walker	2 Aug 1874
Hays	PERKINS, George K. & Maria P.	Rubina	24 Dec 1873
Bastrop	PERKINS, Henry & C. M.	Dora Lee	24 Jul 1873
Nacogd.	PERKINS, J. W. & Susanna	M. M.	3 Sep 1873
		John J.	14 Jul 1875
Hays	PERKINS, John M. & H. M.	Eola	17 Aug 1873
Nacogd.	PERRETTE, John Jr. & Sarah S.	James T.	13 Nov 1873
Burnet	PERRY, O. B. & Sarah M.	Sarah E.	26 Apr 1876
Caldwell	PERRY, P. L. & R. J.	Cyon Clay	15 Dec 1874
Lee	PERTLE, (Pertlee), A. C. & S. E.	A. C.	29 Sep 1875
Gillespie	PETER, George & Clara	Carl Georg	27 Sep 1874
Bell	PETERS, C. A. & M. A.	James H.	2 Nov 1874
Brazos	PETERSON, Martha Ann (See John Marshall Willborn)		
Lavaca	PETERSON, S. D. & E. J.	Thos.	6 Jan 1875
Victoria	PETICOLAS, A. B. &		
	Marion G. (Goodwin)	Sherman G.	1 Jul 1871
		Warner M.	19 Jun 1873
Bexar	PETMECKY, Lina (See Charles Ronnkamp)		
Bexar	PETRICH, N. Z. &		
	A. (Schnetz)	N. Lee	11 Jan 1871
		John R.	19 Nov 1872
		Eugenia E.	7 Oct 1874
Travis	PETTAWAY, Lee &		
	Julia (White)	Margarette	21 Oct 1872
Comanche	PETTET, J. P. & Catharine	William Andrew	16 Jan 1874
Bastrop	PETTY, James M. & Arena	A. A.	13 Feb 1875
Austin	PFEFFER, Charles & Pauline	Max John	Jul 1874
Austin	PFEFFER, Edward & Dora	Emma	9 Dec 1874
Austin	PFEFFER, Fritz & Mary	Minna	27 Jul 1874
Austin	PFEFFER, Wm. F & Johanna	Otto	30 Jul 1874
Austin	PFEIFFER, Ernst & Louisa	Katie Bertha	5 May 1874
Kendall	PFEIFFER, Ernst & Caroline	Carl	16 Mar 1872
		Albert	18 Jul 1873
		Louise	8 Mar 1875
Bexar	PFEIL, Edmund &		
	Adelaide (Stapper)	Bruno	23 Mar 1878
Comal	PFEUFFER, George H. &		
	Susan Elizabeth (Gravis)	Ulric Septim	27 May 1873
Bexar	PFIEFFER, Bertha (See M. Goldfrank)		
Bexar	PFLUGHAUPT, F. W. &		
	Louise (Zitzelmann)	F. W.	13 Jan 1875
Burnet	PHARIS, A. M. & S. E.	James	15 May 1874
		Allen H.	17 Sep 1875
Bexar	PHEIFFER, Adelaide (See Anton Oppenheimer)		

COUNTY	PARENTS	CHILD	DATE
Victoria	PHELPS, Jr. Truman &		
	Moena (Sewell)	Ruth	30 Nov 1873
Kendall	PHILIP, Julius & Margarethe	Julius	29 Jan 1867
		Ottilie	29 Jan 1869
		Christine	4 Jan 1871
		Albert	18 Feb 1873
		Ida	19 Sep 1874
Victoria	PHILIPS, E. M. &		
	M. V. (Bufkin) (?)	Una Cornelia	23 Apr 1874
Kendall	PHILLIP, Joseph & Mina	Anna	13 Aug 1864
		Louise	4 Mar 1866
		Auguste	13 Dec 1867
		Mina	13 Sep 1869
		Adolph	21 Feb 1871
		Charles	27 Dec 1872
Bexar	PHILLIPPE, Mary E. (See Erich Menger)		
Caldwell	PHILLIPS, A. P. & S. J.	Anna Laurette	14 Aug 1873
Bandera	PHILLIPS, J. M. & M. A.	Richard Coke	No date
Travis	PHILLIPS, John Hughston &		
	Mary Elizabeth (McMahan)	Amelia Launa	9 May 1874
Hays	PHILLIPS, John W. &		
	Paralee C.	Paralee	20 Aug 1874
Austin	PIEL, David & Mary	William	7 Dec 1873
Austin	PIER, Samuel & Emilie	Anna Bradford	25 Jan 1875
Bastrop	PIERCE, J. T. & Colinne	Laura	7 Nov 1873
Comanche	PINKORD, D. P. & Sarah C.	Lydia Alma	14 Jun 1874
Bell	PINKSTON, H. W. & Flora	James S.	18 Mar 1874
Bexar	PIPER, F. A. &		
	Minna (Hoerner)	Albert Henry	3 Oct 1875
Victoria	PIPER, John &		
	Frederica (Waber)	Bertha	11 Jun 1873
Bexar	PIPER, Julius & Emilie (Moye)	Otto John	27 Sep 1871
		Frederick Albert	2 Oct 1873
		Max	28 Apr 1878
Bexar	PIPER, William &		
	Mary (Gembler)	??(F)	1 Apr 1876
Bell	PIPES, Abner & Jane	Alice	1 Sep 1873
Bell	PIPPINS, W. C. & Amanda	Andrew Jackson	15 Apr 1874
Fayette	PITSCHKE, Hugo & ??	Edward Wm.	24 Jun 1874
Caldwell	PITTMAN, Ben H. & Maggie	Walter E.	8 Jun 1875
Caldwell	PITTMAN, W. C. & Martha	Marcus Elsworth	29 May 1875
	(Twins)	Mary Emily	29 May 1875
Travis	PITTS, Wm. A. & Samonie	William Wirt	25 Aug 1865
		Henry Curtis	7 Nov 1868
		b. Indianola, Calhoun County	
		Rell Maxey	24 Jan 1874
Gillespie	PLAGE, Bertha (See Rudolph Dressel)		
Nacogd.	PLEASANT, Buford & Node	William B.	1 Oct 1874
Nacogd.	PLEASANT, William F. &		
	Martha	Johnye	1 Oct 1874
Austin	PLEASANTS, Robert &		
	Betsy Catlin	Lila	Oct 1874
DeWitt	PLEDYER, William & Laura	Roberta E.	20 Mar 1876
Austin	PLESS, John & Sophie	Emma	1 Dec 1874
Bexar	PLUMEYER, Louise (See Nicolas Tengg)		
Bexar	POHN, Henrietta (See A. Dullnig)		
Lavaca	POLARSHAK, John & Theresa	Antonio	1 Jan 1874
Hays	POLK, James & Mariah	?? (F)	16 Dec 1873
Brazos	POLK, T. M. & M. J.	H. L.	14 Mar 1874
		M. M.	23 Feb 1876
Lavaca	PONTON, A. C. & Wineford	Walter	15 May 1874
Lavaca	PONTON, Joel & Elizabeth	Lacurgus	24 Feb 1875
Bell	POPE, G. I. & S. J.	Katie R.	15 Aug 1873
Fayette	PORTER, Jackson A. & ??	Charles Seymour	19 Dec 1873
Lavaca	PORTER, Jonathan & L. V.	Ottis Burns	30 Nov 1874
Bastrop	POWELL, Geo. W. & L.	Thomas A.	16 Jan 1874

COUNTY	PARENTS	CHILD	DATE
Nacogd.	POWER, H. B. & Mary Ann	Lawrence H.	25 Dec 1873
Travis	PRATHER, T. F. & C. N.	Chas. F.	6 Sep 1876
Burnet	PRENTICE, John W. & Marcella	John Walter	6 Nov 1874
Bexar	PRESCOTT, Aransas & Anna (Goulon)		
		Annie Eugenie	22 Mar 1869
		Marie Louise	21 Jun 1870
		Wm. Aransas	20 Sep 1871
		Alidice	7 Apr 1873
		Olivia Goulon	9 Aug 1874
Bexar	PRESCOTT, Mary (See E. F. Deaton)		
Bexar	PRESLER, J. (See A. T. Krause)		
Lavaca	PRESNELL, Luke & C. C.	E.	8 Mar 1875
Travis	PRESSLER, Franz & Dora	Hedwig	5 Jul 1874
		Walter	10 Feb 1876
DeWitt	PRESTON, Leonedas & Sarah A.	Frank	19 Apr 1875
Bastrop	PREUSS, John & Maria	Henry	17 Oct 1874
DeWitt	PREUSS, Leo & Maggie	Leonie	9 Sep 1873
Comal	PREUSSER, Emma (See Joseph Rohde)		
Caldwell	PRICE, A. B. & E. M.	Albert Ruskin	8 Sep 1874
Bell	PRICE, H. M. & A. M.	Mary E.	6 Dec 1873
Hays	PRICE, James B. & Laura	Robert Edward	9 Jan 1875
Bastrop	PRICE, Robt. J. & Sarah B.	Stella	18 May 1873
Hays	PRIESTLY, Saml. Grice & Ada	Edward	21 Aug 1874
DeWitt	PRIETZ, F. Frantz & Auguste	Sophi (sic)	11 Apr 1870
Colorado	PRINCE, Werden & Eliza	Ledore	20 Oct 1873
Comal	PROBANDT, Carl Ludwig & Dorothea Marie		
		Charles	12 Sep 1852
		Lewis	16 Jun 1854
		Albert	21 Oct 1856
		Elizabeth	5 Aug 1860
		Felix	31 Dec 1862
Gillespie	PROBST, Georg & Georgine	Georg	11 Jul 1873
		Carl Christian Ludwig	4 Sep 1874
Bell	PROCTOR, W. J. & F. E.	Henry	26 Jul 1874
Austin	PROUTY, L. L. & Lucinda M.	William Austin	9 Jul 1874
Lavaca	PROVAZEK, Joseph & Mary	Rosena	22 Jul 1874
Bandera	PUE, Arthur & Mary	William Arthur	31 Mar 1876
Bell	PUETT, W. E. & S. M.	John Claiborne	18 Jan 1875
Bexar	PULLAM, Wm. & Angeline (Williams)	David	12 Oct 1874
Lavaca	PULLIAM, Wiley & S. Ruth	Ada M.	5 Sep 1874
Comal	PULS, Mina (See J. Albert Kypfer)		
Austin	PUNCHARD, Cornelius & Marginney	Alvin C.	29 Mar 1875
Lee	PURCELL, Peter R. & Nancy (Jones)	Edmund Johnson	15 Dec 1874
Caldwell	PURSER, H. F. & S. J.	James Andrew	18 Sep 1874
San Saba	PYEATT, J. B. & M. J.	Bob Lee	7 Jul 1874
Bexar	PYKA, Francis (See F. C. Kotula)		
Bexar	QUIGLEY, Anne (See Wm. Lyons)		
Burnet	QUINN, R. L. & C. A.	Charles Chester	13 Apr 1873
Lee	QUINNEY, James & Martha A.	Nona Hosea	3 Sep 1875
Gillespie	QUINTEL, Adolph & Maria	Caroline Johanne	8 Nov 1874
Fayette	RABE, C. A. & E.	Emilie W.	10 Feb 1874
Bastrop	RABONE, Isaac & Nancy	Jesse	4 Oct 1874
Victoria	RAGLAND, George & Angeline	Mary Ellen	10 Mar 1873
Victoria	RAGLAND, Jenette (See William Harris)		
Lavaca	RAGSDALE, W. R. & S. P.	Anna	12 Sep 1874
Nacogd.	RAINBOLT, Francis M. & Sarah A.	George F.	Mar 1874
Nacogd.	RAMBAIN, J. L. & Martha A.	Robt. Lee	4 Mar 1875

COUNTY	PARENTS	CHILD	DATE
Bastrop	RAMSEY, Alexander & Susan Jane	Sarah Eveline	22 Apr 1874
Bandera	RAMSEY, Wm. & Martha	George William	3 Jun 1873
Lavaca	RANDOW, Chas. & Louisa	Wilhelmina	1 Oct 1873
Nacogd.	RANEY, Anda A. & ??	E. A.	28 Feb 1869
		Fessie N.	13 Nov 1870
		Anda A.	27 Jul 1876
		Sarah A.	20 Oct 1877
		Newton L.	28 Jul 1879
Nacogd.	RANEY, N. L. & S. J. A. (Legg)	E. L.	5 Nov 1869
		C. E.	21 Nov 1870
		S. Alice	2 Aug 1872
		L. W.	13 Feb 1874
		G. A.	21 Oct 1875
		Mollie L.	6 Sep 1877
		Ella L.	30 Jan 1879
Lee	RANKIN, John D. & Mary M.S.	Rowan Burleson	1 Oct 1873
Grimes	RANKIN, Sam & Alice	Clara	25 Nov 1873
Nacogd.	RATCLIFF, W. G. & Willie F.	W. F.	21 Apr 1876
Caldwell	RATLIFF, J. B. & S. J.	Mary Roberta	4 Feb 1875
Bexar	RATZEL, Mary (See F. Oppermann)		
Kendall	RAUSCH, Heinrich & Maria Sabina	William	3 Jul 1864
		Emilie	25 Dec 1865
		Pauline	7 Feb 1867
Kendall	RAUSCH, John & Maria Sabina	Robert	3 Oct 1868
		Carl	21 Aug 1870
		Bertha	15 Dec 1872
		Gustav Edwin	31 Mar 1875
Kendall	RAUSCH, John Remling & Jane	Mary	27 Dec 1874
		Cathrine	9 Mar 1875
Caldwell	RAY, J. M. & Mary E.	Martha Matilda	19 Jul 1873
Nacogd.	RAY, Reubin & M. J.	Sarah Delpha	29 Oct 1874
Brazos	RAY, Richard & C. P.	Olive Elizabeth	19 Sep 1875
Grimes	REA, Alford F. & Charlotte C.	Alfred Ferdinand	24 Jul 1873
Grimes	READ, Wm. H. & Ella E.	Joseph Benjamin	22 Feb 1874
		Ella Annie	15 Nov 1875
Austin	REASON, Thos. & Kitty	Alice	3 Jul 1873
Bexar	RECHENTIN, August & Louisa	August Willie	19 Sep 1874
Bastrop	REDDING, M. C. & Fany (sic)	Mary H.	28 Nov 1874
Bastrop	REDING, Talitha Jane (See John P. Jones)		
Comanche	REDWIN, L. S. & E. J.	Henry Belton	28 Mar 1875
Austin	REECE, K. W. & Martha	Nancy M.	10 Mar 1875
Bell	REED, E. T. & Malinda E.	Russell	2 Mar 1876
Bell	REED, J. M. & F. I.	Kate	3 Mar 1875
Bandera	REED, Joseph & Amanda	Joseph Nathan	19 Jan 1876
Brazos	REED, Wiley & P. A. E.	Stephen	29 Dec 1875
Lavaca	REES, J. W. & Rophila	Love Alluer	8 Oct 1875
Bell	REESE, J. T. & G. A.	Conway	22 May 1874
Victoria	REEVES, Tobe & Corallie (Williams)	Lee	3 Aug 1873
Travis	REEVES, William D. & Elizabeth	Pearl	22 Jul 1874
Hays	REEVES, William F. & Mary J.	Nellie R.	27 Jan 1874
Austin	REGENBRECHT, Adelbert & Anna	Bernhard	8 Nov 1875
Bexar	REHFINES von, Emmy (See Albrech Dittmar)		
Colorado	REICHART, Charles & Mary	John	8 May 1873
		Charles	26 Sep 1874
Travis	REICHMAN, F. Johann & Ellen M. A.	Emmy	27 Apr 1874
Bell	REID, G. & M. A.	James McGuire	17 Feb 1874
Bastrop	REID, O. H. & Texanna	Thomas	9 Sep 1874
Bell	REID, W. H. & M. S.	Mary G.	29 Jan 1875

COUNTY	PARENTS	CHILD	DATE
DeWitt	REIFFERT, Henry	Elisabeth	7 Nov 1874
Bexar	REINARZ, F. W. & Louisa		
	(Ackermann)	Alfred	20 Sep 1874
Austin	REINECKE, C. F. W. &		
	Wilhelmine	Julius	30 Sep 1873
		Hedwig	25 Jun 1875
Kendall	REINHARD, Louise Christine (See Gustav Willke)		
Austin	REINICKE, William Fred. Chas &		
	Louisa Mary	William Jacob	6 Apr 1875
		Mary Emma Louisa	23 Jul 1876
Travis	REINKE, Paul & Emma	Otto Robert	18 Jan 1873
		Charlotte Emilie	31 Jan 1875
Medina	REITZER, Ambrose & Odilia	Frank Haver	20 Apr 1874
Comal	REMER, William, Dr. &		
	Franziska (Kuehn)	Julius	9 Nov 1852
		Hedwig	13 Aug 1854
		Marie	10 Jun 1856
		Paul	20 Nov 1861
		Olga	4 Feb 1864
Austin	RENEAN, T. S. & Anna	Lustella	18 Oct 1874
Bexar	RENNERT, Augusta (See Fritz Rummel)		
Bexar	REPPA, Juelie (See C. A. Richter)		
Comal	RESCZYNSKI, Adele (See Hieranimus Bernhard)		
Comal	RESZCZYNSKI, Margaretta (See Otto Heilig)		
DeWitt	REUSER, Julius & Mary	Rudolph Leopold	12 Jan 1871
		Ida	9 Dec 1872
Bexar	REVERE, Ellen (See A. I. Murray)		
Bexar	REYES, Roberta (See Juan Pedro Bernal)		
Bexar	REYMANN, Laurence &		
	Margareta (Kehn)	Max Herman	29 Dec 1874
Bastrop	REYNOLDS, A. B. & F. M.	Alley Green	29 Dec 1874
Grimes	RHODA, V. H. & S. E.	Wilmer E.	7 May 1873
	(Twins)	James L. & Don J.	7 Nov 1874
Bexar	RHODIUS, Christoph &		
	Bertha (Degener)	Udo	17 Apr 1855
		Maria	22 Dec 1862
Lee	RHYMES, J. F. & Martha	James Willie	28 Dec 1873
San Saba	RICE, A. G. & Josephine	Davidella	11 Jan 1875
Lavaca	RICE, J. H. & Mollie	Jessie Green	24 Jun 1873
Burnet	RICE, M. L. & Caroline C.	Albert Preston	17 Dec 1874
DeWitt	RICE, Nick & Sally	Virginia	Jan 1874
Bexar	RICE, Rebecca (See Geo. S. Deats)		
Bell	RICH, R. A. & Catharine	Russell	9 May 1873
Bell	RICHARDS, C. B. & E. M.	John B.	10 Dec 1873
Bell	RICHARDS, G. D. & A. G.	Melville W.	14 Sep 1873
		Wm. L.	26 Jul 1875
Grimes	RICHARDS, Geo W. & Fanny	Sarah Jane	28 Sep 1874
Fayette	RICHARDS, Henry B. &		
	Annie E.	Lee Henry	4 Oct 1873
Bandera	RICHARDSON, J.N.B. & N.A.	Joseph R.	16 Sep 1874
Nacogd.	RICHARDSON, James R. &		
	Susan C.	Roberta A.	12 Apr 1875
Bexar	RICHEY, E. L. &		
	Julia (Jaggy)	Fredie	1 Sep 1874
Hays	RICHIE, Henry C. &		
	Temperance R.	William H.	19 Jul 1874
		James Monroe	11 Sep 1874
Bexar	RICHTER, C. A. &		
	Juelie (Rappa)	August Carl	13 Nov 1863
		Amalie Julie	2 Oct 1867
		Louise Auguste	5 Jan 1870
		Ida Catharine	31 Oct 1872
		Edward Carl	2 Jun 1875
Burnet	RICHTER, Herrman & Marie	Pauline Wilhelmine	
		Ottilie	10 Sep 1874
DeWitt	RICHTER, J. H. & Mary	Ledewig	25 May 1874

COUNTY	PARENTS	CHILD	DATE
Comal	RICHTER, Rdulph & Anna (Arnold)	Louise Charlotte	10 Oct 1874
Burnet	RICKETSON, H. & Milley	Albert	28 Jul 1874
Bastrop	RICKS, J. W. & M. H.	Mathias Jones	26 May 1874
Comal	RIDEL, Wendeline (See August Feltner)		
Caldwell	RIDOUT, Gordon & Ella M.	Betty Lola	20 Jan 1876
Caldwell	RIDOUT, M. P. & C. A.	Samuel Horace	27 Dec 1874
Medina	RIEDEN, Frank & Anna	Frank G.	28 Jan 1874
		Anna	5 Jul 1875
Victoria	RIEG, Rosine (See Christian Heck)		
Bandera	RIGGS, Alex & Matilda	Lucy Ann	10 Nov 1873
Lee	RIGGS, E. B. & Nannie M.	Annie Margarit	18 Sep 1875
Bandera	RIGGS, Nelson & Nancy	Priscilla Caroline	8 Nov 1874
Bexar	RIGOLLOT, Josephine L. (See Hy. August Sauvignet)		
Colorado	RILEY, Charles & Sallie M.	Cora	1 Apr 1873
		Marion E.	4 Mar 1875
Bell	RILEY, D. S. & O.S.E.	David Thos. Herbert	10 Aug 1874
Hays	RILEY, E. J. & Jane	Nora Victoria	1 Mar 1875
Bexar	RILLING, John Jacob & Anna M. (Weihnig)	John Jacob	22 Aug 1856
		Katherine Barbara	15 Mar 1858
		Anna Maria	4 Aug 1859
		Juliana	13 Nov 1861
		John George	13 Dec 1863
		Emilie	8 Feb 1870
Hays	RINARD, John & Anne	Bellezora	20 Oct 1873
Austin	RINGENER, Charles & Emilie	Lizette	12 Sep 1875
Bexar	RINGGOLD, Kate (See Geo. R. Dashiell)		
Austin	RINN, Louis & Sophie	Hermann	4 Oct 1873
Bexar	RIPKA, Joseph A. & Juliana (Kozub)	Antonio J.	19 Oct 1874
Bexar	RIPSTEIN, Adolph & Mollie)Dolan)	Laura F.	11 Jan 1875
Bexar	RITTIMANN, George & Catherine (Harlos)	Henry	29 Jun 1875
Bexar	RIVAS, Anta P. & Maria G.	Maria Adelaide	11 Oct 1873
		Edwardo G.	30 Dec 1874
Bexar	RIVAS, Antonio P. & Helena (Castellaw)	Juan Fabio	8 Nov 1874
Bexar	RIVAS, Gertrude (See J. A. Chaves)		
Bexar	RIVAS, Josefa (See Marcos E. Flores)		
Victoria	RIVES, James & Mary Louisa (Brown)	Mervin	18 Feb 1875
Caldwell	ROACH, John A. & Mary M.	Mary Malvina	7 Dec 1875
		Absolom W.	26 Oct 1875
Burnet	ROACH, Thos. A. & Ellen	Jessee Mercer	1 Jun 1875
Colorado	ROBERDEAU, J. D. & W. S.	Ney McCormick	19 Apr 1875
DeWitt	ROBERSON, F. M. & E. J.	Joseph W.	12 Sep 1873
Comanche	ROBERSON, W. T. & M. A.	Lee	1 Nov 1875
Caldwell	ROBERTS, B. F. & Josephine	James	18 Nov 1875
Victoria	ROBERTS, C. T. & Melinda (Webb)	Charles Henry	26 Feb 1874
		William George	17 Nov 1875
Caldwell	ROBERTS, D. P. & A. J.	Martha Pearl	19 Mar 1875
Victoria	ROBERTS, E. S. & Rose (Trusselle)	Gertrude Lucile	15 Nov 1873
Hays	ROBERTS, J. C. & Melia H.	Alice M.	2 Feb 1875
Bell	ROBERTS, J. C. & S. E.	Mary L.	7 Sep 1874
		Robert C.	24 Dec 1875
Brazos	ROBERTS, John D. & Eliza	John Dillen	10 Nov 1873
Victoria	ROBERTS, Louisa F. (See Wm. J. Neely)		
Caldwell	ROBERTS, S. G. & F. R.	George M. Amriah	16 Dec 1874
Lee	ROBERTS, Simeon & Sarah	Annie & Allie	11 May 1874
Caldwell	ROBERTS, W. B. & M. C.	James M.	10 Jun 1874
Caldwell	ROBERTS, W. L. & O. J.	Inez	19 Feb 1875

COUNTY	PARENTS	CHILD	DATE
Bell	ROBERTSON, J. J. & J.	Ira Harmon	15 Sep 1874
Lavaca	ROBERTSON, J. T. & N. E.	M. H.	27 Feb 1875
Menard	ROBERTSON, Peter & ??	Sarah Jane	18 Jan 1863
		Lousa (sic) Anna	3 Jun 1867
		Asa	25 Jun 1869
		Ben	23 Nov 1871
		Nancy	8 Feb 1873
Comanche	ROBINSON, A. A. & E. W.	Stephen Wesley	15 Feb 1874
Nacogd.	ROBINSON, C. H. & A. A.	Car McClure	8 Mar 1874
Comanche	ROBINSON, J. A. & V. A.	Daniel	6 Nov 1875
Bell	ROBINSON, J. G. & E. A.	Daniel	6 Nov 1875
Comanche	ROBINSON, J. M. & Lucinda	John Obediah	2 Jan 1875
Brazos	ROBINSON, Nannie A. (See Jno. W. Coulter)		
Comanche	ROBINSON, O. B. & Catherine	Hima Sucinda Jane	11 Aug 1873
Lee	ROBINSON, R. L. & Jennie E.	Sallie Mary	12 Sep 1875
		Nona Brooks	21 Sep 1875
Fayette	ROBINSON, S. A. & J. A.	Samuel Alexander	1 Dec 1873
Comanche	ROBINSON, Williamson & Mary Jane	Laura Priscilla	26 May 1873
Bexar	ROCABERTE, Ygnacia (See Manuel Bartolome)		
Comanche	ROCH, Ed & Mary A.	Barnard Martin	22 Jul 1873
		Dona Emma	19 Sep 1875
Comanche	ROCH, John & Fannie	Katie	23 Mar 1874
Comanche	ROCH, John & Francis (sic) G.	Mary Adaline	30 Oct 1875
Bexar	RODRIQUEZ, Antonia (See Erasmo J. Chaves)		
Bexar	RODRIGUEZ, Domingo & Martina (Dias)	Domingo	29 Jan 1874
DeWitt	ROEDER, Joachim V. & Louise	William L.	11 Mar 1874
		Ludwig R.	30 Jan 1876
Comal	ROEGE, Wilhelmine (See Ferdinand Gobel)		
Bexar	ROESLER, Bertha (See Elias Rouff)		
Bexar	ROESLER, Robert & Pauline	Wm. Adolph	24 Aug 1871
		Gustav Henry	8 Mar 1872
		George Robert	26 Sep 1879
Caldwell	ROGAN, L. W. & Sarah M.	James Theophilus	23 Nov 1874
Caldwell	ROGERS, R. D. & F. H.	Mary Leona	8 Sep 1874
Burnet	ROGERS, Wm. M. & Nancy M.	Manda Ann	19 Nov 1874
Comal	ROHDE, Joseph & Emma (Preusser)	Tony	9 Sep 1878
Austin	ROHRDORF, Louis & Matilda	Nora	31 Jan 1874
Bexar	ROISE, Margarita (See John Wolfram)		
Bexar	ROMPEL, Charles & Paulina (Weilbacher)	Adolph	23 Jul 1874
Bexar	ROMPEL, Edward & Amelia (Waedner)	Henry Adolph	18 Jul 1869
		Emma Louisa	14 Aug 1870
		Amelia Johanna	28 Sep 1871
		Bertha Augusta	11 Oct 1875
Bexar	ROMPEL, Victor & Martha (Martin	Albert Conrad	2 Jun 1874
Bexar	RONNKAMP, Charles & Lina	Johanna	28 Aug 1875
Burnet	ROPER, Wm. D. & Elizabeth	John Edgar	23 Oct 1873
		Harvy Monroe	17 Sep 1875
Bexar	ROPPERTSBARG, Adolfina (See E. Wehrhahn)		
Colorado	ROSE, A. F. & Sophia	Frank	4 Dec 1874
Bell	ROSE, A. J. & S. A.	Austin	No date
Kendall	ROSE, A. P. & Martha P.	Martha	25 Jul 1874
Kendall	ROSE, James H. & Rebecca Ann	Josianer	7 Mar 1874
Kendall	ROSE, Newton & Lieutilda	Noah	9 Mar 1874
Victoria	ROSE, V. J. & Mary L. (Kay)	Mary Lucinda	31 May 1874
Fayette	ROSENBERG, Carl Walter & Franciska Evon	Walter Albert	26 Mar 1874
Travis	ROSENBERG, von, William & Auguste	Carl Wilhelm	13 Jul 1850
		Arthur	1 Sep 1851

COUNTY	PARENTS	CHILD	DATE
Travis	ROSENBERG, von -- Cont.	Ernst	25 Nov 1852
		Paul	10 Aug 1854
		Laura	26 Feb 1856
		Emma	15 May 1857
		Wilhelm	14 Jan 1859
		Anna	10 Oct 1860
		Maria (d. 7 Aug 1864)	
			31 Jan 1863
		Lina	27 Oct 1864
		Friedrich Cal	3 Nov 1866
		Mina Agnes	17 Jan 1869
Fayette	ROSENHAIN, Frederick &		
	Magdalena	George	12 May 1874
Fayette	ROSENTHAL, Isaac & E.	Eprame	7 Oct 1873
Fayette	ROSS, Oscar & ??	Oscar	2 Aug 1874
Hays	ROSS, Robert A. & Mary M.	Rosa Ovilla	13 Aug 1873
		Mary Elizabeth	20 Aug 1875
Bexar	ROSSMAN, Mathew &		
	Mary (Brewer)	Seward W.	11 Jun 1874
Bexar	ROSSY, Charles & Aminda	Charles	21 Jun 1873
Bexar	ROUFF, Elias & Bertha		
	(Roesler)	Rebecca	29 Feb 1876
Bell	ROULETT, J. B. & Elizabeth	Jamed Earnest	29 Sep 1873
Austin	ROUNDTREE, Daniel & Jane	Polly	15 Jul 1875
Bexar	ROWDEN, L. L. (See B. Stephenson)		
Hays	ROWDEN, William C. &		
	Francis	Eugene Green	4 Mar 1874
Comanche	ROWE, D. J. & M. D.	Hill	11 Feb 1875
Caldwell	ROWE, James E. & Nancy E.	Margaret Erma	25 Oct 1874
Hays	ROY, A. J. & Martha M.	Effie Altah	23 Sep 1874
Bexar	ROY, Lucy (See Lawrence Steward)		
Colorado	ROY, Sam & Martha	George	31 Oct 1875
Bell	RUCKER, Ed. T. & Kate S.	Lucie Edith	19 Jul 1874
Bell	RUCKER, P. G. & M. K.	N. M.	2 Jul 1874
Bell	RUCKER, W. T. & Blanche	Mabel	19 Mar 1874
		Mattie Pendleton	5 Apr 1876
Comal	RUDORF, Casimir &		
	Louise (Schmitz)	Carl	4 Apr 1866
Bexar	RUHENTHIN, August & Louisa	Marie	30 Sep 1876
Austin	RUMMEL, August & Mina	Ernst H.	28 Feb 1874
DeWitt	RUMMEL, Chas. & Gustina	Hellena	11 Aug 1876
DeWitt	RUMMEL, Frederick & Emelia	Frederick	28 Aug 1873
Becar	RUMMEL, Fritz &		
	Augusta (Rennert)	Hulda	6 Dec 1870
		Walter	16 Jan 1874
Nacogd.	RUSK, John & Henrietta L.	Harriet H.	23 Oct 1873
Bell	RUSSELL, B. V. & S. E.	Chas. Brumette	24 Jun 1875
Bastrop	RUSSELL, Geo. D. & M. V.	Dallas Clarence	22 Oct 1874
Brazos	RUSSELL, James & Frances	James	1 Mar 1875
Caldwell	RUSSELL, L. & M. L.	Mary Vidin	19 Oct 1874
Bell	RUSSELL, W. S. & E.	Samuel N.	1 Feb 1876
Bexar	RUSSI, Eliza (See Charles A. Bihl)		
Gillespie	RUTTO, John & Hanna	Martha Jane	15 Feb 1875
Medina	SAATHOFF, F. E. & Gertrude	August	23 Jan 1874
		Engelina	19 Nov 1875
Medina	SAATHOFF, M. & Catharine	Jacob	6 Mar 1874
Gillespie	SAGEBIEL, Aug. &		
	Wilhelmine	Sophie	4 Sep 1873
Gillespie	SAGEBIEL, August & Mina	Wilhelm	20 Oct 1875
Bexar	ST. MARTIN, Caroline (See August Krawietz)		
Bexar	ST. MARTIN, Josephine (See Thomas P. McCall)		
Lee	SAMPLE, M. L. & S. G.	Robert Beverly	2 Mar 1874
Lee	SAMS, Moses & Jaine	Susanah	11 Mar 1874
Travis	SANDEL, D. C. & Zerena	Mattie	27 Jan 1874
Lee	SANDERS, Ephraim T. &		
	Elizabeth	Thomas Franklin	29 Jan 1875

COUNTY	PARENTS	CHILD	DATE
Burnet	SANDERS, M. B. & Annie M.	Nellie May	25 Aug 1875
Hays	SANDHER, Henry & Margaret	Soyed	8 Nov 1874
Burnet	SANFORD, J. T. & Nancy	Dick Hay	6 Mar 1874
Bexar	SANG, Mina (See Ed Kotula)		
Gillespie	SANGER, Wm. & Henriette	Lydia	11 Mar 1874
Bexar	SANNEES, Johanuetta (See Raemond Betzer)		
Kendall	SANSOM, Robert G. & Luana V.	Willis J.	22 Oct 1872
Bexar	SANTLEBEN, Aug. &		
	Mary (Opert)	Sophia	21 Sep 1871
		Fred	12 Nov 1872
		Charlotte	12 Apr 1874
Bexar	SAPINGTON, Mille (See Henry James)		
Fayette	SARRAZIN, Joseph & Louise	Elizabeth	16 Jan 1874
Bexar	SARTOR, Jr. Alexander &		
	Charlotte Baxtor (Leighton)	Alexander Leighton	2 Jan 1855
		Charlotte Isabelle	18 Sep 1856
Bexar	SARTOR, Jr. Alexander &		
	Emilie (Diefenbach)	Luise Emma	
		Katharine Adele	22 Jul 1868
		Henry Bismarck	3 Sep 1870
Bexar	SARTOR, Mary (See Lewis Scheihayen)		
Grimes	SATCHER, Sam & Sarah	Henry Thomas	16 Aug 1874
Comal	SATTLER, Caroline (See Enoch Ben George)		
Fayette	SAUER, Charles & Amalie	Edmond	5 Oct 1873
Fayette	SAUER, Fritz & Mary	David	11 May 1873
Kendall	SAUER, P. D. & Sarah Jane	Lizzie Madora	21 Oct 1874
Bell	SAUNDERS, H. B. & A. E.	Imogene Miriam	30 Aug 1875
Kendall	SAUR, Fritz & Mina	Wilhelm	30 Aug 1860
		Louis	11 Mar 1862
		Theodor	22 May 1864
		Lina	20 Dec 1867
		Georg	24 Aug 1872
Bexar	SAUVIGNET, Hy. August &		
	Josephine L. (Rigollot)	Edmond Henry	19 Jul 1874
Bell	SAWYER, A. H. & N. R.	Mary Elizabeth	29 Jun 1874
Bell	SAWYER, C. & A.	Susa Leola	22 Jun 1874
Austin	SAYNER, Samuel & Mynnara	Darwin	15 Jan 1875
Lavaca	SCAGGS, John C. & Clara E.	Johny Victoria	28 Nov 1873
Austin	SCALES, John H. & Jane E.	Joseph Francis	15 Nov 1873
Bastrop	SCARBOROUGH, L. H. & J. F.	W. L.	16 Jun 1874
Bastrop	SCARBROUGH, T. H. & M. E.	John T.	5 Jul 1873
Lee	SCARBOROUGH, W. T. & Arabella	Thomas Lee	12 Aug 1874
Fayette	SCATES, J. R. & M. J.	Edna Lou S.	4 Dec 1874
Bastrop	SCHAEFER, Chas. & Theresa	Friedrich Wilhelm	18 Jul 1874
Bexar	SCHAEFER, John Henry &		
	Minna (Butz)	Maria Charlotte	24 Jun 1874
		Iva Wilhelmine	6 May 1876
Bexar	SCHAEFFER, Margareta (See Joseph Baetz)		
Bexar	SCHAEZLER, Christian &		
	Gertrude (Lieck)	Amalia	13 Jan 1875
Austin	SCHAFFNER, Jacob & Pauline	Frederick	3 Sep 1873
Gillespie	SCHANDNA, Peter & Margarethe	Clara	17 Jul 1873
Lavaca	SCHANECK, John & Gusta	Emma	16 Mar 1874
Austin	SCHARNBORG, Henry & Louisa	Hedwig	4 Jul 1873
Comal	SCHEIBELICH, Minna (Adolph Tausch)		
Medina	SCHEIDEMANTEL, John Charles &		
	Josephine	Mary Louise	14 Nov 1872
		J. Andrew	9 Mar 1875
Bexar	SCHEIHAYEN, Lewis & Mary		
	(Sartor)	Mary	14 Mar 1873
		Dorithe	30 Nov 1874
Bexar	SCHEILER, Helena (See Adolph Schertz)		
Caldwell	SCHEILEY, John & Malinda	Robert Lee	7 Aug 1874
Lee	SCHELLNIK, John & Anna Mary	Anna Edna Rosalea	1873
Victoria	SCHERER, August &		
	Rosina (Brocker)	Henry Franklin	9 May 1873

COUNTY	PARENTS	CHILD	DATE
Comal	SCHERTZ, Alwine (See Carl Wüst)		
Bexar	SCHERTZ, Adolph &		
	Helena (Scheiler)	Willie	26 Mar 1875
Bexar	SCHERTZ, John E. &		
	Louisa (Groos)	Alvine Eliza	30 Dec 1873
Bexar	SCHIFFERS, Peter &		
	Sophie (Wolcken)	Christian Emil	8 Jul 1874
Kendall	SCHILLING, Ernst & Dorothea	Georg	9 Dec 1870
		Carl	2 Mar 1873
		Edward	26 Dec 1874
DeWitt	SCHIWITZ, Fred & Wilhelemene	Hugo	23 Aug 1874
Bandera	SCHLADER, H. & C. M.	Adelhiad	5 Feb 1874
Gillespie	SCHLANDT, Carl & Caroline	Marie	26 Jun 1875
Gillespie	SCHLANDT, John & Sophie	Emma	7 Jul 1874
Comal	SCHLEICHER, August &		
	Johanna (Timmermann)	Emil	1 Aug 1875
Bexar	SCHLEICHER, Augusta (See Rudolph Dresel)		
DeWitt	SCHLEICHER, George &		
	Elizabeth	Fletcher Stockdale	6 Oct 1874
Bexar	SCHLEUNING, Herman &		
	Louise (Hueffneyer)	Hermann	5 Apr 1875
Bexar	SCHLEUNING, Theo. &		
	Bertha (Meyer)	Bertha	1 Aug 1867
		Theodor	21 Aug 1869
		Louis	28 Jul 1871
		Ernst	15 May 1873
		Fred'k. Chas.	26 Jul 1874
		Erhard	3 Apr 1876
		Ferdinand	19 Jun 1879
Comal	SCHLICHTING, Friedrich &		
	Catharina (Sippel)	Catharine Johanna	
		Olga	22 Jul 1874
Comal	SCHLIPPES, Gertrude (See Joseph Benoit)		
Bexar	SCHLODER, Yattie (See E. Weinhold)		
Austin	SCHLOSSER, H. & Annie	Bernhard	28 Sep 1874
Bexar	SCHMELTZER, G. &		
	Emily Victoria (Eckhardt)	Gustavuss Chas.	18 Sep 1867
		Louisa Johanna	14 Mar 1869
		Cesar Edward	1 Nov 1870
		Emily Matilda	28 Aug 1872
		Ida Julia	18 Aug 1874
		Herman William	
		Robert	9 Dec 1875
Bexar	SCHMIDT, Edward &		
	Pauline (Bauer)	Pauline Eva Marie	13 Dec 1874
Kendall	SCHMIDT, Edward & Wilhelmine	Hulda	25 Jul 1874
		Carl	16 Dec 1875
Medina	SCHMIDT, Ehme & Anna	William	27 Nov 1873
		Andje	27 Feb 1876
Comal	SCHMIDT, Ferdinand &		
	Johanna (Triesch)	Anna	25 Jan 1874
Comal	SCHMIDT, Lisette (See Heinrich Carl Rud. von Specht)		
Gillespie	SCHMIDT, Mathias & Julie	Julie Emma	26 Sep 1875
Comal	SCHMIDT, Paul &		
	Auguste (Leitsch)	Emilie	25 Dec 1873
Victoria	SCHMIDT, Johana (See Charles Weber)		
Austin	SCHMIDT, Joseph & Frances	Minna	4 Jul 1875
Austin	SCHMIDTT, Joseph & Francisca	William	8 Jan 1874
Bexar	SCHMITT, Francisca E. (See Thomas B. Leighton)		
Comal	SCHMITZ, Louise (See Casimir Rudorf)		
Comal	SCHNEIDER, Bacha (See F. W. Foerster)		
Austin	SCHNEIDER, Charles & Theresa	Peter Paul	18 May 1873
Bastrop	SCHNEIDER, G. A. & A. M.	Wm. J. G.	28 Oct 1873
Gillespie	SCHNEIDER, Jacob & Louise	Louis	12 Dec 1874
Comal	SCHNEIDNER, Rosa (See Friedrich Kubel)		
Lavaca	SCHNEIDER, William & Caroline	J. W.	Jan 1873

COUNTY	PARENTS	CHILD	DATE
Bexar	SCHNETZ, A. (See N. Z. Petrich)		
Bexar	SCHOLZ, Adolph & Paulina (Alcog)	Emma	12 Oct 1874
Fayette	SCHOLZ, Henry & Louise	Lina	24 Aug 1875
Austin	SCHOLZ, William & Julia	Frederich	5 Feb 1874
		Anna	11 Sep 1875
Colorado	SCHONFELD, D. & Laura	George	14 Mar 1874
		Marion Freddie	18 Mar 1876
Bexar	SCHORF, Louisa (See Peter Ball)		
DeWitt	SCHORLEMMER, Charles &		
	Caroline	Chirstian Wm.	2 Feb 1874
DeWitt	SCHORLEMMER, Henry & Lina	Bertha E. D.	19 Dec 1873
		O. L. W.	8 Oct 1875
Comal	SCHORN, Heinrich Wilhelm &	Adolph	4 Oct 1869
	Magdalena (Hombach)	Theodor	28 Mar 1872
		Emma	7 Mar 1874
Bexar	SCHORRE, Lina (See F. C. Grothaus)		
Lavaca	SCHOTT, Henry & Hermeine	Anna	23 Aug 1873
		Anna	29 Dec 1875
Colorado	SCHOTT, Valentine &		
	Franziska	Justice Henry	20 Jul 1873
		Elise Hermine	28 Nov 1875
Colorado	SCHOTT, Wm. & Bertha	Carl	8 Oct 1874
Comal	SCHRAMM, Edgar Ernst &		
	Tony (Benner)	Paula Emilie	28 Apr 1868
		Gilbert Ernst	20 Aug 1869
		Edgar Ernst	31 Dec 1870
		Herha Edgarda	
		Agnes	14 Jan 1875
		Tony Blanch	5 Nov 1877
Bexar	SCHREINER, Louisa (See Ignacio Morales)		
Lee	SCHROEDER, E. J. & Louisa	Ernst Christian	
		Robert Lee	16 Apr 1874
Austin	SCHROEDER, Frederick &		
	Charlotte	Paul	22 Jul 1876
Austin	SCHROEDER, Fritz & Charlotte	Charlotte Maria	
		Elizabeth	1 May 1874
Bexar	SCHROEDER, Geo &		
	Matilda (Huebner)	Eliza	15 Oct 1874
Austin	SCHROEDER, Joachim & Minna	Charles	2 Nov 1874
Burnet	SCHROETER, August & Hedwig	Irmgard	21 Mar 1875
Austin	SCHUBERT, August & Marie	Charles	23 May 1873
		August	28 Mar 1875
DeWitt	SCHUBOECK, Charles Leopold & ??	Leopoldine	9 Jan 1875
Bexar	SCHUCTE, Mina (See Jacob Winkler)		
Austin	SCHUERER, Charles & Emily	Clotilda	18 Feb 1875
Fayette	SCHUHMANN, G.P. & Augusta	Auguste Pauline	17 Feb 1874
DeWitt	SCHULTZ, Charles & Augusta	Friedrich	4 Aug 1873
Lavaca	SCHULTZ, Chas. & Charlotte	Charlotte	28 Feb 1874
Bexar	SCHULZ, Mary Bollwick (See Christn. Dullnig)		
Comal	SCHULZE, Friedrich &		
	Frederike (Grupe)	Wilhelm	18 Mar 1874
		Ludwig	15 Dec 1875
Gillespie	SCHUMACHER, Gottlieb &		
	Caroline	Emil	5 Sep 1874
Gillespie	SCHUSSLER, Louis & Mina	Henry	13 Dec 1874
Travis	SCHUTZE, Julius & Julia	Adolf	4 Sep 1873
Austin	SCHWANBECK, Christian &		
	Caroline	Chas. Frederick	
		Henry	9 Apr 1874
Lavaca	SCHWARTZ, M. & Sarah	Sam	3 Dec 1874
Kendall	SCHWARZ, Adam & Marie	Albert	8 Jan 1872
		Dorothea	6 Feb 1875
Kendall	SCHWARZ, Mathias &		
	Maria Genoveva	Maria Gertrude	5 Feb 1874
Medina	SCHWERS, Henry & Johanna	Christina Wil'mina	6 Jan 1874
		Henry	8 Jul 1875

COUNTY	PARENTS	CHILD	DATE
Medina	SCHWERS, Heye & Margaretha	Anna Catharine	4 Mar 1875
Medina	SCHWERS, William & Elizabeth	Catharine	3 Mar 1875
Bastrop	SCOTT, Abner & Louisa	David B.	28 Jul 1875
Bandera	SCOTT, J. W. & Malenda	Walter	16 Oct 1875
Hays	SCOTT, Julia (See John Bunton)		
Bell	SCOTT, L. C. & Emily O.	Frederick B.	7 Sep 1874
Kendall	SCOTT, Thomas Jefferson & Laura Eliza	Rosa Jane	6 Feb 1874
Nacogd.	SEALE, J. T. & Mary	Julia	1 Apr 1874
Lee	SEALE, Joseph H. & Francis A.	Susan Frances	22 Feb 1874
Grimes	SEALE, W. H. & Mary E.	John D. H.	23 Oct 1875
Caldwell	SEARCY, O. O. & Ann	Shelby Overton	2 Dec 1874
Austin	SECHTING, August & Marie	Louise	18 Oct 1874
Lavaca	SECREST, W. H. & S. E.	Minnie E.	8 Nov 1874
Comal	SEEKATZ, Auguste (See Gottlieb Elbel)		
Comal	SEEKATZ, Franzisca (See Eduard Naegelin)		
Bexar	SEFFEL, Anton & Anna	Anton	24 Jan 1874
Bexar	SEFFEL, Edward Anton & Susana (Benner)	Eliese	No date
		Hugo	No date
		Edward Frank	No date
Bexar	SEFFEL, Wenzel & Josephine (Keolvassa)	Bernard	11 Jun 1874
Fayette	SEIDEL, Gustav & Louise	Pauline	28 Nov 1866
		Charles	3 Aug 1870
		Emma	2 May 1873
Kendall	SEIDEMANN, Peter & Genoeva	Ferdinand	17 Jan 1870
		Louise	2 May 1871
		Franz	28 Oct 1872
		Anna	4 Aug 1874
Kendall	SEIDENSTICKER, Heinrich & Juliana	Carl	28 Feb 1863
		Fanny	4 Feb 1865
		Louise	15 Feb 1867
		Hedwig	3 Mar 1869
		Otto	22 Mar 1871
		Heinrich	31 Jan 1873
		Juliana	22 Jan 1875
Lee	SEIFERT, J. D. & M.	Dora	2 May 1876
Bexar	SEMLINGER, Henry & Winnifred (Baldwin)	Lydia	17 May 1874
		Charles & Fred'k	9 Dec 1876
Bexar	SENGENBERGER, George & Anna	George	30 Oct 1873
San Saba	SENTERFITT, M.M. & M.C.A.	Reuben S.	12 Aug 1875
		James Franklin	7 May 1876
Kendall	SERGER, E.W. Emil & Marie E. A.	Elise M. H.	24 Jan 1870
		Paul D. E.	26 Mar 1871
		Emil J. B.	13 Jul 1872
		Franz C. R.	11 Jul 1874
Bexar	SETTLES, Cora (See Haywood Boyd)		
Bell	SEWELL, M. B. & S.	Silas Boon	10 Apr 1875
Victoria	SEWELL, Moena (See Truman Phelps, Jr.)		
Fayette	SEYDLER, Frederic & Amalia	Emma	12 Jan 1862
		Lina	11 Jan 1866
		Robert	1 Apr 1868
		Edmund	12 May 1870
		Martha	17 Dec 1872
Gillespie	SEYNER, Johann & Elizabeth	Carie	3 Aug 1873
Hays	SHANE, Oscar G. & Isabella	Anna Lee	6 Mar 1875
		Luneta	15 Aug 1876
Lee	SHAW, James & Courtney Ann	William G.	28 Apr 1875
Bastrop	SHEASLEY, Saml. & F. E.	Florence Idell	16 Feb 1874
Austin	SHELBURNE, James H. & Mary A.	Mary Ann (?)	12 Jul 1873

COUNTY	PARENTS	CHILD	DATE
Austin	SHELBURNE, Wm. L. & Mary C.	Micajah	31 Jul 1874
Lee	SHELTON, C. P. & A. S.	Lena A.	24 Dec 1874
Bastrop	SHEPARD, J. W. & M. E.	F. A.	23 Jun 1875
Bastrop	SHEPARD, John S. & A. M. J.	Mary L.	8 Jan 1874
Bastrop	SHEPHERD, G. F. & Elizabeth	Jourdan	22 Aug 1876
Bastrop	SHEPHERD, J. S. & Anna	J. H.	12 Aug 1876
Bastrop	SHEPHERD, J. W. & Mary E.	Adda	23 Nov 1876
Bandera	SHEPPARD, Wm. A. & Lydia	Asa Frederich	5 Dec 1874
Victoria	SHERER, John & Julia (Golla)	Anna Mary	30 Jul 1873
		Adolph	21 Dec 1874
Bell	SHERMAN, J. O. & M. E.	Perry G.	16 Feb 1874
Victoria	SHERRER, Joseph & Elizabeth (Meiss)	F. Joseph	19 Mar 1871
		Wilhelm	28 Jun 1874
Bexar	SHERRER, Stephen & Agath (Muller)	Maria Rosa	23 Jan 1875
Austin	SHERROD, Caroline (See Adam Davis)		
Austin	SHERROD, W. A. & Cornelia	Edna	17 Mar 1876
Lavaca	SHINER, H. B. & Lonie(?)	Emma May	21 Jan 1875
Bexar	SHINER, Joseph Volney & Irene (Brown)	Joseph Davenport	10 Apr 1876
Lavaca	SHINFILD, John & Matilda	Matilda	3 Apr 1874
Nacogd.	SHIP, Wiley & Maria	Chedrick M.	7 Jan 1874
Bell	SHIRES, G. C. & Bettie	Joshua Alfred	10 Aug 1875
Caldwell	SHOAF, George C. & Betty C.	Henry George	17 Jan 1875
Comanche	SHOCKLEY, A. P. & E. A.	Olive Rebecca	10 Aug 1873
Bexar	SHOEMAN, Frederick & Mary (Woolfert)	Lina	9 Jul 1875
DeWitt	SHORT, P. P. & J. A.	Joe Preston	30 Aug 1874
Kendall	SHORT, Thomas & Margaret E.	Frank Lee	23 Dec 1873
DeWitt	SHOWS(?), Adam & Christener (sic)	James Madison	30 Sep 1873
Victoria	SHRY, William & Annie F. (Baggett)	Lilias Gregg	3 Jul 1873
Lavaca	SHUTZ, Wm. & Susan	Charles	4 Mar 1874
Bexar	SIBERT, C. M. (See F. Mc. C. Newton)		
Lavaca	SIDNEY, Essex & Candess	Wm. Butler	8 Dec 1873
Bexar	SIELHER, Wilhelma Sophie (See Franz Joseph Ludwig)		
Bexar	SIEMERING, Anna (See Frederick Groos)		
Hays	SIES, John & Zilla	Texana (sic)	30 Feb 1873
		John Westley	3 Jan 1875
Victoria	SIFFERMAN, Mary (See Baldy Luder)		
Lee	SIKES, W. A. & M. C.	Lena Bertha	18 Feb 1876
Victoria	SILVERSTUN, Adelein (See Daniel Alexander)		
Bastrop	SIMMONS, B. P. & M. H.	Wm. H.	6 Jan 1874
Bell	SIMMONS, J. M. & Martha E.	G. H.	18 Oct 1874
Lavaca	SIMMONS, J. P. & Fannie	Vincent	15 May 1874
Austin	SIMMONS, John R. & Phillepena	Anna Phillepena	12 Dec 1874
Brazos	SIMNS, W. K. & Mary S.	Huey Lee	9 Aug 1873
		Ida Lillian	9 Mar 1875
Comal	SIMON, Ferdinand & Marie (Oelkers)	Lidia & Thekla	10 Sep 1873
Bell	SIMPSON, J. H. & A. F.	James A.	4 Jan 1874
Nacogd.	SIMPSON, Martin & Martha	Jeff	5 Dec 1873
Fayette	SIMS, Frederic & Emma	Dietrich	12 Mar 1874
Nacogd.	SIMS, J. L. & Mary Ann	Tally Ann	4 Jan 1874
Bell	SIMS, L. G. & S. S.	Lewis G.	18 May 1873
Brazos	SIMS, M. W. & T. F.	Laura Wilson	19 Sep 1873
Burnet	SINGLETON, J. L. & Emily C.	Emory	2 Dec 1874
Brazos	SINUS, G. W. & ??	Lula	17 May 1876
Comal	SIPPEL, Catharina (See Friedrich Schlighting)		
Comal	SIPPEL, Johann & Johanna (Gruene)	Henry Ernst	23 Oct 1874
Victoria	SITTERLE, Blaise & Haide (Volder)	Louis	9 Dec 1874

COUNTY	PARENTS	CHILD	DATE
Victoria	SITTERLE, Louis & Catherine (Timble)	Victor	28 Sep 1874
Victoria	SITTERLE, Mary Louisa (See Herman A. Neumeyer)		
Victoria	SITTERLE, Sophia (See John Fay)		
Travis	SJOBERG, Herman & Martha	John Herbert	2 Jul 1873
Victoria	SKAGGS, Mary (See Richard S. Chapley)		
Nacogd.	SKILLERN, James S. & Eliza	James A.	17 May 1874
Nacogd.	SKILLERN, Radford B. & Nancy J.	William A.	12 Nov 1873
Nacogd.	SKILLERN, Wm. A. & P. M.	John R.	23 Feb 1875
Lavaca	SLAUGHTER, R. & E.	Geo.	25 Jul 1874
San Saba	SLOAN, T. A. & Emma	Laura R.	22 Apr 1875
San Saba	SLOAN, Wm. P. & Lucinda L.	Sarah Elizabeth	28 Nov 1874
Bexar	SMALL, Wm. & Eliza (Feldtmann)	Matilda	19 Feb 1874
Bexar	SMALLWOOD, Lucy (See George Miller)		
Nacogd.	SMELLEY, J. E. & Emaline J.	Rosana E.	7 Apr 1874
		John W.	16 Apr 1876
Nacogd.	SMELLEY, W. M. & Lucinda	(Twins) Wm. D. & Margret R.	22 Mar 1875
Bell	SMITH, A. F. & M. E.	Alma Eschol	11 Jul 1873
Hays	SMITH, Charles & Mary Ann	Anthony	25 Feb 1875
Lee	SMITH, Christopher Columbus & Amanda M.	Columbus Seaborn	5 Sep 1875
Lavaca	SMITH, E. M. & L. C.	Sumpter	9 Oct 1873
Lavaca	SMITH, Eli & Lydia	Wm.	15 Jun 1876
Bexar	SMITH, Elijah B. & Viney H. (Hester)	David	10 Sep 1873
		Minnie Lee	12 Jan 1875
Fayette	SMITH, F. M. & Mary A.	Trumann M.	5 Aug 1873
Bandera	SMITH, George F. & Isabella	James Herbert	29 Oct 1874
DeWitt	SMITH, H. N. & E. A.	George Henry	14 Sep 1874
Austin	SMITH, J. B. & Clara	Oscar Lougee	3 Mar 1876
Comanche	SMITH, J. E. & Hattie	William Robert	3 Sep 1874
Travis	SMITH, J. F. & Laura M.	Walter Franklin	23 Jun 1874
Bell	SMITH, J. Z. T. & M. E.	Cicero Prentice	6 Jun 1875
Bastrop	SMITH, James & Ann A.	James Edward	9 Nov 1873
Lavaca	SMITH, James & Cloey	Laura	2 Aug 1874
		Minnie	20 Mar 1876
Hays	SMITH, James A. & Rue Ann	Lula Etta	3 Apr 1874
Bexar	SMITH, James S. & Sarah(Carothers)	Hulda S.	3 May 1874
Bexar	SMITH, Joseph & Eliza L.	Albert Sidney	20 May 1873
Bexar	SMITH, Lucinda E. (See. H. M. Newton)		
Bastrop	SMITH, M. A. & Caroline	Geo. A.	7 Aug 1873
Austin	SMITH, Mike & Annie	Mary E.	11 Dec 1874
Hays	SMITH, P. J. C. & M. E.	Johnny Mary	2 Sep 1879
Lee	SMITH, Pryton R. & Martha J.	Seth Elbert	2 Feb 1875
Travis	SMITH, R. B. & Mary E.	Myrtie H.	6 Jul 1874
Caldwell	SMITH, Robt. & Fanny L.	Crawford L.	9 Dec 1874
Caldwell	SMITH, W. C. & Edney	William C.	11 Nov 1874
Caldwell	SMITH, W. K. & M. L.	Della Docenia	10 May 1874
Caldwell	SMITH, W. R. & Melissa	E. P.	18 Jan 1876
Bastrop	SMITH, Wm. C. & Anna M.	Buford A.	18 Dec 1876
Burnet	SMITHHART, Miles A. & Nancy A.	Dora Lee	11 Feb 1874
		Nannie Alice	6 May 1876
Bexar	SMYLIE, Mary A. (See Junius Means)		
Bastrop	SMYTHIA, H. M. & Jane	James L.	6 Jan 1874
Bell	SNEAD, A. H. & L. V. B.	Margaret Bridges	7 Jul 1874
Bexar	SOLMS, Otto & Sophia (Maxfeld)	Otto Gustav	24 Jan 1877
		Hermina	28 Apr 1879
Bexar	SOOKENS, Gabriel & Mary Taylor)	Cora	10 Apr 1874

COUNTY	PARENTS	CHILD	DATE
Bexar	SORGE, Henrietta (See William H. Bitters)		
Bastrop	SORRELL, W. L. & E. D.	Hester	20 Jan 1874
Bastrop	SORRELLS, M. & D. P.	Fanny	4 Mar 1874
Bexar	SOUTER, Christian & Johanna (Crawley)	John Stephen	17 Sep 1873
Bexar	SOUZA, Isabelle (See Leon Moke)		
Bexar	SOWA, John & Amelia (Loworka)	Hedwig Teresa	5 Oct 1874
Comal	SPANGENBERG, Sophie (See Bernhard Kuhn)		
Colorado	SPANN, G. C. & Nancy A.	Eason Andrew	12 Mar 1875
Lee	SPARKS, W. A. & M. S.	Thurston Ross	21 Jan 1875
Austin	SPATES, Robert & Zella	Price	17 Apr 1875
Austin	SPATES, Thomas & Hattie	Elias	12 Apr 1875
Bastrop	SPAULDING, Wm. & Sallie (Mexican)	Vieliana	9 Aug 1874
Lavaca	SPEAKARMANN, David & A. E.	J. E.	12 Nov 1873
Lavaca	SPEARY, John & Matilda	Mina	6 Nov 1873
Comal	SPECHT, Heinrich Carl Rud. von & Lisette (Schmidt)	Elise Natalie	14 May 1854
		Bertha Marie	9 Feb 1856
		Hedwig Minna	18 Oct 1858
		Ida Antonie	10 Dec 1859
		Hans Erich	23 May 1862
		Rudolph Carl	10 Mar 1868
		Ottilie Clara	4 Jun 1871
		Max August	9 Jun 1875
Hays	SPENCE, Henry & Mary Ann	Mary Etta	17 Mar 1873
		James Henry	28 Jun 1875
Burnet	SPENCER, E. L. & Fanny	Francis M.	25 Jun 1875
Burnet	SPENCER, J. W. & Sarah	Wm. Laswell	23 Oct 1874
Comal	SPIESS, Molly Catharina (See F. Hermann Heffter)		
Bastrop	SPITLER, Wm. M. & Sarah	Ruth	6 Apr 1875
Bell	SPOONTZ, W. W. & L. C.	Laura Emma	8 May 1874
Austin	SPRAIN, Henry & Henriette	Ida	Aug 1874
Austin	SPRINGFIELD, Wm. L. & Mary (Matthews)	William	25 May 1873
Bexar	SPROUL, Wm. W. & Margaret E. (Edins)	Robert Augustin	26 May 1874
Comal	STAATS, Emilie (See Eilhelm Geue)		
Caldwell	STAGNER, J. N. & Luella	Robert Tyre	9 Jul 1875
Travis	STALNAKER, J. W. & A. B.	Anna Rebecca	2 Feb 1875
Bastrop	STANDIFER, J. E. & F. A.	Alzada	20 Nov 1873
Bexar	STANDON, Emma (See Thomas Joseph)		
Bexar	STANDT, George & Sophie	Friedricke	13 Aug 1874
Gillespie	STANDT, Peter A. & Mina	Henry	21 Feb 1874
		Johann	29 Jan 1876
Bexar	STANFIELD, J. C. & T. A. (Nuckolls)	Hugh Baylor	Jun 1874
DeWitt	STANFORD, J. M. & Emilia	Margaret E.	26 Aug 1873
Burnet	STANLEY, W. P. & N. E.	Jackson	20 Dec 1875
Bexar	STANISH, Josephine (Henry Collmann)		
Hays	STAPLES, Thomas J. & Louisa	Margaret L.	13 Jul 1873
Comal	STARTZ, Caroline (See Emil Von Bose)		
Victoria	STAPP, Haidee (See Sol Halfin)		
Bexar	STAPPER, Adelaide (See Edmund Pfeil)		
Bexar	STAPPER, Robert & Elisa	Oscar	15 Dec 1876
Austin	STECK, Edwd. & Marie	Henrietta Berta	30 Apr 1873
Fayette	STEELE, J. S. & M. E.	John Noble	15 Mar 1874
Fayette	STEELE, W. H. & H.	Etta	31 Dec 1874
Caldwell	STEELEDON, W. M. & Rosa M.	Mary Sue	4 Sep 1875
Nacogd.	STEEN, James & Sarah L.	Jackolina	5 Apr 1875
Hays	STEIN, Alfred Vom & Charlotte	Alfred Vom Jr.	11 May 1876
Austin	STEIN, Henry & Marie	Emma Caroline Marie	2 Mar 1875
Bexar	STEINER, Jette (See F. Mayer)		
Gillespie	STENDEBACH, Anton & Catharine	Anna	1 Feb 1875

COUNTY	PARENTS	CHILD	DATE
Kendall	STENDEBACH, John F. & Cathrine	Wm. P.	7 Nov 1854
		Anna Barbara	4 Feb 1860
		August	11 Aug 1866
		Maria	17 Oct 1868
		Geo. Washington	23 Feb 1871
		Emma	8 Jul 1873
		Caroline	22 Sep 1875
DeWitt	STEPHAN, Christian & W.	Herman	27 May 1873
Bell	STEPHENS, E. S. & M. L.	Melinda	4 Nov 1874
Comanche	STEPHENS, John W. & Ann Eliza	John Baptist	23 Jan 1874
Lee	STEPHENS, T. A. & M. D.	Richard Lee	6 Oct 1874
Bexar	STEPHENSON, B. & L. L. (Rowden)	Dudley Gilland	7 Sep 1873
DeWitt	STEPHENSON, H. J. & Martha	William White	6 Aug 1874
		Areadana	12 Sep 1876
Austin	STERNENBERG, F. W. & Pauline B.	Wm. Frederick	22 Aug 1875
Travis	STERZING, Fred & Anges	Fred Herbert	23 Jul 1875
Comal	STEUER, Heinrich & Dorothea (Dreyer)	Sophie Auguste	15 Aug 1873
Bandera	STEVENS, Henry & Margaret	Mitty Dell	26 Nov 1874
Austin	STEVENS, Janes E. & Fannie A.	Thomas Lewis	10 Nov 1874
Bandera	STEVENS, Thomas M. & Margaret	Quill Lyson(?)	2 Dec 1874
Bexar	STEWARD, Lawrence & Lucy (Roy)	Francis Veste	24 Nov 1874
Comanche	STEWART, A. J. & A. T. C.	William Jackson	20 Sep 1873
		George Pierce	23 Sep 1875
Burnet	STEWART, C. C. & Marian W.	William Franklin	11 Dec 1874
Burnet	STEWART, J. L. & Martha J.	Holly Hudson	30 Mar 1874
Brazos	STEWART, J. R. & Mary S.	Henry M.	19 Sep 1874
Comanche	STEWART, J. S. & Lucretia	Nancy Elizabeth	6 Apr 1873
Burnet	STEWART, John G. & Amanda	Robert Lee	25 Oct 1874
Burnet	STEWART, Samuel K. & Mary E.	Arthur Bowman	18 Jan 1875
Medina	STIEGLER, Gottlieb & Johanna	Louis William	14 Jan 1874
Burnet	STILES, S. T. & Francis M.	Wm. Virgil	18 Nov 1873
		Sidney	29 Mar 1875
Victoria	STILL, Hiram & Eliza	Mary	11 Jul 1873
Lavaca	STINCHCOMB, J. D. & C.	Malcolm	16 Jun 1873
Burnet	STINNETT, A. & Sarah E.	Nancy Jane	19 Oct 1874
Burnet	STINNETT, Geo. M. & N. J.	Florence M.	27 Aug 1874
Bell	STITH, C. H. & M. L.	Marucs	29 Nov 1875
Lavaca	STOCKTON, T. J. & Lucy M.	David A.	30 Nov 1874
Austin	STOKES, James P. & Mary M.	Mary Ella	7 Feb 1874
	(1875 Entry reads James P. & Melissa M.)	John Walter	17 Jul 1875
Travis	STOKES, John F. & Julia	Agnes Augusta	30 Jul 1873
		John Fernando	11 Mar 1875
Lee	STOKES, R. & Anna	William	Feb 1874
Austin	STOKES, Washington & Sallie	Sylvia	21 Oct 1874
Comal	STOLTE, Caroline (See Heinrich Wetz)		
Austin	STOLTZE, Houston & Mary	Rudolph	12 Jul 1874
Austin	STONE, Jr., A. B. & Mollie O.	James William	27 Jan 1874
Comanche	STONE, A. L. & E. E.	Laura Bama	24 Jul 1873
Caldwell	STONE, C. W. & M. E.	Charles Austin	6 Mar 1875
Nacogd.	STONE, James & Martha Susan	Katie Jane	No date
Comanche	STONE, R. & H. S.	Bertie Lee	13 Feb 1875
Nacogd.	STONE, S. H. & Sultania	Martha S.	29 Jun 1876
Comanche	STONE, W. A. & Sarah	Harvey Monroe Wesley	5 Sep 1873
Bell	STONE, W. G. W. & Sarah A.	Sallie	20 May 1873

73

COUNTY	PARENTS	CHILD	DATE
Bexar	STORBECK, Robert & Lena (Jagge)	Emelia	14 May 1862
		Julia	19 Jun 1865
		Robert	2 Jan 1873
Hays	STOREY, Jas. G. & Sallie B.	Lellia Lou	18 Jun 1875
Caldwell	STOREY, L. J. & Lou J.	Stella Lee	9 Jun 1874
Bexar	STORMS, Gerard & Auguste (Pape)	Arthur	17 Sep 1873
		Gerard Fred	26 Jun 1875
Burnet	STOUT, S. S. & Alice	Lucy	15 Jun 1875
Lee	STOVALL, A. A. & ??	Joseph S.	26 Dec 1874
Hays	STOVEALL, William B. & Minerva J.	Andrew Marvin	11 Jun 1874
Gillespie	STRACKBEIN, Christian & Catharine	Maria	19 Oct 1874
Travis	STRAHLEY, Andrew & Anna	Susan Augusta	14 May 1874
Bexar	STRANDT, M. Anna (See F. Ignace Meyer)		
Bexar	STRASSER, Emelia (See Chas. F. Ziegler)		
Bastrop	STRAUS, W. O. & H.	Carrie	Sep
Austin	STRAUSS, Henry & Emma	Richard	3 Jan 1876
Lavaca	STREICH, T. H. & M. L.	Thos. H.	9 Aug 1874
Gillespie	STRIEGLER, Ove & Anna	Robert	1 Mar 1874
Travis	STROETER, Ernst F. & Carrie G.	Luella Elizabeth	25 Aug 1875
Kendall	STROHACKER, Conrad & Anna	Emilie	19 Apr 1876
Kendall	STROHACKER, Louis & Juliana	Oscar Heinrich	21 Jun 1872
Bexar	STROMEYER, Mary (See Leopold Langwell)		
Bexar	STRON, Sarah (See Louis Bernheim)		
Burnet	STROUP, John E. & Lena B.	Jenny Veav	3 Sep 1874
Bexar	STROYHMEYER, Josephine (See Henry Borchers)		
DeWitt	STRUEBER, A. & Mary	Gustave	26 Mar 1875
Burnet	STRUVE, Armand & Christiane	Henry	30 Jul 1874
		Stephen Louis	22 May 1876
Travis	STUBBS, B. J. & Minerva	Thomas Nicholas	14 Jun 1873
DeWitt	STUBER, Charles & Mary	Caroline	26 Nov 1873
Bexar	STUBING, Mathilda (See Henry Grote)		
Bexar	STUDER, Benedict & Dorotea (Trwlick)	Ida	1 Jun 1875
Bexar	STUMBERY, George B. & Dora	Herman D.	31 Aug 1874
Bell	STURDEVANT, A. H. & N. R.	Ida Gray	22 Sep 1873
	(Twins)	Ira Randolph	22 Sep 1873
Bell	STURDIVANT, G. T. & S. M.	R. L.	13 May 1874
Victoria	STURGESS, M. (See F. A. Turner)		
Victoria	STURGESS, Mssie (See F. A. Fenner)		
Bell	STUTON, W. A. & M. A.	Uler Wilhite	2 Nov 1874
Burnet	STYRE, D. N. & N. D. (or S.	Nora V.	23 Sep 1873
Comal	SUCHE, Moritz & Louise (Hoerhold)	Karl	20 Jul 1866
		Louise	14 Nov 1867
		Edward	25 Jul 1869
Comanche	SUGGS, Wm. & Catharine	William Seleros(?)	4 Aug 1874
Caldwell	SULLIVAN, B. F. & E. M.	Lou Ella	14 Mar 1875
DeWitt	SULLIVAN, Geo H. & Phillis	Maria	19 Oct 1873
		William	10 Nov 1874
Caldwell	SULLIVAN, J. W. & M. J. J.	Margaret J.	25 Mar 1874
Bexar	SULNON, Sala & Rosa (Friedlander)	Max	4 Feb 1871
		Rebecca	5 Feb 1873
		Estella	1 Dec 1874
Travis	SUMMERROW, M. P. & N. A.	Kate	28 Oct 1873
Bell	SUPPLE, J. B. B. & M. F. (T)	James	27 Jul 1873
Hays	SUTOR, M. Martin & Mattie A.	Mary Belle	28 Aug 1875
Caldwell	SWEARINGEN, Jesse & A. M.	Jesse Morgan	24 May 1873
Caldwell	SWEARINGEN, John & Mary M.	Matilda Elizabeth	4 May 1875

COUNTY	PARENTS	CHILD	DATE
Bexar	SWEENEY, J. B. & Mary (Johnson)	Charlotte Pudenciana	14 Sep 1873
Travis	SWISHER, John Milton & Nellie	Annie Elise	13 Oct 1873
Austin	SWITZER, H. C. & Eustacia	Salome	No date
Travis	SWOFFORD, John & Mary Susan	Ann Mandy	30 Oct 1873
	(1875 Entry sepelled Swoford)	Lena	26 Mar 1875
Austin	SYLVESTUS, August & Harriet	August	7 Jul 1875
Bexar	SYMINGTON, Robert C. & Virginia (Byrn)	Edith Crawford	27 Jun 1872
		Robert Byrn	27 Nov 1874
Bell	SYPERT, J. M. & Virginia C.	Texana D.	1873
Bell	SYPERT, Wm. R. & Etna	Jefferson R.	21 Jan 1875
Lavaca	TADLOCK, S. & Aurila	Ida M.	22 Oct 1874
Caldwell	TALLEY, J. R. & M. A.	Fred H.	4 Jan 1876
Hays	TANNER, Solomon & Cynthia A.	Daniel P.	29 Apr 1874
Bell	TARVER, L. K. & A. J.	Edward Morris	20 Sep 1874
Comanche	TATE, Robt. & Julia Ann	Laura	17 Aug 1873
Lee	TATE, Turner & Elizabeth	James William	19 Jul 1875
Gillespie	TATSCH, Adam & Louise	Caroline	4 May 1874
		Anna Emilie	23 Apr 1875
Gillespie	TATSCH, Julius & Wilhelmine	Ernst	12 May 1874
Gillespie	TATSCH, Peter & Conradine	Heinrich	15 Sep 1874
Fayette	TAUCH, Henry & Augusta	Emma	13 Dec 1858
		Wilhelm	2 Feb 1859
		Ida	27 Nov 1861
		Hermann	2 Nov 1863
		Henry	11 Jan 1865
		Agnes	11 Jan 1865
		Bettie	20 Oct 1866
		Emil	7 Sep 1868
		Charles	27 Dec 1869
		Paul	27 Feb 1872
	(Twins)	Albert	4 Jun 1874
		Olga	4 Jun 1874
Brazos	TAULMAN, J. A. & Emma J.	Joseph Edwin	18 Jul 1867
		Oscar Evan	4 Aug 1868
		Julia Laura Pearl	20 Jun 1875
Comal	TAUSCH, Adolph & Minna (Scheibelich)	Ada	22 Jan 1873
		Antonio	21 Mar 1875
		Nelda	22 Mar 1876
Bexar	TAUSH, Emelia (See Christian Zizlemann)		
Brazos	TAYLOR, ?? & ??	Lizzir Missie	30 May 1876
Caldwell	TAYLOR, B. T. & M. A.	John Hugh	13 Jan 1875
Hays	TAYLOR, Benjamin W. & Mary	John Melvin	3 Aug 1873
San Saba	TAYLOR, J. A. & N. E.	William O.	5 Jan 1875
San Saba	TAYLOR, John A. & Artemissa	John A.	9 Mar 1874
Nacogd.	TAYLOR, L. S. & Harriet D. (Irvin)	Lawrence Sterne	4 Jun 1873
		Robert Irion	9 Sep 1875
Bexar	TAYLOR, Lina (See John Thomas)		
Bexar	TAYLOR, Mary (See Gabriel Sookens)		
Bandera	TAYLOR, R. M. & N. J.	Walter Hugh	22 Apr 1874
Comanche	TAYLOR, Wm. & Julia A.	Harvey Walter	12 Mar 1874
Medina	TAYLOR, William C. & Sarah E.	James Edward	20 Sep 1875
Lee	TEAGUE, W. P. & A. M.	Dick Francis	27 Jul 1874
Victoria	TEAL, Julia (See M. Murphy)		
Bexar	TEEL, T. T. & Emily F. (Wynans)	Catharine	1874
Fayette	TEICHMULLER, H. & Augusta	Anna	Oct 1871
Lee	TEINERT, Ernst & Magdalina	Bernath	
Lee	TEINERT, John & Ann	John Ernst Ferchtegoth	11 Apr 1873
		Emma Theresia	
		Johanna Magdalena	7 Aug 1875

COUNTY	PARENTS	CHILD	DATE
Bastrop	TEMPLETON, Ben P. & Addie	Lee Brooks	6 Mar 1874
Bexar	TENGG, Nicolas &		
	Louise (Plumeyer)	Julius	15 Feb 1867
		Anna	15 Jul 1869
	(Note: Later entry dated as 15 Feb 1872)		
		Nicolas	16 Feb 1872
		Thomas	13 Nov 1874
		William	7 Aug 1877
DeWitt	TERRY, J. A. & Julia A.	Lula	4 Jul 1873
DeWitt	TERRY, J. D. & Kate	A. M.	25 Aug 1875
Austin	TESCH, Chas. & Charlotte	William	4 Jul 1873
Austin	TESCH, Louis & Bertha	Louisa	20 Jun 1874
Bexar	TEST, Mary (See Aaron Pancost)		
Nacogd.	TEUTSCH, Lewis & Rebecca C.	Clara O.(?)	4 Apr 1874
Nacogd.	TEUTSCH, Robert & Sarah	William R.	1 Aug 1874
Burnet	THACKSTON, H. C. & H. C.	Edward Oscar	31 Dec 1874
Lavaca	THAMES, J. C. & Mary A.	James H.	25 Feb 1874
Fayette	THAULEMEYER, F. & B.	Martha	16 Mar 1875
Kendall	THEIS, Henry & Johanne	Bruna Henry	2 Nov 1874
		Helene Johanne	15 Jun 1876
		Hilmar Friedrich	No date
Kendall	THEIS, Jacob & Wilhelmine	Robert	21 Jun 1861
		Anna	1 Mar 1865
		Emma	7 Jul 1867
		Rudolph	28 Feb 1869
		Alma	4 Apr 1871
		Lina	16 Jul 1873
Austin	THIELAN, R. & ??	Anna	13 Aug 1874
Comanche	THIGPIN, N. J. & Ella	Jas. Nathaniel	11 May 1875
Burnet	THOMAS, E. F. & Elvira	Kate	22 Mar 1874
Austin	THOMAS, E. R. & Mittie (Veal)	Sallie Wolcott	16 May 1876
Colorado	THOMAS, F. & Rhode	Lizzie	29 Jan 1875
Brazos	THOMAS, J. B. & Lullie E.	Annie Lee	19 Oct 1876
Bell	THOMAS, J. C. & M. M.	Valera Estella	31 Dec 1874
Brazos	THOMAS, J. D. & Sarah F.	Bruce	28 Feb 1874
Lavaca	THOMAS, J. H. & Frances E.	Elona D.	7 Nov 1873
Nacogd.	THOMAS, J. H. & Ella E.	Leon	15 Jul 1873
Lee	THOMAS, James & Eliza	Tempe	8 Feb 1874
Bexar	THOMAS, John & Lina (Taylor)	Willie	5 Mar 1874
Victoria	THOMAS, Peter &		
	Mary (Walker)	Alfred Thomas	12 Nov 1872
Hays	THOMAS, Robert & Elizabeth	Joshua	8 Apr 1873
Nacogd.	THOMAS, S. B. & ??	Samuel	No date
Nacogd.	THOMAS, S. B. & Mary E.	Robert L.	24 Dec 1873
Caldwell	THOMAS, T. & Jane K.	Willie F.	23 Nov 1874
Nacogd.	THOMASON, J. H. & Elizabeth	James Robert	Feb 1875
Nacogd.	THOMASON, Robert & M. A.	Harvy Lafayette	18 Oct 1873
Nacogd.	THOMASON, William A. &		
	Martha J.	Edna J.	28 Aug 1873
Menard	THOMERSON, D. P. & M. P.	S. H.	23 Jun 1862
		R. S.	23 Aug 1866
		A. P.	6 Nov 1868
		A. B.	16 Apr 1870
		C. A.	10 Feb 1873
Bexar	THOMPSON, Annie (See M. H. Bradford)		
Bell	THOMPSON, C. B. & V.	Robt. E. Lee	3 Nov 1873
		Bettie A.	26 Apr 1875
Lavaca	THOMPKINS, Chas. & Julia F.	Frances E.	17 Oct 1873
Bell	THOMPSON, D. P. & M. J.	Martha E.	8 Jan 1874
Austin	THOMPSON, Frederick &		
	Christiana	Augusta	5 Aug 1874
Bell	THOMPSON, J. Q. & M.	John Newton	8 Mar 1874
DeWitt	THOMPSON, S. J. & Mary Ann	John Anderson	25 Oct 1875
Burnet	THOMPSON, Wm. R. &		
	Sophronia C.	William L.	19 Sep 1874
Nacogd.	THORN, C. H. & M. A.	Charles E.	29 Mar 1876

COUNTY	PARENTS	CHILD	DATE
Lavaca	THORNTON, Ben & Mary	Elija	28 Mar 1874
Colorado	THORNTON, Richad A. & Mattie	John Francis	12 May 1873
		Lyle Guinn	14 Oct 1874
Bexar	THRALL, Frances L. (See W. R. Gibson)		
Bastrop	THRASHER, T. J. & M. E.	Samuel Robert	8 Dec 1873
Travis	THURMAN, H. G. & M. C.	Mary Caroline	28 Dec 1873
Travis	THURMAN, Thomas & Malissa	Charles Andrew	14 May 1874
Victoria	THURMOND, C. L. &		
	Margaret A. (McGrew)	George Murat	14 Dec 1873
DeWitt	TIETZ, Lebrecht & Mathilda	Mathilda	3 Sep 1873
Caldwell	TILLER, Alex & Alice Belle	George Benton	6 Nov 1874
Victoria	TIMBLE, Catherine (See Louis Sitterle)		
Comal	TIMMERMANN, Friederike (See Christian Hansmann)		
Comal	TIMMERMANN, Johanna (See August Schleicher)		
Nacogd.	TINDALL, John E. & Mary E.	Wm. R.	20 Aug 1874
Colorado	TINKLER, J. W. & Izora E.	Jesse	12 Oct 1874
Bastrop	TINNIN, John & Eliza	Granville	10 Feb 1874
Nacogd.	TINSLEY, Simon & Ann	Melvina	15 Nov 1873
Comal	TIPS, Julius & Anan (Peltzer)	Alfred	15 Aug 1866
Burnet	TOBEY, Samuel & Martha E.	Mary Frances	22 Mar 1866
Bexar	TOBIN, Chaney (See Aaron Anderson)		
Bell	TOBLER, Julius & Julia (Twins)	Julius & Henry	5 Jun 1875
		Nannie Rebecca	25 Nov 1874
		Mamy Amanda	24 Aug 1876
Kendall	TOEPPERWEIN, E. A. F. &		
	Johanne	Adolph	17 Oct 1869
		Clara	27 Oct 1874
Kendall	TOEPPERWEIN, Gustav A. &		
	Charlotte	Emma Marie	14 Aug 1868
		Arnold Sophus	1 Feb 1870
		Alma Charlotte	10 May 1872
		Hedwig Wilhelmina	19 Feb 1875
Colorado	TOLAND, Ed. & Nellie	Samuel	9 Nov 1874
Colorado	TOLIVER, J. A. & E. F.	John F.	7 Oct 1875
Colorado	TOLIVER, John D. & E. H.	Annie Pearl	2 Jan 1873
		Jessie Dale	1 Jan 1875
Medina	TOMERLIN, W. J. & Elizabeth	Samuel C.	21 Feb 1875
		William J.	21 Feb 1875
Bexar	TOMPKINS, M. E. (See S. G. Newton)		
Bexar	TORES, Susan (See Burton Wilkins)		
Travis	TOWNSEND, A. B. &		
	Caroline (Twins)	Charlie & George	20 Aug 1873
Travis	TOWNSEND, Drewry & Naricopa	Mary	4 Sep 1873
Comanche	TOWNSEND, J. V. & Sarah A.	John Samuel	21 Sep 1873
Hays	TOWNSEND, Samuel L. &		
	Mary E.	Zula	5 Apr 1874
Gillespie	TRACHNORO, August & Albertine	Ida Anna	20 Dec 1876
Caldwell	TRAMMEL, Wm. F. & Lizzie	Dorah Cardelia	20 Oct 1875
Austin	TRAVICK, Frank & Mary	Rosa	1 Jan 1875
Comanche	TRAWEEK, A. I. & G. F.	Albert Carroll	1 Dec 1875
Bell	TRAYLER, J. T. & M. J.	Alverta	1 Nov 1873
Lavaca	TRAYLOR, R. B. & Mary E.	Benj. K.	6 Feb 1874
Gillespie	TREIBS, Jacob & Catharine	Otto	30 Apr 1876
DeWitt	TRENCK, F. P. & Minna	Louis	19 Aug 1873
		Edwin	1 Oct 1874
Austin	TRENCKMANN, Anna F. (See Fritz Engelking)		
Bexar	TREUER, Joseph & Annie		
	(Baumberger)	Amelia	6 May 1874
		Daniel	31 Mar 1875
Comal	TRIESCH, Adolph &		
	Ernestine (Wallhoefer)	Otto	5 May 1873
		Albert	5 May 1873
Comal	TRIESCH, Johanna (See Ferdinand Schmidt)		
Gillespie	TRIESS, C. F. & Dina	Hulda	6 Feb 1876
Bell	TRIMMIER, T. J. & L. R.	Paul August	3 Dec 1874
San Saba	TROWBRIDGE, B. & A. M.	Mary A.	22 Apr 1875

COUNTY	PARENTS	CHILD	DATE
Burnet	TRUE, L. P. & Mary E.	Philipp Shilo	8 Apr 1874
Fayette	TRUESDALE, Jim & Ann	Dora	1 Apr 1870
Colorado	TRUITT, John H. & Mary E.	Marcus Clayton	13 Jan 1875
Victoria	TRUSSELLE, Rose (See E. S. Roberts)		
Bexar	TRWLICK, Dorotea (See Benedict Studer)		
Lavaca	TUCKER, Michael & Elizabeth	Ellen C.	5 Aug 1874
Comanche	TURNER, Burr D. & Emma	Carrie Bell	22 Jun 1874
Colorado	TURNER, D. F. & Alice E.	Luria Leetta	21 Dec 1873
Burnet	TURNER, E. P. & Nancy R.	Louisa Sonora	8 Apr 1874
Victoria	TURNER, F. A. & M. (Sturgess)	Louise Martha	13 Nov 1873
Lavaca	TURNER, F. W. & S. A.	F. W.	10 May 1874
Bell	TURNER, J. W. & M. M.	J. Boyd	3 May 1875
Hays	TURNER, Littleton & Calidonia	Peter Littleton	7 Dec 1875
Brazos	TURNER, Martin & Frances	Wanona	20 Sep 1874
Hays	TURNER, Pass R. & Martha C.	Nellie Antoinette	21 Feb 1875
Bell	TURNER, R. H. & Ella B.	Robt. Lee	14 Jun 1875
Caldwell	TURNER, W. M. & M. E.	Thomas E.	10 Feb 1874
Bexar	TURQUAND, Michael Glynn & Eleanor T. (Duff)	William	30 Apr 1878
Hays	TYSON, E. M. & Lucy A.	Pattie R.	28 Oct 1874
Austin	UECKERT, Charles & Minna	Henry Ferdinand Fritz	8 Dec 1873
		Louis William	20 Feb 1875
Austin	UECKERT, Ferdinand & Julie	Henry Julius Edward	31 Jul 1873
Austin	UECKERT, Fritz & Catherine	Lena	25 Dec 1874
Austin	UECKERT, Harmon & Dorothea A.	Mary	20 Nov 1874
Austin	UECKERT, Hermann & Dorothea	Fritz	16 Nov 1873
		Hermann	7 Feb 1876
Austin	UECKERT, William & Minna	Anna Clara Ernestina	11 Jan 1874
		Frederick Wilhelm	2 Dec 1875
Bexar	UHL, E. C. Alexander & Emma	Henrica Lina	23 Jun 1875
Bexar	UHL, Emma (See E. C. Alexander Uhl)		
Lavaca	ULBIG, Frank & Mary	Bertha	17 Feb 1874
Comal	ULLRICH, Wilhelm & Sophie (Penshorn)	Ida Friederika	5 Sep 1873
Austin	UMLAND(?), Julius C. & Louisa	Charles Henry	4 Sep 1873
		Elizabeth	25 Aug 1875
Lee	UMLANG, Adolph & Augusta	William Otto	8 Mar 1875
Bexar	UPSON, Columbus & Martha (Vance)	Charles	18 Jun 1874
Victoria	URBAN, Emeil & Anna (Bilstein)	Fritz	28 Nov 1874
Austin	URBAN, H. C. & M. M.	Royal Raymundo	24 Aug 1873
Gillespie	USENER, Ludwig & Elise	August	30 Sep 1875
Lavaca	VAIL, Mary (See Wm. H. Hennessey)		
Bell	VALLIANT, J. T. & M. J.	Rosanah	13 Sep 1873
Bexar	VANCE, Martha (See Columbus Upson)		
Bell	VANNESS, J. A. & M. A.	Armstead T.	25 Oct 1874
Bell	VANNESS, T. E. & F. C.	Katie Ann	No date
Victoria	VAN NORMAN, Joseph M. & Martha M. (Halsel)	Claude Henry	6 Feb 1874
DeWitt	VANNOTE, John William & Mary E.	Thomas Whitfield	10 Dec 1874
Lavaca	VANPELT, Geo. G. & Martha A.	Ophelia	24 Jan 1874
Bexar	VAN PELT, Katie (See Robt. McPherson McKie)		
Hays	VAUGHAN, Felix G. & Laura A.	Cora	16 Sep 1873
Nacogd.	VAUGHTER, W. J. & Annie	Elbert	20 Aug 1873
Austin	VEAL, Mittie (See E. R. Thomas)		
Bexar	VENGER, Cathrine (See F. Hahn)		
Grimes	VENTESS, Geo. & Elizabeth	Willie	12 Aug 1869
		Ida	15 May 1873

COUNTY	PARENTS	CHILD	DATE
Grimes	VENTESS, Jack & Airy	Dinah	12 Nov 1874
Bexar	VENTLAND, Minna (See Ventelin Lutz)		
Hays	VERNETTA, Julia (See Wm. A. McGehee)		
Burnet	VEST, B. C. & S. E.	Richard Washington	1 Sep 1874
Lee	VICK, H. D. & Julia	McDuff	11 Apr 1874
		Clifford Hines	16 Jan 1876
Lee	VICK, J. T. & Judy Ann	Judy Emma	22 May 1875
Lee	VICK, Joseph H. &		
	Susan Elizabeth	Hugh Nathaniel	28 Jan 1874
		William Fletcher	16 Dec 1875
San Saba	VICKUS, C. M. & T. C.	Thomas Cloud	8 Apr 1875
Bexar	VIDAL, Santiago &		
	Rosa (Huerta)	Jose	22 Jun 1874
Austin	VOEKEL, William & Anna	Edmond	30 Aug 1874
Austin	VOGELSANG, Fritz & Augusta	Ida H. M.	30 Jan 1875
Hays	VOGELSANG, Gustav & Mary	Peter H.	18 Feb 1873
		Gustav	12 Apr 1875
Bexar	VOGES, Amelia (See Charles Voges)		
Bexar	VOGES, Augusta (See Daniel Hofheinz)		
Bexar	VOGES, Charles & Amelia		
	(Voges)	Clara	6 Jan 1875
Comal	VOGES, Friedrich &		
	Sophie (Koch)	Otto	17 May 1870
		Sophie	24 Apr 1873
Bexar	VOGES, Mena (See Friedrich Koch)		
Bastrop	VOGHT, Charles & Caroline	Maximillian C.	7 Mar 1873
		Maria	10 Aug 1875
Austin	VOITEK, Martin &		
	Franciska	Franciska	10 Mar 1875
Burnet	VOLAND, H. V. & Elizabeth	Minnie	29 Nov 1875
Victoria	VOLDER, Haide (See Blaise Sitterle)		
Lavaca	VOLLENTINE, James & Emma J.	Arthur	15 Aug 1873
Kendall	VOLLMERING, Fritz &		
	Catharine	Emma	No date
		Gustav	No date
		Walter	No date
	VON BOECKMANN see BOECKMANN		
Comal	VOM STEIN, Emilie (See Louis August Henne)		
Comal	VON COLL, Kathinka (See Wilhelm Elemens)		
Bastrop	VOSS, J. W. & A. S.	H.	4 Jan 1874
Travis	WADDELL, Daniel & George Ann	Elkin	17 Nov 1873
Lee	WADE, F. S. & Rosina	Homer	Mar 1874
Nacogd.	WADE, Isaac E. & Fanny J.	Walter Eugene	2 Dec 1873
Nacogd.	WADE, N. G. & Mary Ann	Elizabeth	3 May 1874
Bexar	WAEDNER, Amelia (See Edward Rompel)		
Bexar	WAELDER, Jacob & Ada (Bradley)	Pauline Minter	28 Oct 1871
		Frederick Jacob	4 Aug 1873
Colorado	WAGENFUHR, Henry &		
	Henrietta	T. J. P. C.	6 Dec 1873
		Henry Ernst	
		Helment Chas.	9 Oct 1875
Austin	WAGGE, Charles & Mary	Sophia	23 May 1875
Victoria	WAGNER, Caroline (See Henry Widmier)		
Bexar	WAGNER, Henry & Meena		
	(Wagner)	Sophie	10 Apr 1875
DeWitt	WAGNER, J. & E.	Sigmund P. T.	29 Dec 1851
		William	23 Apr 1854
		Sophia	14 Jun 1855
		Paulina	15 Mar 1857
		Caroline	4 Jun 1859
		C. F. Richard	15 Jan 1863
Bexar	WAGNER, Meena (See Henry Wagner)		
Victoria	WAGNER, Victoria (See Phillip Baecker)		
Bell	WAGONER, W. J. & S. A.	Henry B.	9 Dec 1873
Gillespie	WAHRMUND, Charles & Dorothea	Henry Theodor	27 Jun 1873
Bell	WAKEFIELD, W. A. & J. G.	Wm. O.	13 Jul 1873

COUNTY	PARENTS	CHILD	DATE
Brazos	WALDROP, W. V. & Sallie	Leonard	26 Apr 1875
Gillespie	WALKER, Heinrich & Wilhelmine	Otto	13 Jan 1875
Victoria	WALKER, Mary (See Peter Thomas)		
Hays	WALKER, Robert & Louisa	Mary Jane	2 Jan 1875
Bell	WALKER, W. W. & R.	Mabel Della	6 Feb 1875
Bell	WALLACE, G. R. & C. J.	Mattie Mernerva	9 Mar 1874
Brazos	WALLACE, Geo. & F. E.	Julia S.	7 Feb 1876
Bell	WALLACE, J. L. & Eliza E.	Mariam Amanda	13 Jun 1875
Bell	WALLACE, Jas M. & M. A. J.	John C.	9 Aug 1873
Travis	WALLACE, R. G. & Millie	Mary Ann Rachel	15 Feb 1874
Bexar	WALLACE, W. A. &		
	Annie B. (Bolding)	Frank B.	8 Jun 1874
		Willis Albert	4 May 1876
DeWitt	WALLACE, W. C. & Amelia R.	Ada	3 Mar 1876
Bexar	WALLACE, William &		
	Jane (Harding)	?? (F)	26 Mar 1875
Caldwell	WALLER, A. P. & L. A.	Robert J. T.	3 Jan 1876
Caldwell	WALLER, W. A. & F. U.	Fannie E.	19 May 1874
Comal	WALLHOEFER, Ernestine (See Adolph Triesch)		
San Saba	WALLING, Vance & Sarah A.	Lutitia	7 May 1875
DeWitt	WALLINGFORD, Y. & A.	Elizabeth	3 Jun 1873
Comal	WALLIS, Emma (See Clemens August Conrads)		
Burnet	WALTERS, Moses & Mary E.	Lula B.	5 Jul 1874
		Robert Joel	28 Jan 1876
Austin	WALTON, C. R. & Leenora	Mattie Louisa	12 Sep 1873
Nacogd.	WALTON, Culberson & Malinda	Francis E.	15 Aug 1871
Nacogd.	WALTON, John & Harriet	Asilee	Nov 1873
Bell	WALTON, S. L. & N. M.	Lee O'Conner	17 Jun 1872
		Nora Belle	11 Jul 1874
Bandera	WARD, C. C. & M. E.	Perry Nelson	5 Nov 1875
Fayette	WARD, E. G. & M. L.	Wm. L.	10 Dec 1873
Austin	WARD, Edward & Charlotte	John Oliver	Nov 1874
Lee	WARD, J. J. & Masa	Ettie	13 Jan 1875
Austin	WARD, Ruffin & Narcissus	Walter Scott	30 Apr 1875
Austin	WARNASCH, August & Ernestine	Anna	24 Sep 1874
Austin	WARNASCH, Henry & Justine	Pauline	27 May 1874
San Saba	WARREN, B. G. & Eppa	Richard Murray	31 Dec 1874
Lee	WARREN, R. H. & Mary C.	William C.	11 Jan 1875
Bell	WARRICK, J. K. & M. J.	John Edward	23 Jul 1875
Austin	WASHAM, William B. & Susan E.	Ella	No date
Travis	WASHBURN, Wm. & Polly Ann	Charles Bird	20 May 1874
Nacogd.	WATKINS, J. J. & L. A.	Mary W.	19 Feb 1875
Nacogd.	WATKINS, John & Martha	Annie D.	26 Aug 1874
Nacogd.	WATKINS, John H. & Mattie L.	Robert O.	26 Nov 1875
Bexar	WATSON, Eliza (See German Watson)		
Bexar	WATSON, German & Eliza	Mary Ella	7 Nov 1874
Austin	WATSON, James & Hannah	Harriett	16 Aug 1875
Comal	WATSON, John D. & Fanny		
	(Wheat)	Augustus	16 Jun 1875
Brazos	WATSON, Rubin & Rose	Mary	22 Apr 1875
San Saba	WAYLAND, James & Mary A.	Edwin Homer	3 Nov 1875
Bandera	WEAVER, David J. & C.	Elizabeth	17 Jul 1874
Bandera	WEAVER, F. A. & C.	Samuel	19 May 1874
Hays	WEAVER, John G. & Sarah	Frederic	28 Mar 1876
Bastrop	WEAVER, Wm. & E. E.	Wayne L.	22 Jan 1874
DeWitt	WEBB, Albert & Mary Jane	Thomas Henry	8 Mar 1875
Burnet	WEBB, E. L. & Martha J.	Elijah Edgar	11 May 1875
Victoria	WEBB, Melinda (See Charles Thomas Roberts)		
DeWitt	WEBB, Samuel P. & Ellen	Sam	28 Feb 1876
Caldwell	WEBB, W. J. & A. E.	William	1 Oct 1875
Bexar	WEBB, Wm. & Francis (Clark)	Lottie	8 Sep 1874
Austin	WEBBER, Robert &		
	Johann Juliane	Emilie	1 Sep 1873
Bexar	WEBER, Adolph & Emma (Burg)	Bavette Emma	13 May 1874
Victoria	WEBER, Charles &		
	Johanna (Schmidt)	Rudolph	22 Jun 1873

COUNTY	PARENTS	CHILD	DATE
Fayette	WEBER, D. H. & L. H.	Daniel	7 Jun 1876
Victoria	WEBER, Frederica (See John Piper)		
Kendall	WEBER, Heinrich & Marie	Alwine	4 Dec 1860
		Friedrich	30 Oct 1862
		Natalie	8 Feb 1865
		Georg	7 Dec 1866
		Louis	10 May 1869
		Hermann	26 May 1872
Gillespie	WEBER, John Jacob & Mathilda	Anna	17 Aug 1874
Victoria	WEBER, Michael & Catharina (Fuhrman)	Justhina	5 Jan 1874
Austin	WEBER, Robert & Juliana	Julia	19 Jun 1875
Bexar	WEDEMEYER, Henry F. D. & Clara M. S. (Klenner)	Maria Cecilia	28 Apr 1876
		Henry	1 Jan 1878
Travis	WEED, V. A. & Bell	Hattie Catherine	17 Jan 1875
DeWitt	WEHE, Louis W. & Caroline	Helena K. M.	30 Oct 1873
		Charles Willie Fred	20 May 1875
Gillespie	WEHMEYER, Conrad & Louise	Emma	25 May 1873
Gillespie	WEHMEYER, Fried. & Sophie	Isidor	16 Nov 1873
Bexar	WEHRHAHN, E. & Adolfina (Roppertsbarg)	Ordof	5 Nov 1871
		Ernestina	2 Feb 1875
DeWitt	WEICHMANN, Theo. & Mina	Ernst	7 Aug 1874
DeWitt	WEICHSEL, Fred. & Williamene	Louise Helen	14 Dec 1874
Gillespie	WEIDENFELLER, Johann & Mary	Jacob	10 Apr 1874
Comal	WEIDNER, Lebrecht & Louise (Foerster)	Auguste	21 Jul 1874
Bexar	WEIHNIG, Anna M. (See John Jacob Rilling)		
Bexar	WEIK, John & Ellen (Atkinson)	Annie	31 Dec 1873
Bexar	WEILBACHER, Paulina (See Charles Rompel)		
Bexar	WEINHOLD, E. & Yattie (Schloder)	Ernst	9 Jun 1875
Bexar	WEIR, Henry & Sally (Evans)	Lilly Lee	6 Nov 1874
	WEISIGER, W. J. & Susan H.	Evan Rochester	19 Aug 1876
Bexar	WEISSELBERG, G. F. & Maria (Weisselberg)	Ida	4 Jan 1861
		Emma	4 Nov 1862
Bexar	WEISSELBERG, Maria (See G. F. Weisselberg)		
Lee	WELBURN, W. J. & Mary C.	Caleb	11 Dec 1875
Comanche	WELCH, James & Nancy	Octalie	17 May 1875
Comanche	WELCH, Silas & A. N.	James William	1 Jan 1869
		Simeon Gilmore	27 Aug 1871
		Ceclia Elizabeth	22 Feb 1874
Fayette	WELHAUSEN, Charles & Eliza (Amsler)	Charles	17 May 1871
		Phillip W.	9 Aug 1874
Medina	WEMETTE, John B. & Elise	Elisa	5 Jul 1870
		Josephine	23 Oct 1872
		Eugenia	19 Nov 1874
Gillespie	WENDEL, Adam & Elisabeth	Gustav Leonard	3 Oct 1873
		Sarah	21 Nov 1875
Kendall	WENDLER, C. F. & Pauline	Max Otto	22 Jun 1861
		Clara Ida	18 Nov 1862
		Antonie Hulda	15 May 1864
		Bertha Anna	23 Apr 1867
		Eugenie Lina	19 Mar 1870
		Pauline Hedwig	6 Nov 1871
		Philip Rudolph	21 Jun 1873
		Margarethe Pauline	22 May 1875
Kendall	WENDLER, Henry & Pauline	Hugo	1 Jan 1866

COUNTY	PARENTS	CHILD	DATE
Kendall	WENDLER, Henry -- Cont.	Theodor	8 Feb 1867
		Adolph	16 Jan 1869
		Olga	23 Mar 1870
		Albert	23 Oct 1871
		Bruno	17 Jan 1875
Austin	WERLLA, Charles Louis &		
	Julia	Gustav Charles	8 Sep 1875
Bexar	WERNER, Francis (sic) (See George Dullnig)		
Kendall	WERNER, George &		
	Friederike Caroline	Otto	12 Oct 1874
		August Richard	12 May 1877
Kendall	WERNER, Johannes & Helene	Carl Fr.	17 Dec 1870
		Rich'd Adolph	2 Dec 1872
		Bertha	17 Jan 1875
Bexar	WERNER, Lena (See G. A. Duerler)		
Comal	WERSTERFER, Franz &		
	Alvine (Burkhardt)	Paulina	19 May 1874
Victoria	WERTHEIMER, Charles A. &		
	Blonndi (Halfin)	Jacob	15 Apr 1856
		Sophie	26 Dec 1867
		Solomon	4 Jun 1871
		Isaac	18 Oct 1873
Caldwell	WEST, Hamilton & S. J.	Elah	25 Oct 1874
	(Twins) Marg't E. & Sam'l G.		
			16 Feb 1875
Caldwell	WEST, Harrison H. &		
	Lavenia	Harrison H.	21 Jan 1874
Kendall	WEST, Jacob & ??	E. Pinkney	27 Nov 1873
Brazos	WESTBROCKS, Frank & Harriett	Sissio	5 Mar 1874
		Frank	5 Feb 1876
Lee	WESTBROOK, Joseph Warren &		
	Mary Eleanor	Bula Florinia	6 Jan 1875
Comal	WETZ, Heinrich &		
	Caroline (Stolte)	Alma Auguste	15 Jan 1874
		Alvine Wilh. Cath	24 Sep 1875
Comal	WETZEL, Hugo Bruno &		
	Bertha (Penshorn)	Hugo Gustav	14 Sep 1873
Fayette	WEYAND, John & Susana	John	5 Sep 1873
Comal	WHEAT, Fanny (See John D. Watson)		
Bell	WHEAT, W. J. & S. M.	Samuel	Apr 1873
		William	Mar 1876
Brazos	WHEELER, John Henry &		
	Clara Elizabeth	Henry Walter	2 Sep 1869
	(Keith? Keifer?)	Clara Elizabeth	18 Jul 1877
Victoria	WHEELER, Louis C. &		
	Bettie (Cain)	Miriam Estelle	13 Nov 1874
		Eugene Sibley	23 Apr 1873
Nacogd.	WHITAKER, A. & Francis	Frederick	28 Aug 1873
Nacogd.	WHITAKER, Dock & Sophia	Henry H.	Mar 1875
Burnet	WHITAKER, Geo. & Nancy C.	Thomas	25 May 1874
Nacogd.	WHITAKER, J. P. & Mary S.	Clara Ileta	Jul 1873
Nacogd.	WHITAKER, Madison F. &		
	Malissa A.	William W. (sic)	31 Sep 1873
Nacogd.	WHITAKER, William & Mary	Lillie	15 Nov 1873
Colorado	WHITFIELD, E. Paud (sic) &		
	Sarah J.	Etta	25 Dec 1873
DeWitt	WHITE, A. C.& Fanny	Julia	25 Sep 1875
Travis	WHITE, C. W. & M. J. (Sallie?)	Sillie Pearl	7 Feb 1873
Comanche	WHITE, H. H. & Martha	Oscar	19 Aug 1874
		Ella	19 Aug 1874
Comanche	WHITE, J. B. & S. F.	Lavina Ann	6 Jul 1871
		Charles Rufus	5 Nov 1873
Bandera	WHITE, J. H. & M. E.	David Herter	27 Jun 1875
DeWitt	WHITE, John & Keziah	Daniel Joe	17 Jan 1876
Hays	WHITE, Jno C. & Martha	Sarah Lucinda	17 Feb 1875
Travis	WHITE, Julia (See Lee Pettaway)		

COUNTY	PARENTS	CHILD	DATE
Austin	WHITE, R. M. & C. H.	Emma J.	22 Oct 1874
Nacogd.	WHITE, Thomas D. & Annie E.	Bennett B.	7 Jun 1875
Brazos	WHITE, Tom & Laura	G. B.	3 Mar 1856
Bandera	WHITE, W. H. & Mary A.	David Willey	27 Nov 1873
		James Claborne	18 Jun 1875
Bastrop	WHITE, Warren & Melinda	Rutha	27 Feb 1875
Bexar	WHITELEY, Ellen H. (See R. C. Norton)		
Bexar	WHITHOFF, Fred & Louisa (Drish)	Albert	20 Aug 1875
Austin	WHITLEY, Jesse & Virginia	Nancy Elizabeth	11 Aug 1873
Comanche	WHITNEY, E. D. & R. R.	Americus Texana	3 Jan 1874
Bell	WHITSON, N. M. & Louisa	Lucy Clay	4 Jun 1874
Travis	WHITTEN, Aaron Hill & Martha Elizabeth (Hotchkiss)	Aaron Stuart	27 Oct 1877
Caldwell	WHITTENBURG, J. B. & Sallie	Thomas Searcy	10 Oct 1873
		Luella	13 Sep 1875
Bell	WHITTINGTON, W. R. & M. E.	H. A.	5 Nov 1874
Kendall	WHITWORTH, Robt. W. & Francis	Arthur	Jul 1875
Victoria	WIDMIER, Henry & Caroline (Wagner)	Robert	27 Oct 1873
Kendall	WIEDENFELD, Theodore & Magdalina	Anna	23 Jan 1853
		Emil	4 Aug 1855
		Otto	18 May 1857
		Hugo	2 Dec 1859
		Willie	10 Jan 1862
		Frances	5 Oct 1863
		Agnes	27 Feb 1869
		Louis	11 Oct 1872
Bexar	WIER, Lavina (See John Dobbin)		
Austin	WIESTER, Hugh & Katherine	Hugh	15 Jun 1875
Nacogd.	WIGGINS, Richard & Sarah	Paralee	Apr 1876
Bexar	WILD, Fridolin & Lina (Hoyer)	Josefa	29 Oct 1872
		Sophie	2 Jul 1874
Bexar	WILDENSTEIN, Carie (See Jacob Landman)		
Gillespie	WILEY, Isaac & Nancy Ann	Nancy Jane Charity	13 Jan 1875
Bell	WILEY, J. N. & M. A.	Martha J.	11 Sep 1873
Caldwell	WILEY, Jas. A. & Altah D.	Altah Delena	25 Jan 1876
Bastrop	WILHELM, John & Elizabeth	Peter	23 Dec 1873
Bell	WILKERSON, Mart & Anna W.	Rena J.	4 Dec 1874
Fayette	WILKERSON, R. D. & ??	Yowell M.	11 Feb 1874
San Saba	WILKES, F. D. & M. A.	A. N.	6 Nov 1875
Bastrop	WILKES, R. B. & L. J.	Josie May	27 Nov 1875
Bexar	WILKINS, Burton & Susan (Tores)	Jacob	24 Dec 1874
		Burton	21 Sep 1876
Bell	WILKINSON, S. E. & M. E.	Malcolm Eugene	3 Jul 1873
		Robert Alvin	30 May 1875
Bell	WILKS, F. D. & M. A.	W. A.	17 May 1874
Brazos	WILLBORN, John Marshall & Martha Ann (Peterson)	Eugenia	4 Apr 1869
Kendall	WILLE, Hermann & Marie	Auguste	16 Aug 1855
		Louise	16 Apr 1857
		Sarah	16 Jan 1859
	(Twins)	Bertha & Hermine	7 Feb 1861
		Otto	3 Apr 1864
		Hugo	22 Feb 1867
		Ida	25 Jan 1869
Victoria	WILLEMIEN, Eugenia (See Henry Kuhne)		
Fayette	WILLENBERG, A. E. & P. K.	Anna Dorothea	14 Jan 1867
		Auguste Pauline	21 Aug 1868

COUNTY	PARENTS	CHILD	DATE
Fayette	WILLENBERG, A. E. -- Cont.	Charles Robert Edward	25 May 1871
		Gustav Adolph Richard	9 Nov 1873
Bexar	WILLGEHAUSEN, Frederick & Juliana (Eicke)	Conrad	28 Aug 1838
		Christina	2 Aug 1849
		Julius	12 Jun 1856
Bastrop	WILLIAMS, Alfred & Victoria	John	3 Jan 1874
Bexar	WILLIAMS, Angeline (See Wm. Pullam)		
Victoria	WILLIAMS, Corallie (See Tobe Reeves)		
Lavaca	WILLIAMS, E. O. & V. E.	Wm. H.	24 May 1874
Lavaca	WILLIAMS, Jr., E. U. & Susan A.	Walter Lee	8 Oct 1873
Hays	WILLIAMS, F. S. & Fannie C.	Lightfoot Early	22 Mar 1875
Bexar	WILLIAMS, George & Bell (Hopkins)	Martha	18 Jan 1875
Bastrop	WILLIAMS, H. H. & A. T.	Anna T.	18 Jun 1874
Colorado	WILLIAMS, Henry & Mary	Ned	15 Jan 1874
DeWitt	WILLIAMS, J. & Hyat	Allice (sic)	14 Sep 1874
Bastrop	WILLIAMS, J. H. & Permelia	Mary A.	28 Feb 1874
Bell	WILLIAMS, J. S. & A. E.	Arthur Edwin	19 Jul 1874
Bastrop	WILLIAMS, J. W. & Martha	Rosa Alice	17 Aug 1874
Lavaca	WILLIAMS, J. W. & H.	Carly	1 Mar 1871
Austin	WILLIAMS, James & Amanda	Willie	Dec 1873
San Saba	WILLIAMS, Jas. H. & Martha A.	Wm. Doran	28 Dec 1874
Lavaca	WILLIAMS, Jno. & C. S.	Marg't	18 Jul 1874
Nacogd.	WILLIAMS, John & Eliza J.	Flora B.	10 Oct 1873
Brazos	WILLIAMS, Johnson C. & Bettie M.	Ella Pink	20 Jul 1874
Lavaca	WILLIAMS, Julia Ann (See John Harrison Zumwalt)		
Bexar	WILLIAMS, Lydia E. (See Geo. W. Caldwell)		
Lavaca	WILLIAMS, Robt. S. & Marg't	M. S. L.	1 Oct 1873
Victoria	WILLIAMS, Rosanna (See Thomas Barns)		
Brazos	WILLIAMS, S. B. & M. J.	Clifford	Sep 1874
		Whit	4 1876
Burnet	WILLIAMSON, A. D. F. & Sarah	Dora	19 Nov 1874
Bell	WILLIS, J. J. & Jane	Laura I.	6 Nov 1874
Kendall	WILLKE, Gustav & Louise Christine (Reinhard)	William John	19 Jan 1875
		Louise Emma	27 Dec 1876
Bexar	WILLRICH, Anna (See Gustav Groos)		
Austin	WILLRODT, Deutof & Elizabeth	Hermann	8 Jul 1874
Bell	WILLS, D. C. & C. J. H.	Walter Livingston	9 Sep 1875
Brazos	WILLSEN, I. D. & L. B.	Thos. B.	24 Jan 1874
		Ellen D.	10 Feb 1876
Lee	WILLSON, F. W. & Margaret	Mary Magnalin	13 Jan 1875
Bastrop	WILSON, A. J. & Emily	Mattie Nona	30 Oct 1874
Lee	WILSON, C. S. & E. C.	W. T.	27 Dec 1873
Bastrop	WILSON, G. S. & Sarah F.	Lander	7 Jan 1875
Comanche	WILSON, G. W. & Mary	Benjamin Wright	27 Jun 1873
Grimes	WILSON, H. H. & M. M.	Alice Mabel	20 Mar 1874
Colorado	WILSON, J. C. & Emma L.	Eliza R.	1 Aug 1873
Brazos	WILSON, J. H. & Josephine F.	Fannie	4 Sep 1875
Bell	WILSON, J. L. & L.	Calvin Coulter	21 Sep 1873
Bastrop	WILSON, James M. & Virg. A.	Mary Madison	24 Jan 1875
Lee	WILSON, John H. & Emily F.	John Thomas	1 May 1874
Nacogd.	WILSON, Jno. W. & Leah	Della	14 Nov 1869
		Eva	3 Dec 1871
		Benton H.	2 Aug 1875
Lee	WILSON, Joe J. & Viola	Carrie Ella	14 Jan 1875
Colorado	WILSON, N. C. & Mary E.	Mary Elizabeth	8 Dec 1873
Brazos	WILSON, Tony & Alberta (Harris)	Georgia Mae	No date
Comanche	WILSON, V. & Sarah E.	Sarah Ann	24 Jan 1875

COUNTY	PARENTS	CHILD	DATE
Brazos	WILSON, W. D. & E.	John Irvin	1 Jun 1875
Hays	WIMBERLY, Joseph & Alice	Isaac N.	12 Oct 1873
Bexar	WINCKLER, Francisca (See H. W. Bitter)		
Grimes	WINGARD, F. J. & Charlotte	Mary Caroline	2 Jun 1874
DeWitt	WINKLER, H. & Therese	Katharine	28 Jun 1874
Bexar	WINKLER, Jacob & Mina (Schucte)	Peter	9 Feb 1874
Comal	WIPPRECHT, Rudolph & Julie (Kapp)	Ida H.	11 Sep 1856
		Paul L.	25 Sep 1858
		Walter R.	3 Jan 1864
		Elsbeth J.	20 Feb 1872
Bastrop	WISEMAN, A. & Jasaphin	Fred A.	27 Oct 1874
Bexar	WISOFF, Amanda Marie (See Dan Hader)		
Caldwell	WITHERS, Richard & Cordelia	Mary Birdie	16 Aug 1874
Austin	WITTE, Charles & Minna	Anna	26 Sep 1873
		Ella	24 Mar 1875
Bexar	WITTE, George & Mary (Kleine)	Lilly Lousa(sic)	12 Aug 1860
		Alfred George	18 Aug 1862
		Edwin Henry	10 Oct 1866
		Emma Mary	14 Aug 1868
Austin	WITTENBURG, Fritz & Sophie	Albert	16 Nov 1872
		Mathilde	4 Nov 1874
Austin	WITTENBURG, Joachim & Marie	Ludwig	26 Dec 1872
		Antonia	26 Nov 1874
Austin	WITTENBURG, John & Marie	Charles	28 Mar 1873
Colorado	WITTING, George & Sophia (his 1st wife)	Helene	27 May 1855
		Elise	4 Jun 1858
Colorado	WITTING, George & Augusta	Gustav	24 Mar 1861
		Sophie	6 Nov 1862
		Pauline	13 Oct 1864
		Regine	20 May 1870
		Mathilde	12 Dec 1871
		Robert	7 Oct 1874
		Georg	15 Aug 1877
Austin	WOEST, John & Dorothea	August	16 Jun 1873
DeWitt	WOFFORD, John T. & Josephine	Mitchie J.	7 Dec 1873
		Ala Blanche	29 Nov 1875
Austin	WOHLEB, Seraphim & Augusta	Seraphina Augusta	24 Jan 1874
Bexar	WOLCKEN, Christian M. & Mary (Cotulla)	Stephen	1 Jul 1866
		Rosa	16 Feb 1873
		Martin	16 Jul 1875
Bexar	WOLCKEN, Sophie (See Peter Schiffers)		
Bastrop	WOLF, Michael & Rebecca (Hill)	William Michael	23 Aug 1874
Lee	WOLF, William & Amelia	Minnie	19 Feb 1874
Bexar	WOLFRAM, John & Margarita (Roise)	John	18 Nov 1865
		Emma	16 Nov 1867
		Adolph	5 Nov 1869
		Ferdinand	2 Jan 1873
Comal	WOLFSHOHL, Jacobine (See Friedrich Hampe)		
Austin	WOLGAST, Charles & Dora	Anna	9 Jan 1875
Kendall	WOLLSCHLAEGER, Andreas, Jr. & Clara	Richard	3 Apr 1878
Austin	WOLTERS, Edward & Wilhelmine	Josephine	21 Mar 1874
Fayette	WOLTERS, R. & Adolphine	Elizabeth	4 Jul 1873
	(Twins)	Ferdinand	4 Jul 1873
Bexar	WOLTERSDORF, Christine (See Hermann Woltersdorf)		
Bexar	WOLTERSDORF, Hermann & Christine	R. A.	10 Aug 1874
Grimes	WOMACK, M. S. & C. C.	Cornelia Gertrude	20 Dec 1873

COUNTY	PARENTS	CHILD	DATE
Bell	WOOD, J. H. & E.	Ammon O.	22 Nov 1874
Bastrop	WOOD, S. W. & Jane	Chas. A.	27 Feb 1874
Lavaca	WOODALL, M. B. & Fannie	Willie	17 Sep 1873
Lavaca	WOODLEY, T. J. & M. A.	Oscar E.	2 Jun 1874
Caldwell	WOODRIDGE, E. C. & S. J.	Josie Fitch	18 Feb 1875
Caldwell	WOODRUFF, H. R. & Sarah R.	Nora C.	15 Jan 1875
Hays	WOODS, Mattie & Father Unknown	John	20 Nov 1874
Bell	WOOLEY, P. V. & M. C.	Walter	2 Jun 1874
Bexar	WOOLFERT, Mary (See Frederick Shoeman)		
Lee	WOOLTON, Daniel & Mollie Jane	Edward Taylor	17 Oct 1875
Bell	WRAY, W. B. & C. D.	Wm. Boland	11 Jun 1874
Bexar	WREDE, Maria C. (See Friederick C. Haueisen)		
Hays	WREN, James A. & Matilda	John Killen	1 Jul 1875
Comanche	WRIGHT, B. F. & F. J.	John William James	May 1873
Kendall	WRIGHT, Jos. S. &		
	Minerva Elizab.	Sam. Edward	9 Feb 1873
		Geo. Pickens	30 Sep 1874
Caldwell	WRIGHT, L. B. & S. A.	Thomas W.	5 Apr 1875
Bell	WRIGHT, R. N. & A. E.	Kate	No date
DeWitt	WRIGHT, S. B. & Ann E.	J. T.	25 Jan 1875
Bell	WRIGHT, T. C. & Elizabeth	Mary Elizabeth	23 Jan 1874
Bexar	WROBEL, Maria (See Ed. Kurka)		
Medina	WURZBACH, Adolf Carl &		
	Anna Doris	Marie Louise	28 Sep 1873
Bexar	WURZBACH, C. L. &		
	Kate (Fink)	H. M.	19 May 1874
Medina	WURZBACH, Julius Franz &		
	Caroline Charlotte	Anna Marie Louise	18 Oct 1869
	Justine	Heinrich Adolf	10 Jan 1871
		Bertha Renathe	
		Rosalie	1 Oct 1873
Comal	WÜST, Carl &		
	Alwine (Schertz)	Lydia	6 Feb 1874
Austin	WYATT, James & Hester	Mose	2 Jul 1875
Bell	WYBRANTS, S. W. Jr., & E. C.	Maggie	14 Apr 1874
Bexar	XIMENES, Micaela (See Placido Ollivarri)		
Lee	YARBOROUGH, E. A. & T. E.	Felix Marion	26 Feb 1874
Bell	YARBROUGH, J. C. & L. A.	Yancy Young	13 Mar 1874
Caldwell	YATES, James & Susan J.	Dora Elizabeth	6 Jun 1873
		Willie Bruce	20 Jul 1875
Bastrop	YAWS, Chas. & Mary	Andrew L.	16 Jan 1874
Bastrop	YAWS, Wm. & Nancy	Willm. Thos.	17 Nov 1873
Lee	YORK, M. G. & M. A.	Nettie Maud	12 Jul 1874
Lee	YORK, Samuel W. &		
	Mary Catherine	William Henry	12 Dec 1874
Austin	YORKE, Willis & Josephine	Richard	Jan 1875
Bastrop	YOUNG, Adam & Patsey	Henry	26 Mar 1874
Hays	YOUNG, D. A. & ??	David W.	2 Aug 1873
Bastrop	YOUNG, G. K. & Sarah J.	Mattie Kemper	6 Dec 1874
Nacogd.	YOUNG, Henry L. & Mary C.	Ezekiel	21 Jan 1874
Fayette	YOUNG, James & Mary	William T.	1874
Lavaca	YOUNG, Jas. W. & N. E.	Ida L.	21 Oct 1873
Austin	YOUNG, M. A. & Margaret Ann	Georgie Ann	29 Jul 1875
Bell	YOUNG, P. G. & R. E.	Mary Estella	11 Apr 1874
Travis	YOUNG, Richard S. & Orlenia	Mattie Ella	26 Feb 1874
Bexar	YOUNG, Wm. H. &		
	Fanny K. (Kemper)	Hugh Hampton	18 Sep 1870
Lavaca	YOUNG, Wm. H. & Mary A.	Ida Irene	21 Oct 1873
Victoria	ZAHN, Aurelia (See Frederick Miller)		
Gillespie	ZANKER, Dorothea	Charles William	
		Otto	9 Nov 1874
DeWitt	ZEDLER, Ferdinand & Ida	Paul Edwin	12 Aug 1873
DeWitt	ZEDLER, Gustav & Paulina	Louis	1 Jun 1874
		Margarett	18 Feb 1876
Gillespie	ZENNER, Peter & Clara	Anna	22 Sep 1874
Austin	ZEPTNER, Charles & Theresia	Carl Wilhelm	7 Jul 1873

COUNTY	PARENTS	CHILD	DATE
Bexar	ZIEGLER, Chas. F. &		
	Emelia (Strasser)	Marie Emelia	27 Mar 1870
		Barbara Louise	23 Apr 1872
		Katharina F.	12 Jul 1874
		Emma Barbara	10 Aug 1876
Colorado	ZIEGLER, George S. & Sarah	Georgia W.	27 Jul 1874
Gillespie	ZIMMER, Adam & Catharine	August	13 Mar 1875
Brazos	ZIMMERMAN, James &		
	Caroline	Mary Susan	6 Jan 1874
Bexar	ZINCK, Augusta (See Joseph Maurer)		
Bexar	ZINSMEIR, Emil &		
	Mary (Nestor)	Eda	29 Mar 1874
		Otto Jo.	1875
Bexar	ZITZELMANN, Louise (See F. W. Pflughaupt)		
Bexar	ZIZLEMANN, Christian &		
	Emelia (Taush)	Agnes	8 Nov 1872
		Emilia	16 Jan 1874
Kendall	ZOELLER, Adolph & Auguste	George	13 Mar 1861
		Bertha	11 Nov 1867
		Max	27 Dec 1870
		Lizzie	10 Mar 1872
		Louis	28 Jun 1874
		Charles	16 Aug 1876
		Katie	4 Aug 1878
Kendall	ZOELLER, Philipp &		
	Margarethe	Helwig	1 Oct 1855
		Margarethe	8 Jul 1857
		Ferdinand	19 May 1859
		Ernst	9 Mar 1861
		Heinrich	22 Dec 1862
		Friedrich	24 Oct 1865
		Wilhelm	26 Apr 1868
		Helene	22 Dec 1869
Bexar	ZOLLER, M. & Mary (Beppert)	Oto	19 Oct 1875
Bexar	ZORK, Ada (See Adolph Krakauer)		
Lavaca	ZUMWALT, John & Julia	Fannie	12 Nov 1873
Fayette	ZWERNEMANN, Louis & Eliza	Ernst S.	25 Feb 1873
Fayette	ZWERNEMANN, Martin & Sophia	Conrad H. M.	22 Dec 1873

VOLUME II

COUNTY	PARENTS	CHILD	DATE
Fannin	_____, C. B. & Hellen	M. J.	10 Oct 1875
Fannin	_____, Correlius & Elnyra	W. T.	20 Feb 1875
Fannin	_____, J. L. & S. J.	R. E.	2 Jun 1873
Fannin	_____, J. T. & G. A.	A. B.	29 Jan 1874
Upshur	_____, S. N. & S. C. (twins)	Thos.	21 Dec 1874
		Elijah E.	21 Dec 1874
Fannin	_____, W. T. & Malissa	O. T.	19 Mar 1875
Cameron	ABADIE, Basile &		
	Josephine (Daverede)	Abadie	18 Mar 1875
		Guillermo D.	27 Aug 1876
		Cecile	7 Nov 1877
Washington	ABBOTT, E. C. & H. E.	W. H.	2 Jan(?) 1874
Cass	ABERMATHE (sic), M. R. &		
	F. A.	Earle Brentford	13 Jun 1875
Fannin	ABERNATHY, John B. &		
	Henrietta	Henry Buckner	8 Apr 1874
		Robert Edgar	19 Oct 1875
Cass	ABERNATHY, M. R. & G. A.	Oretta	6 Dec 1873
Kaufman	ABLES, A. J. & A. J.		18 Jan 1874
Fannin	ABSHIRE, M. & M. N.	Thomas Milton	3 Jan 1874
		Effie E.	10 Mar 1875
Rusk	ACSEY, Wesley & D. H.	John Henry	2 Oct 1873
Jasper	ADAMS, Abel, Jr. & Sudie	Robert C.	18 Aug 1874
Jasper	ADAMS, Adam & Roxana P.	Museta	29 Dec 1874
Rusk	ADAMS, E. J. &		
	Roda Ann (Carter)		
Rusk	ADAMS, E. S. & R. A.	Lillie C.	20 Apr 1875
	Note: This birth is later recorded as Lilly C.		
	and the mother's initial is R.		
Rusk	ADAMS, James A. and M. E.	Sam R.	25 Oct 1874
Rusk	ADAMS, John Q. and Martha	Miller	18 Jan 1874
Gregg	ADAMS, Silas W. & Mary F.	Gussie	5 Oct 1871
		Lemuel	6 Feb 1875
Fannin	AGNEW, W. B. & D. H.	W. E.	8 May 1875
Webb	AGUIRRE, Librado & Juana E.	Eusebio	5 Mar 1874
Upshur	AILLS, T. P. & Elizabeth	V. A.	15 May 1873
Rusk	AKIN, J. D. and Eva	Thomas Jefferson	5 Dec 1874
Kaufman	AKIN, James P. and Z. A.	Tobitha Elizabeth	11 May 1873
Rusk	AKIN, Thomas G. &		
	Elizabeth H.	John Walton	12 Aug 1873
Webb	ALCARAS, Leandro &		
	Esteban A.	Merejeda	3 Apr 1874
		Antonio	
Webb	ALCARAS, Maria Rita (See Nicholas Charo)		
Rusk	ALEXANDER, Amos & Sylva	Willie	2 Apr 1874
Fannin	ALEXANDER, J. N. & Mary	Carrie Alice	9 Sep 1875
Webb	ALEXANDER, Julian &		
	Salidad (Gusman)	Ramon	27 Jun 1875
Rusk	ALEXANDER, Stephen & Harriett	Emily	17 Feb 1875
Rusk	ALEXANDER, W. T. & Nancy	Louisa	12 Nov 1875
Fannin	ALFORD, J. F. & Anna E.		1875
Cass	ALLDAY, James R. &		
	J. J. or (I.?)	James F.	30 Sep 1873
Kaufman	ALLEN, A. & R.	Alpha Gertrude	Feb 1874
Fannin	ALLEN, J. W. & Mary J.	Barbara	27 Sep 1874
Rusk	ALLEN, LaFayette & Louisa	Robert L.	28 Jun 1875
Lamar	ALLEN, N. O. & Sarah E.	Charles Orren	25 Sep 1875
Fannin	ALLEN, R. E. & S. M.	Fay	16 Sep 1874
Fannin	ALLEN, Thomas & N. J.	M. M.	14 Feb 1875
Fannin	ALLEN, W. A. & M. E.	Theodore	25 Jun 1875
Kaufman	ALLEN, W. V. & E. J.	Dillah	22 Dec 1874
Fannin	ALLEN, Wm. &	Anna R.	29 Jan 1874
Rusk	ALLISON, Richard & Mariah	John	7 Aug 1873
		Maria	14 May 1875
Lamar	ALSTON, Jos. J. & Louisa	William Henry	27 Aug 1873
Upshur	AMOS, J. T. & M. E. B.	U. P.	23 Oct 1874

COUNTY	PARENTS	CHILD	DATE
Rusk	ANDERSON, Charlie & Martha	Melvina	28 Nov 1873
Rusk	ANDERSON, F. S. & M. E.	W. F.	10 Oct 1873
Rusk	ANDERSON, Ike & Louiza	George	1 Aug 1873
		Allen	1 Dec 1874
Rusk	ANDERSON, J. A. and Orra E.	Lena May	4 Oct 1875
Navarro	ANDERSON, John and Amy	John Henry	20 Oct 1873
Rusk	ANDERSON, Joseph & Lucinda	Lucinda E.	2 Feb 1874
Lamar	ANDERSON, R. M. & M. A.	Herbert W.	8 Apr 1875
Lamar	ANDERSON, T. J. & C. A.	C. A.	3 Jun 1874
Rusk	ANDERSON, Walton & Angeline	Walton	1 Aug 1873
Navarro	ANDERSON, William and Almira	Christopher Winsellew	23 Aug 1874
Washington	ANDREW(?), P. & Hellany(?)	Arabella Malinda	25 Dec 1873
Navarro	ANDREW, S. D. and Irene	Willie Irene	23 Apr 1874
Kaufman	ANDREWS, A. G. & E.	William G.	14 Jul 1874
Rusk	ANDREWS, Abe Searls & Manday	Jerry	28 Oct 1875
Rusk	ANDREWS, John B. and Sarah	John	21 Jan 1874
Cameron	ANGELINE, Christopher and Amanda	Delfine Euphemia	13 Oct 1874
Washington	APPLEWHITE, J. B. & Martha Ella	Edda	27 Aug 1873
Gregg	ARDIS, Thomas A. & Sarah J.	James Love	10 Oct 1875
Fannin	ARLEDGE, George W. & Fannie E.	Thomas E.	19 May 1875
Anderson	ARMSTRONG, J. B. and C. or E. A.	_____	19 Dec 1875
Jasper	ARMSTRONG, James T. and Sarah Ann	Katy May	14 Apr 1874
Cherokee	ARMSTRONG, M.(?) W. and Alinena(?)	Annilla	29 Dec 1873
Rusk	ARMSTRONG, Thomas E. and Annie E.	John Henry	29 Jul 1875
Rusk	ARMSTRONG, W. T. & Isabella	Edie	22 Apr 1875
Rusk	ARNETT, D. W. & Eudora	Denver	28 Dec 1874
Fannin	ARNOLD, G. J. & M. B.	Laura N.	18 Jun 1875
Fannin	ARNOLD, J. S. & M. F.	Lucy Lee	19 Jan 1875
Rusk	ARNOLD, J. T. & E. C.	John	24 Apr 1874
		James	24 Apr 1874
Upshur	ARNOLD, J. T. & M. E.	F. A.	24 Jun 1875
Rusk	ARNOLD, James H. & Clarinda	Mary J.	28 Jul 1874
Rusk	ARNOLD, Moses and Malissa C.	Nancy Jane	22 Jun 1873
		George D.	16 Apr 1875
Webb	ARRAGA, Manuel & Babarra G.	Elvi	1 Dec 1875
Webb	ARTHUR, Joshua P. & Amanda T.	Florence Marian	16 Oct 1873
Rusk	ASH, James F. and M. E.	John Henry	
		Thomas F.	
Lamar	ASKLEY, J. L. M. & M. E.	Minnie Jane	5(or 3) Oct 1873
Cherokee	ATKINS, L. D. & M. A.	John P.	4 Feb 1875
Lamar	ATKINSON, J. D. & C. F.	Willie Hooper	6 Jan 1876
Rusk	AUSTON, D. M. and Nancy L.	Edgar	10 Mar 1875
Kaufman	AVERITT, W. W. & M. T.	D. F.	7 Oct 1873
Gregg	AWALT, S. or L. H. & Ann E.	Anna Pearl	28 Mar 1874
Fannin	AYERS, John G. & R. J.	Anna A.	24 Jul 1874
Nueces	AYERS, The Rev. Nelson & Martha D.	Morrison	25 Mar 1874
Navarro	BAGBY, A. C. and Mildred A.	Robert Sneed	15 Nov 1873
		Mailand	28 Mar 1875
Fannin	BAGBY, Benj. M. & Mary E.	Roda Edler	2 Dec 1873
Fannin	BAGBY, Wm. & Amanda J.	Eva	2 Sep 1873
Rusk	BAGNELL, B. J. & M. V.	Mary	30 Aug 1873
		John E.	6 Sep 1875
Rusk	BAGWELL, Benj. J. & M. Virginia	John Elliott	6 Sep 1875
Fannin	BAILEY, J. S. & J. A.	Eldora J.	18 Jul 1874
Anderson	BAILEY, John & Francis	John	15 Jan 1876
Anderson	BAILEY, Jno. T. & Eliza A.	Delia Josephine	23 May 1873

COUNTY	PARENTS	CHILD	DATE
Rusk	BAILEY, W. H. & M.	Cora	20 Mar 1874
Navarro	BAIRD, J. C. S. and Bettie	Mariah M.	7 Apr 1874
		Frederick Lee	24 Oct 1875
	Note: The mother is called "Elizabeth" on the 1875 listing.		
Fannin	BAKER, D. W. & R. A.	Houston	13 May 1874
Rusk	BAKER, George T. and Martha E.	Sarah C.	25 Dec 1874
Fannin	BAKER, J. C. & Mary	Lilly	Feb 1874
Fannin	BAKER, J. L. & Mary E.	David E.	I Apr 1874
Navarro	BAKER, J. W. and M. E.	Isaac William	20 Mar 1875
Navarro	BAKER, S. B. and R. A.	James Alvin	25 Mar 1875
Upshur	BAKER, W. L. & Mollie T.	Ida V.	3 Sep 1875
Fannin	BALL, J. Benj. & M. J.	S. C.	3 Feb 1875
Lamar	BALL, Z. G. & A. J.	Jno. B.	1 May 1858
		E. G. (or S.)	29 May 1861
Upshur	BALLARD, J. W. & P. N.	James M.	10 Dec 1873
Rusk	BALLARD, John and Sarah	Matilda C.	9 Oct 1875
Rusk	BALLINGER, Will & Lucinda	Oscar	4 Apr 1874
Fannin	BANETT(?), A. B. & M. E.	G. B.	13 Dec 1874
	Might be BARNETT or BARRETT		
Lamar	BANIN, Moses & Bettie	Frederick	8 Mar 1876
Rusk	BAR, Os & Sealie	Jimmie	19 Sep 1875
Webb	BARAJAS, Evaristo &		
	Segunda M.	Marcelino	2 Jun 1874
		Melecio	12 Feb 1876
Rusk	BARBER, J. W. & Almeda	Gertrude	2 May 1875
Rusk	BARBER, T. J. & Lavinia	Dora Palina	26 May 1873
Rusk	BARBER, T. J. & Nancy L.	William Coleman	5 Oct 1875
Fannin	BARKER, William H. & Elender	Amanda D.	Jan 1874
Rusk	BARKSDALE, A. C. & A. R.	Malissa E.	I4 Mar 1874
Rusk	BARKSDALE, M. M. & Mattie E.	Claud C.	27 Apr 1875
Rusk	BARKSDALE, Nathan S. &		
	Mary H.	Julian	3 Jan 1874
Navarro	BARNABY, Isaac L. and S. E.	John Marvin	19 Jun 1873
Nueces	BARNARD, Francis E. &		
	Mary C.	Jennie Cavins	18 Jan 1872
		Mary H.	17 Dec 1873
		Maggie French	17 Mar 1876
Kaufman	BARNES, J. T. & N. J.	Robert D.	21 Feb 1874
Anderson	BARNES, N. B. and Margaret A.	George P.	8 Oct 1873
Kaufman	BARNES, William H. & E. J.	Abbie Somerby	20 Dec 1874
Navarro	BARNETT, A. B. and Laura L.	William Temple	11 Feb 1874
Washington	BARNETT, J. C. & M. C.	J. C.	29 Oct 1873
Kaufman	BARNETT, R. & M. J.	Joseph E.	22 Oct 1874
Fannin	BARNHILL, Jno. D. & S. C.	Leona	
		Reg. 1 Jan 1875	
Washington	BARNHILL, P. H. & Ann	Tempe M.	26 Apr 1874
Rusk	BARRETT, George & Vina	Mary A.	14 Sep 1875
Fannin	BARRETT, W. J. & Huldah A.	A. L.	13 Sep 1874
Cherokee	BARRON, S. B. & E. C.	Wm. P.	8 Jun 1874
Navarro	BARRY, Amborse and J. A.	Sydenham Bullwere	17 May 1875
Navarro	BARRY, Bryan T. (?) and		
	Odoso E.	Charles Thomas	27 Feb 1875
Navarro	BARRY, P. B. and N. E.	Ada	6 May 1873
Rusk	BARTHOLD, Charles and Jane	Walter B.	4 Feb 1875
Navarro	BARTLETT, J. M. and M. H.	Benjamine	8 Jul 1873
Fannin	BARTLEY, T. D. & Amanda	Della Dora	10 Mar 1874
Kaufman	BARTON, D. M. & C. A.	Lillian E.	2 Dec 1873
Kaufman	BARTON, G. W. & M.	Barbry Alto	15 Apr 1874
Upshur	BARTON, J. W. & A. E.	Ada B.	11 Apr 1874
Rusk	BARTON, R. M. & Mary E.	Arthur Acbar	24 Feb 1874
Fannin	BARTON, Thos. E. & Fannie	Moses Allen	2 Dec 1875
Rusk	BASINGER, H. C. & Mary J.	Clay	5 Dec 1873
Navarro	BASON, George W. and		
	Frances H.	James A.	29 Jul 1873
Webb	BASQUEZ, Josefa (Mrs. Marcos Dovalina)		

COUNTY	PARENTS	CHILD	DATE
Washington	BASSETT, B. H. & M. B.	Jefferson	9 Jan 1874
Upshur	BASSETT, J. N. & L. J.	Thomas R.	29 Sep 1873
Rusk	BATEMAN, B. H. & Mary C.	CLABORNE F.	5 Apr 1875
Navarro	BATES, C. F. and Rebecca	William Fredrick	25 Aug 1874
Navarro	BATES, Fredrick M. and Elizabeth	Joseph Wiley	6 Aug 1873
Navarro	BATES, J. Y and C. A.	Joe Ann	15 Jun 1873
Rusk	BATON, W. T. & M. L.	Olla Rimple	18 Dec 1874
Fannin	BATTLE, J. F. & Louisa	Clifton	8 Nov 1874
Rusk	BAYSINGER, Clay & Jane	William	5 Dec 1875
Navarro	BEALE, W. H. and N. L.	Thomas Edward	8 May 1873
Rusk	BEALL, W. L. & Eugenia	Corinne	4 Aug 1873
	Note: In 1875 the mother's name is "Eugene".		
		Eugene M.	30 Nov 1875
Lamar	BEARD, James M. & Mary	John W. T.	25 Jun 1875
Rusk	BEARD, William & Catherine E.	Willis	26 Jun 1873
Rusk	BEARDEN, Bill & Rose	Johnnie	2 Jul 1875
Upshur	BEASLEY, Tim and Flora	Johney	10 Jun 1874
Fannin	BEATY, T. W. & A. G.	Jesse Lee	12 Dec 1873
Washington	BEAUMONT, A. G. & J. T.	Sterling Henry	6 Aug 1874
Kaufman	BEAVERS, J. A. & R. C.	Dora	24 Aug 1873
Kaufman	BECK, W. J. & A. C.	Jonathan Caleb	13 Mar 1874
Rusk	BECKWORTH, J. T. & Mary	Jerome	26 Jun 1874
Fannin	BEDFORD, S. T. & L. J.	L. M.	3 Apr 1874
Navarro	BEEMAN, C. W. and M. R.	Anna Alena	11 Aug 1874
Dallas	BEEMAN, Peter C. G.and M. C.	Charity E.	4 Jun 1873
Cameron	BELDEN, Samuel T. and Francilea (Garcia)	Samuel	29 Oct 1874
		Samuel T.	18 Oct 1877
Rusk	BELL, Ellen (Mrs. Luke Henderson)		
Gregg	BELL, W. A. & M. A.	W. A.	21 Mar 1875
Lamar	BELLFORD (or BIELFORD?), G. W. & M. J.	Verila	15 Nov 1873
Webb	BENAVIDES, Cristobal & Lamar	Ana Lamar	2 Aug 1873
		Aurelia	24 Nov 1874
Webb	BENAVIDES, Euladio & Teodora	Augustina	5 May 1875
Webb	BENAVIDES, Eulalia (Mrs. Henio Garcia)		
Anderson	BENNETT, Charley and Emily	Elizabeth	8 Aug 1875
Lamar	BENNETT, John T. & M. P.	Robert	28 Sep 1875
Rusk	BENSON, Eliza & Mary	Isaac	6 Nov 1875
Cameron	BENTEN, Jacob and Ma. tndrea (sic) (Moralis)	Maria	16 Jun 1876
Fannin	BENTON, E. H. & M. E.	Mack	10 Feb 1875
Rusk	BERRY, H. C. & Tex. H.	Mary M.	14 Mar 1875
Rusk	BERRY, J. G. & E. J.	Elmer	1 Oct 1873
Lamar	BERRY, Jno. T. & Ellen D.	Margaret Olivia	13 Apr 1874
Fannin	BETTIS, W. S. & S. E.	H. C.	27 Jan 1875
Jasper	BEVIL, George S. and Margarett J.	Louisa T.	26 Sep 1874
Nueces	BEYNON, Thomas & Priscilla B. (Hobbs)	Eugene Meyler	12 Jul 1868
		Arthur Holbein	8 Sep 1870
		Edwin Lettig	8 Feb 1872
		Alice Gertrude	27 Mar 1874
Lamar	BIARD, S. H. & L. E. O.	M. A.	28 Jul 1873
Fannin	BIGGERSTAFF, G. W. & D. M.	E. A.	13 Apr 1874
Fannin	BIGGERSTAFF, J. M. & Sallie	Bocca Fay	28 Aug 1875
Fannin	BIGGERSTAFF, M. M. & M. E.	P. M.	19 Dec 1874
Jasper	BIRD, Samuel and Phoebe (Rhymes)	William Wallace	15 Apr 1876
Rusk	BIRDWELL, John Allen & Elizabeth E.	Bertha Stella	25 Apr 1874
Jasper	BISHOP, A. T. and Sarah Ann	Sarah Bell	17 Dec 1873
		Alice A.	18 Jul 1875
Fannin	BISHOP, E. E. & T. C.	Malcom Edward	27 Oct 1875

COUNTY	PARENTS	CHILD	DATE
Navarro	BISHOP, Horace & Sallie	Tabbie Halbert	24 Aug 1874
		Lavinia Starley	8 Nov 1875
Fannin	BISHOP, S. B. & M. E.	E. A.	22 Dec 1874
Navarro	BISHOP, W. P. and Cora E.	Camilla Blanche	21 Jan 1874
		Joseph Thadius	8 Jun 1875
Upshur	BLACK, Henry & Cal.	Alice	15 Sep 1875
Navarro	BLACK, Henry F. and Fannie	George H.	19 May 1873
Cass	BLACK, Jack &		
	Gennie Isaiah	Oscar	12 Jan 1874
Lamar	BLACK, James H. & E. M.	Tommie Hortense	9 Oct 1874
Navarro	BLACKMAN, D. L. and Sallie E.	Emma	___ 1874
Rusk	BLACKMON, W. J. & Agnes E.	Frances	15 Jun 1874
Anderson	BLACKSHEAR, R. K. and E. J.	Robt. King (sic)	27 Jan 186
Jasper	BLACKSHEAR, W. R., Jr. &		
	Fannie E.	Beatrice	17 Jul 1875
Rusk	BLAIR, Cas & Adaline	William	30 May 1874
Fannin	BLAIR, D. R. & J. E.	Walter Davie	23 Jan 1876
Fannin	BLAIR, Geo. W. & Fannie C.	Henry T.	6 Oct 1874
Navarro	BLAISDELL, Hersey & Emma	Hersey May	19 Aug 1873
Fannin	BLAKE, L. J. & M. E.	E. L.	26 May 1875
Jasper	BLAKE, W. Wallace and Hester	Guy	14 Mar 1873
Lamar	BLAND, J. G. & K. M.	Emma Lee	26 Sep 1874
Fannin	BLANTON, B. F. & S. L.	___	24 Mar 1874
Rusk	BLANTON, Brisca & Matilda	Charlie	23 Mar 1874
Rusk	BLANTON, Brister & Tilda	Molly	8 Feb 1876
Rusk	BLANTON, Henry & Nancy	Henry Hart	2 Feb
		Louvina	13 Aug 1874
Rusk	BLANTON, J. H. & Mildred	Emmett B.	13 Jul 1874
Rusk	BLANTON, J. S. & Mary	Metawe	30 Sep 1875
Rusk	BLANTON, Jacob D. &		
	Elizabeth W.	Margaret C.	28 Mar 1874
Rusk	BLANTON, John & Lucinda	Chapman	7 Apr 1874
Fannin	BLANTON, T. J. & L. J.	W. F.	6 May 1874
Cherokee	BLEVIN, Larkin and		
	Marry (sic)	Martin	15 Dec 1873
Lamar	BLOCKER, J. M. & A. W.	Ira Allen	20 Jul 1875
Washington	BLOUNT, W. C. & Clara	F. D.	25 Feb 1874
Rusk	BOATMAN, J. D. & Susan J.	J. L. E.	28 Dec 1874
Rusk	BOATMAN, Solomon & Mandy	Franklin M.	Jan 1875
Rusk	BOATRIGHT, R. T. & M. T.	Laura R.	22 May 1875
Cass	BOAZMAN, Z. G. & Ida A.	Wm. T.	6 Feb 1874
Rusk	BOBER, Marion & Bell	Burnan Ruben	
		Henry	19 Jul 1875
Cameron	BOESH, Mary Eugenie (Mrs. George Brulay)		
Rusk	BOGGESS, Allen &		
	Marina (Gay)	Ben Franklin	19 Dec 1874
Kaufman	BOGGESS, Bennett and Texana	Bennett	___ ___ ___
Kaufman	BOGGS, James A. & Helen C.	James	
		Throckmorton	29 Aug 1877
Kaufman	BOGGS, James A. and Jane E.	James Anderson	1 Jun 1849
Lamar	BOHRENS, H. & D.	Jemmy Amelia	20 Aug 1875
Cameron	BOLLACKE, Henry and		
	Pauline	Julia Emilia	4 Jul 1878
Washington	BOLTON, D. D. & Martha	Marsha Ayers	17 May 1875
Rusk	BOLTON, J. A. & Mollie J.	Anna Bell	18 Nov 1874
Rusk	BOMAR, W. J. & Sallie K.	Mattie May	25 Nov 1873
Cherokee	BONE, R. D. and G. M.	Nevi L.	3 Feb 1875
Cherokee	BONNER, F. W. and Georgia	Georgia	26 Feb 1874
Upshur	BONNER, W. D. & M. F.	Harrett (sic) V.	5 Jun 1875
Rusk	BOOKER, Felix & Jully Ann	Sally Ann Nisy	27 Feb 1874
Rusk	BOOKER, Jim & Emaline	John	29 Apr 1874
Rusk	BOOKER, Paul & Martha	Gabriel	9 Jul 1875
Anderson	BOONE, E. F. and Mrs.	Gertrude	8 Dec 1875
Lamar	BOONE, J. M. & C. C.	Nora E.	15 Feb 1875
Lamar	BOOTH, J. H. & H. (or A?) I.	E. H.	21 Dec 1874
Rusk	BORDERS, W. R. & Rachel	Laura	18 Feb 1874

92

COUNTY	PARENTS	CHILD	DATE
Rusk	BORDERS, W. R. -- Cont.		5 Jun 1875
Webb	BOTES, Antonio & Ignacia	Maria	3 Dec 1873
Anderson	BOWEN, W. H. and C.	Jimie C.	19 Jun 1875
Navarro	BOWEN, Wilson P. and		
	Sarah Ann	Thomas P.	29 Sep 1873
		Mary Elizabeth	18 Oct 1876
Washington	BOWERS, D. G. & S. R.	Lavenia	31 Mar 1874
Rusk	BOWLING, Gaines & Susan Ann	Pearl	14 Feb 1875
Dallas	BOWMAN, Geo. A. & Olivia	Mary M.	14 May 1877
Anderson	BOX, S. D. and N. L.	Frank M.	3 Feb 1874
Navarro	BOYD, G. W. and Sarah E.	David Lindley	6 Nov 1873
Navarro	BOYD, George W. and H. A.	George Forrest	5 Apr
Washington	BOYD, J. S. & Julia A.	Waller E.	15 Mar 1874
Upshur	BOYD, James & Fannie	Charles Watson	18 Mar 1876
Upshur	BOYD, Walter & Margaret	Emma	8 Jan 1875
Cass	BOYETER, E. M. & Mary A.	Mittie	18 May 1875
Jasper	BOYETT, Noah and Susan	James A.	13 Jun 1874
Kaufman	BOYKIN, W. L. and Jane	J. Emmett	20 Nov 1859
		Eddie N.	8 Aug 1873
Rusk	BOYNTON, A. J. & M. E.	Leila E.	29 Aug 1874
Anderson	BRACKEN, W. Y. and Willie A.	Lotta Dixon	26 Sep 1873
Gregg	BRADBERRY, Joseph E. &		
	Mary E.	Rosa Udora	1 Feb 1876
Lamar	BRADEN, C. C. & M. J.	Horace T.	16 Apr 1875
Anderson	BRADFORD, P. L. and Scattie	John	1 Feb 1874
			26 Mar 1876
Rusk	BRADLEY, Doct & Julia	Eda	6 Oct 1873
Rusk	BRADLEY, Jim & Kittie	Easter	7 Jun 1874
Dallas	BRADLEY, S. M. G. and A. E.	Mattie Gaw	30 Jun 1874
Upshur	BRADSHAW, J. B. & E. T.	Ethel F.	10 Nov 1875
Gregg	BRADSHAW, J. K. P. & Annie	James Carlton	15 Sep 1875
Upshur	BRADSHAW, R. O. & S. L.	Neusome	15 Mar 1875
Cass	BRALEY, J. W. & V. A.	C. K.	15 Nov 1873
Washington	BRANNON, L. & Ellen	J.L.? (orJ.S.?)	10 Apr 1874
Dallas	BRASWELL, S. N.(W.) and		
	Mary A.	Emma Anne	29 Sep 1874
Cass	BRAYLEY, J. W. & V. A.	John B. Gordon	10 or 15
			Jul 1875
Washington	BRENNEN, L. & Helen S.	Lawrence	10 Feb 1875
Navarro	BREWSTER, John &		
	Elizabeth A.	James Oscar	30 Aug 1873
Lamar	BREWTON, I. H. & Eva	Elizabeth	— — —
		Thomas Perry	— — —
		M. Pauline	
Marion	BRIANT, G. & Helen A.	Robert T.	14 Mar 1875
Rusk	BRIDWELL, S. and Sarah	G. C. F. E.	10 May 1875
Rusk	BRIDWELL, S. H. & Frances	James H.	4 Jul 1874
Kaufman	BRISCOE, W. J. & N. E.	William Bird	16 May 1874
Upshur	BRISON, G. R. A. & Sarah A.	Ruthie J. E.	15 Nov 1874
Upshur	BRISON, J. A. & M. J. (twins)	Frances O.	30 Jan 1874
		Mary J.	30 Jan 1874
Upshur	BRISON, R. T. & Mary	Sarah A.	15 Jul 1874
Fannin	BRIZANCE, M. R. & Sarah F.	Dorsey L.	7 Mar 1875
Navarro	BROADAWAY, W. M. and M. A.	Barto	5 Jun 1874
Rusk	BROMLEY, S. H. & Lizzie A.	Alleta Estella	8 Jan 1875
Lamar	BROOKS, A. D. & M. E.	A. D.	15 Sep 1874
Washington	BROOKS, G. W. & Sue	Thomas Dewley	9 Feb 1874
		(Dudley?)	
Marion	BROOKS, M. N. & R. W.	Matilde W.	12 Dec 1873
Rusk	BROOKS, Samuel & America	Elnora	11 Feb 1874
Fannin	BROTHERTON, L. C. & M. C.	Andy	15 Jul 1875
Kaufman	BROUGHTEN, T. J.and Ella	Laura May	12 Feb 1876
Fannin	BROWN, B. E. & E. E. (Sims)	Tom Bowman	29 Jun 1869
		Florine Allen	31 Aug 1874
Fannin	BROWN, C. A. & Sarah E.	Calvin E.	17 Nov 1875
Cass	BROWN(?), C.A.J. & Rocky M.	Elener	11 Aug 1873

COUNTY	PARENTS	CHILD	DATE
Anderson	BROWN, D. and wife	Q. D.	8 Jun 1874
Kaufman	BROWN, E. B. & L. M.	J. F.	6 Aug 1875
Rusk	BROWN, Ellick Garrison & Easter	Emma Mary E.	31 Jan 1875
Jasper	BROWN, Enoch W. and Sallie L.	Elizabeth Jane	18 Feb 1876
Anderson	BROWN, J. R. and Matilla	J. R.	5 May 1875
Washington	BROWN, J. T. & H. M.	Hariet Milton	15 Jul 1873
Kaufman	BROWN, J. W. & A. R.	Joella	9 Oct 1873
Brown	BROWN, James D. and Artemisia	James Marion	19 Sep 1874
Rusk	BROWN, Peter & Ellen (Redwin)	Mattie	13 Jun 1875
Rusk	BROWN, Peter & Winnie	Richard	1 Sep 1873
Rusk	BROWN, Peter & Winnie	Robert	1 Sep 1875
Rusk	BROWN, Richard & Jane	Catherine	Jan 1875
Fannin	BROWNLEE, W. W. & M. S.	Una	22 Sep 1872
		Mary	12 Jan 1875
Anderson	BROYLES, R. W. and Georgia V.	Dan	29 Nov 1875
Cameron	BRULAY, George and Mary Eugenie (Boesh)	Eugenie	18 Mar 1878
		Louis	3 Jul 1879
Navarro	BRUMBELOW, J. K. and M. E.	James Edward	27 Dec 1873
Navarro	BRUMBELOW, J. T. (?) and S. E.	Margaret Lucinda	31 May 1875
Rusk	BRYAN, B. B. & Margaret E.	Sidney E.	4 Nov 1874
Navarro	BRYAN, G. W. and M. L.	Callie Florence	16 Oct 1874
Anderson	BRYAN, J. T. and C. C.	M. E.	9 Jul 1873
Kaufman	BRYANT, A. & M.	Lee	5 Dec 1873
Kaufman	BRYANT, F.(?) B. and Eliza J.	Leonidas C.	14 Aug 1873
	Note: The surname is spelled "Bryant" for the child but "Bryan" for the parents		
Lamar	BRYANT, G. & Hlene (sic) A.	Paul Henderson	14 Aug 1873
Kaufman	BRYANT, L. H. and Kate E.	Victor H.	23 Dec 1874
Washington	BUCK, Robert & Ida	Sophia	28 Jul 1873
Rusk	BUCKNER, J. E. & Martha	Nora	22 Sep 1875
Washington	BURCH, J. H. & E.	James Thomas	22 Aug 1875
Fannin	BURDEN, A. J. & Erma	Ruth B.	1874
Dallas	BURFORD, N. M. and Mary J.	Jeff Mallard	Aug 1874
Navarro	BURGESS, M. M. and Ellen J.	Eta Isla	4 Aug 1873
		Bertha	8 Oct 1876
Navarro	BURLESON, A. L. and M. A.	Laura B.	22 Dec 1873
Navarro	BURLESON, James E. and Margaret	James Franklin Lorenzo Dow	26 Jan 1874
		Eliza Jane	1 Sep 1875
Navarro	BURNETT, J. E. and L. C.	Henry Edward	
Fannin	BURNETT, Tom R. & Lou O.	J. Earl	Jan 1874
Cherokee	BURNETT, Z. V. and M. T.	W. W.	9 Jul 1873
Rusk	BURNEY, John & Louisa	Mathew	12 Jan 1875
Navarro	BURRIS, R. M. and Bettie J.	William L.	23 Oct 1873
Kaufman	BURTON, J. T. & S. A.	Caleb	7 May 1873
		J. T.	24 Dec 1874
Rusk	BURTON, Oliver & Florence	John	10 Feb 1875
Fannin	BURUM, P. K. & Mary A.	Mary M.	24 Apr 1874
Kaufman	BUSH, A. J. & M. E.	Martha Lula	28 Jul 1873
Lamar	BUSTER, D. W. & M. M.	Jennie B.	25 Jun 1873
Washington	BUSTER, Smith & Mary J.	William Howard	21 Oct 1873
Rusk	BUTLER, A. M. & R. A.	Laura A.	20 Jan 1876
Rusk	BUTLER, Brister & Mintie	Commodore	1 Dec 1874
Anderson	BUTLER, D. M. and M. F.	Kate May	12 Nov 1874
Anderson	BUTLER, George W. and Florence A.	Eva E.	31 May 1873
Fannin	BUTLER, J. T. & Mary	Charley	4 Aug 1874
Gregg	BUTTS, James T. & Amanda I.	James Floyd	27 Apr 1875
Jasper	BYERLY, James R. and Louize (sic) M.	Louiz (sic) Eda Rebecca	27 May 1874

COUNTY	PARENTS	CHILD	DATE
Jasper	BYERLY, William and Martha A.	Sarah E.	
	Note: This birth was registered 8 Mar 1875.		— — —
Cherokee	BYRD, M. L. & M. A.	Mary Lewis	21 Mar 1876
Cherokee	BYRD, Wm. L. and Mary A.	Edwin E.	21 Sep 1873
Marion	BYSON(?), D. N. & H. M.	Alley Nancy	8 Feb 1874
Fannin	CABINESS, L. R. & R. A.	Charles H.	25 Jul 1873
Webb	CABRA, Lucia (Mrs. Ynocencio Medina)		
Jasper	CADE, Jerry and Hulda	Sallie	15 Oct 1875
Upshur	CALWAY, J. A. & Ida	Ollie	29 Oct 1873
		Minnie	14 May 1874
Fannin	CALDWELL, David & Lucy	Martha S.	15 Jun 1874
Fannin	CALDWELL, T. J. & M. P.	L. E.	Mar 1876
Navarro	CALLAWAY, R. C. & E. K.	Ada Ophelia	24 Feb 1874
Anderson	CALLOWAY, Newton and Ann	W. J.	17 Oct 1875
Anderson	CALLOWAY, Wm. A. and Flora E.	Elizabeth J.	22 Sep 1875
Upshur	CALVERT, D. E. & N. J.	W. E.	9 Oct 1875
Webb	CAMACHO, Eleuteria & Apolonia	Elpidia	4 Mar 1876
Dallas	CAMERON, D. T. and Suzana	David R.	13 Apr 1866
		Emly (sic) A.	1 Nov 1868
		Debora J.	10 Feb 1870
Cass	CAMERON, G. M. & E. E.	Ewla F. or (L?)	3 Mar 1874
Rusk	CAMERON, Isaac & Margaret	Matilda	16 Apr 1875
Rusk	CAMERON, J. M. & M. S. E.	Ewing F.	7 Nov 1873
Upshur	CAMP, W. S. & M. J.	James Oscar	30 Jun 1875
Lamar	CAMPBELL, G. W. & M. P.	Lee James	26 Oct 1874
Rusk	CAMPBELL, George W. & Mariah H.	George R.	2 Jul 1874
Anderson	CAMPBELL, J. I. and Florance M.	Cyrus Albynus	24 Mar 1874
		Donald	17 Feb 1876
Navarro	CAMPBELL, J. P. & Lutitia (sic)	Minnie	1 Dec 1873
Rusk	CAMPBELL, Jerry & Martha	Mary E.	Apr 1875
Anderson	CAMPBELL, John and M. E.	Joseph A.	23 Aug 1874
		Ada S.	12 Nov 1875
Fannin	CAMPBELL, R. W. & Mallie C.	Eunice	14 Jun 1873
Gregg	CAMPBELL, Thomas D. & Cynthis D.	Thomas Duncan	26 Jul 1874
Anderson	CANFIELD, P. A. and Sarah V.	Eugene A.	9 Oct 1874
Rusk	CANNON, Robert T. and Caroline M.	Carrie May	1874
Fannin	CANTWELL, James & Sallie	J. H.	30 Jan 1875
Rusk	CAPPS, T. J. & M. W.	Albert B.	4 Sep 1875
Upshur	CAPS, M. C. & F. C.	J. W.	25 Nov 1873
Fannin	CARAWAY, James E. & Eliza B.	Ann Eliza	May 1876
Webb	CARDENES, George & Rita E.	Rumaldo	7 Feb 1876
		Florencia	7 Feb 1876
Fannin	CARDER, W. I. & Nancy	Samuel E.	28 Nov 1874
Washington	CARMEAN, J. N. & M. A.	John	23 Aug 1874
Kaufman	CARPENTER, P. M. & M. E.	Albert Lewis	23 Feb 1874
Rusk	CARR, W. L. & Mary V.	John Forrest	14 Apr 1874
Gregg	CARRIE, Constantine B. & Franis Y.	Licia	7 Feb 1876
Navarro	CARROLL, B. F. & G. A.	May	1 May 1874
Navarro	CARROLL(?), Isaac & Celia	Harriet Susan Mary Fillis	9 Dec 1873
Rusk	CARROLL, Joseph A. & Emily	James W.	9 Mar 1875
Upshur	CARROLL, S. G. & S. C.	Jacob R.	29 Dec 1873
Fannin	CARROWAY, D. O. & Mary	William D.	5 Feb 1875
Rusk	CARTER, Hubbard & ___	Edgar Hubbard	
Fannin	CARTER, James W. & Sallie A.	William B.	28 Feb 1875
Rusk	CARTER, Robert & Mandy	Robert Lee	15 May 1873
Rusk	CARTER, Roda Ann (Mrs. E. J. Adams)		

COUNTY	PARENTS	CHILD	DATE
Fannin	CARTER, S. L. & <u>Soc</u>	Dorset DeGress	26 Dec 1873
Navarro	CARTER, Wm. L. &		
	Elizabeth J.	Jemima Izora	12 Oct 1873
Rusk	CARY, Jack and Mahala	Green	Oct 1874
Navarro	CASADY, John & F. A.	Maggie Florence	8 Nov 1874
Cherokee	CASEY, Albert & Martha	James H.	19 Mar 1874
Cherokee	CASEY, W. L. and H. D.	E. E.	31 Jan 1874
Navarro	CASKEY, J. G. & L. A.	John Robert	28 Jan 1874
		Emery Cicero	30 Nov 1875
Upshur	CASTELL, B. L. and T. L.	Clara F.	29 Jan 1874
Cameron	CASTILLO, Alvino and		
	Franca (Martinez)	Espiridon	14 Dec 1873
		Macedonio	3 Aug 1876
Navarro	CASTLES, Geo. W. & Sallie E.	James Andrew	4 May 1874
Navarro	CASTLES, J. J. & Elizabeth A.	Walter Marvin	6 Feb 1875
Rusk	CATHY, Ross and Isabella	Gova H.	24 Aug 1875
Fannin	CATNER (or COTNER?), Marcos &		
	C. C.	Kirk	21 Feb 1875
Jasper	CAUSEY, Thomas W. and		
	Eliza D.	Fany (sic) D.	26 Jul 1874
Cherokee	CAUSEY, W. C. and T. C.	Z. D.	3 Dec 1873
Gregg	CAUSEY, W. R. & Puss	Eula Ann	29 Sep 1875
Fannin	CAYLOR, J. L. & Jennie	Frederick Lee	16 Nov 1874
Anderson	CELY, B. C. and M. C.	Cara E.	9 Jul 1875
Rusk	CENTER, Charles & Clara	Charles	Sep 1874
Navarro	CERF, Lewis & Rachael	Isaac N.	23 Dec 1873
Rusk	CHAMBERLAIN, Hubbard & Sue	Ellwyn H.	16 Feb 1875
Anderson	CHAMBERS, B. F. and Amanda	Franklin	9 Jul 1873
Cass	CHAMBLISS, W. P. & Laura	Lola	30 Sep 1874
Rusk	CHAMNESS, B. C. & Amanda	William J.	2 Feb 1875
Rusk	CHAMNESS, Ben C. & Maudy	V. P.	— — —
		J. Knox	— — —
		W. J.	— — —
Rusk	CHANNEL, Zack and Harriett	Lula	16 Dec 1875
Cameron	CHAPA, Delfina (Mrs. Francisco Sarrasquita)		
Rusk	CHAPMAN, W. M. & Martha J.	Luella	21 Jun 1875
Nueces	CHAPMAN, Wm. B. & Jessie R.	Jessie Blair	8 Jan 1869
		Helen Preston	21 Nov 1874
Webb	CHARO, Nicholas &		
	Maria Rita (Alcaras)	Nicholas	4 Dec 1875
Cherokee	CHESHER, A. J. & Malvina	John B.	26 Nov 1874
Upshur	CHRISTIAN, Cid or Arid &		
	C. K.	C. H.	10 Sep 1875
Rusk	CHRISTIE, Monroe & Agnes	Antnette(sic)	2 Sep 1875
Navarro	CHURCH, E. H. & L. H.	Eva Payne	23 Jan 1876
		Ruth	28 Feb 1877
Navarro	CHURCH, W. L. & Victoria	Shelby Loyd (sic)	15 Jul 1874
Fannin	CLAGHORN, M. C. & A. E.	J. P.	1 Jul 1875
Jasper	CLAND, Benjamin F. &		
	Nancy A.	John C.	15 Jun 1874
Fannin	CLARK, E. J. & Nancy k.	Nathaniel	1 Jan 1875
Lamar	CLARK, F. H. & Mary A.	Anna Narcissa	14 Oct 1874
Navarro	CLARK, G. W. & Martha T.	Mary Elizabeth	20 Jul 1873
Lamar	CLARK, H. L. & O (orQ?) T.	Henry Clinton	13 Sep 1873
		Emma Fort	4 Nov 1874
Gregg	CLARK, Thomas B. &		
	Virginia B.	Thomas	12 Mar 1876
Fannin	CLARK, W. T. & L. B.	Mary Alice	26 Jun 1874
Dallas	CLARKE, Jno. G. and Narcie M.	Jesse Gaw	19 Mar 1876
Fannin	CLARY, John J. & T. E.	Samuel O.	3 Dec 1874
Navarro	CLARY, John T. & Mary V.	John Hemon(sic)	10 Aug 1873
Navarro	CLARY, M. P. & L. E.	Allie Bina	6 Jun 1874
Navarro	CLARY, M. P. & S. E.	Susannah	16 Jul 1875
Rusk	CLEMENTS, T. J. & Harriet	R. H.	3 Mar 1875
Rusk	CLEMONS, Julius & Josephine	Susan Ann	10 Mar 1875

COUNTY	PARENTS	CHILD	DATE
Rusk	CLINTON, James E. &		
	Amanda Jane	Mary Francis	5 Nov 1873
Lamar	CLOUD, R. G. & S. J.	J. F.	4 Jan 1874
Rusk	COATS, O. P. & Ann	W. P.	28 Mar 1874
		Ed	1 Apr 1876
Fannin	COBB, J. M. & Elizabeth	Mary Elizabeth	8 Dec 1874
Dallas	COCHRAN, John H. and		
	Martha Jane	Geo. Washington	17 Jul 1873
Rusk	COCKBURN, H. C. & Nannie E.	Susan F.	25 Nov 1873
Rusk	COCKBURN, William and		
	Emory Jane	Robert Emory	26 Jan 1874
Rusk	COCKRAN, J. Y. & M. C.	Annie	6 Jan 1874
Kaufman	COFFMAN, T. J. & C. A.	Joseph N.	15 Oct 1873
Gregg	COHN, Albert & May	Hana	15 Feb 1868
		Berta	25 Dec 1872
		Minnie	1 Jan 1874
Nueces	COHN, Phillip & Mary	Edwin	20 Feb 1876
Navarro	COKER, Saml. L. & Sarah A.	George Thomas	26 Dec 1873
Navarro	COKER, Wesley & Alice	Eddie Hood	15 Nov 1873
Navarro	COLE, F. P. & Virginia A.	Bertha	22 Aug 1875
Anderson	COLEMAN, T. and H.	Bob	4 Mar 1873
Rusk	COLEMAN, Thomas H. &		
	Francis Georgia		4 Sep 1873
		Matthew W.	18 Nov 1874
Anderson	COLLY, Thos. M. and Mary E.	Paul Sims	12 Aug 1875
Rusk	COLWELL, J. J. & Anvil C.	James R.	24 Dec 1873
Dallas	COMBS, G. E. & Rebecca F.	Bettie	21 Oct 1873
		Charles E.	25 Sep 1875
Navarro	COMPERE, J. L. & M. C.	Mary Allice	23 Nov 1874
Rusk	COMPTON, D. J. & S. E.	James	9 Apr 1874
Washington	COMPTON, G. F. & A. A.	Ruben James	1 Feb 1874
Fannin	COMPTON, Green & Aza	John	26 Jul 1876
Rusk	COMPTON, J. W. & E. C. Carrie	Lewis G.	8 Nov 1874
Anderson	CONAWAY, J. W. and M. A.	Mary Alice	18 Nov 1875
Cass	CONEY (or COVEY?), M. W. &		
	L. H.	E. R.	27 Feb 1874
Navarro	CONNER, Cupid & Easter	Joel	16 Apr 1875
Fannin	COOK, Anderson & Elizabeth	S. R.	Jan 1875
Rusk	COOK, John C. & Sarah Ann	J. C.	22 Jul 1875
Rusk	COOK, John R. and Susan E.	Lucinda	16 Jan 1875
Cherokee	COOK, S. H. and Elizabeth	Manerva	26 Nov 1873
Fannin	COONROD, John & H. L.	M. A. C.	5 May 1875
Lamar	COOPER, B. P. & C. T.		8 Apr 1875
Anderson	COOPER, W. M. and S. E.	James Martin	1 Feb 1875
Cherokee	COPELAND, G. W. and Martha J.	William M.	23 Oct 1873
Jasper	COPELAND, James B. and		
	C. Angiline	James	14 Aug 1874
Fannin	COPELAND, R. M. & M. A.	Austin	9 Jan 1875
Fannin	COPELAND, Sam'l & Mary A.	Newton H.	1 Mar 1874
Fannin	CORDER, C. T. & N. E.	L. A.	28 Aug 1874
Kaufman	CORLEY, John H. and M. P.	Thomas(?) E.	26 May 1873
Marion	CORLEY, W. G. & N. E.	John Edgar	15 Feb 1873
		Ennis Cook	
Rusk	COSS, Westley & Harriet	Lela	20 Aug 1873
Rusk	COST, Westley & Harriett	Kitti	31 Jul 1875
Marion	COTTON, J. P. & G. C.	Edgar	31 Jul 1873
Kaufman	COTTON, W. & M. A.	Edgar	5 Nov 1874
	Note: Must be twins born	Ivan	6 Nov 1874
	on 2 days.		
Fannin	COURSEY, A. J. & Mary E.	John H.	6 Nov 1873
		James T.	20 Sep 1875
Navarro	COURSEY, James Jr. &		
	Nancy C.	James Benjamin	4 Jul 1873
Fannin	COURSEY, W. H. & F. M.	William A.	20 Nov 1875
Rusk	COUSINS, Isaac M. & Abba S.	Sarah H.	3 May 1875
Fannin	COVINGTON, W. A. & N. C.	N. A.	7 Nov 1873

97

COUNTY	PARENTS	CHILD	DATE
Fannin	COWART, Alex & Amelia L.	Arley	16 Sep 1874
Cameron	COWEN, Louis and Isabel Lorena	Louis Rutland William	27 Mar 1863
		Una Anna	9 May 1865
		Alfred Benjamin	21 Jun 1867
		Frederick Neale	22 Apr 1872
		David Elias	27 Apr 1874
Fannin	COX, Burwell & Sallie H.	Philip	1 Jul 1874
Fannin	COX, C. C. & M. H.	William E.	5 Aug 1875
Fannin	COX, John G. & Martha	Emily Ann	2 Mar 1874
Rusk	COX, Mitchell & Mandy	Nellie Grant	25 Nov 1874
	(twins)	Betsy Flanagan	25 Nov 1874
Fannin	COX, T. B. & S. R.	Alice N.	22 Sep 1874
Fannin	COX, T. C. & N. C.	B. W.	25 Feb 1874
		Nute	Sep ___
Fannin	COX, W. B. & M. E.	Lucy Mildred	6 Nov 1873
Rusk	CRAIG, Lewis & Ellen	D.	1 Jun 1875
Rusk	CRAIG, T. B. & Martha J.	Paul	28 May 1875
Rusk	CRAIG, W. D. L. F. & Amanda J.	Amanda Louella R.	20 Mar 1874
Rusk	CRANE, Anderson & Patsy	Amy	11 Nov 1874
Fannin	CRAVENS, W. H. & Mary E.	John A.	24 Dec 1873
Kaufman	CRAWFORD, J. C. & J. B.	John G.	10 Nov 1874
Rusk	CRAWFORD, Wallace & Mariah	Lewis	10 Apr 1874
		Willis	15 Nov 1875
Cass	CRAWSON (or CRONSON?), R. J. & V.	J. H. (or F?)	3 Mar 1873
Cass	CREEKMORE, R. F. & A. J.	Annie M.	30 Sep 1873
Rusk	CRIM, J. P. & Julia A.	Joseph R.	26 Dec 1874
Fannin	CRITTENDEN, Jesse & Lucy	Joel A.	10 Apr 1874
Rusk	CRITTENDON, Wright & Sofa	Easter	3 Jun 1875
Lamar	CROCKETT, W. P. & Mary F.	Benj. Milton	12 Mar 1875
Navarro	CROFT, Wm. & Rebecca	Lily May	20 Feb 1875
Upshur	CROLEY, G. T. & M. A.	Texas B. or P.	15 Feb 1874
Lamar	CROMWELL, John & S. F.	A. J.	11 Oct 1873
Lamar	CROOK, J. D. & Emma	Elgie Ida	30 Sep 1874
Navarro	CROPLAND (CROSSLAND?), H. L. & Lucinda	Halbert L.	4 Jan 1875
Fannin	CROUCH, W. J. & Alice V.	D. G.	28 Dec 1875
Rusk	CROW, D. P. & Nell	Ada Bell	30 Apr 1874
Rusk	CROW, W. J. & Sarah W.	Joel Thomas	22 Apr 1874
Washington	CRUNDMLL(?), J. M. & R.	M. A.	23 Jun 1874
Gregg	CRUTCHER, Isaac H. & Lula T.	Isaac H., Jr.	10 May 1875
	Note: both registered 5/29/1876	Earl	10 May 1875
Fannin	CULBERSON, I. M. & Mollie	Rachel E.	9 Dec 1873
Fannin	CULPEPPER, J. A. & A. J.	E. A.	18 Mar 1875
Nueces	CULVER, Martin S. & Catherine (Pugh)	Martin P.	14 Jan 1875
Upshur	CUNLIFFE, H. C. & P. J.	Maud	24 Nov 1875
Fannin	CUNNINGHAM, John & Fannie	John B.	25 Mar 1874
Lamar	CUNNINGHAM, L. A. & A.	Lizzie Orlena Jackson	8 Jan 1875
Rusk	CURBO, John T. & Lucinda	Millie D.	27 Oct 1874
Rusk	CURBO, Thomas B. & Sarah	Tennessee Jane	8 Nov 1873
Jasper	CURTIS, Richard J. and Aurelia J.	Robert M.	22 Feb 1874
Anderson	CUSON, J. F. and Eliza	S. A.	28 Feb 1874
Anderson	CUTHBERTSON, T. and Angelina	Mary A. E.	5 Feb 1874
Washington	DAFFAN, L. A. & M. A.	Katie L.	29 Jul 1874
Cherokee	DALBY, I. K. & M.	Ida May	12 Jun 1874
Cherokee	DALBY, John M. & Alice	John R.	27 Sep 1874
Cass	DANIEL, John T. & ___	Missouri I.	23 Jul 1873

COUNTY	PARENTS	CHILD	DATE
Rusk	DANIEL, S. A. & R. E.	Irena	27 Nov 1875
Rusk	DANIEL, Wiley & Joanna	Betsey	29 May 1875
Rusk	DANSBY, Harry & Susanna	Peter	1 Mar 1875
Kaufman	DANSBY, Isaac and Sallie	Isaac Jacob	11 Jul 1873
Rusk	DANSBY, Joe Newton & Louisa	Elizabeth M.	*25 Oct 1875
	*Elizabeth M. was recorded 25 Oct 1875		
		John Henry	15 May 1875
Kaufman	DANSBY, R. C. & S. E.	Robbie Estelle Marshall	5 May 1876
Fannin	DARBEY (or DAILEY?), W. E. & J. B.	Richard O.	31 Jan 1874
Fannin	DARNALL, A. H. & Barbara	Melissa A.	2 Apr 1875
Lamar	DAUGHERTY, J. N. & G.		14 May 1873
Fannin	DAUGHERTY, Jason & M. A.	William O.	29 May 1873
		Jason E.	17 Dec 1874
Rusk	DAVENPORT, S. R. & Matilda	Maggie Mae	15 Dec 1873
		William H.	21 Aug 1875
Rusk	DAVENPORT, W. D. & J. M.	Mary E.	10 Dec 1873
		Richard W.	16 Jan 1875
Cameron	DAVEREDE, Josephine (Mrs. Basile Abadie)		
Cherokee	DAVID, W. L. and S. B.	Mary Lou	15 Oct 1873
Fannin	DAVIDSON, Thos. & Mary L.	George A.	16 Dec 1874
Washington	DAVIDSON, Thos. Green & Mary Jane	Martha Isabella	4 Dec 1873
Fannin	DAVIS, Alfred A. & Libbie	Thomas H.	13 Feb 1874
Rusk	DAVIS, B. G. and M. E.	Rebecca	20 May 1875
Lamar	DAVIS, D. C. & C. A.	H. C. (or E?)	2 Apr 1873
		James Edgar	9 Sep 1874
Upshur	DAVIS, E. N. & Elizabeth J.	Lucy	4 Nov 1875
Anderson	DAVIS, Henry and M. E.	Arthur	28 Mar 1874
			2 Apr 1876
Lamar	DAVIS, J. L. & L. G.	Nora	20 Jan 1873
Kaufman	DAVIS, J. L. and Louisa	W. R.	16 Nov 1874
Lamar	DAVIS, J. S. & Laura G.	Izer Felix	31 Dec 1875
Navarro	DAVIS, James &	Thomas Jefferson	26 Aug 1877
Fannin	DAVIS, John R. & Joe (sic)		4 Jul 1875
Upshur	DAVIS, M. F. & M. C.	Abram J.	5 Dec 1873
Fannin	DAVIS, Sam'l & A. E.	Almarias	22 Oct 1873
Rusk	DAVIS, Stepney & Mariah	Ophelia	14 Oct 1874
Rusk	DAVIS, W. H. & Nancy	Martha Ellen	6 Jan 1876
Upshur	DAVIS, W. R. & Beckie	Margaret J.	13 Dec 1875
Rusk	DAVIS, William P. and Julia A. R.	Cora M.	9 Feb 1875
Anderson	DAY, G. N. and Elizabeth	Ida E.	7 Jan 1876
Rusk	DAY, Lawrence and ___		9 Aug 1874
Washington	DAY, Thos. & Allie	Thomas, Jr.	22 Sep 1875
Lamar	DEAN, J. S. & M.	Minnie	9 Jun 1875
Upshur	DEAN, L. L. & E. A.	P. B. 25 or 27 Sep 1874	
Rusk	DEASON, J. H. & Martha	Florence	25 Apr 1874
Rusk	DEASON, W. F. and Annie B.	Edgar	21 Mar 1875
Lamar	DEATHERAGE, A. W. & S. J.	William Walter	6 Jun 1875
Upshur	DEDANE, James & Eugenia	Catharine	23 Jul 1873
Fannin	DEEL, Dillard & M. A.	M. A.	3 Feb ___
		(Reg. 17 May 1875)	
Fannin	DEEL, R. C. & Nancy	P. F.	
		(Reg. 9/7/1875)	
Rusk	DeLAMAR, G. H. and N. M.	Sallie Olivia	6 Sep 1874
Rusk	DeLAMAR, Thomas S. & Amanda M.	Thomas L.	8 May 1875
Webb	DE LEON, Gervacio & Yncela (Garcia)	Roberto	31 Jul 1874
		Ynacia	6 Jul 1875
Cameron	DELGADO, Marcelo and Vicenta	Carlos V.	14 Apr 1870
		Jose P.	7 Jun 1874
Kaufman	DELLIS, W. P. & C. E.	T. S.	4 Jul 1874
		Martin Preston	7 Sep 1875

COUNTY	PARENTS	CHILD	DATE
Gregg	DELOY, Francis Lania & Annie V.	Alice Virginia	1 Nov 1873
		George Edwin	5 Feb 1875
Kaufman	DENMAN, W. M. & M. E.	J. C.	5 Oct 1873
Lamar	DENTON, G. A. & C. M.	Georgia R.	27 Feb 1875
Upshur	DERRICK, Dick & Susan	Achsah(?)	20 May 1874
Fannin	DERRICK, George C. & Mary J.	Vida V.	22 Feb 1875
Upshur	DERRICK, J. A., Jr. & Lucetta C.	Viola W.	9 Oct 1874
Cherokee	DESHLER, C. B. & A. M.	E. M.	14 Dec 1874
Cameron	DeSORIA, Rafael and Josephine	Matilda Adelaide	9 Feb 1865
		Alfred Newton	18 Apr 1867
		Joseph Hiram	18 Jun 1869
Washington	DEVER, N. E. & R. H.	Walter E.	8 Oct 1873
Lamar	DEWEESE, Luke W. & M. A.	J. W. L.	21 Jul 1875
Lamar	DeWITT, C. A. & M. E.	John B.	___ Jul 1874
Gregg	DICKARD, David A. & Sarah J.	David Morse	6 Apr 1876
Kaufman	DICKERSON, M. J. & M.	R. B.	27 Jan 1874
Lamar	DICKEY, J. W. & S. A.	Chas. W.	12 Mar 1875
Kaufman	DICKEY, T. F. & M. J.	Charles Franklin	29 Jan 1874
Rusk	DICKINSON, Benjamin C. & Mariah C.	Benjamin	7 Jan 1874
		William Leonidas	27 May 1876
Kaufman	DICKSON, J. W. & M. P.	C. E.	15 Aug 1873
Rusk	DICKSON, Samuel & Mary	Augusta	
Fannin	DIXON, A. B. & P. N.	James L.	9 Apr 1874
Washington	DOBERT, Frank & A.	Joseph	13 Jul 1875
Fannin	DODD, P. H. & Alberta	Wiley	3 Apr 1875
Lamar	DODSON, B. F. & Lena	Nellie J.	9 Jul 1873
Lamar	DODSON, Jas. B. & Sarah E.	Katherine	26 Aug 1874
Fannin	DOFF, John & Margaret	Callie	Feb 1876
Navarro	DONAHO, F. F. & C.	Charls (sic)	27 Oct 1874
Cherokee	DONAHO, W. L. (?) and H. L. (?)	Orsin	1 Dec 1873
Fannin	DONALDSON, J. S. & E. C.	L. M.	Dec 1874
Navarro	DOOLEN, A. H. & M. M.	Sallie Margaret	22 Apr 1874
Navarro	DOOLEN, J. M. & M. F.	Hettie Eldora	22 Jul 1874
Jasper	DOOM, David W. and Esther P.	John Randolph	2 Aug 1873
Nueces	DORETY, B. P. & Helen	Nellie Viola	25 Jul 1875
Fannin	DORSET, John S. & M. Bud (or Bird?)	William S.	30 May 1874
		J. S.	2 Jan 1876
Navarro	DORSEY, Wm. B. & Mary C.	Mamah Idella	17 Nov 1873
Fannin	DOSS, Charles & Mary Elizabeth	Bird	22 Nov 1873
		Charles Edward	15 Jan 1875
Fannin	DOSS, J. W. & Julia	Lucy	19 Jun 1874
Jasper	DOTSON, Anthony and Cresie (Smith)	Anna	10 Mar 1871
Cameron	DOUGHERTY, James and Mary Ann T.	Elizabeth S.	22 Aug 1873
		Alice S.	16 Dec 1876
Navarro	DOUGHTY, A. J. & L.	Maggie Alice	19 Sep 1874
Anderson	DOUGHTY, H. P. and M. J.	Joanna Edna	23 Nov 1874
Cherokee	DOUGLAS, Jos.(?) P. and Annie	Allen Dorie	
Webb	DOVALINA, Blas & Zaragosa S.	Paulino	19 Nov 1875
Webb	DOVALINA, Espiridion & Alvina	Prajedis	23 Jun 1874
Webb	DOVALINA, Marcos & Josefa (Basquez)	Asuncion	15 Aug 1873
Navarro	DOWDY, W. H. & Margaret	Jasper Newton	11 Aug 1873

COUNTY	PARENTS	CHILD	DATE
Fannin	DOWNEY, John A. & A. E.	Josie Elizabeth	8 Oct 1874
Fannin	DOWNEY, Samuel P. &		
	Louisa J.	James W.	19 Oct 1873
Fannin	DRIGGERS, William & Malinda	Margaret	___ Dec 1874
Fannin	DUCKWORTH, G. G. & F. E.	R. F.	10 Oct 1874
Fannin	DUCKWORTH, P. J. & Jane	Joseph A.	28 Nov 1873
Navarro	DUDNEY, (sic) B. F. & Mary	Joseph Edward	24 Jun 1873
		Mobley	24 May 1875
Navarro	DUKE, T. M. & H. P.	Martha	26 Aug 1874
Fannin	DULANCY, Henry & Julia A.	Mandy	23 Mar 1875
Fannin	DULANEY, William & Mary	Burr	19 Jun 1875
Rusk	DULIN, ___ and Tempy	J. L.	1 Oct 1875
Rusk	DUNCAN, George W. & Nancy	George Ann	8 Jun 1874
		John R.	16 Nov 1875
Fannin	DUNCAN, J. M. & Ida	Ada J.	8 Jul 1873
Cass	DUNCAN, Jesse A. &		
	Caroline	George Asberry	13 Dec 1873
Upshur	DUNEGAN, Thos. S. & Emily	James L.	26 Mar 1874
Fannin	DUNN, J. M. & Lucy	George E.	29 May 1874
Fannin	DUNN, J. W. & Lou L.	Ladonia May	May 1873
		W. G.	28 Apr 1875
Jasper	DUNN, Jeremiah and Elizabeth	William R.	8 Nov 1874
Nueces	DUNN, Joseph W. & Oreanda J.	Mack H.	26 Nov 1873
Anderson	DUPUY, H. M. and Victoria	Francis Anna	24 Feb 1874
		William A.	6 Jan 1876
Rusk	DURAN, Taylor and Everline	Rosetta	25 May 1875
Navarro	DUREN, W. W. & J. P.	Lula Belle	4 Apr 1875
Anderson	DURR, Louis and Mary	Albert G.	29 Dec 1873
Fannin	DYER, J. D. & E. E.	Sallie S.	1 May 1875
Upshur	EARP, Henry H. & Winnie	Carry E.	17 Apr 1874
			or 1870
Rusk	EASLEY, W. M. & Rebecca E.	Susan E.	4 Oct 1875
Dallas	EBLEN, J. G. and L. S.	Eugene	16 Sep 1874
		Raymond Sterrett	28 Oct 1875
Rusk	EDDINGTON, J. O. & Mary A.	J. C.	29 Nov 1874
Navarro	EDGAR, W. A. & Martha	Almeda C.	7 Aug 1874
Rusk	EDMON, Thomas and Whiney	Thomas A.	25 Nov 1874
Rusk	EDMONDSON, Lige & Susan	Lucy	9 Aug 1875
Washington	EDWARDS, Ed & Lucy	Mary Ella	15 Mar 1873
Fannin	EDWARDS, J. J. & Mary E.	Frank	14 Nov 1874
			21 Mar 1875
Fannin	EDWARDS, L. R. &		
	J. (or S?) L.	William L.	27 May 1874
Cameron	EGLY, Victor and		
	Catherine (Mear)	Elmine	25 Mar 1871
		Mary Ann	12 Dec 1873
Fannin	EILAND, J. H. H. & Rebecca	Basie M.	1875
		(Reg. 26 Jul 1875)	
Fannin	ELAM, J. R.& Jennie	Ella H.	5 Apr 1874
Upshur	ELDEN, E. E. & S. A.	Effie A.	28 Dec 1875
Kaufman	ELDER, C. E. & M. E.	N. J.	15 Apr 1875
Navarro	ELIOT, G. W. & R. J.	Minnie	21 Jan 1874
Rusk	ELKINS, T. C. & Mary	Arthur	14 Jun 1875
	(twins)	Ader	14 Jun 1875
Cass	ELLINGTON, T. S. & N. R.	Nancy L.	9 Jul 1873
Navarro	ELLIOTT, C. K. & Leah B.	George Thomas	11 Dec 1874
Rusk	ELLIOTT, E. L. and A. V.	H. L.	16 Aug 1874
Cherokee	ELLIS, A. and Matilda	Elizabeth	29 Jun 1874
Lamar	ELLIS, L. B. & S. J.	Sallie Lewis	17 Jul 1874
Anderson	ELROD, B. L. and C.	Esta Jane	24 May 1876
Anderson	ELROD, J. C. and S. E.	John Madison	13 Dec 1874
Fannin	ELROY, G. J. & Anne	James O.	7 Mar 1874
Anderson	EMERSON, J. M. and S. E.	Caroline	24 Dec 1873
		Chesley R.	28 Nov 1875
Rusk	EMORY, ___ & Needy	Buster	30 Oct 1874
Fannin	ENGLISH, B. B. & Elizabeth	Henry Walter	13 Sep 1873

County	Parents	Child	Date
Fannin	ERSKIN, Mose & Mary	John	20 Feb 1874
Anderson	ERWIN, A. F. and Dora R.	Beulah Belle	13 Sep 1875
Lamar	ERWIN, F. H. & E.	Analiza	6 Sep 1873
Kaufman	ERWIN, Henry and Nancy	John Henry	22 Feb 1876
Anderson	ERWIN, James and M. E.	Willie N.	7 Jan 1873
Rusk	ERWIN, T. C. & J. L.	Mattie Adel	23 Sep 1873
	Note: surname is also spelled ERVIN in this listing.		
Webb	ESCAMILLA, Aniceto & Anastacia T.	Juana	27 May 1874
Nueces	EVANS, George Frederick & Cornelia Maria	Alfred Duce	14 Jan 1874
Nueces	EVANS, H.(?) E. (Mrs. Horwick (?) Gussett)		
Fannin	EVANS, J. C. & Lucy G.	Edna Pearl	26 Nov 1874
Rusk	EVANS, Peter & Harriet	Arthur Webster	22 Jun 1875
Navarro	EVANS, W. J. & M. J.	Elizabeth Jane	22 Jan 1874
Washington	EVANS, Wm. & Lucy	Hally	29 Jun 1873
Rusk	EVANS, Willis & Harriet	Lucinda M.	1 Mar 1875
Washington	EVANSICK, F. & M.	John	1 Nov 1873
Anderson	EVES, John and Oma I.	James	30 Sep 1874
Kaufman	EWING, G. & E.	James F.	20 May 1874
Lamar	EYERS, W. G. & F. E.	Llewellyn Delms	16 Nov 1875
Anderson	FAIRES, J. H. and Emily	C. C.	6 Mar 1875
		Charley	26 Mar 1876
Fannin	FAISON, J. I. & M. A.	C. K.	14 May 1875
Rusk	FALKNER, M. D. & M. A. E.	Harrison L.	11 May 1875
Webb	FARIAS, Francisca & Francisca	Crispina Inocente	25 Oct 1874
Anderson	FARISH, William and Jane	Laura	8 May 1873
Navarro	FARMER, Isaac M. & R. A.	James Edward	11 Feb 1874
Webb	FARRELL, Michael & Duga R.	Mary Ann	14 Jun 1874
Kaufman	FENDER, J. W. & M. A.	Josephine	28 Feb 1874
		Cora	4 Jun 1876
Kaufman	FENDER, R. N. & T. V.	C. D.	7 Jan 1874
Navarro	FERGUSON, J. M. & M. J.	Martha Jane	14 Oct 1873
Jasper	FERGUSON, W. A. and M. F.	E. J.	13 Dec 1874
Jasper	FERGUSON, William F. and Clara E.	William S.	27 Apr 1876
Cameron	FERNANDEZ, Victoriano and Elena (Garza)	Emilia	5 Oct 1871
		Clara	12 Aug 1873
		Elena	12 Jun 1875
Lamar	FEWELL, Z. R. & Mary J.	Howard	27 Nov 1875
Fannin	FIELD, Seaman & Maggie	Millie	4 Jul 1875
Dallas	FIELD, Thos. & Florence	Herbert Quincy	22 Aug 1872
		Caroline	4 Aug 1874
Somervell	FIELD, W. T. and L. J.	Elizabeth Maud	31 Jan 1876
Fannin	FINCHER, D. E. & S. E.	E. E.	8 Mar 1874
Gregg	FINCHER, Wm. J. & Matilda	Clarence Hillard Freeman	10 May 1876
Rusk	FINDLEY, Dick & Puss	Lewis	30 Nov 1875
Rusk	FINDLEY, N. Q. & Rebecca A.	Benjamin W.	13 May 1874
		Cerro Gorda	13 Jan 1876
Cherokee	FINDLEY, S. B. and Jennie	S. C.	12 Jan 1874
Cass	FINLEY, J. R. & E. E.	Wm. Charles	27 May 1875
Washington	FISCHER(?), H. & Mary	Ed. Heinrich	10 Aug 1873
Fannin	FISHER, M. S. & E. G.	W. B. L.	25 Oct 1874
Rusk	FITCH, Henry & Nancy	Sarah A.	11 Jun 1874
Fannin	FITCH, S. T. & A. R.	Arthur E.	25 Jun 1875
Fannin	FITZGERALD, A. B. & Olley	H. A.	22 Apr 1875
Anderson	FITZGERALD, J. E. and R. B.	Margaret J.	13 Oct 1875
Fannin	FITZGERALD, Jaboz & L. E.	John Thomas	25 Jan 1874
Fannin	FITZGERALD, W. P. & Emily	Lorna(?)	15 Apr 1874
Nueces	FITZSIMMONS, Jos. E. & Belle	Ella Eugenia	1 Jul 1874
Webb	FLORES, Inocencia (Mrs. Samuel M. Jarvis)		
Webb	FLORES, Vicenti & Petra	Ascension	15 Aug 1874

COUNTY	PARENTS	CHILD	DATE
Upshur	FLOYD, A. D. & M. A.	Jackson	__ Apr 1874
	Note: Second entry mother's name "Margie"		
Upshur	FLOYD, Emanuel & Catherine	John E.	24 Jan 187_
Upshur	FLUELIN, Ben & R. A.	Monroe	8 Jun 187̄4
Cherokee	FORD, C. E. and S. E.	2nd son, no name	28 Feb 1874
		(sic)	
Upshur	FORD, Charles & Lue	Martha	15 May 1874
		Arthur	18 Jan 1875
Kaufman	FORD, D. L. & I. (?)	Georgia C.	2 Dec 1874
Fannin	FORD, Harrison & Louisa	Alice	
		(Reg. 17 May 1874)	
Upshur	FORD, J. P. & P. A.	R. H.	3 Jul 1874
		E. N.	11 Feb 1876
Upshur	FORE, J. L. and S. A.	Eugene	7 Sep 1872
		Eddie	17 Oct 1874
Cherokee	FOREMAN, B. C. & Emma	J. H.	22 Dec 1874
Rusk	FOREMAN, D. & Mary	Lela M.	12 Feb 1874
Fannin	FORSHER, Geo. & Selphince	Samuel	19 Aug 1874
Navarro	FORTSON, B. F. & M. P.	Benjamin Craven	21 Jul 1874
Anderson	FOSTER, H. S. and Eva	William Mead	9 Jan 1875
Fannin	FOSTER, H. S. & Jane	William E.	11 Dec 1874
Fannin	FOSTER, L. N. & Amanda L.	Robert Lynn	17 Feb
		(Reg. 1 Jul 1876)	
Anderson	FOSTER, P. M. and Jennie	Clara Pearl	27 Feb 1876
Cameron	FOSTER, Robert B. and		
	Henrietta B.	Edith Bigelow	29 Oct 1870
		Margaret	7 Feb 1874
Nueces	FOSTER, S. F. & Mary	Samuel	3 Oct 1873
Fannin	FOSTER, S. P. & Margrett	Delle E.	30 Aug 1874
Navarro	FOUTY, C. & C. A.	Thomas	
		Montraville	18 Apr 1874
Rusk	FOWLER, D. R. & Maggie A.	Maud	__ Jan 1875
Rusk	FOWLER, L. S. & E. F.	Alma F.	̄2 Aug 1875
Kaufman	FOWLER, W. L. & A. N.	Harriet Jane	11 Oct 1873
		Alice	9 Oct 1875
Kaufman	FOX, C. J. & E. M.	Marion Lee	3 Aug 1873
Kaufman	FOX, J. H. and Mollie	Joseph E.	31 Jul 1873
Kaufman	FOX, T. W. & E.	Claudius	7 Jul 1873
		Robert C.	16 Mar 1875
Fannin	FOX, W. B. & M. C.	John C.	11 Jul 1874
Upshur	FOX, W. M. & A. E.	Virgie J. Annie	15 Jun 1875
Upshur	F (or T?) RADNCIA(?), Wm. &		
	Nancy A.	L.	11 Nov 1874
Anderson	FRAME, R. W. and M. J.	Willie Boon	10 Jun 1873
Upshur	FRANCES, A. M. & J. A.	Mary	14 Jul 1874
Cherokee	FRANCIS, C. C. & Brunnitt	Judith O.	__ 1875
Washington	FRANKE, H. & Louise	Fritz	̄1 Nov 1873
Fannin	FRANKFORD, J. F. & J. H.	Sarah A.	12 Apr 1875
Rusk	FRANKLIN, Henry & Harriett	Henrietta	18 Jul 1874
Anderson	FRANKLIN, J. W. and Nancy A.	Mary R.	15 Nov 1876
Navarro	FRANKS, R. J. & Sarah J.	Robert Lafayette	11 Oct 1874
Cass	FRAZIER, A. & S. J.	Lara Franklin	13 Mar 1875
Navarro	FREEMAN, E. R. & O. J.	Edda Cornelia	26 Nov 1874
Dallas	FREEMAN, J. A. and A. L.	James Edward	
		Wilson	21 Sep 1873
Rusk	FREEMAN, J. P. & L. F.	Edward A.	15 Aug 1873
		G. D.	5 Jan 1875
Rusk	FREEMAN, W. D. & S. F.	Mary F.	12 Aug 1873
Rusk	FREENY, Aaron & Anny	Jennie	16 May 1874
Rusk	FREENY, Rolly & Ellen	Kiney	15 Nov 1873
Rusk	FRIDDELL, T. R. & Malinda	Linnie	29 May 1874
Rusk	FRIZZELL, William &		
	Elizabeth	Laura E.	10 Jun 1875
Navarro	FROST, Sam R. &	Kate Marie	8 Aug 1873
	Mary L. (Mary A?)	Angelina (sic)	
		Azalea	29 Jun 1875

COUNTY	PARENTS	CHILD	DATE
Cameron	FUENTES, Geneveta(?) (Mrs. Bernardo Yturria)		
Dallas	FULLER, Aaron and Matilda	Francis M.	8 Jan 1875
Lamar	FULLER, Ben F. & Flora	Theta	7 Sep 1873
		Lenora	17 Dec 1875
Lamar	FULLER, Benjam (sic) & Mary A.	Joseph Harris	31 Dec 1874
Gregg	FULLER, David F. & Hattie E.	Hattie Ella	14 Jan 1875
Fannin	FULLER, H. E. & S. E.	Claudius D.	28 Jul 1873
Navarro	FULLERTON, James & Mary	Wm. H.	8 Mar 1874
Anderson	FULTON, L. D. and Susan F.	Mary Jeannetta	23 Jul 1873
Nueces	FUNK, Wm. L. & Emillia	Walter Lewis	26 Sep 1875
Rusk	FUTCH, G. W. & Callie	George P.	22 Aug 1874
Rusk	GADDY, William M. & Mary A.	Thomas T.	6 Feb 1875
Marion	GAFFORD, A. J. & Rebecca E.	Frederick Wm.	28 Oct 1873
Rusk	GAGE, C. R. & Elizabeth	Alice	6 Jul 1874
Washington	GAINES, Aaron & Lucinda	Amanda	2 Dec 1873
Fannin	GALE, Tom & Anna	William	28 Aug 1874
Rusk	GALES, Larry & Mariah	Westly	3 Aug 1875
Anderson	GALLAGHER, J. N. and M. C.	C. M.	10 Mar 1876
Anderson	GALLAGHER, James and Mary F.	Thomas D.	17 Mar 1874
Rusk	GALLWAY, Alec & Mary	Susan	12 Mar 1875
Rusk	GALLOWAY, Allen H. & Nannie D.	Amos S.	15 Feb 1875
Gregg	GALLOWAY, Clifford L. & Ida W.	Ida Ima	27 May 1875
Rusk	GALLOWAY, L. B. C. &		
	Elizabeth C.	Frank M.	17 Feb 1874
Webb	GAMBOA, Prudencio &		
	Gertrudis	Dario	2 Jan 1875
Anderson	GAMMAGE, T. T. and L. R.	Lula Clorida	7 Jul 1874
		(Clonda)	
Cameron	GARCIA, Francilea (Mrs. Samuel T. Belden)		
Webb	GARCIA, Henio &		
	Eulalia (Benavides)	Henio	18 Dec 1875
Cameron	GARCIA, Macedonio and		
	Guadalupe (Perez)	Ovidio	19 Jun 1874
		Hortencia	25 Dec 1875
		Erlinda	21 Aug 1877
		Macedonio Jose	2 Mar 1879
Webb	GARCIA, Ricaldo & Cerveda G.	Jesusa	1 Nov 1875
Nueces	GARCIA, Rosa (Mrs. Edward N. Gray)		
Webb	GARCIA, Trenidad (Mrs. Luis Telles)		
Webb	GARCIA, Yncela (Mrs. Gervacio Leon)		
Kaufman	GARDNER, A. T. & Lucy	Mary	20 Nov 1875
Rusk	GARLAND, ___ & ___	Hannah Recorded 31 Aug 1875	
	Note: No birth date was shown, but this birth was		
	recorded 31 Aug 1875		
Anderson	GARNER, Arch F. and Dora	Clarence A.	6 Sep 1873
Fannin	GARNER, Jr., O. B. & T. J.	Minnie J.	20 Aug 1874
Fannin	GARNER, P. A. & H. E.	Silas William	12 Sep 1873
Anderson	GARNER, S A. and R. C.	Talo	6 Jun 1872
		Anna Bell	3 Jun 1874
Washington	GARNETT, Aaron & Mary Ann	Savannah (Recorded 27 Oct 1875	
Upshur	GARRATT (or GANOTT?), G. L.		
	& Martha A.	Beny j F. (sic)	3 Apr 1875
Washington	GARRETT, C. C. & Dora	Edward Perry	12 Dec 1873
		Henry Lee	13 Oct 1875
Fannin	GARRETT, W. R. & Ann E.	Alford J.	19 Jan 1874
Rusk	GARRISON, R. F. & Sarah C.	Julius C.	31 Jul 1875
Rusk	GARRISON, W. B. M. &		
	Mary Jane	James S.	12 Aug 1875
	(twins)	F. S.	12 Aug 1875
Rusk	GARRISON, Z. B. & E. H.	Rosa Bonner	23 Nov 1875
Rusk	GARVIN, B. & Mary T.	G. T.	2 Sep 1874
Cass	GARY, Ed & Catharine	Preston	16 Sep 1874
		Bell (twins)	16 Sep 1874
Rusk	GARY, R. H. & Mary	Homer	16 Dec 1874
Webb	GARZA, de la, Cayetano &		
	Felipa	C. Vidal	3 Nov 1873

COUNTY	PARENTS	CHILD	DATE
Cameron	GARZA, Elena (Mrs. Victoriano Fernandez)		
Fannin	GA(or O?)SS, W. T. & Nannie	William Givan	24 Jan 1874
Upshur	GASTON, G. S. & Jane	Edker(?) C.	22 Jul 1874
Rusk	GASTON, J. F. & Pernetta B.	James F.	25 Jan 1875
Jasper	GASWAY, Jefferson and Sarah A.	Robert Houston	28 Jan 1875
Rusk	GATLIN, Henry and Joe A.	Bonnie B.	23 Aug 1873
Fannin	GATLIN, R. M. & Mary E.	Roxan	20 Jul 1874
Fannin	GAULDIN, Josiah & M. J.	J. B.	11 Jan 1875
Nueces	GAUSE, Augusta (Mrs. Richard H. E. Schubert)		
Rusk	GAUT, Samuel & Dicy M.	James Samuel	18 Sep 1873
Cherokee	GAY, C. F. & S. E.	Chas E.	15 Aug 1874
Gregg	GAY, John R. & Louisa M.	Nicholas Oslin	11 Jul 1873
Rusk	GAY, Marina (Mrs. Allen Boggess)		
Lamar	GEARON (or GERON?), S. C. & M. L.	L. K.	2 Mar 1874
Lamar	GEE, J. N. & Tobiatha	M. M.	5 Apr 1875
Rusk	GENTRY, J. F. & Mary L.	Ida	29 Jul 1875
Rusk	GENTRY, W. G. & N. J.	Elbert	7 Oct 1875
Cass	GEORGE, James E. & Mary L.	Stewart E. (or A?)	29 Jun 1873
Fannin	GERMAN, Frank M. & Mary C.	Geneva Jane	7 Jun 1875
Rusk	GERMANY, Robert and Liza	Etter P.	14 Mar 1874
Lamar	GIBSON, D. H. & E.	Charles W.	21 Aug 1873
Upshur	GIBSON, H. J. & Sarah A.	Eluka (or Eleekee?) L.	10 Dec 1873
Cherokee	GIBSON, James P. & Jennie B.	Carl Frank	21 May 1874
Fannin	GIBSON, M. W. & B. A.	W. E.	17 Dec 1874
Upshur	GIBSON, W. A. & A. P.	Lula E.	23 Nov 1874
		Ora Bell	10 Jul 1875
Washington	GIDDINGS, Geo. A. & M. E.	Hellen Estelle	26 Mar 1876
Washington	GIESECKE, G. F. & A. K.	Helene Antonia	5 Dec 1874
Washington	GIESECKE, H. L. & A.	Curt Paul	28 Aug 1874
Webb	GIL, Carlos & Maria (Jesus)	Carlos	15 Feb 1875
Upshur	GILLESPIE, A. T. & V. C.	Luther E.	12 May 1875
Kaufman	GILLESPIE, C. R. & Mary B.	Fannie M.	19 Dec 1874
Fannin	GILLIAM, W. H. & S. A.	Robert	22 Jan 1873
		Walter	13 Sep 1874
Nueces	GIVENS, John S. & Sallie (Torian(?))	John	23 Apr 1876
Rusk	GLADNEY, J. S. & Ronda	Albert T.	25 Oct 1874
		Lillian Lula	19 Jun 1875
Rusk	GLADNEY, T. L. & J. C.	Annie Bell	25 Feb 1875
Cherokee	GLASS, S. A. and Susan	Mary C.	2 Aug 1873
Cass	GLAZE, H. W. (or N?) & A. D.	E. J.	13 Aug 1874
Cass	GLAZE, I. R. & Mary		15 Aug 1873
Cass	GLAZE, J. R. & Mary	Baby	12 Aug 1875
Cass	GLAZE, P. H. & Mary A. E.	John	3 Jan 1874
		Baby	18 Oct 1875
Anderson	GLENN, N. A. and M. E.	Lula	22 Jun 1873
		Laura V.	6 Nov 1874
Cherokee	GLENN, N. B. F. & Susan	Adah Ann	17 Dec 1874
Anderson	GLENN, W. A. and F. S.	Thomas Martin	7 Oct 1874
Navarro	GOBER, Wm. M. & Lydia A.	William Marion	21 Dec 1873
Fannin	GOBLE, T. G. & Catharine	Thomas G.	16 Mar 1875
Lamar	GOFF, G. W. & Emma L.	Frank Perry	13 Nov 1872
Fannin	GOINE, B. F. & Ester	J. M.	10 Feb 1874
Upshur	GOLDEN, J. J. & Moriah(sic)	John A.	22 Jan 1874
Rusk	GOLDSBERRY, William and Rebecca	R. E. Lee	30 Oct 1874
Gregg	GOLDWATER, Henry & Maltilda	Henry Turner	3 Jan 1876
Webb	GOMEZ, Atanacio & Jesusa G.	Gregorio	17 Nov 1873
		Paula	29 Jun 1875
Anderson	GOOCH, Jno. Young and I. M.	Maggie Belle	19 Feb 1875
Fannin	GOOCH, Thos. J. & Mary S.	Charles	20 Jan 1876
Anderson	GOODSON, Jacob & Mary J.	Garnett	28 Feb 1874

COUNTY	PARENTS	CHILD	DATE
Gregg	GOODWIN, Bird Reed & Eliza P.	John Whitson	1 Dec 1873
		George Hamilton	3 Dec 1875
Fannin	GORVELL, T. V. & R. A. (twins)	William	31 Oct 1873
		Lillie	31 Oct 1873
Rusk	GOSSIP, Ed & Susan	Joishup (sic)	5 Oct 1874
Rusk	GOULD, George H. & Allen E.	Ellen	12 Oct 1874
Marion	GOUNAH (Gannah(?)), Ernest & Sallie	Ernest	11 Jul 1873
Dallas	GOW, Jno. J. and Susan A.	Minnie L. Cerelle	1 Sep 1874
Fannin	GOYNE, F. M. & Sarah T.	Mary E.	1 Mar 1874
Fannin	GRAHAM, J. J. & Catherine	Anna M.	6 Jan 1874
Lamar	GRAHAM, J. P. & M. E.	Grace	8 Aug 1873
Anderson	GRAHAM, Jesse and A. B.	Richard L.	1 Sep 1873
		Thos. F.	2 Oct 1876
Rusk	GRAHAM, John M. & Martha V.	Effa V.	10 Feb 1874
Nueces	GRAVIS, Charles R. & Elizabeth J.	John F.	4 Mar 1868
		Charles G.	25 Feb 1870
Rusk	GRAY, Alfred & Agnes	Olena	30 Sep 1873
Nueces	GRAY, Edward N. & Rosa (Garcia)	Sarah Ann	14 Oct 1853
		Edward R.	20 Feb 1857
		Rosa	26 Dec 1860
		John Antonio	2 Apr 1862
		Antonita	3 Sep 1863
		Stephen	8 Apr 1865
		Eliza	17 May 1866
		Alice (12 or)	2 Apr 1868
		Richard	7 Apr 1870
		Alfred	20 Feb 1872
		Henry Nescon(?) Nixon?)	7 Jan 1874
Rusk	GRAY, J. W. & J. A.	Authur	23 Aug 1874
Marion	GRAY, James R. & Sarah H.	John B.	10 Jan 1874
Fannin	GRAY, M. F. & M. A.	William Henry	27 Jan 1876
Fannin	GREEN, A. J. & L. D.	Sofronia	12 Jul 1874
Rusk	GREEN, Ben & Matilda	Robert	20 Oct 1874
Rusk	GREEN, G. W. & S. L.	Margaret Ann	5 Aug 1874
Fannin	GREEN, Henry & Jensie	LaCentenial (Reg. 19 Sep 1876)	
Fannin	GREEN, Henry & Louretta	Larzeman	10 Apr 1875
Anderson	GREEN, Ira N. and Ellen B.	Beatrice	29 Aug 1875
Rusk	GREEN, John C. & Iowa C.	Eunice Ann	13 Feb 1875
Rusk	GREEN, W. B. & Z. B.	Sarah Julia	12 Feb 1875
Kaufman	GREEN, W. G. & E. J. N.	Thomas F.	4 Sep 1873
Rusk	GREEN, W. M. & A. N.	Ella Elizabeth	5 Mar 1874
Navarro	GREEN, Wm. H. & Mary M.	Charles Davis	12 Jun 1873
Anderson	GREENWOOD, T. B. and Lucy	Lydia	11 Feb 1874
Upshur	GREER, R. A. & M. M.	Rugus (or Rufus?)	1 Apr 1874
Upshur	GREER, T. A. & Sarah L.	Thomas A.	12 Sep 1873
Anderson	GRIFFIN, B. F. and N. A.	Wm. Henry	25 Dec 1875
Cass	GRIFFIN, James L. & Mary E.	Richard H.	29 Nov 1873
Navarro	GRIFFIN, John F. & Fidelia E.	Maggie Eleaya	2 Feb 1873
Cass	GRIFFIN, John W. & Mary E.	Joseph F.	1 Jan 1874
Rusk	GRIFFIN, W. C. & Mary J.	Leander Wade	6 Feb 1874
Lamar	GRIFFIN, W. K. & M. C.	Sarah B.	6 Feb 1874
Rusk	GRIFFIN, Wade and Elizabeth	Sarah E.	4 Aug 1875
Navarro	GRIGGS, Wm. & M. E.	Luther Eldrige	4 Nov 1874
Anderson	GRIGSBY, R. H. and A. E.	May	17 Dec 1873
Fannin	GROGAN, E. F. & D. A.	A. E.	22 Sep 1874
Fannin	GROGAN, J. G. & M. C.	L. E.	3 Aug 1874
Dallas	GROSS, James M. and Margaret B.	George M	15 Jun 1873

COUNTY	PARENTS	CHILD	DATE
Fannin	GROVES, John W. & Nancy C.	Eldorado	16 Mar 1876
Webb	GUERRA, Justo & Maria Inez	Natividad	8 Sep 1874
Webb	GUERRERA, Francisca (Mrs. Jesus Olvera)		
Rusk	GUIN, W. V. & Mary Jane	Sarah Ann	9 ___ 1874
		Mary Isabel	15 Aug 1875
Lamar	GULLICK, D. D. &		
	Margaret M.		9 Feb 1874
Lamar	GUNN, F. B. & L. A.	Freeman S. S.	15 Jan 1874
Webb	GUSMAN, Salidad (Mrs. Julian Alexander		
Nueces	GUSSETT, Horwick(?), &		
	H.(?) E. (Evans?)	Josephine	24 Aug 1860
		Susan	26 Aug 1866
		Leona	11 May 1868
		Horwick(?) B.	3 May 1871
		Mary Elise	30 Dec 1873
		Horacio D.	15 Jan 1876
Rusk	GUTHRIE, J. W. & Mary J.	Charles E.	11 May 1875
Lamar	GUTHRIE, John A. &		
	Ophelia J.	Minnie G.	22 Sep 1869
		Annie Laura	6 Oct 1871
		Luther Hook	24 Mar 1874
Lamar	GUTHRIE, R. P. & Mary C.	George Wesley	3 Nov 1874
Rusk	GUTHRIE, T. C. & Mary	Yancy M.	14 Feb 1876
Webb	GUTIERRES, Pedro &		
	Elejia B.	Julio	11 Apr 1876
Lamar	GUTTERY, William & Elizabeth	Mary Ellen	14 Apr 1875
Fannin	GWALTNEY, F. M. & E.	Polly M.	5 Jan 1873
Upshur	HACKLER, J. W. & A. J.	M. A.	30 Nov 1875
Upshur	HACKLER, James & S. E.	M. J. M.	12 Mar 1875
Washington	HACKWORTH, S. A. & M. A.	Rosamond	13 Aug 1875
Navarro	HADEN, Jas. H. & Adeline E.	Grace	28 Mar 1874
Lamar	HAINES, L. J. & N. C.	Genevea Gertrude	30 Aug 1875
Fannin	HALBROOK, Jake T. & Mary	William F.	10 Jun 1875
Rusk	HALE, H. P. & ___	Howell M.	25 Oct 1874
Fannin	HALE, William & Mary A.	Marion F.	13 Feb 1874
Rusk	HALL, Berry & Priscy	Aley	15 Apr 1875
Rusk	HALL, D. B. and Annie M.	Upton Blair	15 Dec 1874
Webb	HALL, Edward F. &		
	Caroline M.	Henry	11 Apr 1875
Upshur	HALL, L. R. & J. A.	J. B.	11 Jun 1874
Rusk	HALL, Mark & Rosie	Milligan	29 Sep 1875
Cass	HALL, Peter & T. F. B.	Royal Lee	13 Jan 1874
Fannin	HALL, W. P. & Rebecca	Thos. William	1 Sep 1873
Anderson	HALLUM, E. Y. and F. E.	Edna L.	30 Nov 1875
Anderson	HALLUM, R. G. and Mary I.	Lillie	21 Dec 1873
Fannin	HAMERICK, James & Mary E.	William S.	21 Jan 1874
Navarro	HAMIL, W. H. & Amelia J.	Emma G.	23 Sep 1874
Navarro	HAMILTON, C. C. & E. J.	Emmet Edgar	3 Oct 1874
Rusk	HAMILTON, J. P. & Mary	James	Oct 1874
Fannin	HAMILTON, J. P. & S. A.	Edgar P.	14 Nov 1873
Navarro	HAMILTON, Jas. D. &		
	Mollie D.	Fluvius Guy	11 Jan 1874
Navarro	HAMILTON, S. W. & M. A.	Erna May	16 May 1875
Anderson	HAMLETT, G. W. and Emmie	Annie	24 May 1876
Anderson	HAMLETTE, Wm. J. and Lizzie	Ermine	1 May 1875
Fannin	HAMMOCK, A. D. & Mary E.	Ruth E.	17 Nov 1874
Lamar	HAMMOND, D. S. (or G.?) &		
	S. A.	G. W.	27 Oct 1873
Lamar	HAMMOND, W. S. & Susan A.	Davis Stone	15 Oct 1875
Navarro	HAMMONDS, C. C. & Bettie	Ambros (sic) Elmo	7 Nov 1873
Lamar	HAMNER, Will J. & Amanda L.	Hal	14 Dec 1871
		Will S.	3 Nov 1873
Fannin	HAMPTON, M. G. & Mollie E.	Mollie G.	7 Jan 1875
Cass	HAMPTON, W. G. & Mary J.	John W.	16 Nov 1873
Lamar	HANCOCK, F. F. & S. V.	Mary P.	18 Dec 1874
		Frank	13 Dec 1875

COUNTY	PARENTS	CHILD	DATE
Kaufman	HAND, J. P. & J. E.	Samuel Burford	11 Feb 1874
Fannin	HANEY, W. J. & Martha A.	Hallie	2 May 1874
		Ema (sic)	29 Sep 1875
Rusk	HANNA, James N. & Sallie	Ella May	19 Oct 1874
Kaufman	HANNA, W. J. & M. J.	Thomas A.	3 Dec 1874
Navarro	HARDEN, W. P. & Sarah	Cintha Alice	1 Aug 1873
	Note: Second time: "Wm. P. & Sarah S. Hardin"		
Fannin	HARDIN, A. M. & Amanda	Fannie E.	7 Jan 1874
Jasper	HARDIN, J. A. and M. E.	John H.	11 Jun 1875
Kaufman	HARDIN, J. J. and Mary F.	Martha E.	19 Mar 1874
Kaufman	HARDIN, John and Jennie(?)	J. J.	26 Feb 1874
Anderson	HARDING, W. H. and M. J.	Wm. Parish	18 Sep 1875
Rusk	HARDY, W. T. & F. E.	James Thomas	1 Jul 1875
Upshur	HARGERS, Oscar & Lucendy	H. R.	19 Dec 1873
		Carrie A.	25 Nov 1875
Fannin	HARLE, Elbrige & S. E.	Fred J.	28 May 1873
Rusk	HARMON, A. J. & Mary M.	Leander	28 May 1874
Rusk	HARMON, James H. and Caroline	Laura	29 ___ 1873
Rusk	HARMON, Jesse P. and		
	Sarah E. C.	Mary C.	10 Dec 1873
Navarro	HARPER, Wm. E. & Nancy A.	Nancy Elizabeth	1 Jul 1873
Kaufman	HARR, C. L. & L. V.	Katie Laura	3 Dec 1874
Rusk	HARRINGTON, William S. &		
	Ange E. F.	Thomas F.	2 Feb 1873
		Walter H.	15 May 1875
Washington	HARRIS, A. & F.	Benjamin	2 Oct 1873
Cherokee	HARRIS, C. B. & S.	Geo. Jackson Lee	13 Sep 1874
Rusk	HARRIS, J. F. & Mary S.	W. A.	26 Sep 1873
		America E.	11 Feb 1876
Rusk	HARRIS, W. H. & M. F.	William D.	28 Nov 1874
Gregg	HARRISON, George D. &		
	Lizzie N.	George Burr	3 Sep 1873
		Charles Robinson	13 Feb 1875
Rusk	HARRISON, J. A. & Susan J.	Thomas T.	4 Aug 1875
Anderson	HARRISON, W. W. and M. E.	C.	11 Jan 1876
		James M.	17 Jan 1874
Fannin	HART, A. G. & Mary P.	J. A. M.	23 Jul 1873
		Mary Etta	9 Nov 1874
Navarro	HART, C. H. & E. A.	Georgianna Irene	23 Sep 1873
Jasper	HART, Nathan M. and Susan	Elbert G.	28 Dec 1873
Rusk	HART, Pinck. & Laura	Wayne	17 Nov 1874
Rusk	HART, William & Nelly	Mary	11 Jan 1875
Rusk	HARTT, W. J. & M. A.	William G.	24 Oct 1874
Rusk	HASKINS, D. H. & P.	Elizabeth J. H.	17 Jul 1875
Rusk	HASKINS, Thomas & Mary E.	Martha J. C.	14 Feb 1875
Anderson	HASSELL, John and E. A.	Jim	27 Mar 1874
Fannin	HATCHER, Sam B. & Josephine	Lillie G.	17 Dec 1873
Fannin	HATCHER, W. T. & Rebecca A.	Martha Elizabeth	21 Nov 1873
Lamar	HATHAWAY, C. F. & Mary G. (or S?)	Charles H.	24 Mar 1875
Lamar	HAWKINS, A. J. & S. P.	Sam Y.	3 Mar 1875
		D. Rielley	10 Jul 1876
Rusk	HAWKINS, Henry & Caroline	Rosetta	4 Jul 1875
Fannin	HAWKINS, J. T. & M. E.	Floyd H.	30 May 1875
Rusk	HAWKINS, Jordan & Jane	Otta	4 Jan 1875
Fannin	HAWKINS, W. T. & Mattie	William B.	28 Aug 1875
Jasper	HAWTHORN, J. C. and Mary F.	Laura Ann	3 Jan 1874
Washington	HAYNIE, W. K. & M. H.	Julia	8 Aug 1874
Rusk	HAYS, B. F. & Sarah	Robert H.	31 Aug 1874
Rusk	HAYS, D. M. & Permelia C.	Henry B.	13 Jan 1874
Anderson	HAYWOOD, M. C. and M. E.	Ada M.	1 Apr 1876
Washington	HEALY, M. A. & E. L.	Norma	8 Dec 1873
Washington	HEINS, Adolph & Rosa	Alma	5 Jun 1874
Washington	HEMMING, C. C. & Lucy	John K.	10 Dec 1874
Rusk	HENDERSON, ___ & Ellen	Maria Jane	___ Dec 1874
Upshur	HENDERSON, Bob & Mary	Alex	8 Dec 1875
Lamar	HENDERSON, C. A. & H.	John P.	20 Jun 1873

COUNTY	PARENTS	CHILD	DATE
Anderson	HENDERSON, Danl. and Martha M.	Lucinda	2 Sep 1872
Lamar	HENDERSON, J. P. & Mattie	L. H.	24 Feb 1874
Rusk	HENDERSON, John & Mary A.	Lee Anna T.	9 Feb 1875
Jasper	HENDERSON, John Rondolph & Emma (Southwell)	John Rondolph	16 Oct 1876
Rusk	HENDERSON, Luke & Ellen (Bell)	Jeff⁻	25 May 1874
Rusk	HENDRICK, Seaborn J. & Ellen A.	Carrie E.	23 Nov 1873
Anderson	HENDRIX, P. H. and M. J.	Wm. Levi	15 Oct 1875
Navarro	HENDRIX, R. C. &	Harold	22 Jun 1874
Lamar	HENLEY, J. T. (or P?) & E. J.	Maggie	16 Oct 1874
Rusk	HENRY, Amos & Ann	Mary J. V.	20 Nov 1873
Rusk	HENRY, Nelson & Margaret Ann	Amos	10 Apr 1875
Rusk	HENRY, Walton & Minie	Aaron	13 Jan 1874
Dallas	HENSLER, John F. and Frances Elizabeth	Rosina Wilhelime	6 Sep 1874
Rusk	HERD, Columbus & Lucy	Virgil	Aug 1875
Somervell	HEREFORD, James S. and P. C.	Penny C.	27 Apr 1875
Cass	HERIN, Wm. & Leila (or Letha?) Ann	Arizenia	26 Nov 1873
Cameron	HERNANDEZ, Petra (Mrs. Jose Rodriquez)		
Webb	HERRERA, Jesus & ___	Guadalupa	24 Apr 1874
		Isidoro	13 Apr 1875
		Jesus	30 Jun 1876
Navarro	HERVEY, R. H. & C. M.	Albert Claud	26 Sep 1874
Cherokee	HESTER, C. G. & Mary	John A. J.	20 Jun 1875
Rusk	HICKEY, James C. and Anna E.	Emma C.	31 Jan 1874
Rusk	HICKEY, John M. and Mary E.	Ross	23 Feb 1874
		James F.	20 May 1875
Fannin	HICKS, A. S. & J. H.	William A.	18 Sep 1874
Fannin	HICKS, E. B. & M. H.	Pearl	27 Mar 1874
Rusk	HIGGINBOTHAM, W. L. & Mary	Seaton H.	14 Oct 1875
Kaufman	HIGGINS, A. J. & E.	Earnest	28 Jan 1874
Cherokee	HIGGINS, Saml. & L. E.	U(?) E. J.	25 Apr 1874
Rusk	HIGGS, S. R. & E.	John A. Phelps	7 Oct 1874
Rusk	HIGHTOWER, Green & Betty Ann. E.	Lula	9 May 1873
Rusk	HIGHTOWER, Jim & Ailsy	Mahala	24 Aug 1873
Rusk	HIGHTOWER, Turner & Mary	Henry	12 Oct 1873
Washington	HILL, C. W. & Lottie	___	24 Sep 1873
Fannin	HILL, J. A. & Mary V.	Thomas Y.	1875
Rusk	HILL, Joseph C. and Mary E.	Edward E.	29 Nov 1874
Rusk	HILL, L. L. & Tennessee	Martha	26 Jul 1874
Rusk	HILL, Manul (sic) and Delpha Fly	Alice M.	Apr 1875
Rusk	HILL, R. S. & M. J.	Mary A.	3 Aug 1875
Anderson	HILL, Wm. & Amanda	Bettie Lula	30 Jul 1874
	q	Reuben Monroe	20 Jun 1876
Rusk	HILLIN, James L. and Mary L.	Fannie D.	28 Mar 1874
Rusk	HILLIN, L. L. & Jane	Almarine	29 Apr 1874
	(twins)	Josephine	29 Apr 1874
Fannin	HINCH, John F. & A. B.	Charles F.	9 Jul 1875
Lamar	HINDS, W. A. & E. A.	Cary Coleman	24 Oct 1873
Cass	HINES, Miles H. & S. E.		Dec 1873
Washington	HINES, Theo. & Maria C.	Albert Victor	26 Apr 1874
Fannin	HITCH, L. H. & Elizabeth	Mary Clementine	9 Jan 1876
Nueces	HOBBS, Priscilla B. (Mrs. Thomas Beynon)		
Nueces	HOBBS, Sarah (Mrs. Reuben Holbein)		
Cass	HODGE, Isham & Jane	Millie	Aug 1875
Navarro	HODGE, Wm. H. & M. E.	Thomas Franklin	6 Feb 1874
Upshur	HODGES, C. A. & L. A. R.	Cornelia J.	7 Mar 1874
Lamar	HODGES, J. C. & C. M.	Roy E.	14 Nov 1875
Upshur	HODGES, J. C. & C. W.	R. R.	18 Jan 1874
Upshur	HODGES, W. C. & Mary	M. H.	30 Apr 1875

COUNTY	PARENTS	CHILD	DATE
Lamar	HOFFMAN, W. C. &		
	H. (or N?) J.	Manias R.	17 Sep 1873
Upshur	HOGAN, Bennett & Eliza B.	Emma A.	1 Nov 1874
Rusk	HOGG, Samuel and Susan E.	Samuel E.	8 Mar 1875
Anderson	HOGUE, Thomas M. and C. C.	Clarence M.	25 Feb 1875
Nueces	HOLBEIN, Reuben &		
	Sarah (Hobbs)	Walter Franklin	30 Mar 1858
		Frances Rebecca	22 Feb 1860
		Lillian Augusta	14 Aug 1862
		Georgina	6 Oct 1865
		Richard King	27 Jul 1868
		John McClane	17 Nov 1872
		Reuben Robert	15 Jul 1875
		(Reg. 6 May 1876)	
Upshur	HOLLAWAY, D. E. & L. A.	S. A. H.	27 Nov 1875
Rusk	HOLLEMAN, C. M. & A. T.	Richard V.	28 Aug 1874
Rusk	HOLLEMAN, Jim & Sarah	Roena	11 Oct 1873
Rusk	HOLLEMAN, Josiah and Martha	G. W.	1 Aug 1873
Rusk	HOLLEMAN, M. V. and M. L.	Mariah L.	19 Dec 1874
Navarro	HOLLINGSWORTH, R. G. &		
	Martha J.	Henry Barnett	7 Mar 1874
Navarro	HOLLINGSWORTH, Saml. & F. E.	James Oscar	21 Aug 1874
Lamar	HOLLINS, William G. & M. A.	Mary Texas	21 May 1874
Cherokee	HOLMES, A. J. and H. A.	Peggie A.	25 Dec 1873
Fannin	HOLMES, J. P. & V. (or N?) R.	Bishop	5 Sep 1874
Fannin	HOLMES, James C. &		
	Virginia D.	C. M.	17 Aug 1874
Anderson	HOLT, Geo. and Maggie	Maggie	12 Sep 1875
Gregg	HOLT, John Thomas & Lavenia W.	John France	13 Apr 1874
		Wm. Lewis	19 May 1876
Lamar	HOLT, P. B. & M. A.	William Bell	28 Nov 1873
Fannin	HOLT, W. A. & Jennie	Marian E.	3 Jan 1874
Fannin	HOOD, F. A. & M. J.	E. E.	6 Apr 1874
Fannin	HOOD, W. J. & Harriett J.	Stella	17 Nov 1874
Cass	HOOTAN, Wm. & Mary E.	Anna Bell	30 Nov 1873
Upshur	HOOTEN, James M. & M. B.	Claudin A.	8 Dec 1873
Cass	HOOTEN, S. R. & Sarah	James	23 Jun 1874
Cass	HOOTEN, Wm. M. & Mary E.	Mary E.	8 Feb 1875
Dallas	HOPKINS, Miles and Elvira E.	Mary Lou	31 Jul 1875
Upshur	HOPKINS, Thos. T. &		
	Josephine C.	John T.	5 Dec 1875
Fannin	HOPPER, John L. & E. P.	Robert E. Lee	5 Feb 1875
Fannin	HORN, F. E. & Pa. (sic)	Mary P.	25 Jul 1875
Washington	HORSTON, Jessie & Julia	Laura	30 Nov 1873
Fannin	HORTON, Jas. L. and Sarah M.	Dora B.	20 Nov 1874
Navarro	HOUSTON, Alex & Fanny	Serena	27 Oct 1876
Rusk	HOUSTON, S. W. & Evaline C.	Luther	— Aug 1873
		Claud	— Jan 1875
Upshur	HOWARD, J. C. & L. A.	Pearle R.	8 Dec 1874
Lamar	HOWELL, A. & S. (or G.?) B.	Bennie L.	30 Sep 1874
Lamar	HOWIE (or HOWIS?) S. L. &		
	S. E. (twins)	Arthur	17 Jun 1873
		Gaither	17 Jun 1873
Navarro	HOWREN, A. L.(?) & M. A.	Alice	11 Mar 1874
		Daisy	30 Apr 1875
Fannin	HOY, A. B. & Lou	Bertie	7 Nov 1874
Kaufman	HOY, M. L. & M. M.	Henry H.	5 Nov 1873
Navarro	HUCHERSON, Geo. & Martha J.	David	2 Aug 1874
Anderson	HUDDLESTON, Danl. C. & M.A.	Daniel C.	6 Feb 1874
Anderson	HUDDLESTON, J. A. & Sarah C.	James Newel	19 Jul 1874
		Andrew W.	1 Mar 1875
Anderson	HUDDLESTON, W. E. and M.	Sam Houston	2 Aug 1873
Upshur	HUDGINS, P. E. & Harriet	Mattie	14 Sep 1874
Kaufman	HUDMAN, J. J. & S. M.	Preston	30 Jun 1874
Cherokee	HUDSON, S. R. & S. L.	Ida J.	6 Jun 1875

COUNTY	PARENTS	CHILD	DATE
Jasper	HUFFMAN, Eddy P. and Catherine B.	Mary L.	22 Jul 1875
Jasper	HUGHES, Edward J. and Louisa E.	Ausker (sic) Newton	1873
Anderson	HUGHES, I. M. and Margaret A.	Richard Long	3 Jan 1875
Rusk	HUGHES, J. C. & Elizabeth	Virgil	5 Jul 1875
Lamar	HUGHES, J. C. & M. E.	Dora	7 Nov 1873
Upshur	HUGHES, J. W. & M. E.	J. W.	16 Dec 1873
Rusk	HUGHES, Jasper C. and Sophronia J.	Giles Coffee	29 Nov 1874
Rusk	HUMPHREY, Jim & Emiline	Mattie	2 Nov 1875
Jasper	HUMPHREY, Richard M. and Lizzie	John Auther(sic)	10 May 1875
Rusk	HUMPHREYS, ___ & Arnes	Ose	21 Mar 1875
Upshur	HUMPHREYS, B. T. & L. R.	Rosa T.	27 Mar 1874
Upshur	HUMPHREYS, Dave & Sallie	Lizzie	5 Dec 1875
Upshur	HUMPHREYS, J. A. & Nancy A.	Reglus	21 Mar 1875
		Lusun(or Luxim?)	26 Apr 1876
Rusk	HUMPHREYS, John & Hettey	Betsie	28 Dec 1874
		Mary Eliza	18 Mar 1875
Fannin	HUNT, Geo. H. & Mary L.	Charley G.	29 Feb 1874
Rusk	HUNT, John W. and Amanda C.	Virginia A.	2 May 1874
Lamar	HUNT, L. B. & A. J.	William T.	12 Sep 1866
		Lucy Marje(?)	12 May 1869
		Thomas Wooten	4 Feb 1872
		Analiza	4 Feb 1872
		Larkin B., Jr.	2 Nov 1874
Fannin	HUNT, M. R. & N. M.	A. W.	25 Dec 1874
Rusk	HUNT, Thomas & Nancy	J. T.	7 Sep 1875
Fannin	HUNTER, John W. & Fannie	Robert M.	17 Aug 1873
Rusk	HUTTO, J. E. & S. E.	Francis M.	7 Apr 1875
Lamar	HYLER, G. W. & Emily L.	James W.	8 Apr 1875
Fannin	INGE, John W. & Mary A. C.	Bettie A.	15 Mar 1875
Washington	INGLEHART, E. J. & C.	Jesse Harreld	3 Jan 1875
Fannin	INGLISH, Riley & Caroline	Lilah	25 Sep 1873
Anderson	INGRAM, M. and R.	Washington	4 Apr 1875
Navarro	INGRAM, W. C. & L.(?) A.	Lillie Lorena	27 Dec 1874
Nueces	INMORE, Mary Augusta (Mrs. Felix A. von Blucher)		
Rusk	IRBY, J. H. & Fannie	Sallie	27 Sep 1873
		Henry	11 Mar 1875
Rusk	IRBY, Jasper and Nancy	Mary Lucy	29 Nov 1873
Rusk	IRBY, Newton and Mary	Netty Lee	20 Mar 1875
Lamar	IRWIN, A. M. & M. C.	Willie P.	4 Apr 1871
		Martha P.	Mar 1875
Rusk	IRWIN, C. C. & Mariah S.	Virginia L.	20 Aug 1874
Rusk	IRWIN, J. B. & Mary Jane	James Decatur	9 Jul 1875
Rusk	IRWIN, W. M. & Eliza N.	Minnie Lee	6 Feb 1875
Rusk	JACKSON, ___ & ___	Elizabeth J.	22 Jan 187
Lamar	JACKSON, G. W. & M. J.	Cevena	27 Apr 1874
Rusk	JACKSON, J.A.D. & Margaret E.	William A.(?)	26 Oct 1875
Rusk	JACKSON, Jonas & Laura	Joanna	30 Aug 1873
		Nettie	21 Mar 1875
Rusk	JACKSON, R. W. & M. M.	William F.	19 Oct 1875
Anderson	JACKSON, Toak and Jetty	Sofa	17 Sep 1875
Navarro	JACKSON, W. A. & Catherine	Charles	26 May 1873
Kaufman	JACKSON, W. H.& A. E.	Ada O.	2 Aug 1874
Rusk	JACOBS, John E. and Mary E.	Minnie E.	2 Mar 1875
Marion	JAMES, D. W. & Virginia	D. J. W.	24 Apr 1873
Jasper	JAMES, E. S. and M. W.	Benjamin Franklin	4 Aug 1874
		Edward Elie	28 May 1876
Fannin	JAMES, I. S. (J.G.?) & Fannie	L. S.	8 Dec 1873
		I. A.	27 Mar 1875
Kaufman	JAMES, J. G. & S. P.	Thom. Broughton	11 Feb 1874
Rusk	JAMES, William & Nancy	Bosie	1 Jul 1875
Cherokee	JARRETT, H. M. and N. C.	David	15 Apr 1874

Webb	JARVIS, Samuel M. &		
	Inocencia (Flores)	Samuel	12 Mar 1874
Navarro	JAY, D. W. & Atha	Mary Elizabeth	16 Feb 1874
Rusk	JEFFERSON, W. R. & N. C.	Walter G.	28 May 1875
Anderson	JEMISON, Ennis and Margaret	Howard	21 Dec 1875
		Toby J.	20 Dec 1876
Rusk	JENKINS, Cook & Mary	Henry	20 Jan 1875
Fannin	JENNINGS, E. G. & M. A.	Claud Gibson	6 Sep 1875
Rusk	JERNIGAN, S.(?) D. & Mary	William M.	8 Feb 1875
Navarro	JESSEE, Danl. & Julia	Susan	12 Nov 1873
Webb	JESUS, Maria (Mrs. Carlos Gil)		
Dallas	JETT, B. P. and Lula B.	Edward	2 Mar 1873
		Pendleton	21 Nov 1875
Rusk	JIMMERSON, W. A. & Patsey A.	Robert E.	4 Dec 1873
		D. E.	21 Dec 1875
Rusk	JOB, Moses and Ann F.	D. Ella	8 Feb 1876
Kaufman	JOHNSON, ___ & Evaline A.	Helen Caroline	18 Jul 1854
Fannin	JOHNSON, A. & B. D.	Minnie Lee	4 Feb 1874
Fannin	JOHNSON, Abraham & Nannie	Albert	22 May 1873
		Joseph E.	10 Sep 1874
Rusk	JOHNSON, Charles & Ellen	Archy	10 May 1875
		Elbert (sic)	8 Jul 1875
Rusk	JOHNSON, Charlie & Caroline	Sam E.	29 Sep 1874
Navarro	JOHNSON, E. W. &		
	Frances Louise (McMillan)	Luther Alexander	29 Oct 1875
Upshur	JOHNSON, G. W. & Sallie	Etter Lee	25 Feb 1874
		Prentice	2 Feb 1876
Fannin	JOHNSON, G. W. & T. A.	T. E.	2 Feb 1875
Rusk	JOHNSON, Hampton & Jane	Ned	19 Jun 1873
Fannin	JOHNSON, Isaac & M. V.	Edna	18 Sep 1873
Kaufman	JOHNSON, J. and Aletha J.	Mary Jane	24 Dec 1873
Fannin	JOHNSON, J. C. & Maggie	James A.	11 Aug 1875
Cass	JOHNSON, J. D. & N. E.	Henry Wilkins	14 Dec 1874
Fannin	JOHNSON, J. K. & Mary B.	Frank E.	11 Jan 1875
Navarro	JOHNSON, J. M. & E. H.	Joseph Henry	2 Feb 1874
Washington	JOHNSON, John H. &		
	Nannie M. C.	William Lee	26 Jun 1874
Fannin	JOHNSON, M. L. & N. J.	L. M.	20 Jul 1875
Anderson	JOHNSON, M. P. and V. A.	James W.	9 Feb 1874
Kaufman	JOHNSON, P. H. & E.	David B.	22 Jan 1874
	Note: Mother's initial is		
	"S.E." in 1875.		
Navarro	JOHNSON, W. D. & C. E.	Wiley Doug	28 Sep 1875
Kaufman	JOHNSON, W. O. and Agnes E.	Dudley	4 Mar 1875
Fannin	JOHNSON, William & M. E.	Martha Jane	6 Aug 1873
		Robert Lee	29 Jun 1875
Fannin	JOHNSON, Wm. & Polly	Harriet	20 Feb 1874
Anderson	JOHNSTON, W. H. and S. E.	Lillian Roberter	1 Jul 1875
Fannin	JOLLY, J. W. & Mary E.	Alice	13 May 1873
		Sarah J.	20 Mar 1875
Upshur	JONES, Alex & Cannie (sic)	Andrew	24 Oct 1875
Fannin	JONES, C. C. & Sarah E.	John S.	13 Feb 1874
Rusk	JONES, Ed & Joanne	Robert	25 Dec 1873
Rusk	JONES, Ellick & Manday	Amie	15 Nov 1874
Rusk	JONES, Fizer (or Rizer?) and		
	Adice (sic)	William	__ May 1875
Rusk	JONES, G. M. & M. F.	V M E	6 Oct 1874
Rusk	JONES, Griff and	Frenetta A.	__ Jan 1875
Navarro	JONES, J. C. & Martha E.	Mattie Beatrice	30 Aug 1873
Fannin	JONES, J. C. & Melovia	John M.	1 Sep 1874
Lamar	JONES, J. F. & F. C.	James Y.	10 Jan 1874
Rusk	JONES, J. P. & Nannie C.	Edgood Dudley	14 Dec 1873
Fannin	JONES, J. W. & M. J.	Charley A.	6 Sep 1875
Rusk	JONES, James H. & Eliza D.	Lee Tipton	16 Jan 1874
Navarro	JONES, John L.(?) & Izora	Hester Virginia	4 Mar 1874
Fannin	JONES, John W. & Mary H.	Ida	22 Dec 1873

COUNTY	PARENTS	CHILD	DATE
Fannin	JONES, M. M. & Francis A.	Martha Jane	11 Sep 1875
Rusk	JONES, M. M. & M. A.	Marcellus Arden	4 Jan 1875
	(twins)	Grace Etherton	4 Jan 1875
Navarro	JONES, M. N. & E. C.	Adele Lee	8 May 1873
		Samuel Dabney	13 Arp 1875
Fannin	JONES, M. R. & F. J.	W. N.	1 May 1875
Rusk	JONES, Martha (Mrs. Jack Blount Monroe)		
Navarro	JONES, Martin & Lucinda	Sarah Bellezora	26 Jun 1874
Dallas	JONES, Mary Snydor (Mrs. Charles Frederick Tucker)		
Fannin	JONES, N. A. & E.	Isaac F.	5 Jun 1874
Rusk	JONES, R. L. & Elliott	Benjamin F.	May 1874
Fannin	JONES, R. W. & Lula	Samuel Mabel(sic)	28 Jan 1876
Lamar	JONES, Richard & Martha	Julia Ada	19 Nov 1873
Fannin	JONES, W. C. & Ellen O.	Harriett	2 Jun 1874
Navarro	JONES, W. H. & Celestia	Ada	3 Apr 1874
Upshur	JONES, W. H. & P. A.	Attar	14 May 1875
Fannin	JONES, W. M. & Frances A. E.	John Richard	17 Nov 1873
Kaufman	JONES, W. R. & C. S.	Henry P.	Jun
Jasper	JONES, William and Margaret	Thomas D.	1 May 1873
Anderson	JONES, Wm. and Mary	Henry	28 Jul 1875
Navarro	JORDAN, J. T.(?) & M. P.	Samuel	9 Dec 1874
Washington	JORDAN, Willis & Maria	Lizzie	3 Apr 1873
Washington	JORDON, F. D. & Virginia	John Gray	6 Dec 1869
		Virginia	8 May 1872
		Florens(?)	1 Apr 1874
Webb	JOSEPH, Rudolph & Rosalia	Helen	30 Sep 1873
Fannin	JOURNEY, Israel & M.A.E.	Altha	31 Dec 1874
Webb	JUAREZ, Silvestre (Mrs. Roque Rodrigues)		
Fannin	JUNIE, T. A. & _____	Josie	12 Mar 1875
Rusk	KAVANAUGH, J. H. & Emma	Eugenia	28 Mar 1875
Rusk	KEE, J. D. & Fanny B.	Mary Z. C.	10 Jun 1873
Fannin	KEENE, George W. & Mary M.	Emma	4 Jul 1875
Fannin	KEENE, J. T. & Cordelia	Bruce	29 Aug 1874
Rusk	KEENER, C. A. & J. M.	Mary H.	30 Oct 1874
Navarro	KEITH, J. M. & Leanora	Willie Leonora	11 Apr 1874
Fannin	KEITHLEY, M. & H. E.	Calvin Dio	26 Feb 1874
Navarro	KELLEY, W. C. & J. V.	Wiley Newton	12 Apr 1874
Jasper	KELLIE, Edward J. and M. S.	Bertha	17 Oct 1874
Navarro	KELLY, A. S. & M. A. C.	Adazoo	2 Dec 1873
Rusk	KELLY, Allen and Martha M. (Knight)	Dudley A.	29 Mar 1874
Rusk	KELLY, Martillus J. and Feriba M.	Martha M.	22 Sep 1873
Rusk	KELLY, Seth C. and Frances E.	William F.	15 Jun 1874
Cameron	KELLY, William and Mary Ann	William	14 Jun 1873
Anderson	KENMORE, John G. and _____	Kirksey	27 Jul 1876
Upshur	KENNARD, G. T. & S. V.	T. V.	12 Apr 1874
Gregg	KENNARD, Taylor E. & Sarah E.	Charles D.	9 Oct 1875
Cherokee	KENNEDY, Israel & Lucinda	Wm. P.	19 Sep 1874
Rusk	KENT, W. H. & Amanda C.	Caroline A.	19 Feb 1875
Fannin	KERR, A. J. & L. G.	Lenora	18 Jan 1873
		Ida	29 Mar 1875
Navarro	KERR, J. A. & T. C.	John Mortimer	1 Nov 1874
Fannin	KERR, Levi & Nora	W. A.	1 Jun 1874
Fannin	KERR, Robert R. & Sarah L.	Sam Edgar	24 Sep 1873
Navarro	KERR, W. J. W. & Mattie C.	James Wade	1 Mar 1875
Marion	KESSELER, C. A. & Lunette I.	Charles Wm.	15 Sep 1873
		Mary Elizabeth	3 Jul 1875
Navarro	KEY, J. H. E. & Zenoba	Joseph Henry Emanuel	21 Jan 1874
Navarro	KEY, R. L. & Sarah Jane	Lovic Pierce	11 Aug 1873
		Thomas Henry Austin	24 Aug 1876
Fannin	KINCAID, William & Mattie	William F.	17 Apr 1874
Kaufman	KINCHEN, J. M. & J. M.	Alzadia	28 Jan 1875

COUNTY	PARENTS	CHILD	DATE
Kaufman	KING, C. M. & A. M.	C. C.	28 Jun 1874
Navarro	KING, E. H. & M. G.	Guy	23 Dec 1873
Navarro	KING, J. C. & E. A.	George	16 Nov 1874
Upshur	KING, John W. and A. J.	John T.	16 May 1873
	(twins)	James W.	16 May 1873
Fannin	KIRK, I. W. & M. M.	Charles Levi	23 Aug 1875
Marion	KNEELAND (KNULAND?), W. E. & Eva	Kie	21 Nov 1873
		Wm. O.	3 Jan 1875
Rusk	KNIGHT, Martha M. (Mrs. Allen Kelly)		
Rusk	KNIGHT, W. A. G. & Sarah Jane	Emma Nora	27 Jan 1875
Upshur	KNOWLES, A. J. & Margaret	Edward	10 Aug 1874
Washington	KNOX, W. A. & Betty	Wm. Alexander	31 Aug 1873
Cameron	KOWALSKI, Louis and Amelia	Rosalie	30 Apr 1877
		Joseph	18 Jul 1878
Washington	KRUG, K. & Dora	Rudolph	2 May 1874
Rusk	KYLES, Jeems & Adaline	Florence	31 Mar 1874
		Mandy	9 May 1875
Rusk	LACEY, Turner & Tan	Henry	15 May 1873
		Laura	15 May 1875
Anderson	LACY, Alfred and Mary	Tisha Anna	25 Nov 1874
Rusk	LACY, Jerry & Mary	William	1 Dec 1875
Rusk	LACY, Si & Elizabeth	Bennie	1 Jun 1875
Rusk	LACY, Thomas R. and Emily A.	James William	9 Oct 1875
Rusk	LANDAR, Washington & Caroline	Nat	5 Feb 1875
Rusk	LANDRU, ___ & Minerva	Mary	23 Jun 1875
Rusk	LANDSBERRY, William H. & Susan C.	Charlie Arthur	7 Feb 1874
Fannin	LANE, J. L. V. & N. D.	Lillie	5 Jan 1870
		John G.	14 Mar 1872
		James D.	30 Aug 1874
Fannin	LANE, R. P. & E. M.	Robert H.	4 Oct 1874
Webb	LANG, Thomas & Santas G.	John S.	17 Jun 1873
Dallas	LANGE, Herman & Eliza	Louis	17 Jan 1874
Rusk	LANGHORN, James & Emma	Georgia	23 Nov 1874
Rusk	LANGSTON, A. & Dionitia	Effie E.	16 Aug 1873
Anderson	LANGSTON, Jim and Maggie	James Dennis	14 Oct 1875
Anderson	LANGSTON, Silas and Tennessee	Thos. Franklin	11 Mar 1874
		Marion Kary	4 Apr 1876
Fannin	LANIUS, Phillip & Joanah I.	Ara Minta	9 Sep 1875
Fannin	LANIUS, William & N. P.	C. A.	2 Dec 1875
Navarro	LANKFORD, Jas. H. & Le Manda	Matilda Emma Leonia Victoria	30 Jan 1874
Fannin	LANKFORD, William A. & L. E.	John S.	8 Feb 1874
Cameron	LAREADE, Joseph & Margarette	Annette Noeli	25 Dec 1872
Fannin	LARISON, J. H. & Hattie N.	T. S.	8 Mar 1874
Kaufman	LAROE(?), A. A. & M. E.	George Albert	___ Dec 1873
Fannin	LASSITER, Wm. & Martha	Thomas	18 Oct 1873
Washington	LATHEM(?), Eras & Anna(?)	Erasima	30 Dec 1875
Lamar	LATIMER, T. H. & F. L.	William	15 Aug 1874
Lamar	LATTIMER, Alex H. & Mattie J.	Louisa Lee	14 Aug 1875
Rusk	LAWLER, J. H. & L. E.	Ida E.	13 Jun 1874
Rusk	LAWRENCE, Augustus and Alice M.	George F.	___ Sep 1874
Fannin	LAWRENCE, T. H. & Sarah J.	Eula	31 Mar 1874
Dallas	LAWS, ___	John James	19 Jun 1876
Navarro	LEA, P. M. & L. M.	Preston Joel	21 Jan 1876
Fannin	LEAIRCE(?), W. M. & S. J.	Ida V.	27 May 1873
Navarro	LEARMONTH, Jas. & Jenney	Alexander Charles	11 Jun 1874
Rusk	LEATH, B. D. & Levicie	Elliott Drean	7 Apr 1874
Dallas	LEDBETTER, W. C. & R. A.	John Wm.	6 Jul 1875

COUNTY	PARENTS	CHILD	DATE
Rusk	LEE, Austin & Sidney	Joseph	1 Apr 1874
Navarro	LEE, Blake & Mary Ann	Britton Isaiah	18 Oct 1873
Navarro	LEE, C. E. & N. C.	Mittie	15 Mar 1875
Rusk	LEE, Clark & Mariah	Annie	20 Dec 1874
		Clark	14 Sep 1875
Fannin	LEE, James A. & Mary M.	Lenah M.	3 Mar 1875
Rusk	LEE, Richmond & Mary	Ida D.	2 Mar 1875
Navarro	LEE, T. J. & Mary L.	Uriah M.	11 Oct 1874
Fannin	LEENER, Oliver & Sarah J.	Sarah Elizabeth	4 May 1876
Fannin	LEETHE, Josiah & M. A.	William H.	12 Oct 1873
Lamar	LENOIR, Jos. Y. & Matilda	Thomas English	1 Dec 1873
Lamar	LENORE, I. & M. E.	E. C.	1 Apr 1874
Rusk	LESLIE, B. F. & E. A.	Willie D.	28 Aug 1875
	Note: obviously (twins)	Birty Lee	28 Aug 1875
	dates are incorrect.	Howard J.	3 Oct 1875
Rusk	LEWIS, George & Tennessee	Emma	26 May 1875
Washington	LEWIS, Henry & Levina	Norah	29 Oct 1874
Rusk	LEWIS, Morton & Lucy	Jane	4 Jun 1875
Webb	LEYENDECKER, John Z. &		
	Juliana B.	Miguel T. M.	22 Sep 1873
Lamar	LIDDELL, N. S. & Mary W.	Sarah Shoppeson	30 Jul 1874
Lamar	LIGHTFOOT, W. H. & Dora M.	Maxey Bell	15 Nov 1875
Kaufman	LILES, ___ & ___	Mary Jane	16 Apr 1874
Fannin	LINDSEY, J. T. & M. J.	Thos. Sidney	26 Jan 1875
Upshur	LINDSEY, Joseph & M. J.	Amanulha E. J.	23 Feb 1875
Navarro	LINDSEY, Wm. B. & Sarah J.	Robert Preston	9 Aug 1873
Rusk	LINTHICIN, Harrison & Eda	Calvin	19 Oct 1875
Rusk	LINTON, W. F. & Mary	M. S.	18 Aug 1874
Washington	LIPSCOMB, Joel A. &		
	Fannie A.	Rob. Upshaw	5 Mar 1873
Fannin	LIPSCOMB, Smith & W. S.	E. E.	1 Feb 1875
Cherokee	LISEMBY, J. T. & F. J.	C. W.	11 Aug 1872
		Misouri	12 Oct 1874
Anderson	LITTLE, Ben and Sallie	Ella	5 Dec 1875
Rusk	LITTLE, J. R. & M. C.	Emory Jane	5 Nov 1875
Fannin	LITTLE, L. H. & M. A.	Louallen	24 Nov 1874
Cass	LIVINGSTON, B. T. & F. A.	Z. A.	30 Jan 1874
Rusk	LIVSEY, W. E. and Mary P.	Mary M.	11 May 1875
Cherokee	LLOYD, T. N. and S. M.	Arnett	9 Oct 1873
Fannin	LOCKE, W. H. & N. I.	Mary E.	23 Jul 1875
Washington	LOCKETT, C. C. & F. A.	V. W.	3 Feb 1875
Anderson	LOFLIN, James and Margaret J.	Sarah Francis	28 Jan 1874
Jasper	LOGGINS, Lewis L. and Mary E.	John Edger(sic)	23 Nov 1873
		Maudie E. J.	27 Aug 1875
Rusk	LOLLAR, James and J. F.	Emma	15 Oct 1875
Rusk	LOLLAR, William and M. J.	H. M.	15 Nov 1875
Cherokee	LONG, Ben A. & B. W.	Wade S.	15 Jan 1875
Fannin	LONG, Geo. W. & Mary A.	Cora A.	12 Mar 1874
Anderson	LONG, J. H. and L. or T. E.	R. B.	3 Apr 1875
Rusk	LONG, J. N. & Cinderella	Alexander G.	13 Aug 1874
Lamar	LONG, James M. & Mary E.	Robert James	26 Oct 1873
Rusk	LONG, Retman & Clara	William Horace	5 Feb 1875
Cass	LONG, Solomon & Carcas A.	Ora May	5 Mar 1875
Upshur	LONGSHORE, L. W. & E. L.	J. O.	16 Feb 1874
Upshur	LOONEY, M. H. & Anna	Oran M.	3 Sep 1875
	(twins)	Bearnice Achsah	3 Sep 1875
Webb	LOPEZ, Evarista &		
	Decideria M.	Antonio	18 Dec 1875
Cameron	LOPEZ, Manuel Parra and		
	Demetria (Moreno)	Jose Ma.	10 ___ 1878
Webb	LOPEZ, Vivian & Segun da J.	Maria Guadalupe	1 Sep 1875
Navarro	LOVE, J. R. & Harriet E.	Lena Ellen	20 Mar 1874
	Second entry: "J. R. & H. E."	Mattie Beeler	22 Mar 1876
Fannin	LOVELACE, Chas. D. & Lou A.	Emma	29 May 1874
Fannin	LOVELACE, D. W. & M. M.	Alpha C.	24 Nov 1873
Fannin	LOVELACE, I. G. & Martha	B. F. P.	7 Feb 1875

COUNTY	PARENTS	CHILD	DATE
Fannin	LOVELACE, J. E. & S. J.	Albert E.	10 Nov 1874
Cherokee	LOVELADY, W. H. & H. J.	R. L.	18 Apr 1875
Fannin	LOWERY, M. P. & Nannie E.	John M.	24 Aug 1873
Rusk	LOWERY, W. B. & E. A. C.	John A. D.	18 Sep 1874
Rusk	LOWRIE, A. P., Jr. and F. E.	Luella	5 Nov 1874
Rusk	LOWRIE, A. P., Sr. and L. A.	Samuel H.	26 Oct 1874
Rusk	LOWRIE, John B. and Clarissa E.	Clarissa E.	24 Apr 1874
Upshur	LUEL (or TUEL?), W. H. & Indiana	S. E.	21 Aug 1875
Navarro	LUMMUS, T. L. & Margaret W.	Margaret Ann	13 Sep 1873
Fannin	LUMPKIN, R. W. & Sarah	J. W.	27 Aug 1874
Fannin	LUSK, R. M. & Clara	Maud P.	27 May 1875
Fannin	LUTON, J. K. & S. B.	Mary Julia	7 Mar 1874
		Clarence Eugene	21 Dec 1875
Fannin	LYDAY, Jas. H. & Josie	David Russell	29 Nov 1873
Rusk	LYLES, W. P. & Martha L.	Laura W.	20 Apr 1874
		Archard(sic) D.	11 Sep 1875
Rusk	LYLES, Z. T. & T. J.	S. L.	2 Nov 1873
		A. D.	21 May 1875
Fannin	LYNCH, Green & Zelpha	Monroe	3 Jun 1875
Rusk	LYNCH, W. T. & Mary Ann	Emily	4 Jul 1873
		James Francis	19 Mar 1876
Lamar	LYNN, S. & M.	Mary Elizabeth	20 Aug 1874
Lamar	LYNN, W. F. & M. E.	Mary E.	22 Feb 1875
Washington	LYONS, Henry &	Martha Ann	8 May 1873
Lamar	LYONS, R. C. & G. A.	E. A.	30 Jan 1874
Rusk	McANULTY, James L. and Louiza J.	John E.	May 1874
Cherokee	McCALL, E. S. & Mary	Gordon C.	22 Mar 1875
Rusk	McCAMMON, Ben & Amelia	John A. Giles	18 Apr 1875
Nueces	McCAMPBELL, John S. & Anna E.	Eva	1 Aug 1874
Rusk	McCARTER, John C. and V. A.	John O.	29 Dec 1874
Rusk	McCAULEY, Bill & Delia (Still)	William Richard	17 Jul 1875
Navarro	McCAULLEY, D. C. & Sarah J.	John Rouden	9 Sep 1873
Rusk	MCCLELLAN, Tom & Ellen	Dolph	28 Dec 1875
Fannin	MCCLENDON, A. J. & Elizabeth J.	John H.	28 Nov 1873
Rusk	McCLENNAN, Thomas & Ellen	Gus	12 Mar 1874
Upshur	McCLUNG, R. L. & M. A.	J. H. 7 (or 17?)	Feb 1874
Upshur	McCLUNG, Richard & M. A.	J. B.	6 Feb 1876
Upshur	McCLUNG, W. B. & M. A.	Mary Ella	10 Mar 1874
Rusk	McCLURE, A. C. & A. C.	W. R.	20 Jul 1874
Anderson	McCLURE, R. and M. M.	Fila	30 Jul 1873
Webb	McCOMBS, J. H. & Rosaria	Charles Richard	26 Apr 1875
Navarro	McCONICO, Chas. T. & S.(?) A.	Jessie Helvetia	6 Feb 1874
Upshur	McCOOK, J. H. & Sarah A.	Wm. H.	15 Sep 1873
Anderson	McCOOL, M. and Jane	Jimmie	18 Feb 1874
Gregg	McCORD, Felix J. & Gabrella A.	Earl Mortimer	21 Jan 1875
Rusk	McCORD, John W. and Nancy C.	Nancy S.	29 Nov 1875
Rusk	McCORD, Patterson & Lucy Ann	Andrew P.	30 Aug 1875
Washington	McCOWEN, Ben. & Cath.	Mary	6 Aug 1873
Somervell	McCOWN, J. J. and A. E.	Mary S.	28 Sep 1875
Rusk	McCRARY, N. D. & E. M.	William B.	6 Feb 1875
Fannin	McCRAW, W. B. & Josephine	William Edgar	6 Mar 1874
Navarro	McCUISTIAN, Charles & Leora T.	Lula	30 Dec 1873
Cherokee	McCUISTION, A. J. and Julia	Eugenia J.	3 Sep 1873
Navarro	McCUISTION, J. A. and M. E.	John Jay	12 Mar 1875
		Maggie May	21 May 1875
Rusk	McCURLEY, Ben & Luckey	Luram	25 Sep 1874
Upshur	McDANAL, J. A. & S. C.	James M.	13 Mar 1875
Fannin	McDANIEL, J. L. & E. A.	William L.	27 Jun 1874

COUNTY	PARENTS	CHILD	DATE
Rusk	McDAVID, J. M. & Susan M.	James Walter	15 Jun 1873
		John Etherel	19 Nov 1874
Rusk	McDAVID, James & Ellen	M L E	18 Jan 1874
Rusk	McDAVID, James & Tilly E.	Edna	1874
Anderson	McDONALD, E. P. and Su	Edward M.	13 Aug 1874
Fannin	McDONALD, J. C. and M. J.	O. V.	Oct 1874
Kaufman	McDONALD, J. H. & G.	Mary M.	13 Jul 1874
Upshur	McDONALD, J. W. & Alla	J. M. (or I.M.?)	10 Jun 1874
Somervell	McDONALD, W. A. and A.	Gabrel	22 Jan 1875
Rusk	McDONOUGH, Calvin R. and Isabella	Cornelia A.	5 Dec 1873
Rusk	McDONOUGH, Ed. & Adeline	Willie	4 Mar 1875
Fannin	McDOWELL, Ira & Sarah	James B.	Feb 1875
Fannin	McDUFFEY, John & Nancy N.	Avner(sic) Clark	19 Dec 1873
Jasper	McFARLANE, William M. and Amanda M.	Mary	Nov 1873
Rusk	McGARRITY, W. A. & M. H.	John Homer	8 Jan 1874
Upshur	McGEE, J. H. & R. K.	L (or Q?) G.	19 May 1874
Lamar	McGLOSSON, L. G. & L. H.	Kate K.	23 Aug 1875
Lamar	McGLOSSON, P. C. & A. A.	P. C.	28 Oct 1874
Kaufman	McGOWEN, J. M. and Maggie	Nannie K.	7 Aug 1874
Anderson	McGRIFF, Ben and Susan	Gorge (sic)	6 May 1874
Fannin	McHENRY, Robert & Mary J.	R. L.	3 Feb 1875
		Harvey Rush	25 Apr 1876
Upshur	McINTARSH(?), A. W. & L. A.	G. T.	27 May 1874
Upshur	McINTOSH, A. W. & Texan	Viola Clara	11 Apr 1876
Nueces	McKENZIE, James & Catherine (Rankin)	Josephine Brown	16 Dec 1871
		Jessie R.	13 Jul 1873
		James Junr.	8 Oct 1874
Fannin	McKINNEY, J. R. & J. H.	Dana A.	14 Apr 1875
Upshur	McKISICK, T. F. & S. A.	Mira	15 Feb 1875
Navarro	McLAIN, G. W. & P. A.	Samuel Dennis	28 May 1874
Webb	McLANE, Albert L. & Kate	Paul Waelder	19 Jul 1874
Cameron	McMANUS, Francis E. and Emily	Gerald O'Connell	10 Jul 1873
Navarro	McMILLAN, Frances Louise (Mrs. E. W. Johnson)		
Navarro	McMILLAN, Wm. C. & M. E.	Mary Diamond	19 Apr 1875
Anderson	McMORRIS, G. W. and Julia A.	Alla Harrison	4 Dec 1874
Lamar	McMURRAY, J. F. & Juliett	Julia Louisa	31 Jul 1873
Lamar	McMURRY, A. L. (or H?) & Adelia	Frank A.	22 Feb 1875
Gregg	McNEALY, Thomas & Geneva	William	15 Jul 1875
Washington	McNEESE, J. L. & Annie	L. L.	14 Feb 1874
Fannin	McPHERSON, James & Mary	Annie J.	30 Nov 1873
Fannin	McPHERSON, William & Fannie	Licy (sic)	10 Oct 1875
		John F.	25 Feb 1875
Fannin	McRAE, A. R. & M. F.	Charles Douglas	7 Jan 1874
Fannin	McRAE, F. L. & F. A.	Rosella	27 Sep 1874
Cass	McWHORTER, J. D. & N. H.	Damon B.	4 Oct 1875
		Daisy	4 Oct 1875
Navarro	McWHORTER, W. H. & Emma	Willie	26 Dec 1873
Fannin	McWILLIAMS, D. R. & S. A.	J. M.	1 Mar 1874
Fannin	McWILLIAMS, G. W. & Charlotte	Leonus	31 Oct 1872
		Oscar	30 Aug 1874
		Albert	10 Oct 1875
Upshur	MACKEY, E. A. & M. A.	J. B.	15 Feb 1876
Fannin	MADDREY, Peter B. & S. A.	James D.	13 Nov 1873
Rusk	MADDUX, Allin & Sarah	Lucretia	30 Oct 1874
Rusk	MADDUX, Jacob & Frances	Olley	Mar 1873
Rusk	MADDUX, John T. and Julia T.	Edgar Thomas	1 Jan 1874
Navarro	MAGGARD, John & M. K.	John	4 Aug 1873
Navarro	MAGNESS, W. M. & Mary J.	Joanna	3 Jun 1873
Cameron	MAILHE(?), Dolphine (Mrs. Celestin Tagou)		
Rusk	MAJOR, E. F. & S. A.	Ermin C.	5 Aug 1874
Navarro	MALLORY, S. T. & F. E.	Eldred Love	16 Jan 1875

COUNTY	PARENTS	CHILD	DATE
Anderson	MALONE, A. H. and M.	Sam C. Wood	26 Sep 1873
		Thomas	3 Jan 1874
Rusk	MALONEY, David and Frances	Susan	15 May 1874
Kaufman	MANION, George D. and		
	Texana	George D.	1 Jun 1875
Lamar	MANN, J. H. & Mary	Edward Levy	5 Aug 1875
Cherokee	MANNING, A. J. and Virginia	Carrie Rosanna	14 May 1873
Cherokee	MANNING, E. D. & Florence	C. C.	12 Apr 1874
Cherokee	MANNING, W. M. & M. A.	Emma	5 Jan 1874
Fannin	MANS (or MARRS?), J. R. &		
	Jane	John	12 May 1874
Rusk	MANSINGER, John and Sarah	John L.	19 Jan 1875
Navarro	MARABLE, W. C. & L. B.	Eufaula Buckner	13 Jul 1876
Rusk	MARCH, Giles & Dilsy	Carrie L.	27 Dec 1874
Rusk	MARCH, Jack & Margaret	____	6 Aug 1875
Navarro	MARCHBANKS, B. F. & Mary N.	Mattie Florine	20 Jun 1873
		Boling Ford	11 Jul 1875
Fannin	MARR (or MAN?), J. M. & S. A.	James	22 Dec 1873
Fannin	MARRS, (or MANS?), W. M. and		
	L. J.	C. W.	15 Feb 1875
Navarro	MARSH, R. B. & Sallie	James Dean	11 Jul 1874
Navarro	MARSH, W. H. & M. M.	Blanche	22 May 1874
Upshur	MARSHALL, Ed P. & L. V.	Ida P.	19 Jun 1873
Upshur	MARSHALL, J. M. & L. P.	Lillie	29 Nov 1873
		Wm. H.	27 Jun 1875
		Frank	17 Aug 1876
Upshur	MARSHALL, John S. & E. J.	James Marion	19 Sep 1875
Lamar	MARTIN, J. H. & S. J.	William N.	15 Sep 1873
Cherokee	MARTIN, M. W. and A. S. D.	Alice Ike	21 May 1874
Cherokee	MARTIN, R. B. and E. B.	W. B.	23 Nov 1873
Webb	MARTIN, Raymond & Tersa (sic)	Raymond Victor	6 Mar 1874
Cherokee	MARTIN, W. C. & S. C.	C. E.	2 May 1874
Webb	MARTINES, Proceso & Maria Jesusa Eusebio		30 Aug 1874
Cameron	MARTINEZ, Franca (Mrs. Alvino Castillo)		
Cass	MASEY, S. B. & Mary Ann	Mattie Elizabeth	30 Jan 1875
Anderson	MATHEWS, Anderson and Mary	Peter	8 Nov 1874
Washington	MATHEWS, J. F. & M. W.	William W.	18 Nov 1874
Rusk	MATHEWS, J. W. & Mary A. B.	C. G.	4 Apr 1874
Fannin	MATHEWS, James & Jane	James D.	17 Aug 1874
Rusk	MATHEWS, Wiley and Alice E.	Gertrude Eugenia	22 Jan 1875
Upshur	MATHIS, Charles & Susan	Jimey	5 Apr 1875
Kaufman	MATHIS, T. E. & M. E.	William Leonard	20 Jul 1873
Fannin	MATLOCK, Wm. F. & Henrietta	James D.	8 Sep 1874
Navarro	NATTHEWS, Joseph C. &		
	Margaret A.	Willie Augustus	4 Aug 1873
Marion	MATTHEWS, Paul & Ann J.	Eliza B.	19 Aug 1875
Rusk	MATTHEWS, Thomas M. and Emma	Henry P.	21 Oct 1873
		Conrad Longard	25 Oct 1875
Rusk	MATTHEWS, W. A. P. & Ellen D.	John C.	17 Oct 1875
Marion	MATTHEWS, Wm. T. & Indianna	Allicah P.	11 Mar 1874
Cass	MAXEY, L. N. & M. A.	Ellis	5 Mar 1874
Lamar	MAXWELL, J. A. & D. E.	J. P.	9 Jan 1875
Fannin	MAXWELL, J. D. & G. A.	James Lee	13 Jun 1874
Fannin	MAY, J. M. & A. J.	J. B.	12 Feb 1874
Navarro	MAY, Wm. S. & Rebecca E.	Jonathan Pickens	1 Jul 1873
Rusk	MAYERS, Gustave and Emma C.	Emma C.	22 Sep 1875
Kaufman	MAYES, T. J. & F. E.	Joseph Irving	25 Nov 1874
Upshur	MAYFIELD, Asa & Hannah	Adaline	15 Oct 1873
Rusk	MAYFIELD, George Williams &		
	Tisha	Wilson W.	10 Jun 1874
Fannin	MAYFIELD, James R. &		
	Euginia (sic)	William H.	29 Jul 1873
Navarro	MAYS, J. W. & J. C.	John Richard	31 Jul 1871
		Ruth	28 Feb 1873
		Janie	16 Jan 1875
Cherokee	MEADER, A.(?) and Agnes	Willis K.	24 Oct 1873

118

COUNTY	PARENTS	CHILD	DATE
Cherokee	MEADLETON or MAALETON ?),		
	E. H. and M. C.	Carrie M.	12 Feb 1874
Navarro	MEADOR, J. J. & L.	Elizabeth Jane	7 Sep 1875
Navarro	MEADOR, Joel J. & Susan M.(sic)	Thomas Meridith	11 Jul 1873
Navarro	MEADOR, W. P. & Mary	Thomas Esau	20 Dec 1875
Navarro	MEADOR, W. P. & Mollie	Mattie	12 Feb 1874
Lamar	MEANS, D. F. & M. J.	Ludella	28 Jan 1874
Lamar	MEANS, L. W. & Mary F.	R. E.	22 Sep 1874
	Note: the date __ Aug 1873 is written under		
	the above date		
Cameron	MEAR, Catherine (Mrs. Victor Egly)		
Cherokee	MEAZEL, Wm. and A. V.	E. L.	17 Nov 1873
Cherokee	MEDOFRD, R. and Malvina	George S.	29 Sep 1873
Webb	MEDINA, Ynocencio &		
	Lucia (Cabra)	Guellermo	25 Jun 1876
Navarro	MELTON, ___ & Melia(?)	Lydia	31 May 1874
Navarro	MELTON, Geo. & Katy	Trudy	27 Aug 1874
Rusk	MELTON, J. F. & Martha A.	Ann E.	13 Apr 1874
Navarro	MELTON, James & Mary J.	Mary Anna	18 Feb 1874
Navarro	MELTON, Lavatar & Lucy	Hiram Lavatar	6 Aug 1873
Navarro	MELTON, Melton & Harriet	Jane	19 Jun 1875
Navarro	MELTON, W. R. & E. J.	Arthur	11 Jul 1874
Cherokee	MENDELL, S. C. & M. D.	Bennie C.	28 Nov 1875
Webb	MENDIOLA, Bernardo &		
	Doratea	Ipolita	17 Oct 1874
Webb	MENDIOLA, Valentin &		
	Eulalia N.	Andrez	31 Dec 1875
Rusk	MENEFEE, Garrison & Ednie	Edie	1 Sep 1875
Rusk	MENEFEE, L. F. & Alice	William W.	2 Aug 1874
Rusk	MENEFEE, S. F. & Alice	Elizabeth	30 Nov 1875
Dallas	MENZCER, Jacob and Regina	Edward Arnold	1 Jul 1875
		Nena Rose	14 Sep 1876
Nueces	MERCER, Edward T. B. &		
	Emma L.	Robert L.	27 Mar 1874
	Note: Both reg. 21 Jun 1875	Wm. H.	13 Nov 1874
	Obviously dates in error		
Navarro	METZGAR, Amos C. & Susan R.	John Clinton	14 May 1873
Cass	MILES, A. & A. B.	Wm. M.	8 Jun 1874
Cherokee	MILLER, Chas. A. and Lou A.	Chas. Isaac	5 Oct 1872
Cameron	MILLER, George William and		
	Twanda C.	George William, Jr.	16 Aug 1872
		Robert S.	30 ___ 1874
		Juna Jane	6 Jul 1875
		Lilly Amanda	7 Aug 1877
Navarro	MILLER, John &		
	Elizabeth Esther	Cora Lee	1 Sep 1873
Anderson	MILLER, John A. and Texanna	Mary H.	14 Jan 1876
Fannin	MILLER, Nichlas & Ida(sic)	Mary Elizabeth	7 Nov 1874
Lamar	MILLER, R. M. & M. J.	F. Joe	29 Nov 1875
Navarro	MILLER, R. M. & Mary D.	Katie E.	19 Jun 1873
Fannin	MILLER, W. C. & Elizabeth	Coney	1874
		(Reg. 28 Jun 1875)	
Fannin	MILLER, William & Nannie	Lillie	Feb 1876
Cass	MILLS, J. P. & Mary F.	Netta Emma	1 Sep 1873
Cass	MILLS, John T. & Mary F.	John S.	15 Mar 1876
Lamar	MINEN, Fred W. & A.	Alura	14 Sep 1866
	Note: Alura died 17 Nov 1870		
	Ella died 2 Oct 1870		
		Ella	26 Aug 1868
		Mary Alice	6 Dec 1871
		Carrie Adela	1 Apr 1874
Navarro	MINTER, Albert & Hannah	Nancy	9 Feb 1874
		Elijah Stafford	2 Apr 1875
Kaufman	MIXON, R. D. & S. E.	Lena	30 Jan 1874
Washington	MOLVENHAEUR (MOLDENHAM?),		
	Henry & Emma	Louise	11 Dec 1873

COUNTY	PARENTS	CHILD	DATE
Kaufman	MONDAY, W. H. & M. J.	Henry A.	10 Mar 1876
Fannin	MONKS, J. & Amanda	Josephine	22 Jul 1874
Rusk	MONROE, Jack Blount and Martha (Jones)	E.	15 Sep 1875
Somervell	MONTGOMERY, J. H. and M. J.	Frances Maybell	20 Dec 1875
Navarro	MONTGOMERY, W. C. & Nancy E.	Cora Caroline	12 Apr 1876
Upshur	MONTGOMERY, W. W. & Mary A.	Estella V.	23 Nov 1873
		James Edward	22 Apr 1876
Upshur	MOODY, W. H. & A. E.	Martha J.	26 Feb 1875
Fannin	MOORE, G. N. & Annie	Samuel P.	1874
Fannin	MOORE, George & Palsie	King	6 Jul 1874
	(twins)	Cain	6 Jul 1874
Fannin	MOORE, J. R. & Martha	Viola	24 Oct 1874
Rusk	MOORE, Joseph and Julia	Martha A.	25 Feb 1875
Fannin	MOORE, P. G. & M. J.	Lelia	29 Sep 1874
Fannin	MOORE, R. S. & E. J.	Richard	30 Mar 1874
Rusk	MOORE, Seton and Levic V.	John Romulus	20 Apr 1875
		Jeems Remus	20 Apr 1875
Rusk	MOORE, Silas M. and Mary Ann	Maudy Elizabeth	27 Feb 1875
Rusk	MOORE, Simpson and Martha F.		8 May 1874
Anderson	MOORE, T. W. and M. E.	Turner	3 Feb 1874
Fannin	MOORE, W. C. & Emily	Charles T.	26 Feb 1874
Kaufman	MOORE, W. J. & D.(?) J.	James Alexander	8 Nov 1873
Rusk	MOORE, William and Amanda J.	George W.	23 Jun 1874
Cameron	MORALIS, Ma. tndrea (sic) (Mrs. Jacob Benten)		
Webb	MORAN, Valente & Maria (Munos)	Catarina	30 Apr 1876
Cameron	MORENO, Demetria (Mrs. Manuel Parra Lopez)		
Fannin	MORGAN, A. J. & Sarah	Martha E.	8 May 1874
Fannin	MORGAN, Charles & E. V.	M. E.	21 Jul 1874
Jasper	MORGAN, Malachi and Eliza F.	Salura Eudora	
Lamar	MORGAN, R. B. & M. E.	John W.	22 Jun 1874
Upshur	MORGAN, S. P. & M. A.	Seburn (or Schern?) C.	17 Oct 1873
Washington	MORGAN, W. L. & T. D.	N. P.	5 Jan 1875
Cherokee	MORRIS, Charles and M. E.	Norah A.	21 Feb 1874
Rusk	MORRIS, D. L. & S. C.	Elizabeth A.	10 Aug 1874
		Lizzie	10 Aug 1875
Rusk	MORRIS, James C. and Sarah J.	James A.	8 Aug 1874
Rusk	MORRIS, John M. and Mary E.	Joseph G.	9 Jun 1875
Cass	MORRIS, R. A. & S. L.	Saml. E.	2 Oct 1874
Nueces	MORRIS, Simon & Ellen	Delphine	6 Jan 1875
Anderson	MORROW, J. B. and O. P.	Laura L.	2 May 1875
Anderson	MORROW, W. T. and C. S.	Robt. L.	7 Aug 1875
Navarro	MORSE, A. E. & S. T.	Susie Floy	28 Feb 1874
Cherokee	MOSELY, E. R. and R. A.	Elijah Marion	4 Nov 1873
Fannin	MOSS, C. C. & F. I.	Mattie	Jun 1875
Navarro	MOUNT, W. T. & M. A. E.	William Finis	4 Jan 1875
Rusk	MOYERS, Isham B. and Jacintha	Willie R. M.	28 Feb 1875
Kaufman	MUCKLEROY, J. H. & M. R.	Lilla	21 Dec 1873
Rusk	MUCKLEROY, Ras & Melia	Benton	1 Sep 1874
Webb	MUNOS, Maria (Mrs. Valente Moran)		
Nueces	MURPHY, David M. & Catherine M.	Mary Geneveive(sic)	15 Oct 1874
		David Lee	13 Apr 1876
Lamar	MURPHY, N. G. & M. P.	James Clinton	2 Apr 1875
Upshur	MUSICK, J. A. & M. E.	Thos. F.	23 Aug 1874
Upshur	MUSICK, J. T. & S. C.	Robert H.	3 Aug 1875
Fannin	MYERS, G. W. & M. F.	Brock	10 Dec 1874
Rusk	NALL, J. M. & M. J.	James W.	25 Aug 1874
Fannin	NANNOY, L. J. & E. M.	M. E.	5 Apr 1874
Rusk	NEAL, Aaron & Mary	Julia Ann	20 Jul 1875
Fannin	NEAL, T. D. & Lucreta(sic)	Mildred	Jan 1875
Lamar	NEATHERY, Chas. S. & Isabella	Mowice(?) G.	3 Jul 1874
Rusk	NEEDHAM, W. H. & Catharine	Robert E. Lee	25 Nov 1873

COUNTY	PARENTS	CHILD	DATE
Rusk	NEELEY, J. W. & M. A.	Luther O.	14 Dec 1873
		Eunice E.	9 Mar 1875
Rusk	NEELEY, John and M. E.	Charles W.	18 Feb 1874
Dallas	NEELY, ___ & ___	Martha Lucinda	18 Oct 1872
		Mary Elizabeth	18 Jul 1874
		Ella Ada	10 Mar 1876
Rusk	NEELY, W. B. & Mary	James R.	4 Sep 1874
Fannin	NELMS, A. L. & M. J.	Robert C.	16 May 1874
Navarro	NELMS, J. A. & Ophelia L.	S. Stephen	20 Oct 1874
Lamar	NELSON, Thomas M. & S. J.	Thomas Marion	3 Mar 1875
Lamar	NELSON, W. D. & L. V.	Thomas Uriah	20 May 1875
Rusk	NEVILLS, Calvin R. and		
	Permelia E.	Julia Lee	8 Feb 1875
Fannin	NEWBERRY, A. G. & Jemmia J.	W. H.	18 Sep 1873
Fannin	NEWBURY, E. R. & Elza	George F.	8 Nov 1873
Fannin	NEWMAN, J. W. & C. J.	Beulah	14 Nov 1873
Anderson	NEWSOM, F. F. and Caroline	Florence	24 Mar 1875
Rusk	NEWSOM, G. H. B. & M. W.	James M.	23 Aug 1873
Rusk	NEWSOM, J. E. & M. Q.	Lamma E.	20 Jul 1873
Kaufman	NEWTON, D. H. and Mina	Walter Brison	11 Nov 1873
Rusk	NEWTON, W. T. & Liza E.	Thomas F.	25 Feb 1875
Rusk	NICHOLAS, Columbus & Hester	Jesse E.	7 Nov 1875
Rusk	NICHOLAS, Thomas and Sarah	Nellie	15 Oct 1875
Rusk	NICHOLS, John T. and Sarah L.	John Gaston	17 Feb 1874
Washington	NICHOLS, John V. & H. E.	Robt. M.	24 Mar 1874
Rusk	NICKERSON, Daniel & Harriet	Daniel	10 May 1874
Fannin	NOBLE, R. E. & Kate	Lizzie	17 Oct 1874
Rusk	NOBLE, S. E. & Kate	Simon E.	19 Feb 1875
Cameron	NODRI, Maximina (Mrs. Santos Valdez)		
Gregg	NORTHCUTT, Wm. G. &		
	Julia Ann	Charley Coleman	24 Dec 1875
Navarro	NORVELL, E. & Cornelia J.	Sarah Ann	7 May 1874
	Note: Second entry: "Dr. E. & C. J."		
		John Williams	3 Apr 1876
Rusk	NORVELL, John E. and Kesiah T.	Charles	4 Jun 1873
Lamar	NOWELL, J. B. & M. E.	Emily E.	18 Jan 1874
Rusk	NUNNALLY, C. L. & H. A.	Carry E.	13 Apr 1875
Anderson	NYETT, W. R. and S. O.	Dora Bell	27 Nov 1875
Rusk	OBERTHIER, E. C. & Margaret	Sallie H.	23 Dec 1873
Rusk	OBERTHIER, H. L. & E. V.	Susan M.	18 Jun 1874
Navarro	ODEN, G. A. & M. J.	Robert Clifford	22 Mar 1876
Washington	OGBURN, L. H. & Julia	Josiah	8 Jan 1874
Anderson	OGG, Anderson and Kessy	Hilliard C.	28 Nov 1875
Gregg	OGILVIE, Norman C. & Ada C.		26 Feb 1875
Fannin	OLDHAM, Samuel Z. & E. J.	William C.	31 Dec 1874
Fannin	OLIVER, Albert & C. M. (sic)	Ema L.	6 Sep 1874
Rusk	OLIVER, M. D. & Nancy	M. H.	1 Apr 1875
Fannin	OLIVER, N. T. & M. C.	Andrew A.	24 Jan 1874
Rusk	OLIVER, William R. and Mary E.	Joseph O.	31 May 1874
Lamar	OLLIVER, A. K. & Mary(sic)	William Allen	1875
Kaufman	OLSEN, O. and Annie	Julius Mathis	20 Nov 1874
Webb	OLVERA, Jesus &		
	Francisca (Guerrera)	Refugia	5 Jul 1875
Navarro	ONSTOTT, J. H. & N. L.	Marion Lee	25 Nov 1873
Rusk	ORANGE, Allen & Elvinie	Alfred	1 Mar 1875
Kaufman	ORR, D. J. and Annie	Nannie Dashiell	20 Dec 1873
		Hattie Sue	14 Feb 1875
Navarro	OUTLAW, L. B. & H. V.	Mary Caroline	12 May 1874
Cherokee	OWEN, W. S. & A. E.	Elias S.	1 Feb 1875
Navarro	OWENS, F. G. & Martha Ann	Mary E.	25 Sep 1873
Lamar	OWENS, M. J. and M. J.	Joel	3 Dec 1874
Jasper	OWENS, S. H. and Minerva (Pace)	S. H., Jr.	
	Note: Parents' names given	Cora Ollie	14 Jan 1879
	for Cora Ollie were		
	Stephen Oliver Owens		
	and Minerva (Pace)		

COUNTY	PARENTS	CHILD	DATE
Fannin	OWENS, T. B. & Sarah A.	William H.	14 May 1874
Cherokee	OWENS, W. W. and wife	Fannie J.	7 Jan 1874
Jasper	PACE, Minerva (Mrs. Stephen Oliver Owens)		
Washington	PAHL, H. F. & Virginia E.	William Henry	19 Aug 1873
Neuces	PALACIOS, George & Sarah Ann	Edward	4 Jul 1873
		George	19 Feb 1875
Anderson	PALMER, Levi and Mary	Pleasant Hugh	5 Oct 1875
Rusk	PALMER, W. H. & Elizabeth	J. H.	12 Feb 1875
Lamar	PARIS, J. D. & M. C.	T. Click	1 Nov 1873
Upshur	PARISH, J. B. & Carrie	James W.	1 Apr 1875
Upshur	PARISH, L. C. H. & Ardella	Willie	4 Apr 1875
Kaufman	PARISH, N. H. and H. A.	N. H.	16 Feb 1874
	Note: surname is spelled "Parrish" in 1876		
Rusk	PARKER, E. W. H & Martha A.	Alice B.	25 Aug 1873
Rusk	PARKER, F. M. H. & Nancy L.	James T.	7 Nov 1873
		Lula V.	7 Nov 1875
Rusk	PARKER, H. R. T. & Mary C.	Mary A.	9 May 1874
Rusk	PARKER, J. F. & Sarah A.	C. A.	24 Oct 1875
Rusk	PARKER, J. H. & Ella P.	Aldora O.	15 Aug 1875
Rusk	PARKER, Jacob and Clarissa	James H.	24 Feb 1875
Rusk	PARKER, James F. and Amanda A.	Louis F.	3 Dec 1874
		Minnie L.	24 Jan 1876
Anderson	PARKER, John and C. F.	Wm. Franklin	11 Feb 1875
Rusk	PARKER, John and Mary E.	Nicholas	29 Nov 1874
Fannin	PARKER, William & Sarah A.	William Clarence	9 Jan 1875
	(Twins)	Anna Clara	
Navarro	PARRISH, Wm. & Margaret M.	Joseph Manly	28 Feb 1874
Cass	PATMAN, Wm. H. & M. R.	David Elios	27 Jan 1874
Rusk	PATRICK, R. D. & Frances P.	Minnie A.	8 Jul 1874
Rusk	PATTERSON, Alex & Cyntha	Mary	1 Apr 1874
Navarro	PATTERSON, Ben Mc. & Charlotte	McIntosh	Jan 1874
Anderson	PATTERSON, J. A. and M. A.	Belzoria	3 Apr 1874
Rusk	PATTERSON, L. H. & Martha	Robert W.	30 Oct 1875
Navarro	PATTERSON, Thos. H. & E. M.	Charlotte	24 Feb 1874
		John M.	13 Nov 1875
Anderson	PAYNE, J. B. and ___	Dudley	27 Feb 1874
Rusk	PEACAW, John and Mary A.	Minaola	29 Jul 1874
Fannin	PEAKS, George W. & Elizabeth	William W.	28 May 1874
Kaufman	PEARSON, P. and Helen		27 Aug 1874
Fannin	PEAY, J. M. & Easter	C. Jane	7 Jan 1875
Fannin	PEA(Y), Jim & Easter	Minnie Magnolia	24 Jun 1876
Navarro	PEEK, John & Hannah	Dow Perry	18 Dec 1873
Lamar	PEEVEY, L. J. & M. J.	Waity Emma	11 Nov 1875
	(twins)	Mary Arlena	11 Nov 1875
Gregg	PEGUIS(?), Dock & Eliza M.	Oliver	2 Apr 1875
Upshur	PELGRAN, J. P. & Hannah B.	Frances V.	7 Sep 1874
Navarro	PELTON, D. C. & E. J.	Flora	19 Oct 1873
Cameron	PENA, de la, Miguel and Doloris (de la Portilla)	Juana J.	13 Aug 1873
	(triplets)	Rita A.	13 Aug 1873
		Maria Guadalupe	13 Aug 1873
Upshur	PENDER, H. B. & F. E.	H. E.	9 Jan 1873
		E. M.	26 Feb 1876
Upshur	PENDER (or PENDEE?), R. C. & E. J.	Wm. R.	15 Nov 1875
Rusk	PENN, William & Jennie	Martha	21 Sep 1873
Fannin	PENNINGTON, A. & M. E.	Theopluss(sic)	15 May 1875
Fannin	PENWELL, L. C. & R. E.	Lutie Dell	22 Oct 1875
Navarro	PERDUE, G. M. & Gracie	Liney Evline	3 Jun 1873
Cameron	PEREZ, Guadalupe (Mrs. Macedonio Garcia)		
Kaufman	PERKINS, A. H. and D. E. J.	E. D.	17 Feb 1874
Cass	PERKINS, D. W. & E. J.	Jno. A. (or K.?)	15 Jan 1874
Rusk	PERKINS, J. A. and Jane	O. H. A.	2 Feb 1875
Rusk	PERNELL, W. A. & A. B.	John William	26 Aug 1875
Navarro	PERRY, J. M. & Laura M.	Louisa Josephine	10 Aug 1875

COUNTY	PARENTS	CHILD	DATE
Lamar	PERRY, M. & M.	J. T. (or F.?)	15 Jun 1874
Somervell	PERRY, O. H. and L. (or S.)	George W.	26 Dec 1873
Rusk	PERRY, R. B. & Emma J.	Janie Irene	28 Oct 1873
Rusk	PERRY, W. R. & Eliza A.	George	1 Apr 1875
Cherokee	PERRY, Wm. & Elizabeth	Mary A.	20 Feb 1874
Gregg	PERRY, Wm. F. & Elizabeth E.	Wm. Florence	7 Jun 1873
Gregg	PERRY, Wm. F. & Mittie E.	Lula May	13 Jan 1875
Fannin	PERSONS, Abrams & Sarah	Marion	1 Oct 1875
Fannin	PETERS, Elijah & Elizabeth	Tinnie C.	1 Jan 1874
Rusk	PETERSON, G. W. & Lucinda	Effie S.	6 Aug 1875
Anderson	PETIT, B. W. and M. J.	Henry R.	7 Feb 1876
Navarro	PETTY, J. T. & Elizabeth	George Edward	11 Jun 1874
		Alice	1 Jan 1876
Anderson	PETTY, Jno. N. and Mary E.	Nelia	15 Feb 1875
Anderson	PETTY, William M. and Margaret	John A.	1 Apr 1876
Fannin	PEYTON, J. A. & M. J.	D. W.	10 Jun 1875
Washington	PFENNEGER, Henry & Pauline	Henry Emanuel	12 Dec 1873
		Samuel Jacobus	19 Mar 1875
Cass	PHELPS, E. C. & M. T.	James S.	26 Nov 1873
Lamar	PHILIPS, Jno. T. & Mary E.	F. A.	5 Jan 1874
Upshur	PHILLIPS, A. M. & M. E.	Elizabeth	24 Dec 1874
Upshur	PHILLIPS, A. P. & E. E.	Erastus	29 Jan 1876
Rusk	PHILLIPS, D. J. & Eudora E.	Lucinda E.	16 Jan 1875
Rusk	PHILLIPS, J. L. & Zera	Ida	8 Jun 1874
Upshur	PHILLIPS, J. W. & Jane P.	Rosalee	24 Nov 1875
Anderson	PHILLIPS, James and F. J.	Thomas	19 Aug 1873
		Mary L.	16 Dec 1875
Rusk	PHILLIPS, R. N. & Missouri	John Clark	20 Mar 1875
Fannin	PICKENS, A. H. & M. J.	M. A.	26 Sep 1875
Anderson	PICKLE, James A. and Kittie	Albert W.	2 Aug 1874
		Jesse P.	12 Apr 1876
Fannin	PIERCE, Robert N. & Laura	John M.	8 Nov 1874
Rusk	PIERCE, W. M. and N. J.	Mollie F.	14 Jan 1874
Fannin	PINER, J. W. & ___	Mary Belle	19 Oct 1874
Fannin	PINER, John & Dora B.	F. E. Piner, Jr. (sic)	12 Jan 1875
Dallas	PINKNEY, Jas. H. and Eunice A.	Eugene Allbretton	19 Mar 1875
Upshur	PINSON (or Pierson?), W. C. & Julia	Joseph F.	18 Nov 1873
Navarro	PITTMAN, J. N. & Emily V.	Robert Asa	10 Apr 1875
Navarro	PITTMAN, W. N. & Winnie C.	Cora Elizabeth	1875
Washington	PLUMMER, W. M. & Clemon(?)	Malcolm Augustus	11 Apr 1874
Rusk	POE, J. A. & Elizabeth	Edgar A.	7 May 1874
Rusk	POLK, David & Ellen	Noma	22 Sep 1873
Kaufman	POLK, K. F. & S. E.	Fannie Paralee	4 Mar 1874
Rusk	POLK, Moses & Josephine	Jimmie	1 Jun 1874
Rusk	POLK, Sam & Ellen	Mary	12 May 1874
Fannin	POPE, John E. & L. W.	William A.	17 Sep 1875
Rusk	POPE, Lewis & Barbara	James T. W.	10 Jan 1874
Lamar	PORTER, S. A. and F. A.	Lucy	3 Jul 1873
		William	13 Sep 1875
Cameron	PORTILLA, de la, Doloris (Mrs. Miguel de la Pena)		
Rusk	POTTER, E. D. & M. F.	James W.	17 Dec 1875
Jasper	POWELL, William N. and Charlotte C.	Mary Matilda	31 May 1876
	(twins)	William J.	31 May 1876
Rusk	PRATHER, David and Eliza J.	Hattie O.	11 Feb 1876
Fannin	PRATT, Saml. & Susan E.	George P.	26 Dec 1873
Navarro	PRESLEY, T. M. & Belle M.	Emmett L.	22 Apr 1874
Fannin	PRESTON, Geo. A. & M. S.	Mary	27 Oct 1874
Rusk	PREWITT, W. H. & Mary Elizabeth	Mary	14 Mar 1874
Washington	PRICE, A. & E. O.	Archalous	24 Nov 1874
Anderson	PRICE, C. L. and E. A.	W. S.	18 Feb 1875

COUNTY	PARENTS	CHILD	DATE
Fannin	PRICE, James O. & Mosella	Henry	24 Apr 1875
	(twins)	James	24 Apr 1875
Fannin	PRICE, Robert A. & M. D.	Bob	11 May 1873
Fannin	PRICE, T. D. & S. E.	Ella	25 Jul 1874
Navarro	PRICE, Wm. & Mary A.	Thomas S.(?)	7 Jan 1874
Navarro	PRIDDY, E. & M. M.	Winnie Florence	22 Oct 1874
Rusk	PROCTOR, Allen and Francis	Rabon Hamilton	6 Jun 1875
Rusk	PROPES, John A. and Tempey L.	Duncan S.	21 Aug 1875
Rusk	PROTHRO, George E. and Ann E.	Mary E.	13 Sep 1875
Jasper	PRUETT, A. M. and Crissy Ann	James M.	11 Mar 1875
	(twins)	M. E.	11 Mar 1875
Rusk	PRUITT, Henry H. and Sarah E.	Mary E.	6 Oct 1873
Navarro	PRUITT, James & Caroline	Joseph Stephen	24 Sep 1873
Rusk	PRUITT, Riley & Kittie	Mary	28 Feb 1875
Rusk	PRYOR, A. H. & M. J.	E. J.	4 Dec 1874
Nueces	PUGH, Catherine (Mrs. Martin S. Culver)		
Navarro	PURSLEY, George & Sarah E.	Alsbury	15 Feb 1874
Navarro	PURSLEY, J. M. & Elizabeth	Henry	5 Sep 1873
Cameron	PUTEGNAR, Joseph L. and Rosa	Henry Samuel	14 Jul 1873
Nueces	RABB, John & Martha	Elizabeth J.	5 Mar 1849
	Note: Registered 2 Jan 1875 in Nueces Co., but born in Fayette County--first two children. Next three children b. in Karnes County. Frank b. in Nueces Co.		
		Margaret A.	11 Feb 1851
		Green A.	― ― 1854
		Thomas L.	― ― 1856
		Mary L.	― ― 1858
		Frank	― ― 1866
Rusk	RAGLAND, L. S. & L. T.	John	― Feb 1875
Fannin	Ragsdale, A. T. & Nancy A.	Belle	30 Mar 1874
Fannin	RAGSDALE, T. W. & Nannie S.	Mary Blair	7 Jan 1875
Marion	RAINEY, G. D., Jr. & E. L. Reg. 6 May 1874	Dara Alice	22 Nov 1873
Rusk	RAINWATER, L. B. M. & S. A. M.	B. A.	16 Jun 1875
Navarro	RAKESTRAW, G. A. & D. R.	George Albert	9 Apr 1875
Jasper	RALPH, Henry and Nancy P.	Sophia M.	15 Mar 1874
Fannin	RAMSEY, J. R. & ――	Flora Ida	2 Sep 1873
Fannin	RANDALL, H. I. & E. B.	H. T.	― Feb 1874
Webb	RANGEL, Luciano & Magdalena M.	Bruno	6 Mar 1876
Nueces	RANKIN, Catherine (Mrs. James McKenzie)		
Washington	RANSOM, H. & C. T.	Ruth	27 Oct 1873
Navarro	RAPHAEL, E. & Mina	Sophia	29 Aug 1873
Washington	RASMUSSEN, Peter & Dorothea	Louise	22 Jan?1874
Lamar	RATLIFF, Robert P. & D. T.	Robert Eli	7 Dec 1873
Navarro	RATTAN, C. C. & Mary W.	Frederick	15 Sep 1873
Fannin	RATTON, Oscar & Mollie J.	Lou Ella	24 May 1875
Rusk	RAWLINGS, Richard T. and Nancy J.	Fannie E.	8 Jan 1875
Dallas	RAWLINS, Edwin C. and Sarah E.	Henry Leslie	11 Dec 1873
Dallas	RAWLINS, R. D. and Henrietta C.	Jessie Alex	12 Sep 1873
Upshur	RAY, L. P., Jr. and M. F.	W. A.	13 Aug 1875
Upshur	RAY, W. W. & Laura E.	Henrietta E.	3 May 1874
Upshur	READ, L. M. & E. E.	Susan A. 21 (or 22?)Mar 1874
Rusk	READY, G. A. & E. H.	William J.	3 Oct 1874
Cherokee	REAGAN, B. & M. A.	Richard B., Jr.	18 Sep 1874
Kaufman	REASONOVER, J. J. & M. E.	J. J.	5 Dec 1873
Navarro	REDDEN, J. T. & Sarah A.	John David	21 Dec 1876
		D. W.	26 Apr 1878
Rusk	REDWIN, Ellen (Mrs. Peter Brown)		
Rusk	REDWIN, Isham & Caroline (Willis) Joseph Anderson 20 Apr1875		

COUNTY	PARENTS	CHILD	DATE
Fannin	REED, Syl & Ema	Syl	1 Sep 1874
	(twins)	Henry	1 Sep 1874
Jasper	REESE, Jordan & Sarah M.	Buenavita	26 Nov 1874
		Louvenia	Oct 1875
Cherokee	REESE, Wm. & M. J.	T(r)essa C.	7 Sep 1874
Fannin	REEVES, S. T. & E. A.	Cora Ann	31 Dec 1874
Fannin	REEVES, Thompson & A. M.	Josephine	17 Jul 1874
Kaufman	REEVES, W. A. & E. T.(?)	Lahrenah	30 Nov 1873
haufman	REIERSON, J. H. & A. V.	Royal Reinert	17 May 1876
Navarro	REMONTE, J. & E.	Bennie	4 Jul 1874
Rusk	RETTIG, Bob & Catherine	Persey	1 Oct 1875
Rusk	RETTIG, Ellick & Jane	Albert	9 Jan 1875
Rusk	RETTIG, Paul & Martha S.	Edward	25 Sep 1873
		Frank	20 Feb 1875
Lamar	REUSS, E. W. & H.	Edward	22 Apr 1877
		Max	1 Jan 1876
Fannin	REVELL, T. B. & V. J.	Pearl L.	7 Oct 1874
Cameron	REYES, Hermerejildo &		
	Gregoria (Villareal)	Jose de la Paz	8 Jun 1879
Dallas	REYNAUD, Wm. H. & L. M.	Henry Farrot	26 Jul 1876
Gregg	REYNOLDS, John F. &		
	Elizabeth E.	Thomas Josiah	7 Aug 1866
		Levi Dennis	20 Dec 1873
Cherokee	REYNOLDS, Wm. & Martha	George Z.	19 Nov 1873
Fannin	RHINE, David & Florence C.	Sophia	20 Jan 1874
Lamar	RHUDASIL, James C. &		
	Annie E.	Ella Lee	15 Feb 1874
Jasper	RHYMES, Phoebe (Mrs. Samuel Bird)		
Webb	RIAS, Tiburcia (Mrs. Porciano Romero)		
Fannin	RICE, J. M. & S. E.	Rosie L.	21 Sep 1874
Lamar	RICE, W. A. & L. R.		
	(or R. L.?)	B. F.	14 Nov 1874
Jasper	RICH, George L. and		
	Rebecca J.	Walter L.	5 Sep 1874
Fannin	RICHARDS, George & ___	Luanie	20 Oct 1874
Upshur	RICHARDSON, B. F. & E. T.	L. A.	31 Dec 1873
Upshur	RICHARDSON, D. & M. M.	Jackanasus(?) A.	1 Mar 1874
Jasper	RICHARDSON, Larkin A. &		
	Mary Jane	Larkin A.	10 Aug 1873
Upshur	RICHARDSON, W. W. & L. E.	Mary Ella	1 Mar 1876
Fannin	RICHESON, John O. & Mary A.	Minnie I. or Q?)	23 Jan 1874
Lamar	RICHEY, A. J. & Sarah A.	Edith Lucinda	
		Ellinor	29 Oct 1875
Lamar	RICHEY, W. L. & Mary C.	William Oscar	22 Dec 1875
Lamar	RICHEY, William L. & M. C.	Ophelia J.	Mar 1873
Lamar	RIDLEY, D. & Mary F.	Eugene Drengoole	16 Mar 1876
Lamar	RIDLEY, H.(?) & Mary	W. T.	3 Spe 1873
Lamar	RIGNEY, J. M. & Virginia	Sallie	17 Nov 1875
Washington	RISHER(?), John F. &		
	Margaret	Eliza Jane	31 Oct 1875
Lamar	RITCHIE, N. J. & M. W.	Frances Hellin	25 Oct 1875
		(sic)	
Rusk	RIVES, Henry J. and Mary A.	Colby	26 Dec 1873
Lamar	RIVES, Littlebery W. &	William Thomas	23 Sep 1874
	Francis J. (twins)	Francis Marion	23 Sep 1874
Navarro	ROBERTS, E. & Mary L.	Eliza Prudence	3 Aug 1874
Rusk	ROBERTS, G. W. & Martha W.	James M.	6 May 1875
Rusk	ROBERTS, George A. and M. A.	___	2 Dec 1874
Navarro	ROBERTS, H. G. & America	Thomas Hood	1 Sep 1875
Navarro	ROBERTS, J. R. & N. C.	Thomas Jefferson	10 May 1874
Lamar	ROBERTS, John E. & Narcissa C.	Louie	21 Oct 1867
		Edward W.	8 Aug 1869
		Ida	21 Oct 1872
		Albert B.	
		(or G.?)	4 Feb 1875
Fannin	ROBERTS, R. C. & J. O.	Henry	1 Mar 1874

125

COUNTY	PARENTS	CHILD	DATE
Rusk	ROBERTSON, Calvin & Charity	Harrison	8 Feb 1876
Rusk	ROBERTSON, Jerry & Ellen (Bell)	Laura	15 Apr 1875
Lamar	ROBERTSON, W. C. & D. E.	Laura Rebecca	17 Jul 1874
Cass	ROBIN (or RAHIER?), J.P. & Eugenia A. (or H.?)	Joseph A.	16 Nov 1873
Fannin	ROBINSON, D. C. & P. J.	John B.	22 Jun 1874
Anderson	ROBINSON, J. D. and Sadie	Richard L.	20 Dec 1872
		Saml. D.	17 Aug 1875
Fannin	ROBINSON, M. L. & T.	Minnie C.	17 Jul 1874
Lamar	ROCHELL, F. M. & M. V.	Jno. W. (or C? or R?)	10 Apr 1874
Kaufman	ORDDEN, D. B. & S. C.	Ethan	9 Sep 1873
		Finis	25 Jul 1875
Gregg	RODDEN, Joseph T. & Darthula L. or S.	Nancy Augusta	1 Aug 1875
Webb	RODRIGUEZ, Jesus ma & Regina (Salinas)	Crisolfo	10 May 1874
Cameron	RODRIGUEZ, Jose and Petra (Hernandez)	Justo	9 Aug 1873
Webb	RODRIGUEZ, Roque & Silvestre (Juarez)	Roque	25 Jan 1874
Fannin	ROGERS, E. G. & Josephine	E. E.	17 Nov 1874
Anderson	ROGERS, J. A. and Mary G.	Ann Eliza	31 May 1874
Rusk	ROGERS, James T. and Annie C.	George W.	1 Dec 1874
Fannin	ROGERS, S. M. N. & E. R.	Martha A.	30 Apr 1875
Kaufman	ROGERS, T. J. & E. F.	T. H.	24 May 1873
	(twins)	J. S.	24 May 1873
Anderson	ROGERS, W. R. and M. J.	Ewell Neal	3 Feb 1874
Lamar	ROLEND, B. S. & H. R.	Robert Edger(sic)14 Mar 1874	
	Note: "Hattie" on second entry. Albert R.		
Lamar	ROLEND, W. H. & L. E.	W. H.	8 Jan 1874
Rusk	ROLLINS, ___ & ___	Gracy, Jr.	
	Note: No birth date was given, but this birth was recorded 10 Nov. 1875.		
Anderson	ROLLINS, Sam A. and Mary E.	Jesse	3 Aug 1874
		Mary	6 Mar 1876
Webb	ROMERO, Porciano & Tiburcia (Rias)	Agapita	19 Mar 1876
Navarro	RORIE, W. J. & M. C.	Rufus Elonzo	28 Feb 1874
Fannin	ROSE, Wm. & Mary J.	Laura J.	9 Oct 1874
Rusk	ROSS, Albert & Beckie	Arthur	18 Feb 1874
		James Davis	18 Jun 1875
Navarro	ROSS, H. H. & Mary E.	William Eliphas	11 Feb 1874
Rusk	ROSS, J. P. & R. T.	Adella	11 Oct 1873
Fannin	ROSS, Joseph N. & Fanny E.	Mary M.	1 Sep 1873
Rusk	ROSS, Thomas & Ellen	James A.	21 Aug 1874
Gregg	ROSSAN, Thomas Jefferson & Elmira	William Gregg	3 Jul 1874
Gregg	ROSSON, Joseph B. & Nancy	Leonora	13 Sep 1874
		Carrie Elizabeth	5 Mar 1876
Cass	ROUNTREE, S. J. & M. C.	Martha S.	29 Jul 1873
Cameron	ROUSETTE, Louis Amadie and Mary Alice	Ida Annie	3 Oct 1869
		James Louis	18 Sep 1871
		Elia	16 Aug 1873
Rusk	ROUSSEAU, T. & J. A. T.	Aaron	6 Mar 1874
	(twins)	Eugenia	6 Mar 1874
Fannin	ROWLAND, C. F. & D. E.	Edna	6 Mar 1875
Rusk	ROWLAND, L. B. & Mary J.	Edgar	10 Oct 1875
Marion	ROWLEY, Edwin R. & Jane F.	Elizabeth E.	5 Dec 1873
		(Reg. 28 Mar 1874)	
Anderson	ROYAL, N. R. and Anna	Lucy	23 Oct 1874
Anderson	ROYAL, R. J. and A. A.	John P.	24 Mar 1874
Fannin	ROYSE, B. L. and M. T.	Vista	15 May 1874

COUNTY	PARENTS	CHILD	DATE
Rusk	RUARK, E. L. & M. C.	Hattie Magnolia	22 Dec 1874
Gregg	RUCKER, Asa B. & Mary E.	Waddie Wilborne	27 Feb 1874
Washington	RUCKER, J. E. & S. E.	Henry	29 May 1875
Washington	RUFFIN, Charles & Mariah	Sarah	25 Nov 1873
Kaufman	RUSHING, J. A. & H. O.	Charles Cornelius	5 Aug 1873
Lamar	RUSSELL, E. A. & S. E.	Neometta	10 Jan 1875
Fannin	RUSSELL, J. L. & Susan J.	Walter C.	8 May 1875
Rusk	RUTHERFORD, M. L. & Emma M.	John W.	29 Nov 1873
		Trammell P.	28 Odt 1875
Fannin	RYAN, W. A. & A. D.	Mary S.	3 Mar 1875
Kaufman	SADLER, T. C. and Abi	Maud Yates	2 Mar 1874
Webb	SALAS, Damacio & Octaviana	Saragosa	3 Oct 1873
Webb	SALINAS, Augustin & Pablo G.	Pedro	13 May 1873
	Second entry: mother's name spelled "Paula Garcia"	Maria Antonia	9 May 1876
Webb	SALINAS, Carlos & Pabla M.	Virgenia (sic)	3 Dec 1875
Webb	SALINAS, Pilar & Concepcion	Porfiria	8 Aug 1873
Nueces	SALINAS, Rafael F. & Jane R.	Rachel G.	6 Dec 1867
Webb	SALINAS, Regina (Mrs. Jesus Rodriguez)		
Rusk	SAMPLE, A. W. & M. L.	Genie	19 Sep 1875
Webb	SANCHEZ, Damacio & Dorotea T.	Concepcion	31 Dec 1875
Cherokee	SANDERLIN, E. J. and J. W.	J. A.	11 Feb 1874
Rusk	SANDERS, Henry & Sarah	Sallie	15 May 1873
Cass	SANDERS, J. H. & M. A.	Genette	1 Mar 1874
Rusk	SANDERS, T. J. Jordan & Ann E.	J. C.	21 Jul 1875
Webb	SANDOVAL, Sylvestro & Juana	Margarita	15 Feb 1874
		Josefita	5 Apr 1876
Cass	SAPER, Jacob & Caroline	Texanna	23 Oct 1873
Washington	DAPP, York & Rosa	Martha (Marsha?)	8 Sep 1872
Jasper	SARGENT, James K. and Cassey A.	Richard I.	30 Jan 1875
Jasper	SARGENT, Mayfield & Catherine	Early B.	11 Oct 1874
Cameron	SARRASQUITA, Francisco & Delfina (Chapa)	Vicenta	25 Jul 1875
Cass	SARRATT, L. W. & E. M.	J. E.	4 Apr 1873
Rusk	SARTAIN, G. W. & Flora	Lazy	18 May 1875
Upshur	SAUNDERS, W. H. & M. V.	Lizzie	23 Jul 1875
Nueces	SAVAGE, Robert R. & Mary A.	Lottie Scott	16 Oct 1875
Washington	SAYLES, B. G. & M. J.	Henry	11 Jun 1873
Lamar	SCALES, E. D. & L. L.	Wallace Bryan	5 Dec 1875
Navarro	SCALES, J. A. & S. E.	Lou Allice	13 Oct 1874
Jasper	SCARBOROUGH, L. D. & Martha E.	Martha A.	6 Sep 1873
Navarro	SCARBROUGH, T. J. & Nancy J.	George Byron	25 Mar 1875
	(twins)	James Warren	25 Mar 1875
Nueces	SCHUBERT, Richard H. E. & Augusta (Gause)	Annie Maria	20 Apr 1871
		Charles Frederick Richard	17 Oct 1872
		Lucy Jane	22 Mar 1874
Washington	SCHUERENBERG(?), W. F. & E.	Rudolph	29 Sep 1873
Navarro	SCOTT, H. B. & S. C.	Sarah Macedonia	21 Apr 1874
Dallas	SCOTT, R. B. and J. M.	Harry D.	6 Feb 1874
Upshur	SCOTT, S. B. & M. F.	Carrie	Feb 1875
Anderson	SEAGLER, J. Y and S. E.	M. M.	20 Sep 1873
Jasper	SEALE, Elias T. and Emily A.	Emily S.	2 Apr 1874
Rusk	SEALEY, J. T. & M. H.	George F.	5 Oct 1874
Rusk	SEARLES, Taton & Bettie	Elbert	20 Apr 1874
Rusk	SEARLS, Abram & Manda E.	Wm. F.	17 Dec 1873
Fannin	SEARS, J. D. & E. L.	Clarence	17 Dec 1874
Fannin	SEARS, J. J. & M. A.	Clara Lake	31 May 1875

COUNTY	PARENTS	CHILD	DATE
Cameron	SEAT, Benton & Louisa	William H.(?) Benton	10 Nov 1874
Dallas	SEAY, R. B. & Lura	Roberta S.	21 Aug 1876
Cameron	SECUNDINA, ___ and (Susarri)	Romana	
Navarro	SEDGELEY, ___ & ___	Benna V.	3 Jun 1870
Cherokee	SELMAN, B. F. and E. H.	Carrie	28 Dec 1873
Cherokee	SELMAN, J. W. and S.	W. G.	23 Dec 1873
Fannin	SEMPLE, Richard B. & Martha M.	Robert Baylor	5 Oct 1874
Cass	SERRATT, Jonas & Lucinda	Thos. Jefferson	19 Aug 1873
Kaufman	SHANKLE, W. H. & M. C.	C. A.	___ Dec 1874
Fannin	SHANKS, Ben & Malinda	Lorena	18 May 1875
Lamar	SHANNON, J. A. & Nancy E.	John E.	10 Aug 1874
Kaufman	SHARP, Joseph H. and O. A.	Joseph B.	7 Jul 1873
Anderson	SHATTUCK, J. S. and Julia P.	Ed S.	4 Mar 1875
Fannin	SHAW, G. W. & Parelee	L. G.	8 Feb 1875
Lamar	SHAW, J. H. & Alice W.	Samuel M.	27 Oct 1875
Nueces	SHAW, Joseph W. & Margaret	Flora B.	4 Feb 1876
Kaufman	SHEHEE, T. J. & J. C.	Henryetta	2 Jan ___
Jasper	SHELBY, Robert P. and Nancy E.	Zerah E.	27 Jan 1873 or 1876
	Note: The year was either 1873 or 1876; one figure was written over the other and it was impossible to tell which was intended; the birth was reg. in 1876.		
Lamar	SHELTON, J. R. & E. E. (or A. E.)	Jenuay(?) Scott	11 Nov 1875
Lamar	SHELTON, Jessie R. & Ann E.	Laura Irene	2 Sep 1874
Fannin	SHEPARD, Henry & Mary	Gilbert	3 Feb 1875
Upshur	SHEPHERD, W. W. & M. A.	J. R.	1 Dec 1875
Navarro	SHERRILL, W. D. & M. L.	McNichols	17 Oct 1874
Navarro	SHERRILLE, James T. & Mary E.	Virda	5 Nov 1873
Upshur	SHIELDS, W. B. & L. L.	W. B.	25 Jul 1874
Fannin	SHIPLEY, Isaac & Harriett	Nally	___ Apr 1874
Fannin	SHIPMAN, Henry A. & Clara	Hattie	24 Dec 1874
Upshur	SHIPMAN, J. P. & S. A.	Anna L.	25 Jul 1874
Lamar	SHIPMAN, Monroe & Jane	Stella	8 Aug 1875
Somervell	SHOEMAKER, N. A. & L. H.	M. D. (girl)	14 Aug 1873
Jasper	SHOLARS, Samuel W. & Sarah E.	Arthur R.	27 Jan 1875
Cherokee	SHOOK, J. E. & M. B.	Jeff	3 Feb 1875
Fannin	SHORTRIDGE, J. B. & Belle	Warnita	7 Sep 1873
Upshur	SHRUM, John & Mary E.	Charity F.	4 Mar 1874
Rusk	SHULER, C. J. & B. R.	Mary F.	25 Jul 1874
Cameron	SHUTTER, A. A. and Lena	Augustino Emilio	10 Jan 1872
Cherokee	SICKENBERGER, J. V. & N. R.	Mary Jane C.	24 Feb 1874
Webb	SIELSKI, Joseph & Margaret L.	Joseph Clinton	23 Jul 1872
		Violet	23 Mar 1874
		Jno. Stewart	10 Nov 1875
Fannin	SIKES, R. C. & Ada	Mary	25 Dec 1874
Cherokee	SIMMONS, A. A. and Lydia	William H.	10 Jan 1874
Anderson	SIMMONS, Austin and Angelina	Bob	31 Oct 1874
		John Lowry	31 Oct 1875
Rusk	SIMMONS, J. & Rachel	Louisa J.	8 Nov 1875
Rusk	SIMMONS, John & E. J.	Martha J.	15 Mar 1874
Gregg	SIMMONS, Wm. D. & Emma	Joseph Boring	9 Apr 1875
Fannin	SIMPSON, Jo. M. & M. E.	John H.	31 Jan 1874
Fannin	SIMS, E. B. & Ann L.	Harry Clay	___ Jul 1874
Fannin	SIMS, E. E. (Mrs. B. E. Brown)		
Kaufman	SIMS, J. H. & A. J.	William Oscar	9 Jun 1876
Cherokee	SINGLETARY, F. H. & S. M.	I. A.	17 Dec 1874
Fannin	SINK, David & Emeline	T. A.	25 Jan 1875

COUNTY	PARENTS	CHILD	DATE
Navarro	SKILES, T. M. & S. J.	Elijah E.	23 Nov 1873
Fannin	SLACK, O. P. & Manerva(sic)	M. A.	2 May 1875
Washington	SLATER, Jas. E. & Geoga. A.	Grace	23 Jan 1874
Rusk	SLAUGHTER, ___ & ___	Thomas E.	___ ___ ___
	Note: No birth date was given but this birth as recorded on 22 Jun 1875		
Navarro	SLAYTEN, John & Minerva	Minnie	7 Oct 1874
Navarro	SLOAN, A. C. & L. N.	Alexander Younger	10 Apr 1874
Rusk	SLOVER, W. P. & Virginia	E. C.	23 Oct 1874
Upshur	SMART, L. D. & Ella	Robert E.	15 Jan 1874
Upshur	SMART, Nathan & Malenda	Nathan	14 Dec 1875
Navarro	SMITH, Alexander & Phoeba (sic)	Benjamin Martin	17 Sep 1873
Rusk	SMITH, Bob & Mary	Benjamin Thomas	11 Nov 1874
Lamar	SMITH, C. & C.	E. P.	8 May 1874
Jasper	SMITH, Cresie (Mrs. Anthony Dotson)		
Navarro	SMITH, D. B. & Harriet E.	Maud	24 Sep 1874
Upshur	SMITH, David & Julia A.	Emma R.	25 Jan 1874
Jasper	SMITH, David Y. and Ava A.	Sarah J.	3 Dec 1874
Washington	SMITH, E. N. & Nancy(?)	Nora Va.	22 Sep 1875
Dallas	SMITH, Edward & Anna	Edward	11 Oct 1874
Rusk	SMITH, Frank & Susan	Mary	31 Dec 1874
Rusk	SMITH, G. M. & Susan T.	Wilbur	13 Nov 1875
Rusk	SMITH, G. R. & Mary E.	Green D.	4 Feb 1875
aNavarro	SMITH, G. W. & M. E.	Albert G.	30 May 1873
Upshur	SMITH, George & E. J.	Thomas	4 Aug 1875
Fannin	SMITH, George W. & Mary	Edgar F.	(Reg. 19 Jun 1875)
Washington	SMITH, H. L. & Ella	Lula	15 Jun 1875
Fannin	SMITH, H. W. & H. E.	Samuel M. Klingle	27 Aug 1874
Anderson	SMITH, Houston and Susan	Houston	3 Mar 1873
		Golias	2 Feb 1874
		Lurenda	28 Jan 1875
Kaufman	SMITH, J. A. & M. E.	Lilie	26 Apr 1873
Navarro	SMITH, J. J. & M. A.	Eli David	29 Nov 1874
Jasper	SMITH, J. J. & Nancy	Dozier F.	___ Dec 1870
		William A.	___ Dec 1872
		Mary E. J.	___ Oct 1874
Lamar	SMITH, J. K. P. & S. A.	T. B.	30 Dec 1873
Cass	SMITH, J. M. & Ida	Edwin Ovestus	21 Jan 1875
Washington	SMITH, J. S. & C. P.	John S.	8 Mar 1874
Cass	SMITH, J. W. & C. H.	D. I.	13 Jan 1874
Navarro	SMITH, James & Emma	Arthur Bertrum	3 Jan 1874
Rusk	SMITH, Jasper F. & Annie C.	Carrie	29 Dec 1874
Rusk	SMITH, John and Caroline	Martha Ann	11 Jul 1875
Fannin	SMITH, John E. & Josephine E.	Harold O.	24 May 1873
Navarro	SMITH, Jno. R. & Francis A.	Patrick C.	30 Oct 1873
Fannin	SMITH, N. B. & Martha U.	Robert L.	11 Jan 1874
Kaufman	SMITH, R. B. & L. A.	Edward D.	18 Dec 1874
Lamar	SMITH, R. O. & N. A.	C. (or S.?)	5 Mar 1874
Rusk	SMITH, R. P. & M. E.	Mary A.	17 Jul 1874
Upshur	SMITH, R. W. & S. A.	Zue (or Zell?)	25 Jun 1875
Fannin	SMITH, T. F. & S. L.	W. E.	8 Apr 1875
Lamar	SMITH, T. M. & M. S.	Charley E.	17 Sep 1873
Rusk	SMITH, W. D. & Amanda A.	Lula	15 Oct 1875
Fannin	SMITH, W. E. & M. C.	Sam Bell Maxie	16 May 1875
Fannin	SMITH, W. H. F. & Pollie	Blanch P.	14 Apr 1874
Upshur	SMITH, W. R. & Eliza	Mary O.	27 Aug 1875
Anderson	SMYTH, Jos. J. and M. A.	J. T.	10 Nov 1874
Jasper	SOUTHWELL, Emma (Mrs. John Rondolph Henderson)		
Kaufman	SOWELL, C. B. & T.	Pearl	28 Aug 1874
Fannin	SOWELL, J. W. & Lizzie A.	Mandy Rebecca	12 Nov 1875
Fannin	SPARGER, John & Eliza	B. A.	15 Nov 1874
Kaufman	SPARKS, G. W. & S. A.	Henry A.	18 Nov 1874
Lamar	SPEAIRS, B. T. & M. A.	B. P.	12 ___ 1875
Lamar	SPEAIRS, P. M. & Mary S.	William Fulton	25 Dec 1870
		Phil Adams	18 Feb 1874

COUNTY	PARENTS	CHILD	DATE
Rusk	SPEAR, Fannie (Mrs. W. P. Young)		
Fannin	SPELCE, J. L. & M. M.	Ira	19 Jun 1873
Rusk	SPENCE, I. J. & S. A.	Edwin J. M.	16 Jul 1873
		Carrie Ella(sic)	31 Apr 1875
Rusk	SPENCER, Alfred & Sarah	Carrie	28 Dec 1873
Washington	SPENCER, G. & E. E.	A. E.	1 Jan 1874
Washington	SPENER, Robert & Puss	Lewellen	17 Dec 1874
Rusk	SPIVEY, W. W. & Sallie A.	W. W.	
Navarro	SPIVY, D. F. & Alcy	George B.	13 Feb 1874
Navarro	SPIVY, P. P. & Cintha	Bettie	7 Jun 1873
	Second entry: "P.P. & Cynthia"		
		Tank Melton	15 Nov 1874
Fannin	SQUIRES, G. W. & V.	Ethel	10 Jun 1874
Anderson	STAFFORD, U. M. and M.	Clem Munroe	13 Oct 1875
Fannin	STALLER, Soloman & Mary	Charles E.	19 Sep 1874
Lamar	STALLINGS, E. D. & V. E.	L. J.	4 Apr 1874
Fannin	STANDIFER, B. F. & S. A.	Sarah L.	28 Jan 1875
Rusk	STANFORD, J. M. & S. C.	J. W.	21 Aug 1874
Navarro	STANFORD, Richard & Eliza	John Elbert	19 Apr 1875
Navarro	STANLEY, G. A. & S. C.	Henry Austin	22 Aug 1874
Rusk	STANLEY, J. C. & N. E.	J. C.	25 Aug 1875
Fannin	STANSBURY, M. A. & Nettie	Elbert N.	14 Jun 1874
Upshur	STARKEY, James & Parilie	Leila	20 Jan 1875
Rusk	STARLING, Joe & Lizzie	William	Dec 1874
Anderson	STARR, Daniel P. & Martha E.	Peo.(?) Edwin	9 Jan 1863
Lamar	STARR, Francis R. & Sarah W.	Homer	31 Mar 1875
Anderson	STARR, Perry and Martha A.	Sarah	26 Jul 1875
		Perry	1 Mar 1876
Navarro	STARWATER, Robert & Rebecca	Joseph	20 Sep 1873
Fannin	STEENE, J. T. & Nicie	Mary Bell	11 Sep 1874
Webb	STEFFIAN, Peter & Refugia G.	Peter A.	1 Jul 1874
Upshur	STEPHENS, A. C. & Emily	Malinda T.	5 Oct 1874
			1875 or 1877
Rusk	STEPHENS, Jerry & Margaret	Oscar	25 Jan 1875
Kaufman	STEPHENSON, E. H. & S. E.	Cyrus F.	2 Oct 1874
Nueces	STEPHENSON, Frank &		
	Mary Anges	Mary Anges	5 Dec 1866
		Lydia Levinia	17 May 1870
		John Mercer	3 Jun 1872
Fannin	STEPHENSON, L. E. &		
	Lauora (sic)	Champ	10 Dec 1873
Lamar	STEPHENSON, R. B. & M. H.	D. D.	23 Nov 1874
Lamar	STEPHENSON, R. G. & M. H.	L. L.	19 Mar 1875
Lamar	STEPHENSON, W. H. & E. J.	Rich'd Lee	18 Feb 1876
Dallas	STERRETT, W. G. & Fanny L.	Elizabeth Holt	20 Apr 1874
Rusk	STEVENS, L. D. & Sarah J.	Evangeline	14 Aug 1874
Kaufman	STEVENSON, J. E. & M. M.	W. E.	5 Nov 1873
Fannin	STEVENSON, John & Eliza A.	Lemuel J.	5 Jan 1874
		Jesse F.	17 Dec 1875
Upshur	STEWART, J. G. & J. A.	Harry H.	2 Mar 1874
Fannin	STEWART, John and Mary	William	22 Jan 1875
Rusk	STEWART, John S. L. and Ann E.	Robert L.	25 May 1873
Navarro	STEWART, R. H. & Sarah P.	James Polk	29 Jan 1874
Kaufman	STILL, A. J. & M. B.	Maud	17 Mar 1874
Rusk	STILL, Delia (Mrs. Bill McCauley)		
Rusk	STILL, J. A. & Mary Caroline	B. R.	28 Sep 1874
Rusk	STILL, J. N. & Eliza J.	Mary	2 Apr 1874
Rusk	STILL, Joseph & Sarah E.	Helen A.	15 Jun 1875
Kaufman	STILL, W. T. & A. E.	Emma Laura	18 Aug 1874
Fannin	STIMPSON, T. B. & R. E.	Madie E.	17 Sep 1874
Gregg	STINCHCOMB, Thomas &		
	Mollie A.	Thomas	2 Aug 1874
Upshur	STINSON, Andrew & Ellen	Effy T.	12 Jan 1876
Navarro	STOCKARD, Jas. H. & Luesa	Hiram Claudius	9 Mar 1874
Navarro	STOKES, D. & Mary	Lydiann ONeal	21 Aug 1874
Navarro	STOKES, Joseph & Ann	Etta	6 Sep 1873

COUNTY	PARENTS	CHILD	DATE
Navarro	STOKES, R. S.(?) & Elizabeth	Richard Middleton	15 Jun 1873
Navarro	STOKES, S. W. & E. A. E.	George Everett	1 Sep 1874
Navarro	STOKES, Willis & Mary	Willie Columbus	26 Sep 1875
Fannin	STONE, J. W. & Nannie	John B.	10 Apr 1875
Cass	STONE, James N. & Amanda	Sallie K?(or R.)	20 Oct 1873
Anderson	STONE, John and Hannah	Kitty Clara	5 May 1873
Fannin	STONE, John A. & Sarah N.	J. T. W.	31 Jan 1875
Navarro	STONE, O. W. & Marion	Mary Ollie	18 Sep 1873
Washington	STONE, Sam & Bettie V.	Robert Alex	24 Apr 1875
Jasper	STONE, Stephen K. and		
	Susan L.	Thomas A.	9 Jun 1873
		Bula	3 Apr 1875
Jasper	STONE, Thomas M. and Emily F.	Arthur Kyle	11 Nov 1874
Gregg	STONE, Thomas M. &		
	Lou S. (Stroud)	Foy Stroud	4 Oct 1875
Cass	STONE, W. A. & Laura B.	Mary H.	10 Sep 1874
Rusk	STONE, W. J. & Annie B.	Carl Oti	18 Dec 1874
Navarro	STORY, D. M. & T. F.	Lou Allene	23 Mar 1874
Cherokee	STOUT, H. C. & E. J.	Harrison	5 Dec 1875
Fannin	STOUT, John & Josephine	J. D.	28 Mar 1874
Kaufman	STOVALL, A. J. & M. F.	Anna May	10 Mar 1875
		Oval(sic) Ingram	21 Apr 1876
Kaufman	STOVALL, F. M. & N. J.	Richard Coke	1 Feb 1876
Kaufman	STOVALL, G. D. & N. C.	Nova Lee	6 Feb 1875
Kaufman	STOVALL, J. R. & M. E.	John Boyd	2 Oct 1875
Rusk	STOVALL, S. K. & Anni(sic) H.	Sims Henry	2 Feb 1875
Kaufman	STOVALL, W. J. & M. W.	Virgil Ugene	4 Nov 1875
Rusk	STRICKLAND, Lyman and S. L.	Jean Graham	4 Aug 1875
Rusk	STRONG, C. J. & Mary	R. E.	1 Nov 1875
Rusk	STRONG, John and Sarah	Mary H.	25 Mar 1875
Rusk	STROUD, A. D. & F. G.	John Pope	12 Apr 1875
Gregg	STROUD, Lou S. (Mrs. Thomas M. Stone)		
Dallas	STULTS, Wm. and Lou G.	Ida May	7 Mar 1874
Fannin	STUTSMAN, A. L . & May J.	Minnie Bell	5 Sep 1874
Fannin	SUDDUTH, D. G. & Martha	Ellen	25 Apr 1875
Cherokee	SUMMERS, J. M. & Eliza	Jno. R.	23 Oct 1875
Rusk	SUMMERS, R. W. & M. F.	Birdie	18 Jul 1875
Navarro	SUMMERS, T. J. & S. T.	Taylor Augustus	16 May 1873
Cameron	SUSARRI, ____ (Mrs. ____ Secundina)		
Cass	SUTTON, E. D. & Delia	William	11 Mar 1875
Rusk	SUTTON, Robert D. and Syntha J.	Lucinda Pruett	12 Oct 1874
Washington	SWAIN, Henry C. & Jennie E.	Robert J.	24 Oct 1873
Washington	SWEARINGEN, J. T. & Ada	Annie	21 Sep 1874
Navarro	SWEARINGEN, R. J. &		
	Mallissa	Andrew Bettis	1 Oct 1877
Navarro	SWINDAL, S. L. & Mary E.	Samuel L.	12 Mar 1875
Dallas	SWINDELL, Jno. W. and M. H.	Archibald G.	21 Oct 1874
Rusk	SWINNEY, T. J. & Tennessee	J. H.	31 Oct 1874
Rusk	SWINNEY, T. T. & Frances C.	Lula A.	11 Oct 1875
Rusk	SWINNEY, William & Mary F.	Edwin	24 Oct 1873
Navarro	TADLOCK, J. A. & M. M.	John O.	17 Oct 1873
Cameron	TAGOU, Celestin &		
	Dophine (Mailhe)(?)	Adolph Louis	24 Mar 1869
		Albert Dominique	20 Jul 1872
		Michel Vincent	21 Oct 1874
		Christine Marie	15 Jan 1878
Rusk	TALBERT, Andrew & Sallie	Ellie	20 Nov 1875
	(Twins)	Eddie	20 Nov 1875
Rusk	TALBERT, Levi & Mary	Fannie	26 Feb 1875
Navarro	TALLEY, James & Kate	James	5 Nov 1873
Kaufman	TAPP, V. J. and Amira(?) J.	Robert McMurry	1 Oct 1874
Marion	TAYLOR, F. M. & Jennie	Marion DeKalb	29 Aug 1873
Rusk	TAYLOR, George & Mary Jane	Lily	28 Sep 1873
		Dory	10 Apr 1875
Rusk	TAYLOR, Henderson & Frozine	William	26 Oct 1874
Rusk	TAYLOR, J. T. & Eliza Jane	William Jackson	15 Jan 1875

131

COUNTY	PARENTS	CHILD	DATE
Marion	TAYLOR, John M. & A. M.	Lou Pearl	10 Sep 1874
	(triplets)	Eliza	10 Sep 1874
		Urbie	10 Sep 1874
		Agnes	
Kaufman	TAYLOR, M.I.(?) & L.A.	Alice Burtie	3 Jul 1875
Fannin	TAYLOR, M. L. & Mary J.	Louisa R.	1 Nov 1874
Fannin	TAYLOR, P. G. & M. E.	L. C.	19 May 1873
Dallas	TAYLOR, P. W. (or N.?) and		
	E. D.	Forest	1 Apr 1874
Fannin	TAYLOR, Perry & Sue	Lanell	Jan 1875
Fannin	TAYLOR, Reuben & Nannie J.	Moses Newton	31 Jan 1876
Cass	TAYLOR, W. H. & E. W.	James Mc.	Nov 1873
Navarro	TAYLOR, Wm. B. & G. J.	Willie E.	27 Sep 1872
		Annie	28 Sep 1875
Kaufman	TEAGUE, H. P. & F.	Henry Pitts	11 Jul 1874
Fannin	TEAGUE, J. N. & Virginia	Ira C.	18 Sep 1873
Webb	TELLES, Luis &		
	Trenidad (Garcia)	Jesusa	2 Apr 1874
		Teadosa	29 May 1876
Cherokee	TEMPLETON, J. F. & H. C.	James D.	9 Feb 1874
		David A.	20 Nov 1875
Gregg	TERRY, Evans G. &	James Archibald	
	Eugenia L.	Burke	1 Jan 1875
Fannin	TERRY, T. B. & S. A.	Thomas F.	17 Jan 1875
Fannin	TERRY, W. H. & Mollie	Iva	Jan 1875
Lamar	TERRY, W. S. & A. E.	H. S.	9 Nov 1873
Fannin	THACKER, J. R. & S. E.	Ida C.	18 Jan 1875
Cameron	THIELAN, Frank and Louisa	Peter T.	30 Aug 1873
		Martin Nicholas	23 Dec 1874
Navarro	THOMAS, Crockett &		
	Eeveline (sic)	Willie	Sep 1874
Fannin	THOMAS, F. M. & M. I.	M. M.	4 Aug 1874
Navarro	THOMAS, James D. & Mary	William Samuel	30 Jul 1873
Navarro	THOMAS, Jno. M. & M. J.	Daniel A.	4 Apr 1874
Rusk	THOMAS, Kissic & Nancy	John	18 Jul 1873
Fannin	THOMAS, T. & M. A.	James R.	Jun 1873
		Ora R.	Mar 1875
Navarro	THOMASON, ___ & ___	G. W.	
Navarro	THOMASON, George & Amantha	Joshua Eliott	28 Jan 1876
Navarro	THOMASSON, P. W. & Martha	Alex Gowan	22 Mar 1874
Rusk	THOMPSON, Benonie & Martha J.	Beall	15 Jun 1875
Rusk	THOMPSON, George & Rhoda	George	12 Oct 1874
Cherokee	THOMPSON, J. & Emily	Elias	25 Dec 1874
Fannin	THOMPSON, J. N. & Nancy L.	Lucy E.	1875
		(Reg. 24 Sep 1875)	
Rusk	THOMPSON, John & Susan	Mary	27 Jul 1874
Fannin	THOMPSON, Robert C. & M. J.	Robert E.	3 Jan 1874
		John Buckner	20 Dec 1875
Marion	THOMPSON, S. A. & Bettie	Samuel McKelvey	18 Aug 1873
Cherokee	THOMPSON, S. A. and Celeste	Maggie	19 Mar 1874
Rusk	THOMPSON, Squire & Lucy Ann	Mary Jane E.	25 Oct 1875
Cherokee	THOMPSON, Thomas and Maggie	Emmett M.	14 Oct 1873
Rusk	THOMPSON, W. W. & Rebecca	Charles Harris	6 Apr 1874
Rusk	THOMPSON, Wade & Jane	Amber	15 Aug 1874
Fannin	THORNTON, E. W. &		
	Mary R. (or P.?)	Edward W.	29 Aug 1875
Rusk	THORPE, William T. and Mary H.	Tynes Hall	9 Apr 1875
Lamar	THROOP(?), M. M. & M. O.	Allie T.	17 Dec 1875
Fannin	THURSTON, D. L. & F. A.	William Cok	
		(or Cook)	29 Apr 1875
Navarro	TICKLE, Andrew & Mildred C.	Cornelia E.	27 Sep 1873
Navarro	TICKLE, James & Louisa	Lu Ida	26 Aug 1873
Dallas	TILLMAN, E. M. and		
	Francis (sic)	Cecilia Bell	16 May 1874?
	Note: obviously dates in	Sidney Hess	10 Sep 1874?
	error		

COUNTY	PARENTS	CHILD	DATE
Rusk	TINKLE, W. M. & Nannie	Lucy	27 Feb 1876
Nueces	TINNEY, Wm. A.(?) & C. S.	Sarah Mary	19 Jul 1876
	Note: Sarah Mary - b. in	Martha Jane	28 Jul 1878
	Duval Co., Martha Jane b.	Cerro Gorda	16 Sep 1880
	in Corpus Christie,		
	Cerro Gorda b. in Piedras Pintas,		
	Duval Co.		
Rusk	TIPPS, C. C. & Frances A.	Jesse	30 Jul 1874
	(twins)	Charlie	30 Jul 1874
Rusk	TIPPS, Edmond & Charlottie	Jessee	10 Jun 1875
Rusk	TIPPS, L. E. & Mary C.	Henry Parker	16 Mar 1874
		Sarah	4 Sep 1875
Anderson	TIPPSEN, B. F. and M.	William Oliver	3 Mar 1874
	(Tissen?)		
Fannin	TISDALE (or LISDALE?), J. W. &		
	Louisa	J. L. J.	13 Oct 1874
Fannin	TITSWORTH, L. N. & M. J.	Tina	19 May 1874
Rusk	TODD, A. R. & N. J.	William Marian	27 Jan 1876
Cherokee	TORBETT, S. R. & __	Mary C.	6 Jun 1875
Nueces	TORIAN, Sallie (Mrs. John S. Givens)		
Gregg	TOSSON, Thomas J. & Ellen	Thomas Percy	18 Jan 1876
Rusk	TOWISKEE, Josh & Sealy	Jefferson	25 Nov 1874
Navarro	TOWNSEND, J. & A. &		
	E. H. (sic)	Wilmot	1 Nov 1874
Cameron	TOYO, Ventura and Covine	Nosa Eulalia	27 Sep 1871
		Mary Dolores	31 Jan 1873
Rusk	TRAMMEL, G. W. & Texas A.	Clara	20 Oct 1874
Rusk	TRAMMELL, T. J., Jr. and		
	M. A.	John Thomas	9 Jan 1876
Navarro	TRAMMELL, Thos. & Mary J.	James Philip	20 Nov 1873
Fannin	TRAUT, J. C. & E. C.	M. M. Z.	1 Jul 1874
Rusk	TREADWELL, G. A. & M. J.	Lawrence	12 Oct 1874
Fannin	TRICE, B. A. & D. E.	Arthur B.	1 Jan 1875
Fannin	TRIPLETT, G. W. & Permelia	Ida May	23 Dec 1873
Fannin	TROTTER, William F. &		
	Mary M.	William H.	24 Feb 1874
Fannin	TROUT, G. M. & E. R.	Josie B.	24 May 1875
Fannin	TRUSS, G. W. & Josephine	Lolar	Dec 1873
Fannin	TRUSS, John & Mattie	Tommie	12 Nov 1874
Anderson	TUBBS, Peter and Easter	Sarah	15 Aug 1873
Dallas	TUCKER, Charles Frederick &		
	Mary Snydor (Jones)	St. George Brooke	1 Oct 1875
		Snydor Jones	22 Jan 1877
Fannin	TUCKER, Ellis & Lutitia	Jessie	3 Jan 1875
Rusk	TUCKER, Henry & Isabella	Arthur	11 Apr 1874
Anderson	TUCKER, R. and A. E.	James E.	6 Oct 1875
Kaufman	TURK, J. T. & P. A.	Thomas E.	6 Apr 1874
Rusk	TURNER, A. B. & Lizzie	Minnie	20 Jan 1874
Rusk	TURNER, Allen & Mary Jane	Bob	30 Jun 1873
Anderson	TURNER, Benton and Eliza	Edmund	5 May 1874
Rusk	TURNER, Edward & Amanda	Mary C.	7 Jul 1875
Fannin	TURNER, Henry E. & Anna J.	J. C.	22 Sep 1873
Gregg	TURNER, Jerry C. & Fannie	William	4 Oct 1872
		Annie	25 Nov 1873
		Fannie	20 Jul 1875
Rusk	TURNER, L. J. W. & Sarah C.	Mary Francis	28 May 1874
Rusk	TURNER, Sam & Rachel	Mandy	1 Feb 1875
Anderson	TYLER, James & Mary	Secelia	17 Sep 1875
Fannin	TYLER, R. K. & Mary M.	M. E. C.	29 Nov 1873
Lamar	ULRICH, Peter &		
	Mancy (sic) A.	Angeline Theresa	20 Aug 1874
Fannin	UNDERWOOD, F. & I. E.	Frank	21 Sep 1875
Cameron	UZEDA, Franco &		
	Guadalupe (Villerreal)	Franco	21 Jul 1876
Cameron	VALDEZ, Santos &		
	Maximina (Nodri)	Santos U.	27 Jan 1877

COUNTY	PARENTS	CHILD	DATE
Washington	VAN DREISS, F. & Matty	Julius W. H.	15 Feb 1874
Cameron	VANDERVEER, John L. &		
	Mary Amanda	Annie Rosina	16 Oct 1870
		Mary Elizabeth	19 Nov 1871
		Cornelius	24 Mar 1873
Navarro	VANDVER, A. T. & Mary	Mary Melissa	19 Nov 1875
Washington	VANESS, J. B. & F. A.	Julius Olen	3 May 1874
Rusk	VANSICKLE, A. K. & Sarah E.	Hershell V.	6 Nov 1874
Cass	VAUGHAN, George T. &		
	Vesteola O.	Adine Lewis	13 Oct 1874
Cameron	VILLAREAL, Gregoria (Mrs. Hermerejildo Reyes)		
Camerson	VILLERREAL, Faustino &		
	Regina (Necio)	Porfirio	15 Sep 1876
Cameron	VILLERREAL, Guadalupe (Mrs. Franco Uzeda)		
Fannin	VINCENT, B. V. & S. E.	Arthur	27 Apr 1874
Cherokee	VINING, B. F. and L. C.	Wm. E.	2 Jun 1874
Rusk	VINSON, John B. and Laura A.	William B.	7 Mar 1874
Rusk	VINSON, Nathan & Polly	Benjmain	26 Apr 1874
Navarro	VINYARD, Geo. & L. F.	Jessie	17 Oct 1874
Cameron	VIRANSJE, George &		
	Henrietta Augusta	Amanda Augusta	
	Teresa (sic)	Theresa (sic)	21 Sep 1874
Upshur	VIVIAN, J. L. & S. E.	William L.	25 Apr 1876
Nueces	VON BLUCHER, Felix A. &		
	Mary Augusta (Inmore)	Maria Felicia	14 Jan 1851
		Julia Augusta	6 Jan 1853
		Charles Frederick	10 Feb 1856
		Richard Paul	20 Mar 1858
		George Antonio	3 Oct 1861
		Anna Elizabeth	26 Aug 1864
Navarro	WADE, Wm. J. & A. F.	Fannie	20 Aug 1873
Fannin	WAFFORD, A. W. &		
	Josephine W.	Amelia W.	29 Sep 1874
Rusk	WAFFORD, Jake & Liza	Cornelius	14 Dec 1874
Anderson	WAGGONER, Chas. G. and Alice V.	Reathe	17 Dec 1874
Rusk	WAGGONER, Daniel & Emma A.	Doctor John J.	14 Dec 1873
Rusk	WAIR, James Henry &		
	Julia Ann	James Henry	2 Jul 1875
Fannin	WALCOTT, Chrles (sic) H. &		
	Nancy J.	B. J.	22 Oct 1873
		K. E.	18 Jan 1875
Navarro	WALDRON, Thos. H. & M. E.	Jacob Allen	13 Dec 1873
Rusk	WALDROP, A. W. & M. M.	Laura P.	31 Oct 1873
Fannin	WALKER, J. T. & J. A.	Addie	3 Sep 1873
Lamar	WALKER, J. W. & V.	Allen Lee	17 Sep 1873
Rusk	WALKER, M. H. & Ann	Malinda O.	3 Jan 1875
Fannin	WALKER, Wm. R. & L. N.	Katie	3 Aug 1874
Fannin	WALL, Charley & Ann	George	1 Aug 1874
Fannin	WALL, D. D. & Mary	James N.	___ Oct 1874
Fannin	WALL, W. D. & Mary	Charles Edward	___ Feb 1876
Rusk	WALLACE, C. J. &		
	Minerva A.	W. L. D. D.	
		W. J. D. D.	25 Nov 1874
		Susan M. A.	21 Mar 1875
Kaufman	WALLACE, J. P. and Ann M.	Letha N.	17 Mar 1874
Rusk	WALLACE, LeRoy & Lou J.	Liza Ann	16 Jul 1875
Rusk	WALLACE, S. W. & H. E.	L. M.	17 Jul 1875
Kaufman	WALLACE, W. S. & V. V.	Hilliard	11 Mar 1874
Cherokee	WALLER, James(?) & Rhoda	Mary F.(?)	15 Feb 1874
Rusk	WALTON, J. B. & Mary	Theresa	18 Mar 1875
Kaufman	WARD, James and ___	Coriell	2 Oct 1873
Nueces	WARD, James W. & Alice G.	Thomas Dudley	26 Jun 1873
Jasper	WARD, Stephen D. &		
	Elizabeth	Nancy E.	11 Nov 1874
Anderson	WARD, W. J. and N. C.	Ottie	30 Jan 1876
		(twins) Ollie	30 Jan 1876

COUNTY	PARENTS	CHILD	DATE
Anderson	WARREN, Henry Clay and Mollie V.	Elizabeth Glenn	10 Dec 1873
Marion	WARREN, Wm. H. & Laura L.	Holmes L.	19 May 1874
		Infant	3 Jan 1876
			d.11 Jan 1876
		Edward Audley Vines	25 May 1877
		James Alberto	20 Apr 1880
Cass	WARRINGTON, John & Eliza A.	Joshua M.	__ Mar 1874
Rusk	WASHINGTON, George & Sylvie	James	4 Dec 1875
Fannin	WATERS, Geo. & Matilda	John H.	13 Apr 1874
Kaufman	WATKINS, J. A. & O.	Nettie M.	16 Spe 1873
Rusk	WATKINS, John R. & Mary F.	William L.	16 Dec 1874
Kaufman	WATKINS, R. L. & M. L.	William P.	16 Feb 1874
Navarro	WATKINS, Thos. E. & Lavinia F.	Arthur Alexander	27 Apr 1875
Upshur	WATKINS, W. E. & Sadie	Minnie M.	19 Jul 1873
		R. C.	10 Jan 1875
Lamar	WATSON, Andrew & Sarah	John R.	5 Jan 1875
Washington	WATSON, B. A. & A. G.	Quintus Ultimus	2 Jul 1874
Navarro	WATSON, John & Henrietta	George Jefferson	26 Apr 1875
Anderson	WATSON, John and Missouri	Florence A.	10 Nov 1869
		Theadoso	28 Dec 1872
Rusk	WATSON, M. J. & Ann	George H.	15 Mar 1875
Rusk	WATSON, Pomp & Rinda	Leanna C.	__ Oct 1874
Washington	WATSON, W. & C. J.	Mary W.	10 Sep 1873
Rusk	WATSON, William C. & Georgia	George W.	23 Feb 1876
Anderson	WATTS, J. F. and M. E.	Anna Bell	1 Feb 1876
Anderson	WATTS, W. J. and M. S.	Willis L.	21 Feb 1876
Navarro	WAY, J. G. & Laura A.	Laura Jane	6 Jan 1874
Navarro	WEAVER, John M. & Leah	Charlie Oscar	4 Dec 1873
Fannin	WEAVER, S. J. & M. E.	Partheny	27 Mar 1875
Fannin	WEBB, R. S. & Mary E.	Clifton	9 Mar 1874
Kaufman	WEBB, William F. & M.A.E.	W. F. J.	26 Apr 1874
Navarro	WEBSTER, John C. & Susan	Mary Belle	30 Dec 1873
Navarro	WEEKS, D. H. & E. J.	James K. Polk	23 Nov 1873
Navarro	WEEKS, Geo. W. & Delila	Charles Monroe	6 Jan 1875
Navarro	WEEKS, H. N. & Alice	Wm. P.	3 May 1875
Navarro	WEEKS, J. W. & Mary E.	Mary Lena	2 Sep 1875
Navarro	WEEKS, W. J. & Anna	Newman Marshall	25 Jun 1874
Gregg	WEEMS, John & Marize	Cally Elizabeth	1 Jan 1876
Nueces	WEIL, Charles & Sarah	Jonas	22 Sep 1874
		Simon	3 Mar 1876
Rusk	WELCH, A. J. & Nancy A.	Georgia E.	5 Feb 1874
Rusk	WELCH, B. M. & Tabitha	Ida	9 Oct 1874
Rusk	WELCH, F. E. & Mary E.	John T.	23 Aug 1874
Rusk	WELCH, George T. & Missouri H.	Ella May	5 Mar 1874
Rusk	WELCH, J. M. & M. E.	Charles R.	31 Mar 1874
Rusk	WELCH, Joseph & Josephine	M.A.D.	24 Feb 1875
Rusk	WELCH, T. J. & N. J.	J. P.	21 Jul 1875
Upshur	WELLS, Ben & Amey	Joseph A.	22 Dec 1873
Upshur	WELLS, Ben & Anna	Elizabeth M. M.	20 Dec 1875
Fannin	WELLS, John A. & Nancy E.	Samuel A.	5 Aug 1873
Rusk	WEST, A. C. & M. E.	G.A.D.	8 Jan 1875
Navarro	WEST, George E. & Isabel	Virginia Alice	18 Jan 1874
Fannin	WEST, O. C. & C. J.	Ira	3 Nov 1874
Cass	WESTBROOK, J. H. & Z. C.	Mary Eunice	27 Feb 1874
Washington	WEYAND, (or WAYAND or WARGAM?), Ernst & Matilde	Mina	28 Mar 1874
Rusk	WHATLEY, Mack & Angeline	Robert Young	10 Mar 1875
Fannin	WHEDBER, D. B. & M. J.	W. L.	3 Oct 1873
Nueces	WHEELER, E. H. & S. E.	Lydia Elizabeth	18 Mar 1874

COUNTY	PARENTS	CHILD	DATE
Fannin	WHEELER, John & Hattie Ann	Hattie A.	14 Jun 1873
Fannin	WHEELER, S. R. & P. C.	G. W.	29 Dec 1874
Fannin	WHEELER, W. C. & S. C.	Bettie	17 Jun 1875
Lamar	WHEELER, W. T. & M. C.	Mary E.	2 Sep 1874
Gregg	WHILLINGTON, Jefferson B. & Anna E.	Oliver Pegues	2 Apr 1875
Fannin	WHISENHUNT, Jim & J. G.	A. G.	17 Sep 1874
Fannin	WHISENHUNT, N. W. & M. F.	A. H.	27 Feb 1874
		Leora Alma	22 Jan 1876
Fannin	WHITE, C. H. & S. R.	Bertha	19 Jul 1874
Fannin	WHITE, C. W. & M. E.	Ida Gee	3 Oct 1874
		C. W., Jr.	9 Oct 1875
Fannin	WHITE, Charles N. & Emma J.	Mary A.	14 Mar 1875
Rusk	WHITE, Enoch A. and Amanda M.	Mary E. C.	23 Dec 1873
Lamar	WHITE, H. C. & A. C.	L. K.	5 Jan 1874
Kaufman	WHITE, H. H. and Mary G.	Walter Jones	22 Jun 1873
Fannin	WHITE, I. G. & Mary E.	A. W.	29 Dec 1874
Fannin	WHITE, J. F. & M. A.	Charley Mussel	14 Sep 1875
Navarro	WHITE, J. M. & E. R.	Joseph Elijah	28 Dec 1873
Fannin	WHITE, J. M. & Mary A.	Flora E.	23 Feb 1874
Jasper	WHITE, John L. C. & Texanna P.	Willie A.	2 Apr 1874
Navarro	WHITE, L.(?) A. & Elizabeth	John Newton	9 Jan 1874
Fannin	WHITE, Nathaniel & Mary	John Henry	27 Jul 1874
Washington	WHITE, Robt. & H. A.	Minerva	Dec 1874
Fannin	WHITE, Tom & Clema	Mack	7 Jun 1875
Lamar	WHITE, W. A. & J. A.	Tom J.	4 Mar 1876
Navarro	WHITE, W. H. & Mary A.	Ruth	22 Jul 1874
Cass	WHITING, Sandy & Sallie	Elizabeth	13 Feb 1874
Rusk	WHITLEY, John H. & Margaret	Maud	20 Apr 1875
Anderson	WHITTLE, J. C. & Julia M.	Eeppia Campbell	3 Aug 1874
Cass	WHITTLE, J. L. & Sallie M.	Lola Bettie Willie	
Jasper	WIESS, Massena & Elvira E.	Clyde	27 Dec 1874
Cherokee	WIGGINS, Jas. H. & M. J.	Elmo Dabney	10 Apr 1874
Navarro	WIGHTT (or WIGHT), J. T. & M. S.	Ruth	17 May 1874
Jasper	WIGLEY, John M. & Martha A. E.	Viola D.	21 Nov 1874
Anderson	WILDER, H. B. & E. M.	Henry B.	21 Aug 1874
Rusk	WILEY, ___ & ___	Amantha J.	___ Apr ___
	Note: No birth date was given but this birth was recorded on 20 Aug 1875		
Navarro	WILEY, Spenser & Margaret	Isaac	15 Nov 1874
Dallas	WILEY, Thos. H. & Mattie E.	Bessie	16 Apr 1875
Rusk	WILEY, W. E. & Mary E.	Neitus	8 Aug 1874
Rusk	WILEY, W. R. and Mary J.	Andrew F.	4 Mar 1874
Rusk	WILHELM, Benjamin and Mary A.	J. R.	18 Jun 1873
Navarro	WILKINSON, D. W. & A. J.	William Gamer(?)	5 Nov 1873
Fannin	WILKINSON, H. B. & R. A.	Mary H.	28 Apr 1875
Upshur	WILLEFORD, John W. & L. A.	J. W.	21 Feb 1874
		A. B.	10 Aug 1875
Upshur	WILLEFORD, Thos. A. & Mary	Sarah Jane	30 Sep 1875
Navarro	WILLIAM, J.(?) M. & Amanda J.	Jeptha Wood	13 Jun 1873
Fannin	WILLIAMS, B. M. & D. J.	Julia Ann	24 Feb 1875
Lamar	WILLIAM, G. (or S.?) W. & V. A.	Artie Leon	13 Oct 1874
Lamar	WILLIAMS, J. D. & E. J.	John D.	20 Mar 1876
Lamar	WILLIAMS, J. F. R. & Sarah Jane	Eddie	11 Jan 1872
		Z. C.	19 Nov 1874
Lamar	WILLIAMS, J. Q. (or I.?) & E. M.	L. H.	25 Sep 1873
Fannin	WILLIAMS, James & Helen(sic)	Oha Jane	15 Oct 1874

COUNTY	PARENTS	CHILD	DATE
Cherokee	WILLIAMS, Jno L. & C. A.	Lucy Eliza	29 Apr 1874
Lamar	WILLIAMS, N. &		
	Georgiann C.	Zebylon Terrell	30 Jun 1875
Anderson	WILLIAMS, P. E. A. and E. A.	Charity E.	13 Feb 1875
Lamar	WILLIAMS, P. H. & J.	A. L.	16 Nov 1873
Fannin	WILLIAMS, S. B. & S. J.	Benj. M.	19 Feb 1875
Fannin	WILLIAMS, W. T. & E.	Charley	15 Jun 1874
Cass	WILLIAMS, W. W. & O. F.	Lillian Estelle	1 Mar 1875
Rusk	WILLIAMS, Willis &		
	Lucy Ann	Victoria	10 Jan 1874
Cherokee	WILLIAMSON, John & Mattie	M. A. L. E.	24 Apr 1874
Upshur	WILLINGHAM, A. J. & A. E.	A. E.	25 Jan 1874
Anderson	WILLINGHAM, J. E. & Julia A.	Edgar	18 Dec 1875
Upshur	WILLINGHAM, J. W. & M. A.	M. J.	19 Nov 1875
Kaufman	WILLINGHAM, R. W. & A. W.	Fannie Pearl	20 Jul 1874
Rusk	WILLIS, Caroline (Mrs. Isham Redwine)		
Cass	WILLIS, L. R. A. & A. E.	Ruffin T.	14 Feb 1874
Cherokee	WILLSON, S. A. & Elizabeth	Byrdie Vini	6 Dec 1874
Washington	WILSON, A. W. & Annie	John W.	14 Apr 1874
Rusk	WILSON, Barney & Sarah	Sam I.	17 Aug 1875
Fannin	WILSON, D. C. & L. B.	L. B.	16 Feb 1874
Kaufman	WILSON, G. N. & M. C.	Mollie May	15 Jun 1875
Rusk	WILSON, Hughey & Bettie Ann	Hughey	26 Aug 1873
		Mariah E.	1 Sep 1875
Cherokee	WILSON, J. J. and Annie	George W.	28 Sep 1873
Jasper	WILSON, J. T. and Frances J.	Walter C.	8 Sep 1874
Kaufman	WILSON, J. W. & ___	___	___ ___ ___
Fannin	WILSON, J. W. &		
	N. B. (or D.?)	Sarah A. J.	25 Oct 1873
Lamar	WILSON, L. C. & C. F.	Ora Ellen	20 Sep 1873
Fannin	WILSON, L. C. & Josephine	Don Edward	10 Sep 1874
Upshur	WILSON, Lenard & Millie	Martha E.	6 Aug 1875
Fannin	WILSON, M. V. & Polly	Arch	3 Mar 1874
Rusk	WILSON, Oscar & Lou	Josephine	May 1873
Rusk	WILSON, R. H. & Adnanna	Fannie C.	13 Oct 1874
Kaufman	WILSON, S. H. & M. E.	Henry R.	20 Jul 1873
		William C.	16 Feb 1875
Upshur	WILSON, T. C. & M. J.	Thomas C.	7 Jul 1873
Cherokee	WILSON, W. H. & Decie	Mary W.	5 Oct 1874
Kaufman	WILSON, W. J. and Mary E.	Hantance	20 Jan 1874
Rusk	WILSON, William H. &		
	Elizabeth A.	Don Carlos	12 Oct 1873
Navarro	WILSON, Wm. T. & Sarah J.	Mary Alice	15 Oct 1873
	Second entry:		
	"W. T. & Sarah J."	Joseph Alonzo	27 Apr 1875
Navarro	WINKLER, C. M. & A. V.	Harrison Owen	21 Jun 1874
Fannin	WINTER, Alex N. & K. M.	C. A.	17 May 1874
Kaufman	WISDOM, A. J. & M. J.	Charity Jane	7 Oct 1873
Rusk	WITCHER, Mat & Delia	Martha	29 May 1875
Fannin	WITCHER, W. W. & Susan	Martha B.	31 Jul 1875
Lamar	WITT, J. W. & L. C.	R. L.	24 Dec 1873
Upshur	WOLENBINGER, W. & Mary	Thos. W.	23 Mar 1874
		Sarah E.	22 Mar 1875
Rusk	WOLF, Stafford & Catherine	Evie Ann	22 Feb 1875
Rusk	WOLFE, ___ & Hester	John Wallace	2 Aug 1875
Anderson	WOLVERTON, M. B. and S. M.	Ora B.	21 Jul 1875
Gregg	WOMACK, Alonza A. & Eliza H.	Victoria Louise	19 Oct 1875
Fannin	WOMACK, W. G. & Mittie	Emmaetta	25 May 1875
Rusk	WOOD, Geor. R. & Leulla	James H.	2 Aug 1873
	Note: in 1875, mother's	Geor. Edgar	16 Aug 1875
	name is spelled "Louella"		
Washington	WOOD, H. A. & Mattie	V. D.	21 Aug 1873
Cherokee	WOOD, J. C. & M. N.	Felix N.	17 Jul 1873
Rusk	WOOD, J. W. & M. A.	John V.	2 Jun 1875
Rusk	WOOD, R. B. & E. M.	Thomas B.	21 Sep 1874
Washington	WOOD, W. A. & A. P.	Ella Jane	20 Aug 1875

COUNTY	PARENTS	CHILD	DATE
Navarro	WOOD, W. B. & Almarine	Clarah Jenevie	4 May 1875
Navarro	WOOD, W. B. & M. E.	Fleetie Steward	8 Dec 1873
Rusk	WOODALL, Thom & Willy	Gus	15 Jan 1874
Navarro	WOODARD, Wm. & N. O.	Annetta Iraola	29 Jun 1873
Fannin	WOODS, B. F. & Julia J.	William Manley	1 Dec 1875
Rusk	WOOLVERTON, T. B. &		
	Elizabeth Jane	Jesse	28 Aug 1873
		Nellie	11 Mar 1875
Rusk	WOOLVERTON, W. T. &		
	Rebecca Ann	Corah Bell	1 Apr 1874
Fannin	WOOTEN, M. & L. A.	Della	1 Jul 1873
	(twins)	Ida	1 Jul 1873
		Lula	15 Feb 1875
Anderson	WORD, John J. & Kate	Jackson	20 Dec 1874
Anderson	WORD, T. J. and M. L. J.	Eoline	30 Jul 1874
Rusk	WORRELL, H. R. & Barbra Ann	Benjamin F.	7 Feb 1874
Lamar	WORTHAM, J. D. & C. J.	James L.	12 Aug 1873
Somervell	WRAY, James P. and A. F.	Lulia	5 Dec 1874
Kaufman	WREN, A. R. & M. A.	John Leroy	4 Jan 1875
Lamar	WRIGHT, J. H. & Loulah	Edgar B.	1 May 1874
Upshur	WRIGHT, J. M. & M. A.	J. F.	10 Jun 1875
Fannin	WRIGHT, J. S. & Mary E.	G. B.	29 Jan 1875
Upshur	WRIGHT, J. W., Jr. &		
	Mary E.	Jesse Mary	10 Jun 1875
Jasper	WRIGHT, Sharod & Sarah F.	Thomas S.	8 Oct 1873
Jasper	WRIGHT, Stephen & Jane	John O. E.	7 Sep 1871
		Judge A.	15 Apr 1875
		Hetty	16 Mar 1876
Rusk	WRIGHT, W. G. & P. L.	Mary C.	5 Dec 1875
Kaufman	WRIGHT, W. H. & F. A.	Ray Barkley	24 Apr 1874
Jasper	WRIGHT, William S. &		
	Caroline	Alexd. V.	15 Jan?1875
	Note: The month had been written		
	over and was illegible.		
Fannin	WYATT, Joseph & Sorena J.	Ada	23 Dec 1873
Fannin	WYATT, R. H. & L. M.	Serena Otho	8 Aug 1875
Anderson	WYLIE, William & M. N.	Adeline	2 Aug 1874
Rusk	WYNNE, R. M., Sr. &		
	Laura B.	R. M., Jr.	19 Aug 1874
Rusk	YANDLE, William W. &		
	Mary Ann	John M.	4 Oct 1875
Gregg	YANTIS, Robert E. & Helena	Hallie	3 May 1876
Fannin	YARBROUGH,T. B. & Sallie	Mary A.	10 May 1875
Fannin	YARBROUGH, T. P. & S. F.	Thomas Bell	7 Jun 1873
Kaufman	YARRELL, S. L. and Annie	Hugh Henry	13 Nov 1871
Fannin	YEAGER, F. N. & Elizabeth	James A.	12 Jan 1875
Navarro	YORK, R. G. & Mahala	Margaret Susan	May 1873
Navarro	YOUNG, A. T. & M. B.	Delmer Osmund	8 Apr 1874
Rusk	YOUNG, Ben. & Charlotte	Charlit	1 Mar 1875
Rusk	YOUNG, Elhanan W. &		
	Mary L.	Edward F.	5 Jun 1875
Navarro	YOUNG, J. D. & M. J.	John D. Williams	4 Sep 1874
Rusk	YOUNG, John H. W. and		
	Virginia C.	Wallace	21 May 1874
Rusk	YOUNG, W. P. & Fannie (Spear)	Emma Lenore	13 Sep 1875
Gregg	YOUNG, Wm. F. & Fannie S.	Emma Lenore Y.	13 Sep 1873
Lamar	YOUNGBLOOD, Harvey A. &		
	Sarah E.	Harvey H.	13 Dec 1874
Cameron	YTURRIA, Bernardo &		
	Geneveta(?) (Fuentes)	Francisco	10 Nov 1876
Fannin	ZACKARY, B. S. & Hulda	Edith C.	3 Apr 1875
Fannin	ZACKARY, W. H. & Susan	Martha B.	31 Mar 1874
Rusk	ZUBER, D. F. & M. R.	Eugene F.	27 May 1875